Julian of Norwich

GARLAND MEDIEVAL CASEBOOKS
VOLUME 21
GARLAND REFERENCE LIBRARY OF THE HUMANITIES
VOLUME 2034

GARLAND MEDIEVAL CASEBOOKS

JOYCE E. SALISBURY AND CHRISTOPHER KLEINHENZ, *Series Editors*

JULIAN OF NORWICH
A BOOK OF ESSAYS

EDITED BY
SANDRA J. McENTIRE

GARLAND PUBLISHING, INC.
A MEMBER OF THE TAYLOR & FRANCIS GROUP
NEW YORK AND LONDON
1998

Library of Congress Cataloging-in-Publication Data

Julian of Norwich : a book of essays / edited by Sandra J. McEntire.
        p.   cm. — (Garland reference library of the humanities ; vol.
2034. Garland medieval casebooks ; vol. 21)
     Includes bibliographical references and index.
     ISBN 0-8153-2529-0 (alk. paper)
     1. Julian, of Norwich, b. 1343.   I. McEntire, Sandra J.   II. Series:
Garland reference library of the humanities ; vol. 2034.   III. Series:
Garland reference library of the humanities. Garland medieval casebooks ; vol. 21.
BV5095.J84J83   1998
248.2'2'092—dc21   98-12955
                                                                     CIP

Cover illustration: The opening page of Julian of Norwich's *Revelation of Love,*
used by permission of Westminster Cathedral (MS 4, folio 72v).

Printed on acid-free, 250-year-life paper
Manufactured in the United States of America

For Jeff

"a joy, a blisse and endlesse lyking"

Contents

Acknowledgments

A debt of gratitude is due to many without whom this volume would not have been completed in a timely manner. I would like to thank in particular the contributors for their willingness to work under rigorous deadlines. As one of the general editors of the series, Joyce E. Salisbury has been generous in her support and assistance. Rhodes College provided me a faculty grant to complete the editing. Above all, I want to thank Valerie Lagorio for her initial vision of such a volume, and her subsequent encouragement and enthusiasm.

Introduction

Computer technology provides a fair witness to the growing interest in medieval women mystics in general, and Julian of Norwich in particular. A quick web search for "Julian of Norwich" yields nearly 300 sites which include links not only, for example, to the Grace Warrack edition of the Sloane Manuscript, but also to academic course webpages that feature her, and to the Order of Julian of Norwich founded in Norwich, CT in 1982. This more "popular" technological representation mirrors the production of scholarly matter on Julian in the last half of the twentieth century, but especially following the publication of Marion Glasscoe's edition in 1976, Frances Beer's edition in 1978, and the Colledge and Walsh two-volume edition also in 1978. Translations, including paperbound versions, have facilitated the accessibility of Julian's *Showings*. Further stimulating interest in Julian, Roberta Nobleman's dramatic one-woman rendition of J. Janda's *Julian* played to scores of collegiate, monastic, and church-based audiences in the 1980s. Of all the English mystical works, Julian's *Showings*, or *Revelations*, has attracted the most intense interest and scrutiny. This volume recognizes the heightened current awareness of Julian and her text and provides for our readers further access to her intellectual and theological milieu. A series of distinct but related studies, these essays explore various aspects of Julian's work and consider several contexts from which to interpret her text and its meaning.

The facts about Julian, although well known, are limited. At the age of thirty and a half years, she endured a serious illness that culminated on May 13, 1373 in a series of visions or revelations. For twenty years after her visions, she reflected and prayed about their meaning. In 1413 she was an anchoress attached to St. Julian's Church in Norwich, attested to not only by her own text, but by independent witnesses as well. These bequests, as well as the visit of her contemporary Margery Kempe, indicate the reputation Julian enjoyed as a holy woman.[1]

Julian produced two versions of her visions, the first most likely written soon after her sickness and the revelatory experience and the shorter of the two. The second was composed at least twenty years later as a result of her reflections on the meaning of the visions. Denise N. Baker rightly notes, however, that Julian "was probably not well known as an author during her lifetime."[2] Only a single mid-fifteenth-century manuscript of the short text survives, possibly copied from the original or facsimile of it. Around 1500 a heavily edited and excerpted version of the long text was produced, which also may have been abbreviated from an original version. According to the textual evidence, it was not until the mid-seventeenth century that post-Reformation interest in Julian's *Showings* surged. The three extant manuscripts of the long text were copied around 1650, and in 1670 Serenus Cressy printed it. The Cressy edition was subsequently reprinted, once in 1843 and again in 1902. Julian's book circulated not only in England but also on the continent, but "it was the Benedictine devotion to Julian which preserved knowledge of her work" (Colledge and Walsh 18), and most Benedictine libraries were likely to have had copies of the Cressy edition by the late nineteenth century.[3]

Comparison of the earlier and later texts has formed the core of a complex of issues, most of which have centered on Julian's evolving thought and understanding and its expression in the later text. Suppressing some of the earlier material while adding large sections that are both analytically and theologically sophisticated, Julian's Long Text provides not only an expansion of her reflected comprehension of her original experiences but also signifies the multiple perspectives Julian engaged in her revision. The Long Text represents Julian's allegorical and tropological reading of her own earlier text, and, as such, of her represented self in that text. Fully aware of her lettered and unlettered audience, lay and churchly, and of her culture's political and social boundaries, and just as fully committed to the inerrancy of her revelations, Julian's Long Text is a brilliant excursus in medieval thought, spirituality, and poetics.

The essays in this book provide a rich evaluation of this late-fourteenth and early-fifteenth century mystical writer and her *Showings* and consider the construction of her narrative, its theological complexity, and its literary and intellectual contexts. Eleven essays make up the contents, all but one original for this volume. Featuring discussions ranging from audience to rhetoric, genre to eschatology, gynecology to diabology, the casebook features essays by both established scholars and newer voices. While the methodologies may vary, each scholar offers additional facets of appreciation of this complex text. Moments from within the *Showings* are repeatedly evoked; the hazelnut passage, the attack by the devil, the allegory of the Lord and the servant are given equal place in Julian's thought as the oft-cited motherhood of God and the problem of sin sections.

Augustine figures as a large presence in several essays. His theology of the image of God and of the Trinity is foundational in medieval thought, and McEntire, Baker, and Watson all read Julian's *Showings* as deeply engaged in the theological discourse shaped by Augustine's influence. In the first Sandra J. McEntire sees Julian as resisting the "patriarchal discourse" as elaborated by M. M. Bahktin, and writing a theology not only of the Fall as inclusive, merciful, and coherent, but of God as embracing the full spectrum of human experience. Physicality and the metaphor of childbirth inform Julian's representation of God. Couching her insights in a rhetoric of obedience and subordination, Julian nonetheless posits perspectives that are marginally unorthodox.

Denise N. Baker also reads Julian as engaging in a dialogue with Augustine, particularly as she distinctly averred from Walter Hilton's understanding of the soul. In her 1993 essay, "Julian of Norwich and Anchoritic Literature,"[4] Baker first queried the possibility of influence between Julian and her contemporary Walter Hilton. She here takes up the question again. While rejecting the possibility of direct influence, Baker elucidates the distinct ways that both writers derive their mystical theory from Augustine's *De trinitate*. Hilton transmits the Augustinian model of the soul nearly intact; Julian transforms the paradigm and expresses her own unique vision.

Augustine, especially the *De trinitate*, grounds Nicholas Watson's 1992 essay, "The Trinitarian Hermeneutic in Julian of Norwich's *Revelation of Love*," which is here reprinted and is the only essay not original for this volume. Deserving a wider audience than its possibly limited former venue, Watson's analysis challenges fundamentalist approaches heretofore taken to Julian, and indeed, continued to some extent in this volume. Focussing primarily on the Long Text, Watson warns against reading the text as an absolutely literal account of the events that provide the subject of Julian's work. Rather the text signals in Julian a hermeneutical awareness that is intensely sophisticated. It must be seen as not only a recording of her experience but also as a representation of her memory, long years of reflection, and interpretation of those memories and reflections. At the heart of her hermeneutic is the trinity as both divine being and as metaphor for her own synthesis.

Memory, particularly Julian's memory of her visionary experience, and the need to communicate her vision to others by means of simple metaphors, grounds Susan K. Hagen's "St. Cecilia and St. John of Beverly: Julian of Norwich's Early Model and Late Affirmation." Hagen posits the shift in Julian's initial inspirational purpose in the Short Text to her more explicitly didactic intention in the Long Text as mimetically coded by Julian's focus on Saint Cecilia and St. John of Beverly. That Julian shifts her emblematic reference from one to the other reflects her later understanding of her visions and her self as teacher. Noting the expanded visual attention of the longer version and Julian's imbrication of sensual detail and explanatory glosses, Hagen examines the impact devotional images likely had on the medieval contemplative. Shifting the emphasis from a virgin martyr to a locally known teacher enables Julian to appropriate the inspiration accorded to teachers.

Lacanian theory, grounded in orality, language philosophy, and poetics, undergirds Brad Peters's discussion. In particular, the primary speech genres represented in the *Showings* reveal that Julian reinvents dialectics as a result of her intensely focussed *lectio divina,* as it were, whereby she reads the multivalent elements of her own instruction. She thus deconstructs underlying cultural principles inconsistent with her own insights. What results, says Peters, is a woman-positive epistemology, a *jouissance,* in the light of the inherent paradoxes of her revelations that all shall be well but that sin is a given in human life.

Following upon numerous textual notes throughout the edition, a rich vein of information can be found in Colledge and Walsh's Appendix on those rhetorical figures Julian employed. Yet much more remains to be done with this topic. Cynthea Masson's essay examines in detail Julian's suggestive use of two rhetorical figures, *contentio* and *chiasmus,* to structure her experience of the ineffable. At the intersection of her near-death moment and the infusion of divine revelation, Julian is led to the enigmatic and oxymoronic *oppositio contrariorum* whereby humanity and divinity are at one. Elaborating on the "poynte" passages, Masson reads the rift in space and time as an apophatic opportunity, chiastically represented.

Largely overlooked in the extensive discussion of sin and evil in Julian's theology, the otherworldly representation of evil remains a central tenet of medieval belief. Yet while Julian is not granted a vision of hell, she does directly experience an assault by the devil. This encounter centers the discussion of two essays. Counterbalancing the heretofore widespread interest in Julian's representation of Jesus as Mother, Jay Ruud examines the masculine aspects of Julian's male figures in the text, God and the devil. Noting that most of the language about God is male-gendered, Ruud's essay looks to romance to discover the conventions of masculine behavior in Julian's time. Discerning both positive and negative characteristics, Ruud notes that God/Christ is represented as ideal male protector, provider, and lover while the devil, also depicted as masculine, is dominating, deceitful, and aggressively physical to the point of violence. This stereotypical split in masculine representation is, however, more finely nuanced in the light of the fiend's impotence against God's power. If God is androgynous, so is the fiend, but the one embodies positive male- and female-gendered qualities, the other the negative.

David Tinsley also looks at the diabolical encounter of Julian with the devil. His essay, "Julian's Diabology," examines the wide range of spiritual experiences in affective piety as represented by the demonic encounters of Julian and the German women visionaries Christina von Stommeln, Ita von Hohenfels, Elsbeth Stagel, but most especially the Dominican nun Elsbeth von Oye. For Julian, suffering, including the encounter with the fiend, comes from sin and can be transcended. For the German mystic, however, suffering is an end; itself the means of transcendence, suffering dominates not only desire, but theology as well. If the devil is impotent for Julian, her vision ultimately brings her consolation. But for Elsbeth, suffering brings satisfaction not to her but to God, who imposes additional expectations of great suffering. Julian's God is a caring mother, Elsbeth's an insatiable suitor; it is the fiend who links these affective worlds.

By examining the social and textual contexts surrounding a work, we continue to historicize that work. Scientific and medical texts have often been neglected as sources of belief and ideology. Alexandra Barratt reads Julian's text in the context of an early fifteenth-century gynecological and obstetrical treatise, *The Knowing of Woman's Kind* and suggests that Julian's interest in the body might mirror the sort of knowledge that an intelligent and informed woman of her day would possess. In particular, Julian's attitude to pain and suffering and her conception of motherhood were likely a product of her time. Our understanding of these concerns improve with our more nuanced awareness of these issues as they existed for medieval women.

Hugh Kempster's essay examines the editorial practice of the late-fifteenth or early-sixteenth century Westminster manuscript to posit the changing audience of this mystical text. Noting the growth of lay participation in a "mixed life" and the texts that support such a spiritually energetic movement, Kempster's close reading of Westminster's truncated version of the Long Text reveals the possibility of a spiritually active lay audience, hints at the nature of late fifteenth-century lay piety, and provides a lens for viewing the reception of Julian's text.

The coincidence of the experience of the ineffable in Julian and in Eastern Orthodoxy constitutes the subject of Brant Pelphrey's essay. The numerous points of theological correspondence between Julian and Byzantine theologians mark her as a particularly felicitous partner in the dialogue between East and West. Pelphrey's essay also notes liturgical parallels.

It is my hope that the readers of *Julian of Norwich: A Book of Essays* will garner a greater appreciation of Julian and her work and be stimulated to return to the *Showings* itself in order to discover more that can be found there. Medievalists will read these essays with greater critical facility and fluency of the original Middle English. Non-specialists and students will discover the sophistication of this medieval woman and her text, her intellectual precision, her linguistic acumen, her rhetorical strategies. For these readers translations are provided. While this collection covers a number of topics not previously considered in depth elsewhere, they do not in any way provide a comprehensive discussion of Julian and her book.

What becomes clearer and clearer to me as I reread these essays, is that Julian's *Showings* transcends essentialist interpretations. Like the work of her contemporaries Geoffrey Chaucer and William Langland, Julian's text stands up to multivalent scrutiny, and reveals itself as an intensely complex, highly original, and deeply inspired work open to many speculative approaches.

Memphis, TN   SJM

NOTES

1. For the bequests, see Edmund Colledge and James Walsh, *A Book of Showings to the Anchoress Julian of Norwich* (Toronto: Pontifical Institute of Medieval Studies, 1978) 33-35. For Kempe's visit to Julian, see Chapter 18 of *The Book of Margery Kempe*, ed. Sanford Brown Meech and Hope Emily Allen, EETS 212 (Oxford: Oxford UP, 1940).

2. *Julian of Norwich's Book of Showings. From Vision to Book* (Princeton, NJ: Princeton UP, 1994) 3.

3. For thorough discussion of the manuscripts see Colledge and Walsh, 1-18 and Alexandra Barratt, "How Many Children Had Julian of Norwich? Editions, Translations and Versions of Her Revelations," in *Vox Mystica. Essays on Medieval Mysticism*, ed. Anne Clark Bartlett, et al. (Cambridge: Brewer, 1995) 27-39.

4. *Mystics Quarterly* 19 (1993), 156-158.

List of Contributors

Professor of English at the University of North Carolina at Greensboro, *Denise N. Baker* has published *Julian of Norwich's Showings: From Vision to Book* as well as articles about several of Julian's contemporaries, including Langland, Gower, the Pearl poet, and Chaucer.

Alexandra A. T. Barratt, Professor of English at the University of Waikato in Hamilton, New Zealand, serves as editor of *Mystics Quarterly.* Her books include editions of *The Book of Tribulation, Dame Eleanor Hill. The Seven Psalms*; *Women's Writings in Middle English*; and (coedited with John Ayto) *Aelred of Rievaulx's "De Institutione Inclusarum": Two English Versions,* as well as a translation of *Gertrude the Great of Helfta: The Herald of God's Loving-Kindness: Books One and Two.* Published essays cover such topics as the passion lyrics, the *Ancrene Wisse*, Margery Kempe and Elizabeth of Hungary, the sermons of Stephen Langton, and Julian of Norwich.

Professor *Susan K. Hagen* holds the Mary Collett Munger Chair in English at Birmingham-Southern College where she also serves as Chair of the Division of Humanities. In addition to *Allegorical Remembrance,* a book on medieval allegory, she has published articles on Chaucer's Wife of Bath, the Second Nun's and Merchant's tales, and teaching Chaucer.

Hugh Kempster, an Anglican parish priest in Remuera, Auckland, New Zealand, completed his Theol.M. in Church History through Melbourne College of Divinity in 1996. Working towards enrolling for a D.Phil. at the University of Waikato he is researching the fifteenth-century reception of the writings of Richard Rolle. His publications include an edition of the Wesminster text of Julian's *Revelation*.

Cynthea Masson received her Ph.D. from McMaster University (Hamilton, Canada) in 1996 and has taught medieval literature at McMaster and Nipissing University (North Bay, Canada). She is currently working on rhetorical iconography and Margery Kempe.

Sandra J. McEntire is Associate Professor of English at Rhodes College in Memphis, TN. Her books include *The Doctrine of Compunction in Medieval England* and *Margery Kempe: A Book of Essays* (ed). She has also published essays on Chaucer, Dante, and Old English poetry.

Brad Peters is Director of Composition at California State University at Northridge. He has published articles on Julian of Norwich in *Mystics Quarterly*. His scholarly work also focuses on cultural studies and genre theory in rhetoric and composition.

Brant Pelphrey is Administrative Assistant to the President and Academic Dean at Hellenic College, Holy Cross Greek Orthodox School of Theology where he also lectures in Orthodox Theology, Patristic Theology, and World Religions. His publications include *Julian of Norwich: Christ Our Mother* and *Love Was His Meaning: The Theology and Mysticism of Julian of Norwich*.

Jay Ruud is Professor of English and Interim Dean of the College of Arts and Sciences at Northern State University in Aberdeen, South Dakota. He is the author of the book *"Many a Song and Many a Leccherous Lay": Tradition and Individuality in Chaucer's Lyric Poetry* as well as articles on Chaucer, Julian of Norwich, and Arthurian literature.

David F. Tinsley, Professor of German at the University of Puget Sound, is currently working on a book exploring spiritual implications of extreme asceticism in fourteenth-century Dominican convent culture. His publications include studies of Hermann von Sachsenheim, Ulrich von Lichtenstein, and Elsbeth von Oye.

Nicholas Watson is Professor of English at the University of Western Ontario. His books include *Richard Rolle and the Invention of Authority*; *Anchoritic Spirituality: Ancrene Wisse and Associated Works* (co-editor with Anne Savage); and *The Idea of the Vernacular: An Anthology of Middle English Literary Theory and Practice, 1280-1520* (co-editor with Ruth Evans, Andrew Taylor and Jocelyn Wogan-Browne; forthcoming). He has also written articles in the fields of religious history, vernacular theology, mysticism, and literary history.

JULIAN OF NORWICH

The Likeness of God and the Restoration of Humanity in Julian of Norwich's *Showings*

Sandra J. McEntire

The *Showings* of Julian of Norwich depicts the ways, directly and indirectly, that she negotiates both the conformity of and the distance between her personal mystical experience and its subsequent insights and that which is deemed acceptable within the parameters of traditional patriarchal and theological authority. In an age fraught with intense scrutiny from political and ecclesiastial authority,[1] Julian needed to balance her own assertions and the authority of the heresy-sensitive church. Indeed, any text written by a woman in the medieval period necessarily reflects not only an assertion of her own authority but also an awareness of the limits of the discourse she relies on to make her assertion. While subject to the intellectual, cultural, and social frames of reference that contextualize her and her text, her subjective experience coaxes her to embrace new positions vis-a-vis her self, her text, and authority.

The tradition that Julian interiorizes and examines asserts views of the human and the divine identities that are at variance with Julian's post-revelatory experience. How she moves from the traditional discourse to a position of dissent constitutes the topic of this essay. While remaining subject and indeed loyal to the primary tradition, she nonetheless is liberated from it, but only after long and conscientious inner negotiation, particularly in the intervening years between the Short and Long Texts of her book. Indeed, as Lynn Staley observes, the Long Text is "an extended dialogue between her spiritual understanding and her belief in the teachings of Holy Church" (PH 141).[2] Whereas Staley and David Aers probe the politics of Julian's *Showings*, I would like to interrogate further the ways in which Julian and her text negotiate the interior tension between the complex authority she inherits and the original insights of her theology.

This negotiation assumes a dialogue, however unconscious it may be, between the individual and what Mikhail Bakhtin calls "authoritative discourse," that is, the word that has come down as tradition, as established, as resistant to change. Although feminist criticism has been proficient at producing evidence of a body of mysogynist literature, I would like to reference briefly a single source of the powerful discourse that in the course of patriarchal history takes on nearly absolute authority, the exegesis on the Book of Genesis, Chapters 1 through 3.

I. "Authoritative Discourse": Woman as Eve

Although autobiographical texts seem at first glance to be univalent in presentation of voice, a closer look reveals the numerous dialogues that undergird the apparent monologue. Besides recreating actual conversations and dialogue with others, particularly the divine being, mystical revelation is also inherently dialogical, negotiating an internal conversation about the events and experiences taking place. The two loquators of that internal conversation include the inherited word, or in Bakhtin's phrase, the "authoritative discourse," and "one's own," that is, populated with intention and accent, and adapted to a particular "semantic and expressive intention."[3] Explaining further Bakhtin says: "Within the arena of almost every utterance an intense interaction and struggle between one's own and another's word is being waged, a process in which they oppose or dialogically interanimate each other" (354). What is particularly novel about late medieval, often vernacular mystical texts, according to Bernard McGinn, is their dialogue with the older tradition, that is, the Latin "monologic triumph of the authoritative male voice of ecclesiastical authority."[4] Julian's word, her *Showings*, represents both her critique of this misogynous tradition and her interaction and struggle with the inevitably gendered nature of the discourse.

Authoritative discourse shapes behavior and the bases of ideological interrelations with the world. It becomes internally persuasive. Bakhtin says:

The authoritative word demands that we acknowledge it, that we make it our own; it binds us, quite independently of any power it might have to persuade us internally; we encounter it with its authority already fused to it. The authoritative word is located in a distanced zone, organically connected with a past that is felt to be hierarchically higher. It is, so to speak the word of the fathers. Its authority was already *acknowledged* in the past. It is a *prior* discourse. It is therefore not a question of choosing it from among other possible discourses that are its equal . . . .

It is not a free appropriation and assimilation of the word itself that authoritative discourse seeks to elicit from us; rather, it demands our unconditional allegiance. (342-43)

Hard-edged, calcified, inert, authoritative discourse "cannot be represented--it is only transmitted" (344).

One place to look for an example of an authoritative discourse and to situate a discussion of Julian's *Showings* within that discourse can be found in the Biblical exegetical tradition.5 The primary and symbolic locus for the marginalizing of women and the valorizing of a dominant male voice is embedded in the writings on the creation stories of Genesis 1-3, but especially Genesis 2 and 3. This central text defines what it means to be human, what the relationship between men and women, husbands and wives, authority and subordinate should be.

Although a considerable portion of the exegetical literature on Genesis asserts positivist and essentialist theories about the importance of women in the scheme of the created universe, an equally considerable body of misogynistic literature, both more pervasive and thus in some ways more influential, permeates the theological, intellectual, and cultural world view. Augustine, for example, cannot imagine why God created the prelapsarian Eve in the first place. Even as a helper he finds her wanting, thinking it much more agreeable for two male friends to provide each other company and conversation (Clark 29). Other commentators also saw Eve's position as inferior. That Eve was created from the physical body of Adam and not from the earthly dust as he was comes to signify a fundamental inferiority, physical, moral, and intellectual. Only connected with the man can she reflect the image of God; even in that relation she has no authority or autonomy.

If the pre-lapsarian Eve is gendered and suspect, the discussions of the post-lapsarian Eve reveal the definitions of woman which most deeply inform the discourse of authority. Indeed, in these writings, not only does Eve cause the fall of man, but it is precisely because she fails to obey Adam, that is, to maintain the divinely ordained and appropriate order of the man as the head of the women, that sin enters and disrupts the world. Asserting that man fell because of woman, commentators such as Ambrose indicate that woman is the originator of man's wrongdoing (Clark 41). Chrysostom ups the ante by putting into the mouth of God a judgement that extends to all women:

> You did not use your authority well, so consign yourself to a state of subordination. You have not borne your liberty, so accept servitude. Since you do not know how to rule--as you showed in your experiment with the business of life--henceforth be among the governed and acknowledge your husband as lord. (Clark 43)

The conclusion which the fathers draw about Eve's and woman's place in the world is absolute and determined. In a passage which, as Howard Bloch indicates, "shifts the ethical burden of sexuality toward women, making her the passive agent . . . of the seduction of males" (39), Tertullian says in this widely cited text:

> God's judgement on this sex lives on in our age; the guilt necessarily lives on as well. *You* are the devil's gateway; *you* are the unsealer of that tree; *you* are the first foresaker of the divine law; *you* are the one who persuaded him whom the devil was not brave enough to approach; *you* so lightly crushed the image of God, the man Adam; because of your punishment, that is, death, even the Son of God had to die. (Clark 39; also Bloch 40 and O'Faolain 132)

Against this exegetical backdrop, and with a "deep distrust of the body and materiality" (Bloch 45), the ambivalence about sexual values is found. Sexual desire and sexual knowledge followed the fall. The knowledge of good and evil eventuated sexual awareness. Clement and Irenaeus put forth arguments that would influence later generations of apologists and the subsequent ambivalence about sexuality. While confirming the blessedness of marriage, sexual passion had to be purged, thereby dichotomizing the desires of the flesh and the higher functions of will and reason.

Even better, however, than chaste marital relations is virginity. Only then might a woman "become the equal of man" (Bloch 93). The loathing of the flesh, a loathing that overflows in revulsion against the female body, is best found in Augustine and in Jerome, particularly the latter's diatribes against Jovinian, who counsels a more sensible, balanced view. As a result of woman's role in bringing man down to his baser instincts, she must suffer the consequences of childbirth pain.

From this highly summarized overview, a few conclusions might be drawn. As creature woman is conceived in bodily inferiority and intellectual insufficiency. As such she possesses no authority or autonomy of her own. As Howard Bloch points out, "she is, in a sense, as powerfully entangled as the story of the Fall itself, entrapped by the logic of a cultural ideal that, internalized, makes her always already in a state of weakness, lack, guilt, inadequacy, vulnerability" (91). These assumptions constitute the "authoritative discourse" which women struggled with.

That these assumptions and conclusions about woman, the flesh, and the inferiority of the body were widely appropriated can be assumed for the medieval audience. Nevertheless, one document in particular attests to the integration of these ideas as they pertain explicitly to medieval women and their spirituality. An early thirteenth-century treatise, the *Ancrene Riwle*, was intended by its male clerical composer as a guide for three sisters undertaking the life of asceticism and enclosure. In recommending the safeguards for their proper behavior, he betrays the misogynistic and authoritative point of view found in the fathers. According to the writer, perfect cleanness must be preserved not only by her virginity but also by the complete and thorough enclosure of the anchoress, an enclosure that insures that each of the senses will be shut off, but most particularly her mouth. Calling her a jabberer and a magpie, the writer describes the organs of female speech: "her two jaws are the two grinding stones, her tongue is the clapper. See to it, dear sisters, that your jaws never grind anything but soul-food, and your ears never drink anything but soul-tonic."[6]

Explicitly relating speech to Eve's tempting of Adam, the writer ignores the salvific words of Mary, "fiat voluntas tua," and valorizes her near silence over a cackling Eve:

> You, my beloved sisters, follow Our Lady, and not the cackling Eve--because an anchoress, whatever she is, however much she knows, should keep silent. She does not have the nature of a hen. The hen, when she has laid, can only cackle--and what happens on account of it? The crow comes right away and steals her eggs from her, and eats what should bring forth living birds. In just the same way the devil-crow carries off and swallows all the good which cackling anchoresses have given birth to, which should bear them up like birds towards heaven if it had not been cackled away. (73)

The suspicion of the female flesh, her senses, desires, and voice, is hereby incorporated into the very guidebooks for women who wish to live the ascetic or spiritual life.

The subordination of woman, the silencing of her voice and experience, and the complementary authorizing of male points of view find their roots in the traditional teachings about the creation and fall story. These teachings become deeply embedded in the fabric of relations between men and women into the Middle Ages. Even though there is a difference between the discourse of antifeminism and the facts of a culture of exclusion,[7] nevertheless, this authoritative discourse undergirds a cultural frame of reference, a context out of which women and men interpreted the role and place of women in the world. Even though the effort might make them physically ill,[8] some women did succeed in moving beyond the prohibitions. Hildegard of Bingen, Mechtild of Magdeburg, Mechtild of Hackenborn, Gertrude the Great, and Catherine of Siena stand out as teachers and prophets, not silent or repressed, but actively engaged in the work of the Church. Nevertheless, the approbation of even outstanding activity by these exceptional women was slow in coming. As Jean Leclercq notes, "In the disputations of the masters of 13th and 14th-century scholastic theology, the question was often asked whether or not women had a right to be depicted with the halo of the Doctors; the answer was always negative" (3). Although individual women might attain a place of resolution with the overwhelmingly misogynistic point of view, it was not without intense struggle and resistance, internal and external.

II. Julian's Discourse: The Theology of Likeness

Although the source of Julian of Norwich's learning cannot be known, her *Showings* attests to a learned author, one familiar with some of the most important patristic texts and commentaries.9 Further, she would have known the *Ancrene Wisse*. She most certainly heard and read the principal teachings of the fathers about women's inferiority and flawed nature. But only exceptionally does this frame of reference intrude in her text. In both the Short and Long texts, toward the end of her revelations, she tells of an instance when her pain is taken away and she experiences dryness and barrenness. "Thann comm a religiouse personn to me and asked me howe I farde, and I sayde that I hadde raued þat daye ["Then a man of religion came to me and asked me how I did, and I said that during that day I had been raving"].10 The only explanation that she gives is that she did not expect him to believe her:

> I thought: this man takyth sadly the lest worde that I myght sey, that sawe no more therof. And when I saw that he toke it so sadly and with so grete reverence, I waxsyd full grettly ashamyd, and wolde a bene shryven. But I cowlde telle it to no prest, for I thought, how shulde a preste belieue me when I by seaying I ravid, I shewed my selfe nott to belyue oure lorde god? (66.633-34)

> [I thought: This man takes seriously every word I could say, who saw no more of this than I had told him. And when I saw that he treated it so seriously and so respectfully, I was greatly ashamed, and wanted to make my confession. But I could not tell it to any priest, for I thought: How could a priest believe me, when I, by saying that I had been raving, showed that I did not believe our Lord God. (311)]

That this passage remains nearly unrevised suggests the importance it has for her initial awareness of her experience. She names her experience in terms of the expectation the priest might have of her claim: a raving, or madness. Incredulous of the graces she, a woman afraid of pain and suffering, had received, she resists articulating them or claiming insights beyond her place. When he stands outside her expectation, one shaped by the misogynistic authoritative discourse, she immediately repents her folly and wretchedness and unbelief.

A second section of the *Showings* points to a similar interiorization of the negative view of woman and the attending prohibitions against her. Chapter 6 of the Short Text is governed by a self-representation at once apologetic, anxiety filled, and only tentatively assertive. In language completely consistent with the patriarchal rhetoric which sees women as deceptive, subject, subordinate, Julian presents herself as "the wrechid worme, synfulle creature" ["the wretched worm, the sinful creature"], indeed, "a womman, leued, febille and fraille" ["a woman, ignorant, weak and frail"]. Apparently embarrassed by her revelations, she displaces her privileged status as recipient of divine favor and cloaks herself in the language of nothingness:

> For sothly it was nought schewyd vnto me for that god loves me bettere thane the leste sawlle that is in grace. For I am sekere thare ys fulle many that nevere hadde schewynge ne syght botte of the commonn techynge of haly kyrke that loves god better þan I. For ȝif I loke syngulerlye to my selfe I am ryght nought. (6.220)

> [For truly it was not revealed to me because God loves me better than the humblest soul who is in a state of grace. For I am sure that there are very many who never had revelations or visions, but only the common teaching of Holy Church, who love God better than I. If I pay special attention to myself, I am nothing at all. (134)]

Indeed, she asks to be forgotten--"forgette me that am a wrecche" (222)--anxious that she become too noticed or important.

The anxiety that permeates this chapter reflects the deeply inculcated and interiorized sense of inferiority that Julian feels as mystic and as writer. In taking up her pen, she is, as it were, providing insight and information to her reader. But as an ignorant woman, she is, of course, not allowed to teach, a notion she herself acknowledges and assumes: "Botte god for bede that ȝe schulde saye or take it so that I am a techere, for I meene nouȝt soo, no I nevere mente nevere so" ["But God forbid that you should say or assume that I am a teacher, for that is not and never was my intention."] Nevertheless, she asks, "Botte for I am a womann, schulde I therfore leve that I schulde nouȝt telle ȝowe the goodenes of god?" (222) ["But because I am a woman, ought I therefore to believe that I should not tell you of the goodness of God?" (135).] This interrogative provides a merely tentative assertion of her sexed identity and points to the doubled and troubled sense of herself that the Short Text reveals.[11]

In contrast, however, to this negative portrayal of her role in the revelatory experience, the Long Text omits the tone, the language, and the message of this chapter. This omission marks an editorial practice that "displays a hermeneutic awareness . . . at once sophisticated, individual, and impressively of a piece with the rest of her theology" (Watson 81). It argues for Julian's later rejection of traditional misogynistic thought and her reworking of the discourse of patriarchy. While she identifies herself elsewhere in the Long Text as a "symple creature vnlettyrde" (2.285) ["simple, unlettered creature" (177)], this assertion lacks the conviction of inferiority or self-loathing in the prior discourse. Indeed, as Grace Jantzen points out, "all the internalised misogyny, all the self-doubt, all the worry about her gender as a teacher are gone" (178).

With the exception then of Julian's incredulity regarding her interpretation of her uniquely revelatory moment, a credulity which results from a deeply interiorized set of assumptions, the misogynistic teachings undergirding the authoritative discourse are conspicuously absent from the Long Text. It is my contention that this absence reflects not that such assumptions failed to impress upon her their weight and import but that she carefully and consciously resists them as a result of her own experience and revelation. Indeed, as the editorial practice of the Long Text demonstrates, Julian explicitly altered and excised material which she found unacceptable. While she could not directly oppose the teachings of the church, her own spiritual journey led her, particularly during the twenty or more years between the short and long versions of her text, to a set of internally persuasive truths profoundly liberated "from the authority of the other's discourse" (Bakhtin 348).

If authoritative discourse is hard, concrete, and binding, "internally persuasive discourse," according to Bakhtin, is "tightly interwoven with 'one's own word'";

> its creativity and productiveness consist precisely in the fact that such a word awakens new and independent words, that it organizes masses of our words from within, and does not remain in an isolated and static condition. . . . The semantic structure of an internally persuasive discourse is *not finite*, it is *open*; in each of the new contexts that dialogize it, this discourse is able to reveal ever newer *ways to mean*." (345).

By struggling with the prior discourse, indeed stimulated by it, individuals "will sooner or later begin to liberate themselves from the authority of the other's discourse" and come "to ideological consciousness" (348). The *Showings* of Julian of Norwich, particularly the Long Text, testifies to her ideological consciousness and liberation from the patriarchal discourse.

The interior dialogue that Julian undertakes with the dominant discourse encompasses far more, however, than the semantics of self-representation. The structure of resistance and revision is most evident in Julian's exegesis of Genesis. Even though she omits any direct disputation about the Fall, the role of woman in it, or its implications for the body, her text strategizes a dissenting theology from the assumptions previously established and most particularly expressed in the exegesis of Augustine which directly implicates divine and human nature. Augustine, who returns to this Biblical narrative five times in the course of his lifetime,[12] figures as a source Julian both knows and ultimately rewrites. In order to do so, she, like her near contemporary Margery Kempe, needed to disguise her "strongly original and in some cases, destabilizing, insights into systems of theology."[13] The resulting narrative points to a theology that is at once double-gendered and inclusive, divine and human, substantial and sensual.

In the parable of the Servant, Julian provides a reading of Genesis which not only "revises the prevailing Augustinian reading of Genesis 3" (Baker 86), but also expresses disagreement with Augustine's premises about the nature of humankind's likeness to the divinity. Diverging from Augustine's gendered, dualistic interpretation about Adam and Eve as made in the image and likeness of God, Julian adopts an approach at once more relational and more inclusive. It is instructive that she never mentions Eve or her role in the Fall, nor does she assign blame to either party. This omission or gap in the text silences or blocks the authoritative discourse of male privilege and substitutes new meaning. The post-lapsarian Adam has a dual identity of substance and sensuality. And in the new Adam, the sensual is redeemed.

Julian's understanding of the Fall undergoes a significant process of sophistication in the years between the Short and the Long text.[14] Her earlier revelation consists in the simple assertion "that Adammes synne was the maste harme that euer was done or ever schalle to the warldes ende" ["that Adam's sin was the greatest harm ever done or ever to be done until the end of the world"]. Further, she is taught the atonement "is mare plesande to the blissede godhede and mare wyrschipfulle to mannes saluacionn with owten comparysonn than euer was the synne of Adam harmfulle" (14.247) ["is more pleasing to the blessed divinity and more honourable for man's salvation, without comparison, than ever Adam's sin was harmful" (149-50)].[15] But the intervening years of contemplation of this revelation led to her explication of the Servant parable whereby the focus is less on the fall than on the hurt and injury that the servant suffered on the one hand and the compassion and mercy of the lord, on the other. Augustine, in contrast, is preoccupied with the sin and the dispensing of blame as well as the means by which original sin is transmitted to the human race. For Augustine, Adam is the transmitter of original sin through his active seed, for which woman is the passive receptor.[16] But the sin itself was a result, first of Eve's seduction by Satan, and second, of Adam's persuasion by Eve (Børresen 53). Although Adam remains responsible for the Fall, Augustine asserts that the sin began with the woman ("a muliere initium factum est peccati" [Børresen 65]), and it is this latter notion that takes on nearly incantatory force in the tradition. Julian, however, "offers an alternative to the doctrine of original sin crucial to Augustine's juridical theodicy," disagrees with "the Augustinian premises about the nature of sin and the character of God's response to it," and "epitomizes her opposition to retributive theodicy" (Baker 86). Julian finds no cause for blame and "refuses to attribute disobedience to Adam or wrath to God. She presents the original transgression as an inadvertant separation from God rather than a deliberate act of rebellion" (Baker 88). Observing the servant falling, she says: "I behelde with avysement to wytt yf I culde perceyve in hym ony defauȝte, or yf the lorde shuld assigne in hym ony maner of blame; and verely there was none seen, for oonly hys good wyll and his grett desyer was cause of his fallyng" (51.516) ["I looked carefully to know if I could detect any fault in him, or if the lord would impute to him any kind of blame; and truly none was seen, for the only cause of his falling was his good will and his great desire" (268)]. Not only is blame eliminated but he is "rewardyd withoute end" (51.518) that is, above what he would have had he not fallen.

The servant is initially identified as Adam, but by "Adam" Julian does not mean a single individual. She provides a thorough exegesis of the term, allegorizing the identifier: "For in the servannt, that was shewed for Adam as I shall sey, I sawe many dyuerse properteys that myght by no manner be derecte to syngell Adam" (519) ["For in the servant, who was shown in Adam, as I shall say, I saw many different characteristics which could in no way be attributed to Adam, that one man" (269)]. Indeed, Adam represents all humanity, "For in the syghte of god alle man is oone man, and oone man is alle man" (522) ["For in the sight of God all men are one man, and one man is all men" (270)]. Here Julian seems to follow Augustine's anthropology whereby "through all seminal creation, *informatio*, Eve is a human being like Adam, *homo*" (Børresen 18). Her soul, like that of man, says Augustine, is created and derived directly from God and is rational, that is, made in God's image.

What is particularly telling about this inclusiveness is Julian's veiled intention to exonerate Eve from blame as well. Her non-gendered understanding of Adam is made clear when she applies her insights, using such pronouns as "we," "us," and "our," that is, all men and women.[17] Not only is Adam found blameless, but Eve, too, must be included in the compassion and pity of God. Adam, God's "most lovyd creature" (524), includes all, Adam, Eve, and all humanity. The judgement of weakness, deception, subjection, subordination, servitude is not only lacking but also completely and thoroughly dismissed. Julian's disagreement with the traditional interpretation of Genesis 3, while veiled in visionary metaphor, nevertheless demonstrates both her theological sophistication and her resistance to the tradition.

When Julian's revelation moves on to the interpretation of the servant as the new Adam, we find an even more complex set of images. As Denise Baker has demonstrated, Julian is familiar with the notion of the fall as a fall into the "*regio dissimilitudinis*, or land of unlikeness" (88).[18] But Julian goes further. She adds that the new Adam, Christ, fell into humankind and restored likeness: "And what tyme that he of hys goodnesse wyll shew hym to man, he shewyth hym homely *as* man" (51.525) ["And when he of his goodness wishes to show himself to man, he shows himself familiar, *like* a man" (272)] [emphasis added]. The Fall of Adam is complemented by the Fall of Christ:

> When Adam felle godes sonne fell; for the ryght onyng whych was made in hevyn, goddys sonne myght nott be seperath from Adam, for by Adam I vnderstond all man. Adam fell fro lyfe to deth, in to the slade of this wrechyd worlde, and aftyr that in to hell. Goddys son fell with Adam in to the slade of the meydens wombe, whych was the feyerest doughter of Adam, and that for to excuse Adam from blame in hevyn and in erth. (51.533-34)

> [When Adam fell, God's son fell; because of the true union which was made in heaven, God's Son could not be separated from Adam, for by Adam I understand all mankind. Adam fell from life to death, into the valley of this wretched world, and after that into hell. God's Son fell with Adam, into the valley of the womb of the maiden who was the fairest daughter of Adam, and that was to excuse Adam from blame in heaven and on earth. (274-5)]

Julian's exegesis of the servant parable establishes a distinct complementary relationship between the fall whereby humankind became unlike God, and the Incarnation where the new Adam, and God, became like humanity. This likeness is not a similitude, but real. For Augustine, the materiality of the first couple radically differentiates their relationship. Eve, dependent on Adam for her material creation is thus subordinate to him; "she is a woman, *femina*" (Børresen 18). And it is precisely her sexual body (*femina*), that creates the duality not only between the two persons, but within the person of the woman. Since the divine resides in the *homo*, "the inferiority of *femina* prevents woman from showing in her body the superiority of her rational soul" (Børresen 27). Man, however, is not dual; he reflects God's image in both his soul (*homo*), and in his body (*vir*). The feminine is thus subordinate to the masculine.

Julian rejects Augustine's gendered anthropology of redeemed corporal humanity. For Augustine, because of the dualism of his anthropology, woman must wait for the restoration of her full humanity until the resurrection of the flesh (Børresen 82). Julian, extending the servant allegory, says: "The wyth kyrtyll is his fleshe; the singlehede is that ther was ryght noght betwen the godhede and the manhede" (51.535-36) ["The white tunic is his flesh, the scantiness signifies that there was nothing at all separating the divinity from the humanity" (275)]. Adam's "kyrtyll," corporeal humanity, is hereby dignified, not rejected, not gendered, not split. The Incarnation, according to Julian, is a restoration of the dwelling place of God within humanity--"I saw hym heyly enjoye for the worschypfull restoryng that he wyll and shall bryng hys servannt to by hys plentuous grace" (527) ["I saw him greatly rejoice over the honourable restoration to which he wants to bring and will bring his servant by his great and plentiful grace" (272)]--the establishment of a *regio similitudinis*, as it were.

The fall of the second person of the Trinity is not without price: "for the godhed sterte fro þe fader in to þe maydyns wombe, fallyng in to the takyng of oure kynde, and in this fallyng he toke grete soore. The soore that he toke was oure flessche, in whych as sone he had felyng of dedely paynes" (51.540) ["for the divinity rushed from the Father into the maiden's womb, falling to accept our nature, and in this falling he took great hurt. The hurt that he took was our flesh, in which at once he experienced mortal pains" (277)]. While Augustine compares the formation of Christ in the womb of Mary to the formation of Eve from the side of Adam (Børresen 19), he fails to recognize the implications of this detail either in his soteriology or his anthropology. But Julian imparts the significance precisely. The price the Servant pays is the original punishment, labour. Indeed, the Servant is a "laborer," winning peace "with hys hard travayle"; the Father permits the Son to "suffer all mans payne without sparyng of him" (51.540-41). According to Julian, this labour encompasses all human labor, not only of Adam, but also of Eve even to the birthing labor which will bring humankind to its renewed relationship with God. In language distinctly evocative of childbirth, the language Julian uses to encode the death and life struggle of the new Adam is inclusive:

And by the walowyng and wrythyng, gronyng and monyng, is vnderstonde that he myght nevyr ryse all myghtly fro that tyme þat he was fallyn in to the maydyns wombe, tyll his body was sleyne and dede, he yeldyng the soule to the fadyrs hand with alle mankynde for whome he was sent. (51.541-42)

[And by the tossing about and writhing, the groaning and moaning, is understood that he could never with almighty power rise from the time that he fell into the maiden's womb until his body was slain and dead, and he had yielded his soul into the Father's hand, with all mankind for whom he had been sent. (277)]

The transmutation of the Servant Adam into a woman giving birth to humanity transforms the meaning of humanity itself. As Nicholas Watson puts it:

The servant, who is both Adam and Christ, God and human, in effect . . . becomes a woman at the event which is at once Fall and Incarnation, and is thus occasion at once of humanity's greatest grief and greatest glory. For to be "woman" in this sense is, for Julian, simply to be human; it is the inevitable, the proper metaphor for all life that is lived in the flesh. (25)

The birthpains, the suffering and death, result in the reunification of the human with the divine and the transformation of the flesh not awaiting the resurrection of the body but in a realized eschatology, that is, already in the resurrected body of Christ:

And oure foule dedely flessch, that goddes son toke vppon hym, whych was Adams olde kyrtyll, streyte, bare and shorte, then by oure savyoure was made feyer, new, whyt and bryght, and of endlesse clennesse, wyde and seyde, feyer and rychar than was the clothing whych I saw on the fader. (51.543)

[And our foul mortal flesh, which God's Son took upon him, which was Adam's old tunic, tight-fitting, threadbare and short, was then made lovely by our saviour, new, white and bright and forever clean, wide and ample, fairer and richer that the clothing which I saw on the Father. (278)]

Julian appropriates the inferior female body for an image of humanity and its salvation and hereby reverses Augustine's anthropology.

The significance of this reversal might best be uncovered through Bakhtin's explication of the bodily hierarchy of upper and lower strata. The upper stratum localizes bodily reality in the head and the word, that is, in thought and speech. The surface of the body remains closed, smooth, and impenetrable and "limits the body as a separate and completed phenomenon."[19] In Augustinian terms, the upper stratum of the body is notably masculine. The lower stratum of Bakhtin's analysis replicates the Augustinian limits of the female body without undermining its importance. Bahktin calls it the grotesque body. "The gaping mouth, the protruding eyes, sweat, trembling, suffocation, the swollen face--all of these are typical symptoms of the grotesque life of the body" (308). In contrast to the idealized body, "the grotesque body . . . is a body in the act of becoming. It is never finished, never completed; it is continually being built, created, and builds and creates another body" (317). In the lower stratum of the grotesque body, "the entire mechanism of the word is tranferred from the apparatus of speech to the abdomen. . . . It is a miniature satyrical drama of the word, of its material birth, or the drama of the body giving birth to the word" (309). Finally, "in grotesque realism" Bakhtin says, "the bodily element is deeply positive. . . . It makes no pretense to renunciation of the earthly, or independence of the earth and the body" (19). Coinciding as it does with birth, "in the grotesque body . . . death brings nothing to an end" (322).[20]

Not only does Julian appropriate female bodily imagery in her pietistic practice by embracing extreme physical suffering in her own body, but she also goes much further than other female mystics by representing the divinity as having a female body that groans and moans, endures wounding and torture. Translating her own grotesque body onto that of the divine, she sees the divinity assume the grotesque female body. If Augustine sees female humanity as ineluctably dual and that therefore "woman is nearer to the devil and further removed from God" (Børresen 53), Julian envisions a God who exploits the duality of human spirit and physicality. Humanity, as it were, reveals divinity. If the [female] human being is dual, so is God. Thus where traditional theological discussion had been preoccupied with how man is made in the image and likeness of God and woman's inability to reflect that image,[21] Julian articulates an internally persuasive discourse that distinctly revises that prior view and embraces imagery that opposes Augustine's view of the body as limitation. Engaging as it were with the tradition, she adopts not only a more inclusive point of view but also adapts distinctly female imagery to articulate her theology of inclusion. She both appropriates the discourse of gender and, setting it alongside the equally gendered discourse of tradition, decodes the metaphors which comprise the discourse.[22] Her subsequent imagery continues to exploit the notion of similitude.

Julian's theology of likeness sees God conforming to humanity as well as the more usually reversed view. Emphasizing immanence over omniscience, Julian discovers in the family cogent and persuasive imagery for depicting the relationship between God and humanity. God is revealed not only as traditionally depicted as Father, Son and Holy Ghost but also as one who "enjoyeth that he is our fader, and god enjoyeth that he is our moder, and god enjoyeth that he is our very spouse, and our soule his lovyd wyfe" (52.546) ["rejoices that he is our Father, and God rejoices that he is our Mother, and God rejoices that he is our true spouse, and that our soul is his beloved wife" (279)]. While each of these metaphoric anthropomorphisms has its roots in earlier mystical writings--God's paternal character deeply embedded in Biblical revelation, God's motherhood found in Bernard of Clairvaux, and the brautmystik spirituality widespread since the thirteenth century-- Julian's elaboration of the notion of God as Mother takes on a particularly nuanced character. Recasting the Trinity from traditional father, son, and holy spirit into father, mother, and lord, Julian metaphorizes God precisely in terms of human relationships. The relationship between the Trinitarian persons and between the Trinitarian persons and humanity is substantially, that is, essentially, spiritually, the same. Again, and following Augustine's explication of the image of God as the substance of the soul (homo), Julian develops a more inclusive position. God's very substance is the substance of creation, that is, of humanity itself. She says:

I sawe no dyfference betwen god and oure substance, but as it were all god; and yett my vnderstandyng toke that oure substance is in god, that is to sey that god is god and our substance is a creature in god. For the almyghty truth of the trynyte is our fader, for he made vs and kepyth vs in hym. And the depe wysdome of þe trynyte is our moder, in whom we be closyd. And the hye goodnesse of the trynyte is our lord, and in hym we be closyd and he in vs. We be closyd in the fader, and we be closyd in the son, and we are closyd in the holy gost. And the fader is beclosyd in vs, the son is beclosyd in vs, and the holy gost is beclosyd in vs. (54.562-63)

[I saw no difference between God and our substance, but, as it were, all God; and still my understanding accepted that our substance is in God, that is, to say that God is God, and our substance is a creature in God. For the almighty truth of the Trinity is our Father for he made us and keeps us in him. And the deep wisdom of the Trinity is our Mother, in whom we are enclosed. And the high goodness of the Trinity is our Lord, and in him we are enclosed and he in us. We are enclosed in the Father, we are enclosed in the Son, and we are enclosed in the Holy Spirit. And the Father is enclosed in us, the Son is enclosed in us, and the Holy Spirit is enclosed in us. (285)]

This mutual enclosing of the divine in the human and the human in the divine is substantial, that is, the very nature of both the human and the divine. Though the human senses may be faulty, the human is not reduceable to flesh, inferior, unacceptable. Nor is the human a dichotomized creation of soul imprisoned in body. "As anemptis oure substannce it may ryghtly be callyd oure soule and that is by the onyng that it hath in god" (56.572) ["As regards our sensuality, it can rightly be called our soul," says Julian, "and that is by the union which it has with God" (289)]. Joan M. Nuth notes the blurring of the line Julian draws between the sensual soul and the sensual body: "insofar as the 'sensual soul' is linked to the body, Julian's use of the term "sensuality" can at times be interpreted to include the body itself."[23] Indeed, Christ in the Incarnation makes possible "the assumption of human sensuality into union with [the soul's] substance" and thereby completes human nature

(Nuth 111). In contrast to Augustine's anthropology, for Julian the Incarnation is fully efficacious, both for male and female humanity. "Though not the image of God as such" (112), human sensuality is an essential part of the human relationship with the divine.

While also influenced by Augustine's *De Trinitate*,24 Julian rewrites traditional patriarchal formulations of the Trinity in her rearticulation of the Godhead in the terms of Fatherhood, Motherhood, and Lordship. The essential nature of God is creative and maternal. And that creation includes both substance and sensuality:

> And ferthere more I saw that the seconde person, whych is oure moder, substanncyally the same derewurthy person, is now become oure moder sensuall, for we be doubell of gods makyng, that is to sey substannciall and sensuall. . . . The seconde person of the trynyte is oure moder in kynd in oure substanncyall makyng, in whom we be groundyd and rotyd. (58.585-86)

> [And furthermore I saw that the second person, who is our Mother, substantially the same beloved person, has now become our Mother sensually, because we are double by God's creating, that is to say substantial and sensual. . . . The second person of the Trinity is our Mother in nature in our substantial creation, in whom we are founded and rooted. (294)]

Like a mother whose body gives material nature to the unborn child, God, too, substantially gives birth to humanity. Indeed, Julian again adopts the language of birthing to reveal the relationship of the divine to the human. Even more than an earthly mother who bears her child in pain and death,

> oure very moder Jhesu, he alone beryth vs to joye and to endlesse levyng, blessyd mot he be. Thus he susteyneth vs with in hym in loue and traveyle, in to the full tyme þat he wolde suffer the sharpyst thornes and grevous paynes that evyr were or evyr shalle be, and dyed at the last. And whan he had done, and so borne vs to blysse, yett myght nott all thys make a seeth to his mervelous loue. (60.595-96)

[our true Mother Jesus, he alone bears us for joy and for endless life, blessed may he be. So he carries us within him in love and travail, until the full time when he wanted to suffer the sharpest thorns and cruel pains that ever were or will be, and at the last he dies. And when he had finished, and had borne us so for bliss, still all this could not satisfy his wonderful love. (298)]

Embracing an incarnational theology that will come into fullest expression in later centuries, Julian says further: "God is more nerer to vs than oure owne soule, for he is grounde in whome oure soule standyth, and he is mene that kepyth þe substannce and the sensensulyte to geder, so that it shall nevyr departe" (55.571) ["God is closer to us than our own soul, for he is the foundation on which our soul stands, and he is the mean which keeps the substance and the sensuality together, so that they will never separate" (288-89). Our nature "is wholly in God" (291) and we "haue oure beyng of hym, where the ground of moderhed begyn- nyth. . . . As verely as god is oure fader, as verely is god oure moder" (59.589-90) ["have our being from him, where the foundation of motherhood begins. . . . As truly as God is our Father, so truly is God our Mother" (295)].[25]

Thus, when Julian further develops her Jesus as Mother imagery, it is grounded in gendered physicality, the body and the breast in terms of the nature of female maternal nurturing: "Thus Jhesu Crist, that doth good agaynst evyll, is oure very moder" (59.589) ["So Jesus Christ, who opposes good to evil, is our true Mother" (295)]. Jesus as Mother corrects Augustine's anthropology of humanity whereby humanity takes only matter from the mother. As in the Servant parable, Julian here again exploits the grotesque in embodied imagery.

The moder may geue her cylde sucke hyr mylke, but oure precyous moder Jhesu, he my fede vs wyth hym selfe. . . . The moder may ley hyr chylde tenderly to hyr brest, but oure tender mother Jhesu, he may homely lede vs in to his blessyd brest by his swet opyn syde, and shewe vs there in perty of the godhed and þe joyes of hevyn. (60.596-98)

[The mother can give her child to suck of her milk, but our precious Mother Jesus can feed us with himself. . . . The mother can lay her child tenderly to her breast, but our tender Mother Jesus can lead us easily into his blessed breast through his sweet open side, and show us there a part of the godhead and of the joys of heaven. (298)]

This identification sharply contrasts and engages Augustine's anguished view that the child at the breast is a sign of original sin and the fall:

Who can remind me of the sin of my infancy? For, no one is free from sin in Thy presence, not even the infant whose life has lasted but one day on earth. Who can remind me? Does not each tiny child, in whom I see what I do not remember about myself?

What sin, then, did I commit at that time? Was it that I tearfully gaped with longing for the breast? . . . At that time, then, I did things meriting reproof. . . . But if I "was conceived in iniquity, and in sin did my mother nourish me within her womb," where, I beseech Thee, O my God, where, O Lord, where or when was I, your servant, ever innocent? (*Conf* 1,7)[26]

While Augustine avers that even the milk his mother and nurses fed him came from God, this is but an expansion of his gratitude for all the gifts of his life, not any kind of real appreciation for the body or of a nurturing mother and child. Julian challenges Augustine's assumption about the selfishness of the child and his subsequent blame. In appropriating the relationship of a child with its mother she embraces an imminent God uniquely attuned to human physicality.

And thus is Jhesu oure very moder in kynd of oure furst makyng, and he oure very moder in grace by takyng of oure kynde made. Alle the feyer werkyng and all the swete kyndly officis of dereworthy motherhed is in propred to þe seconde person. . . . I vnderstode thre manner of beholdynges of motherhed in god. The furst is grounde of oure kynde makyng, the seconde is takyng of oure kynde, and ther begynnyth the moderhed of grace, the thurde is moderhed in werkyng. And therin is a forth spredyng by the same grace of lengt and brede, of hygh and of depnesse without ende; and alle is one loue. (59.592-93)

[And so Jesus is our true Mother in nature by our first creation, and he is our true Mother in grace by his taking our created nature. All the lovely works and all the sweet loving offices of beloved motherhood are appropriated to the second person. . . . I understand three ways of contemplating motherhood in God. The first is the foundation of our nature's creation; the second is his taking of our nature, where the motherhood of grace begins; the third is the motherhood of work. And in that, by the same grace, everything is penetrated, in length and in breadth, in height and in depth without end; and it is all one love. (296-97)]

Thus does Julian rewrite Augustine and reread the Eucharist as Christ's suckling of his beloved children of himself. The Eucharist is not a merely spriritual event; it requires actual physical eating of the material substance. In her depiction of Christ's motherhood, Julian metaphorizes the physical with the spiritual. It is through the physical that one can experience the spiritual. In its essence, the lovely word "mother" which for Julian means "Kynd, loue, wysdom and knowyng" (60.599) ["nature, love, wisdom and knowledge" (299)], describes the very nature of God. This is a startling understanding. Sallie McFague says, "What is interesting about this theology is that practically alone among extensive medieval attribution of maternal imagery to God, it focuses on an understanding of God as 'substantially' and not just 'accidentally' female. Moreover, as female, God here not only creates but brings her creation to fulfillment through nurture and through redemption."[27] Rather than represent a sign of the Fall, the motherhood of God reveals the redemption.

III. Julian's Text: Strategies of Dissent

When Julian moves from personal revelation to written text she engages in a public way the problematic dialogue of her discourse. Writing her revelations, and that more than once, she invites scrutiny and claims through her authorship power and autonomy. Inscribing her insights requires an acute awareness of her audience, both the devout believer and the eccleciastical sceptic. As Jo Ann McNamara points out, she, like other women writers, must overcome powerful inhibitions against speaking at all, and by exercising "judicious self-censorship" walk the dangerous boundaries between orthodoxy and heterodoxy (13). But the two versions of her revelations and the time intervening between the two texts point to "her own awareness of the tension between her identity as a daughter of Holy Church and as a recluse and author of private visions" (Staley, *MKDF* 24). In an era of intense religious, political, and theological unrest and suspicion, Julian's acts of revision indicate her need, like her contemporary Margery Kempe, for "strategies to conceal or disguise their original and, in some cases, destabilizing, insights into systems of theological or communal ordering" (Staley, *MKDF* 4). If my reading of her exegesis of the parable of the Servant and the Motherhood of God in the Long Text has merit, Julian is locating herself on the margins of heterodoxy. The twenty or more years during which she reflected on her revelations suggest Julian negotiating both her deeper understanding of the revelations and her concern for their coherence with the authoritative discourse of the tradition. Her acts of revision accommodate the internal dialogue, her "inwarde lernyng" (Baker 138).

Julian conscientiously aligns herself with the Church and avers her allegiance to its teachings. But as Staley persuasively argues, this allegiance must not be read ingenuously, but rather as a strategy, or screen, "allowing her to maintain views that, while not heretical, nonetheless give primacy to a theology whose dominant notes are those of mercy, love, forgiveness, and likeness" (*MKDF* 30). That Julian revises the interpretation of the Fall, omitting any mention of Eve or her role, and focusses instead on a servant who comes to represent all humankind as well as the redeemer of that humankind, is a bold stroke revealing an even bolder theology: "human persons, whether male or female, are created by both God the Father and Jesus the Mother as a union of body and soul incorporating qualities associated with both sexes" (Baker 166); God's relationship with humanity, intimately united in the Incarnation, is likened to the most human of human relationships, a mother and her child; women are incorporated into the redemptive plan as persons and, as such, valued.

Julian's theology and anthropology sharply contrast the patriarchal theology of a fallen humankind, distant from God, struggling to shake off the evils of the flesh in order to attain purity of will and mind and thereby unity with God. Yet Julian cannot help but be sensitive to the authoritative power of the Church and cognizant of the need to screen her more controversial insights. Again and again in her book she specifically negotiates between what she has seen and understood in her revelations with the teachings of the Church. Her soul instructed by her visions, she is fully aware that women were themselves not permitted to teach. Indeed she denies that she is teaching: "I sey nott thys to them that be wyse, for they wytt it wele. But I sey it to yow that be symple, for ease and comfort" (I9.321) ["I do not say this to those who are wise, because they know it well. But I say it to you who are simple, to give you comfort and strength" (191)]. Further, Julian strategizes her theology by screening her text as solidly within the traditional teachings of the creed: "We knowe in our feayth and in our beleue, by the teachyng and the prechyng of holy church, that the blessyd fulle trinitie made mankynd to his ymage and to his lykenes. . . . It was the ymage and the lyknes of owr fowle blacke dede where in our feyer bryght blessyd lorde hyd his godhede" (10.329-30) ["We know in our faith and our belief, by the teaching and preaching of Holy Church, that the blessed Trinity made mankind in his image and likeness. . . . It was in the image and likeness of our foul, black deeds where our fair, bright, blessed lord hid his godhead"].[28] Yet this rhetoric of shame and foulness is absent in her own revelatory explications. Indeed, Julian, truly a child of the Church and its teachings, requests a sight of hell and purgatory, the reward of sinners and the fallen.

> It was nott my menyng to take prefe of ony thyng that longyth to oure feyth, for I beleued sothfastly that hel and purgatory is for þe same ende þat holy chyrch techyth for. But my menyng was þat I myght haue seen for lernyng in all thyng that longyth to my feyth, wher by I my3t lyue the more to goddes wurschyppe and to my profy3te. And for ought þat I culde desyer, I ne culde se of thys ryght nou3t but as it is before seyde in þe fyfte shewyng, wher that I saw þe devylle is reprovyd of god and endlessly dampned. (33.427)

> [It was not my intention to make trial of anything which belongs to our faith, for I believed steadfastly that hell and purgatory exist for the same ends as Holy Church teaches. But my intention was to have seen for instruction in everything which belongs to my faith, whereby I could live more to God's glory and to my profit. But for all that I could wish, I could see nothing at all of this

except what has already been said in the fifth revelation, where I saw that the devil is reproved by God and endlessly condemned. (234)]

While averring that she was not drawn from any articles of the faith or of church teaching, Julian nevertheless notes that her revelation was of goodness, not of evil.

Similarly, in her revelation of the passion of Christ she observes that she did not see "so properly specyfyed the Jewes that dyd hym to deth" (33.428) ["so exactly specified concerning the Jews who put him to death" (234) even though she knows by the teachings of the Church that they were "a cursyd and dampnyd" (33.428) eternally. Yet, her conclusion is an oddly incoherent one; she claims to have been "strenghed and lernyd generally" to keep the faith in "evyry poynt" but this general faith seems to leave room for her to explicate her more particular insights. Subtly rejecting the scholastic theological schools, and veiling her more disconcerting insights under the aura of obedience and humility, she avers: "the more we besy vs to know hys prevytes in that or any other thyng, the ferthermore shalle we be from the knowyng" (33.429) ["the more we busy ourselves in that or in anything else, the further we shall be from knowing" (235)]. Nevertheless, despite this caveat, "her avowals of obedience seem designed to function as screens for her own strongly original and oftentimes bold cast of thought" (Staley, *MKDF* 30), and are not to be read literally or simplistically.

Julian also indirectly negotiates the teaching of the church about the mercy of God and what was revealed to her by Christ. "For by the techyng that I had before," she says, "I vnderstode that the mercy of god shalle be forgeuenesse of hys wrath after the tyme that we haue synned" (46.495) ["For by the teaching which I had before, I understood that the mercy of God will be remission of his wrath after we have sinned" (260)]. But it is not a deeper understanding of God's anger and wrath that she discovers. Indeed, she experiences nothing of the sort. Rather she discovers the frailty of humanity:

Man is channgeabyll in this lyfe, and by sympylnesse and vncunnyng fallyth in to synne. He is vnmyghty and vnwyse of hym selfe, and so his wyll of ovyr leyde in thys tyme he is in tempest and in sorow and woe. . . . Yf he saw god conynually,

he shulde haue no myschevous felyng ne no maner steryng, no
sorowyng that servyth to synne." (47.496)

[Man is changeable in this life, and falls into sin through naivete
and ignorance. He is weak and foolish in himself, and also his
will is overpowered in the time when he is assailed and in sorrow
and woe. . . . For if he saw God continually, he would have no
harmful feelings nor any kind of of prompting, no sorrowing
which is conducive to sin. (260)].

It is God's mercy, not anger, that sustains humanity and brings it to
blessedness, a blessedness that Julian hopes for: "And the joyng in hys
syght with this trew hope of hys mercyfull kepyng made me to haue
felyng and comfort, so that mornyng and drede were nott grettly
paynfull" (47.498) ["The rejoicing in his sight, with this true hope of
his merciful protection made me have feeling and comfort, so that the
mourning and fear were not very painful" (261)].

Julian does more, however, than dialogue with the theological and
ecclesiastical culture. As Lynn Staley asserts, "Julian needed to evolve a
rhetorical stretegy that allowed her the freedom to say what she needed
to say" (*PH* 109). In addition to the strategies elucidated by Staley,
Julian adopts a posture of subjectivity which seems to subordinate her
insights and theological interpretations to the larger authority of the
church. This subjectivity is coded in the phrase, "as to my syght," which
punctuates the Long Text. This interpolation, however, often intrudes
at potentially sensitive theological moments and should be read as an
example of another strategy for disguising her unauthorized insights
rather than merely an expression of doubt or inferiority. Indeed, the
language itself denotes interior insight and understanding as distinct
from physical sight or revelation.[29] For example, in Chapter 4, Julian
asserts for the first time her understanding that "wher Jhesu appireth the
blessed trinitie is vnderstand, as to my sight" (295-96) and foreshadows
her later more assertive representation of the trinitarian metaphor and
hermeneutic. Similarly, in Chapter 7, Julian twice locates the phrase
around her soteriology, seeing the Lord Jesus as not only the most high,
noble, and most honorable, but also the lowest, humblest, and most
familiar (314, 315), foreshadowing her more thorough exegesis of the
servant parable. In Chapter 8, her sixth understanding of the bleeding

head of Jesus is that "god is all thyng that is good, as to my syght, and the goodnesse that all thyng hath, it is he" (318) an assertion that will be more fully explicated when she more overtly resists the representation of God as angry and judgemental.

In Chapter 31, Julian couches her introduction of Christ's longing for the bliss of all humanity with the phrase:

> therfore this is his thurste and loue longyng of vs, all to geder here in hym to oure endlesse blysse, as to my syght. . . . For the same thurst and longyng that he had vppe on the rode tre, whych desyre, longying and thurste, as to my sight, was in hym from withou3t begynnyng, the same hath he 3ett and shalle in to the tyme that the last soule that shalle be savyd is come vppe to hys blisse. (31.418, 420)

> [Therefore this is his thirst and his longing in love for us, to gather us all here into him, to our endless joy, as I see it. . . . For he still has that same thirst and longing which he had upon the Cross, which desire, longing and thirst, as I see it, were in him from without beginning; and he will have this until the time that the last soul which will be saved has come up into his bliss. (230-31)]

Open as this passage is to an interpretation of Julian's acceptance of universal salvation, Julian masks her interpretation to subjectively limited insight.[30]

The subjectivity of the expression disguises the assertions which form the core of Julian's teaching. Interpolated into those more interpretive sections of the revelations, Julian subtly blurs the representation of her more unorthodox teachings about Christ and salvation. While pointing as it does to the inner dialogue of Julian with the authority of the Church and superficially ceding that authority, the phrase codes the very concerns that Julian experiences in the revelations and imbricates her own internally persuasive discourse and authority.

For Julian, God both embraces all of human experience, physical experience, male and female, particularly parenting, and rejects that which is faulty in humanity, such as anger and wrath. Since the production of the Short Text, "the unlearned and feeble woman has become a voice aligned with the community of the Church (as her oft repeated phrase 'myn evyn cristen' implies) and speak[s] with the authority of the seer and the teacher" (Staley, *MKDF* 26). She employs strategies and techniques which negotiate her thinking with male readers predisposed to reject her insights. She also asserts and affirms the legitimacy of her othodoxy while refusing to internalize those truisms of patriarchal discourse and doctrine which are not revealed to her. Julian of Norwich nevertheless manages, by means of an intelligent awareness of the need to screen her insights, to balance orthodoxy with heterodoxy as she discovers within her own experiences a mode of spiritual exercise.[31]

NOTES

1. For the most thorough examination to date of the political and social world informing Julian and her text, see Lynn Staley and David Aers, *The Powers of the Holy* (University Park, PA: U of Pennsylvania P, 1996).

2. Barbara Newman, in referencing Nicholas Watson makes a similar observation: "the entire Long Text is constructed as a dialogue not so much between God and Julian as between Julian-the-inspired-visionary (who received the showings) and Julian-the-questing-believer (who struggles to understand them)." See *From Virile Woman to WomanChrist* (Philadelphia: U of Pennsylvania P, 1995) 131.

3. M. M. Bakhtin, *The Dialogic Imagination* (Austin: U of Texas P, 1981) 293.

4. "The Changing Shape of Late Medieval Mysticism," *Church History* 65 (1996): 204. Laurie Finke makes the same observation in her analysis of the way this discourse regulated the female body in *Feminist Theory, Women's Writing* (Ithaca, NY: Cornell UP, 1992) especially 78ff. See also Nicholas Watson's "'Yf wommen be double naturelly': Remaking 'Woman' in Julian of Norwich's Revelation of Love," *Exemplaria* 8 (1996): 1-34.

5. Thorough research on this topic has been summarized in: Alcuin Blamires, ed., *Woman Defamed and Woman Defended* (Oxford: Clarendon, 1992); Elizabeth A. Clark, *Women in the Early Church.*, Message of the Fathers of the Church. Vol 13 (Wilmington, DE: Glazier, 1983; rpt. 1987), Julia O'Faolain and Lauro Martines, eds. *Not in God's Image* (NY: Harper, 1973) and Elaine Pagels, *Adam, Eve, and the Serpent* (New York: Random, 1988). See also Howard Bloch, *Medieval*

Misogyny and the Invention of Western Romantic Love (Chicago: U of Chicago P, 1991).

6. *Anchoritic Spirituality. Ancrene Wisse and Associated Works.* Trans. Anne Savage and Nicholas Watson (New York: Paulist, 1991) 74.

7. See, for example, Laurie Finke's discussion of Leoba and the attending complexity of relations between the prior discourse and the actual empowering of Leoba's embodied speech. *Feminist Theory. Women's Writing* (Ithaca: Cornell UP, 1992) 79-82.

8. For example, "Hildegard concealed her visions for half her life until, in 1141, a sense of irresistible supernatural force overcame her paralysis," Lutgard of Aywières was forced from her sickbed by God, and an angel beat Elisabeth of Schönau "until she agreed to reveal her visions." Jo Ann McNamara, "The Rhetoric of Orthodoxy," *Maps of Flesh and Light*, ed. Ulrike Wiethaus (Syracuse: Syracuse UP, 1993) 11.

9. See, for example, Colledge and Walsh's discussion of Julian's intellectual formation: *A Book of Showings* 43-59. Baker notes that by 1393, the time of the final version of her text, "she had acquired an understanding of moral and mystical theology that enabled her to use this discipline's terminology and adapt its concepts with subtle creativity" (12-13).

10. *A Book of Showings to the Anchoress Julian of Norwich.* 2 vols. Eds. Edmund Colledge and James Walsh (Toronto: Pontifical Institute of Mediaeval Studies, 1978) 22.266; 632. *Julian of Norwich: Showings.* Trans. and eds. Edmund Colledge and James Walsh. Classics of Western Spirituality (New York: Paulist, 1978) 162, 310. Subsequent references will be provided parenthetically within the text.

11. Grace M. Jantzen makes a similar observation: "the passage reads as though Julian feels caught between her gender and her religious duty, and is squirming to find a way forward. . . . Furthermore, it seems that she has interiorized her inferiority as a woman." See *Power, Gender and Christian Mysticism* (Cambridge: Cambridge UP, 1995) 177.

12. *On Genesis against the Manichees, On the Literal Interpretation of Genesis, Confessions, On the Trinity,* and *City of God*. See Roland Teske, *St. Augustine. On Genesis* (Washington, DC: Catholic U of America P, 1991) 3.

13. Lynn Staley, *Margery Kempe's Dissenting Fictions* (University Park, PA: P State UP, 1994) 3.

14. Watson suggests that the intervening time between revisions may well exceed the usually accepted twenty years, "perhaps as many as forty" (82).

15. Baker notes the difficulty Julian must have experienced resolving this vision with the teachings of the Church. She seems to solve these difficulties only at the end of her many years of reflection. "Her failure to mention either the parable or the idea of Jesus as Mother suggests that most of this revelation was composed during the second revision of the short text" (85).

16. Kari Elisabeth Børresen, *Subordination and Equivalence. The Nature and Role of Woman in Augustine and Thomas Aquinas* (Washington, DC: University P of America, 1981) 42.

17. For example, "And this was a begynnyng of techyng whych I saw in the same tyme, wherby I myght come to knowyng in what manner he beholdeth *vs* in *oure* synne. And then I saw that oonly payne blamyth and ponyschyth, and *our* curteyse lorde comfortyth and socurryth, and evyr he is to the soule in glad chere, lovyng and longyng to bryng *vs* to his blysse" (51.522-23) ["And this was a beginning of the teaching which I saw at the same time, whereby I might come to know in what manner he looks on *us* in our sin. And then I saw that only pain blames and punishes, and *our* courteous Lord comforts and succours, and always he is kindly disposed to the soul, loving and longing to bring *us* to his bliss" (271)]. Emphasis added.

18. Also 94-95 and 97-98 where she provides the traditional texts which centerpiece this notion.

19. *Rabelais and His World* (Bloomington, IN: Indiana UP, 1984) 318.

20. Essential reading on this topic include Laurie Finke's two essays: "Mystical Bodies and the Dialogics of Vision" in *Maps of Flesh and Light*, ed. Ulrike Wiethaus, (Syracuse: Syracuse UP, 1993) 28-44; and the chapter "The Grotesque Mystical Body: Representing the Woman Writer" in *Feminst Theory, Women's Writing*, 75-107.

21. Only in relationship with the man can the woman reflect the image of God, asserts Augustine. ". . . Not the woman but the man is the image of God. . . . When she is referred to separately in her quality of helpmate, which regards the woman herself alone, then she is not the image of God; but as regards the man alone, he is the image of God as fully and completely as when the woman too is joined with him" (O'Faolain 130).

22. See Jantzen, esp. 301-303.

23. *Wisdom's Daughter. The Theology of Julian of Norwich* (New York: Crossroad, 1991) 109.

24. See Baker 109.

25. Julian's theology also contrasts with that of Hildegard of Bingen who strategizes her explication of the creation by adopting the Augustinean hierarchy of gender and emphasizing the preordained bodily weakness of Eve which exonerates her from blame. See Joan Cadden, *Meaning of Sex Difference in the Middle Ages* (Cambridge: Cambridge UP, 1993) 190-92 and Gerda Lerner, *The Creation of Feminist Consciousness* (Oxford: Oxford UP, 1993) 58-62.

26. *Saint Augustine. Confessions*, trans. Vernon J. Bourke (Washington, D.C: Catholic U of America P, 1953) 12-13. I am indebted to Karen Cherewatuk for pointing me to this reference.

27. *Models of God. Theology for an Ecological, Nuclear Age* (Philadelphia: Fortress P, 1987) 115.

28. Translation my own.

29. Nicholas Watson observes in his essay in this volume (n. 22) that "while Middle English 'as to my sight' was doubtless sometimes used with the vague generality of the modern English . . . it is more closely similar equivalent to 'in my judgement.' . . . Julian's use of the term is likely to have been especially conscious and serious."

30. See, additionally, the phrase as used in Chapters 32, 41, 45 and 76.

31. This essay was completed with the support of a Rhodes College Faculty Development Grant. I am grateful for the helpful insights and comments of Karen Cherewatuk, Denise N. Baker, and Brad Peters.

The Image of God: Contrasting Configurations in Julian of Norwich's *Showings* and Walter Hilton's *Scale of Perfection*[1]

Denise N. Baker

Two of the most significant Middle English discourses about mysticism were completed during the last quarter of the fourteenth century: Julian of Norwich's *Showings* and Walter Hilton's *Scale of Perfection*. Since Hilton ostensibly addresses his spiritual advice to an anchoress, it is often assumed that Julian was familiar with the *Scale*. Jonathan Hughes, for example, asserts that Hilton directly influenced Julian; John P. H. Clark more cautiously claims that the *Scale* "sets before the reader the program of ascetic theology that the author of *The Cloud of Unknowing* and Julian of Norwich would have taken for granted."[2] The fact that both writers derive their theory from the Augustinian discourse of introspective mysticism seems to further support this hypothesis about influence, either direct as Hughes asserts, or indirect as Clark suggests. As I hope to demonstrate, however, it is highly unlikely that either author knew the work of the other not only because the evidence about dates of composition and manuscript circulation make any such contact improbable but also because the two authors develop the mystical theory they appropriate from Augustine's *De trinitate* (*On the Trinity* 400-416) in antithetical ways. Julian of Norwich and Walter Hilton interrogate rather than affirm each other's interpretation of the theology of the *imago Dei*, her articulation of the Augustinian premises being so different from his more traditional recapitulation as to constitute an innovative contribution to late-medieval theology.

This disclosure of the radically different uses of the same theological commonplace in the *Showings* and *The Scale of Perfection* refutes the assumption that the late-medieval discourse about mysticism was univocal and exemplifies the diversity of vernacular theology in the fourteenth century, a diversity which was suppressed early in the next century by the ecclesiastical reaction against Lollardy.3 Until very recently such suppression was perpetuated by scholars who insisted on evaluating these texts in regard to some universal standard of religious orthodoxy, whether it be the three stages of mystical ascent, the passage through an apophatic "dark night of the soul," or some other criterion of validity.4 Because of this concentration on the issue of legitimacy, texts about mysticism were reduced to their most common features rather than analyzed in terms of their unique points of view and historical contingency. In the last decade or so, however, a shift in the paradigm for inquiry, from a religious to a cultural perspective, has resulted in a recognition of the diversity of medieval spirituality. This new approach emphasizes the varieties of visionary and mystical experiences and their cultural construction and significance. Such an emphasis on the disparate "configurations of holiness" as well as their social and political implications enables scholars to explore the contestation about the meaning and validity of religious experiences, symbols, and terminology in late-medieval England.5 The analysis of Middle English mystical discourse has thus begun to move, as Aers and Staley put it, from reproduction of the dominant orthodoxy to reflection upon its formation. The contrasting interpretations of the *imago Dei* offered by Julian of Norwich and Walter Hilton exemplify the range of opinion allowed in the decade or so prior to the restriction of vernacular theology that resulted from Arundel's *Constitutions* of 1409.

I.

Because Julian of Norwich was an anchorite, at least by 1393, it is tempting to assume, as Hughes does, that she knew Walter Hilton's *Scale of Perfection*, the preeminent Middle English work of spiritual advice about contemplation addressed to a woman recluse. Julian and Hilton were, after all, exact contemporaries, both living in or near East Anglia in the last three decades of the fourteenth century. It is even likely that both were born in same year, 1343. Julian indicates this date of birth when she reports that at the time of her visionary experience in May 1373 she was thirty and one half years old. The only extant manuscript copy of the short text, British Library Additional 37790, is preceded by a scribal note that states she is still alive in 1413, though she probably died two or three years later. Known to have been an anchoress in Norwich from at least 1393/4, it is assumed that she lived in the city or its environs all her life.[6] Hilton's life span, though shorter by about two decades, coincides with Julian's. Documents indicate that he became a Bachelor of Civil Law around 1370. If so, as Clark reasons, "he must have come up to Cambridge by 1357; since fourteen years was the minimum age for entry, he can hardly have been born later than 1343."[7] Though possibly from Lancashire, Hilton spent most of his adult life in East Anglia, either at Cambridge or Ely, until he entered the priory of Augustinian Canons at Thurgarton in Nottinghamshire around 1386.[8] He died there ten years later in 1396.

Julian of Norwich and Walter Hilton both composed texts about mysticism sometime between 1373 and 1386 which they subsequently revised or amplified in the 1390s. Julian's first, short account of the revelations was written within about a decade of her visionary experience, possibly as early as 1373 or as late as 1388.[9] She increases the length of this original version sixfold in the long text finished no earlier than 1393, after she had reflected "for twenty yere after the tyme of the shewyng saue thre monthys" (51.520) ["for twenty years after the time of the revelation except for three months" (270)].[10] During this period that Julian of Norwich was revising her short text, Walter Hilton was writing the two books of *The Scale of Perfection*; the first was completed around 1386 and the second, shortly before his death in 1396. Given this chronology of composition, it is highly unlikely that either author knew the other's final version since both were probably writing during the 1390s. It remains possible, however, that Julian might have consulted Book I of the *Scale* while she was completing her long text or that Hilton could have been influenced by the short text of the *Showings* as he worked on either of his books.

When the evidence of extant manuscripts is taken into consideration, however, both these possibilities seem implausible. Despite the fact that Julian's short text preceded Hilton's Book I, possibly by as many as thirteen years, the single surviving manuscript copy, based on an exemplar produced in 1413, suggests such limited circulation as to make Hilton's knowledge of it highly unlikely. Even Margery Kempe, who reports on her visit to Julian in Norwich around 1413 and refers to her as an anchoress who "good cownsel cowd ʒeuyn" ["could give good advice"] never mentions her *Showings*.[11] On the other hand, although there are over forty extant English copies of Book I of *The Scale of Perfection*, its late date of composition in 1386 would only allow for Julian's knowledge of it during the last stages of her revision of the short text.[12] While the external evidence does not preclude the hypothesis that Julian read Book I of *The Scale of Perfection* between 1386 and 1393, internal evidence, as I will show, proves that she uses the Augustinian discourse of introspective mysticism which Hilton introduces in Book I and develops even more extensively in Book II in such a radically different manner as to foreclose any question of his influence on her, except perhaps as she reacted against his interpretation of their common tradition.

II.

The enabling premise of this self-reflexive mysticism derives from the account of creation at Genesis 1:26-27: "And he said: 'Let us make man to our image and likeness; . . . ' And God created man to his own image; to the image of God he created him. Male and female he created them." These words, as interpreted by Augustine in *De trinitate*, authorize the model of the soul as the *imago Dei* to which both Julian of Norwich and Walter Hilton subscribe. In his effort to understand the divine Trinity that he accepts on faith, Augustine assumes that humankind, created in the image and likeness of God, embodies a similar trinitarian unity or *imago Dei*.[13] Conceding that the human mind is not divine by nature, Augustine asserts that it nonetheless has the potential to participate in divinity. "For [the mind] is His image by the very fact that it is capable of Him, and can be a partaker of Him; and it cannot be so great a good except that it is His image."[14] Augustine's emphasis on capacity inscribes a circular trajectory for self-development, with the goal a fulfillment of the pattern imposed at the beginning. Having been created in the image of their Creator, individuals have the potential for achieving a likeness to God. Such participation in the divine nature is, according to Augustine, the ultimate human destiny.

Despite his vision of humanity's exalted destiny, Augustine is not confident that most individuals will attain a likeness to God. For, in keeping with his theodicy, he believes that Adam's sin obscured the image of God in his descendants; as a result, not only have they lost paradise, but they are also born with their essential nature deformed. While Adam could diminish the image of God created within him, humanity cannot, Augustine argues, restore this image to its original condition nor perfect it into a likeness to God without divine intervention. Only through a process of sanctification, enabled by Christ's atonement and enacted by grace, can humanity be re-created in the image of God and perfected to his likeness.

Although Augustine's definition of the soul as the *imago Dei* pervades the medieval ideology of sin and salvation, the human capacity for deification gains particular prominence in mystical theology. The Victorines and the Cistercians in the twelfth century, the Franciscans and Dominicans in the thirteenth, and the Rhineland mystics in the fourteenth variously develop Augustine's dynamic model of the self as a deformed image with the capacity for likeness to God into the epistemology, ontology, and anthropology of introspective mysticism. In this tradition of introspective mysticism, contemplation is metaphorically spatialized as a paradoxical movement of the mind both upward and inward, "since to ascend in the scale of being is to enter more deeply into oneself, into the centre of one's being."[15] Through introspection, it was believed, the contemplative could gradually and sporadically perfect the inherent image of God into a likeness and attain, though only momentarily, self-fulfillment by participating in the divine nature.

Julian of Norwich and Walter Hilton appropriate these central tenets of introspective mysticism developed from Augustine's *De trinitate*.[16] Both base their mystical theology on a conception of human nature which locates the *imago Dei* within each individual. In Book I, Hilton's account of human creation concludes: "a man's soul, which may be called a created trinity, was filled with memory, sight and love by the uncreated blessed Trinity, who is our Lord."[17] Julian likewise employs the Augustinian vocabulary in the long text: "And thus was my vnderstandyng led of god to se in hym and to wytt, to vnderstonde and to know that oure soule is a made trynyte lyke to the vnmade blessyd trynyte, knowyn and lovyd fro with out begynnyng, and in þe makyng onyd to the maker" (55.568); ["And so my understanding was led by God to see in him and to know, to understand and to recognize that our soul is a created trinity, like the uncreated blessed Trinity, known and loved from without beginning, and in the creation united to the

Creator" (287)]. Similarly, both Hilton and Julian regard contemplative union as the culmination of a process of self-examination which leads the mystic to see the *imago Dei* within. Hilton advises the anchoress to engage in introspection: "That is to enter into your own soul by meditation in order to know what it is, and by the knowledge of it to come to the spiritual knowledge of God. For as St. Augustine says: 'By the knowledge of myself I shall get the knowledge of God'"(I.40.III). Julian alludes to similar statements by Augustine, but with a significant reversal of the procedure:

> And thus I saw full suerly that it is redyer to vs and more esy to come to þe knowyng of god then to know oure owne soule. For oure soule is so depe growndyd in god and so endlesly tresoryd that we may nott come to the knowyng ther of tylle we haue furst knowyng of god, whych is the maker to whome it is onyd. But not withstondyng I saw that we haue kyndly of fulhed to desyer wysely and truly to know oure owne soule, wherby we be lernyd to seke it ther it is, and that is in to god. And thus by the gracious ledyng of the holy gost we shall know hym both in oone: whether we be steryd to know god or oure soule, it is both good and trew. (56.570-71)

> [And so I saw most surely that it is quicker for us and easier to come to the knowledge of God than it is to know our own soul. For our soul is so deeply grounded in God and so endlessly treasured that we cannot come to knowledge of it until we first have knowledge of God, who is the Creator to whom it is united. But nevertheless I saw that we have, naturally from our fulness, to desire wisely and truly to know our own soul, through which we are taught to seek it where it is, and that is in God. And so by the leading through grace of the Holy Spirit we shall know them both in one; whether we are moved to know God or our soul, either motion is good and true. (288)]

Although Hilton and Julian both assert that knowledge of self and of God coincide, he regards the movement as unidirectional, from the soul to God; she, as bidirectional, either from God to the soul or from the soul to God. This difference of opinion about the sequence by which such knowledge is achieved discloses the crucial ideological difference in their interpretations of introspective mysticism.

Hilton develops the concept of the *imago Dei* in a pastoral, ascetic context while Julian explores it from a speculative, metaphysical perspective. He emphasizes the disfiguration of this *imago Dei* caused by transgression and its displacement by the image of sin. Using optical metaphors for the soul and for the deity, he concentrates on the occlusion that separates humankind from God. Julian, though troubled by her conviction of her own sinfulness, insists on the inextricability of the *imago Dei* of the elect from its ontological union with the godhead. She uses tactile metaphors of enclosure and containment to indicate the indivisible bond between humankind and God. In his model of the soul Hilton employs gender-coded language to indicate the hierarchical relationship within the soul. Because of his anxiety about the disfiguration of the *imago Dei* and the diminishment of the individual's divine potential, Hilton insists on the need for ascetic discipline of the sensuality. Julian, on the other hand, is assured that "alle shalle be wele" through the revelation of the godly will of the elect. By tracing out these fault lines that distinguish their interpretations of the *imago Dei*, I hope to show how Julian subtly shifts the theological foundation of introspective mysticism.

Perhaps the best way to begin to articulate the divergence between Hilton's and Julian's orientations is to contrast their representations of the Augustinian model of the soul. In Book XII of *De trinitate*, Augustine distinguishes between two parts of the soul (*mens*), the higher and lower reason; the former, engaged in the contemplation of eternal things, can achieve wisdom (*sapientia*); the latter, directed toward action in the temporal world, can achieve only knowledge (*scientia*). He accounts for this division of labor within the *mens* using the analogy of Eve's creation. Just as the first woman was formed as Adam's helpmate because no suitable companion could be found for him among the animals, so, Augustine argues, "a certain part of our reason, not separated so as to sever unity, but diverted, as it were, so as to help fellowship, is set aside for the performing of its own proper work" (XII.3.3:345). The higher and lower reason are thus gender-coded as Adam and Eve, masculine and feminine. Despite Augustine's insistence that the two parts of reason are one mind as the wedded couple are two in one flesh, he privileges the higher or masculine reason as the locus of the *imago Dei* in humankind: "in that part alone, to which belongs the contemplation of eternal things, there is not only a trinity but also an image of God; but in that which has been diverted to the action upon temporal things, even if a trinity can be found, yet it cannot be an image of God" (XII.4.4:346). Augustine thus situates the *imago Dei* exclusively in that part of the mind which he metaphorically construes as male.

In the subsequent chapters of Book XII, Augustine moves from his initial analogy between the lower reason and Eve as helpmate and equal of Adam (Chapter 3) to an identification of the lower reason with Eve as the temptress to sin (Chapter 12). In his analysis of the psychology of temptation, Augustine regards the female not just as a metaphor of temporality and physicality but as the literal embodiment of them. The historical Eve, deceived by the serpent, lured Adam into eating the forbidden fruit just as the feminine part of the mind, the lower reason, in contact with the body, seduces the higher or masculine reason to sin. In his tropological interpretation the serpent represents "the sensual movement of the soul which is directed to the senses of the body, and which is common to us and to the beasts," but is excluded from reason (XII.12.359). The lower reason, directed toward the corporeal, is the medium of temptation between this sensuality and the higher reason. This tripartite construction gains wide currency in the high Middle Ages because Peter Lombard incorporates it into his *Sentences* (2.24.6-13), where he divides the soul into the sensuality or inferior power and the reason or superior power, which itself consists of higher and lower parts.[18]

Although Walter Hilton and Julian of Norwich both follow the Augustinian model of the bilateral soul and also employ the term "sensuality" to indicate the lower component, a closer examination reveals distinctive modifications that betray the crucial difference between them. In Book II of *The Scale of Perfection*, Hilton describes the two parts of the soul, which he terms the sensuality and the reason. His identification of the lower component as the sensuality reveals that he has been influenced, either directly or indirectly, by Peter Lombard's exposition in the *Sentences*.

> A soul has two parts. One is called the sensuality: that is the
> carnal feeling through the five outward senses which is common
> to man and beast. From this sensuality, when it is irrationally and

inordinately ruled, is made the image of sin, . . . for the sensuality is sin when it is not ruled according to reason. (II.13.213)

Despite Hilton's initial assertion that the sensuality is one of the two parts of the soul, his subsequent insistence on its contamination by sin makes clear that his term refers not to the lower reason as it is defined in Augustine's *De trinitate*, but rather to the motion of the senses emphasized by Lombard.

Hilton then separates the higher part of the soul into two parts, the superior and inferior reason, and reiterates Augustine's distinction between them.

> The other part is called reason, and that is divided in two, into the higher part and the lower part. The higher part is compared to a man, for it should be master and sovereign, and this is properly the image of God, for by that alone the soul knows God and loves him. The lower part is compared to a woman, for it should be obedient to the higher part of reason as woman is obedient to man, and that lies in the knowledge and rule of earthly things, to use them discerningly according to need and to refuse them when there is no need; at the same time always to have an eye raised to the higher part of reason, with reverence and fear, in order to follow it. (II.13.213-14)

In accord with *De trinitate*, Hilton uses a metaphor of gender to describe the relationship between these two parts of the reason. The higher reason should govern the lower reason as the male exercises control over the female. Moreover, the *imago Dei* resides exclusively in the higher or masculine part of reason and the lower or feminine aspect of the soul is the intermediary between the higher reason and the sensuality.

In his subsequent discussion Hilton uses these three parts of the soul to classify the three different states in his hierarchy of spiritual development.

> Now, I can say that a soul living according to the pleasure and lusts of his flesh like a beast without reason . . . is not reformed

to the likeness of God, for it lies and rests wholly in the image of sin, that is, the sensuality. Another soul that fears God, withstands the impulses of the sensuality to mortal sin and does not follow them, but lives rationally in the rule and control of worldly things . . . he is reformed in faith to the likeness of God. . . . But another soul that through grace flees all the stirrings of the sensuality to mortal sin--and to venial sins as well--to such length that he does not feel them: he is reformed in feeling, for he follows the higher part of reason in beholding God and spiritual things. (II.13.214)

For Hilton, the sensuality is that part of the soul common to animals as well as humans; it is associated with the instincts and appetites. As the ground of sin and the locus of the image of sin, the sensuality impels transgression and must be resisted and suppressed. Through the failure of the feminine lower reason, the sensuality's image of sin displaces the image of God in the soul. If, however, the lower reason can resist the temptations of sensuality, succumbing only to minor infractions, it rises to the first rung of Hilton's spiritual scale or ladder, reform in faith. The highest stage of development, reformation in feeling, can only be achieved when the superior component of the soul, the masculine higher reason which contains the *imago Dei*, is perfected by grace. As this passage indicates, Hilton emphasizes the transgressive force of the sensuality and the vulnerability of the lower reason throughout *The Scale of Perfection.*

Although Julian of Norwich bases her model of the soul on the same Augustinian paradigm that Hilton invokes, she develops it in a radically different manner.[19] She terms the higher reason the soul's "substance" and the lower reason its "sensuality." Julian, however, refuses to gender these two parts of the soul as is common in the Augustinian tradition. Furthermore, although she uses the same word as Hilton does, her attitude toward the sensuality is much more positive than his; and, as the term "substance" implies, her exposition is metaphysical rather than moral. In contrast to her male contemporary, Julian insists that both parts are integral to the soul: "and as anemptis oure substannce it may ryghtly be callyd oure soule; and anemptis oure sensualite it may ryghtly be callyd oure soule, and that is by the onyng that it hath in god" (56.572); ["as regards our substance, it can rightly be called our soul, and as regards our sensuality, it can rightly be called our soul, and that is by the union which it has in God" (289).] Her emphasis on this unity reiterates Augustine's initial claim that the division between higher and lower reason is one of function, not essence--a claim which he nonetheless violates in his subsequent analysis of the psychology of temptation. Thus, while Hilton, distinguishing between the lower reason and the motion of the senses, uses "sensuality" to denote the latter, Julian enhances the status of the term "sensuality" by employing it to identify the lower reason.[20]

Julian diverges significantly from the Augustinian tradition by refusing to restrict the *imago Dei* to the higher reason. Rather, she asserts that it informs the sensuality or lower part of the soul.

> I saw that in oure sensualyte god is, for in the same poynt that oure soule is made sensuall, in the same poynt is the cytte of god, ordeyned to hym fro without begynnyng. In whych cytte he comyth, and nevyr shall remeve it, for god is nevyr out of the soule, in whych he shalle dwell blessydly without end. (55.567)

> [I also saw that God is in our sensuality, for in the same instant and place in which our soul is made sensual, in that same instant and place exists the city of God, ordained for him from without beginning. He comes into this city and will never depart from it, for God is never out of the soul, in which he will dwell blessedly without end. (287)]

By locating the image of God in the sensuality, the nexus between the spiritual and the corporeal, Julian indicates that she considers the human person as a union of body and soul.[21] Although she does not gender-code the sensuality female, as Hilton does with the lower reason, she implicitly associates it with women and the body through her metaphor of the motherhood of Jesus; her attitude toward both, however, is much more positive than his. Like a mother, Jesus incorporates the preexistent substance of the soul into its material manifestation or body by uniting it with its lower part or sensuality: "for we be doubell of gods makyng, that is to sey substannciall and sensuall. Oure substannce is þe hyer perty, whych we haue in oure fader god almyghty, and the seconde person of the trynyte is oure moder in kynd in oure substanncyall makyng, in whom we be groundyd and rotyd" (58.585-86); ["because we are double by God's creating, that is to say substantial and sensual. Our substance is the higher part, which we have in our Father, God almighty; and the second person of the Trinity is our Mother in nature in our substantial creation, in whom we are founded and rooted" (294).] When she speaks of God residing in the sensuality from the moment that the substance, predestined for salvation from all eternity, is joined to it, Julian may mean that the substance itself is the *imago Dei* and that it rests in the sensuality while embodied.[22] In any case, she clearly regards salvation as the complementary perfection of body and soul, sensuality and substance.

> And all the gyftes that god may geue to the creature he hath gevyn to his son Jhesu for vs, whych gyftes he wonnyng in vs hath beclosyd in hym in to the tyme that we be waxyn and growyn, oure soule with oure body and oure body with oure soule. Eyther of them take helpe of other tylle we be broughte vp in to stature as kynde werkyth; and than in the ground of kynd with werkyng of mercy þe holy gost gracyously enspirith in to vs gyftes ledyng to endlesse lyfe. (55.567)

> [And all the gifts which God can give to the creature he has given to his Son Jesus for us, which gifts he, dwelling in us, has enclosed in him until the time that we are fully grown, our soul together with our body and our body together with our soul. Let either of them take help from the other, until we have grown to full stature as creative nature brings about; and then in the foundation of creative nature with the operation of mercy, the Holy Spirit by grace breathes into us gifts leading to endless life. (287)]

Using a metaphor of physical growth, Julian emphasizes the mutually invigorating relationship between the body and the soul and their inevitable maturation to their ultimate potential.

Despite her more positive attitude toward the body, Julian concurs with her male contemporary about the deficiencies of the sensuality and its responsibility for transgression. She does not, however, categorically repudiate it, but rather anticipates its elevation to its original sanctity.

And anemptys oure substannce he made vs so nobyll and so rych
þat evyr more we werke his wylle and his worshyppe. Ther I say:
We, it menyth man þat shall be savyd. . . . And of þis grete
rychesse and of this hygh noble, vertues by mesure come to oure
soule, what tyme þat it is knytt to oure body, in whych knyttyng
we are made sensuall. And thus in oure substannce we be full and
in oure sensualyte we feyle, whych feylyng god wylle restore. . . .
And of theyse none shalle be perysschyd, for oure kynde, whych is
the hyer party, is knytte to god in þe makyng, and god is knytt to
oure kynde, whych is the lower party in oure flessch takyng.
(57.576-78)

[And as regards our substance, [God] made us so noble and so
rich that always we achieve his will and his glory. When I say
"we," that means men who will be saved. . . . And from this
high nobility, commensurate powers come into our soul, whilst
it is joined to our body, in which joining we are made sensual.
And so in our substance we are full and in our sensuality we are
lacking, and this lack God will restore. . . . And of these none
will be destroyed, for our nature, which is the higher part, is
joined to God in its creation, and God is joined to our nature,
which is the lower part in taking flesh. (290-91)]

Acknowledging the susceptibility of the sensuality to sin, Julian
nonetheless looks forward not to its suppression and extirpation, as
Hilton does, but to its completion and reunion with the higher part of
the soul or substance. Admittedly, in contrast to him, she refers only to
those predestined for salvation, but for her this category is much more
inclusive than it is for other medieval theologians.[23] In her
representation substance and sensuality are not inherently in conflict but
rather complementary; and holiness is a state of wholeness or integration
of these two parts of the soul.

Furthermore, by using the word "substance" to identify the higher
reason, Julian also indicates the metaphysical orientation of her analysis.
As Aristotle's first category, substantia, the Latin equivalent of the
Middle English "substance," is a word commonly used in scholastic
discourse and by the Rhineland mystics like Eckhart.[24] However, Julian
may also have acquired the term from patristic or prescholastic sources.

Both Augustine and Boethius use it in their texts on the Trinity, and throughout the Middle Ages substance was not regarded as "purely logical" but rather "had metaphysical and theological implications."[25] In *De trinitate*, for example, Augustine uses substance as a synonym for essence.

> But God is without doubt a substance, or perhaps essence would be a better term . . . [because] essence is so called from being [*esse*]. And who possesses being in a higher degree than He, who said to His servant Moses: "I am who am," and "He who is, has sent me to you." . . . Being is in the highest and truest sense of the term proper to Him from whom being derives its name. (*De trinitate* V.2.177)

"Substance" for Augustine thus denotes "the quality of being real or having an actual existence."[26] Julian implies this definition of substance as existence in her claim that God is the ground of the soul's being.

> God is more nerer to vs than oure owne soule, for he is grounde in whome oure soule standyth, and he is mene that kepyth þe substannce and the sensualyte to geder, so that it shall nevyr departe. For oure soule syttyth in god in very rest, and oure soule stondyth in god in suer strenght, and oure soule is kyndely rotyd in god in endlesse loue. And therfore if we wylle haue knowyng of oure soule, and comenyng and dalyance ther with, it behovyth to seke in to oure lord god in whom it is enclosyd. (56.571)

> [God is closer to us than our own soul, for he is the foundation on which our soul stands, and he is the mean which keeps the substance and the sensuality together, so that they will never separate. For our soul sits in God in true rest, and our soul stands in God in sure strength, and our soul is naturally rooted in God in endless love. And therefore if we want to have knowledge of our soul, and communion and discourse with it, we must seek in our Lord God in whom it is enclosed. (288-89)]

Julian's conception of God as the ground of the soul can ultimately be traced back to the doctrine of participation which Augustine adapted from Neoplatonic thought and passed on to his medieval successors. "The centrality of this doctrine," according to Bell, "lies in the fact that if a thing *is*, then it *is* not by virtue of its own being, but simply because it participates in True Being, which is God."[27] Thus to exist means to exist in God: all of creation, by virtue of its existence, shares in God's Being without being God. Augustine interprets God's words in Exodus, "I am that I am," as a statement of creaturely subsistence in the Creator: "For since God is the supreme existence, that is to say, supremely is, and is therefore unchangeable, the things that He made He empowered to be, but not to be supremely like Himself."[28] Julian makes precisely this point when she claims, paradoxically, that she "sawe no dyfference betwen god and oure substance, but as it were all god; and yett my vnderstandyng toke that oure substance is in god, that is to sey that god is god and oure substance is a creature in god" (54.562-63); ["saw no difference between God and our substance, but, as it were, all God; and still my understanding accepted that our substance is in God, that is to say that God is God, and our substance is a creature in God" (285)]. Through the distinction between the Creator and creatures she articulates in the last clause of this sentence, Julian avoids claiming a *unitas indistinctionis* or "absolute oneness of God and the soul," a claim that led to Eckhart's condemnation for heresy early in the fourteenth century.[29] Instead she regards the soul as a substance in the sense that it exists in, without being identical to, God.

Julian's analysis of the nature of the soul is thus more theoretical and speculative than Hilton's. Rather than recapitulating the textbook discussion from Lombard's *Sentences*, she adapts the Augustinian paradigm to express her own unique perspective regarding the sensuality's potential for sanctification and the substance's animation by God. She thus creatively articulates ideas implied by, but seldom expressed as, orthodox beliefs.

The implications of these differences between Hilton's and Julian's appropriation of the Augustinian model become obvious in the metaphors they use to describe the soul's relationship to God and in the program of spiritual development they set out for their readers. Hilton emphasizes the self-loathing and ascetic discipline that should result from the contemplative's recognition that the *imago Dei* has been disfigured into the image of sin through the dominance of the sensuality or ground of sin over the reason.

Through looking inward you will be able to see the honor and dignity [your soul] ought to have from the nature of the first making; and you will see too the wretchedness and misery into which you have fallen through sin; . . . You will also feel a loathing and horror of yourself, with a great will to destroy and suppress yourself and everything that hinders you from that dignity and joy. (I.42.112)

Hilton argues that this repulsion will compel a program of discipline designed to obliterate the ground of sin on which the reason rests. He uses the metaphor of harrowing a field to indicate not only how fundamental and prolific the sensuality's inclination to sin is, but also how intractable.

This is a task for the spirit, hard and sharp in the beginning for anyone who will work vigorously in it, for it is a labor in the soul against the ground of all sins, small or great; and this ground is nothing but a false disordered love of a person for himself . . . and indeed until this ground is thoroughly ransacked and deeply delved, and as if dried up by casting out all fleshly and worldly loves, a soul can never feel spiritually the burning love of God, or have clear sight of spiritual things by the light of understanding. (I.42.112)

Throughout Book I, but especially in Chapters 52 through 90, Hilton painstakingly constructs the image of sin that rests on this ground of sin, analyzing, in the tradition of the *Ancrene Wisse*, the *Scale's* predecessor in the genre of anchoritic literature, the seven deadly sins.[30] Although he advises moderation in ascetic discipline, he concentrates on eradicating this ground of sin in the sensuality.

Regarding sanctification as the suppression of the sensuality, Hilton not only focuses on the conflict between the two parts of the soul and between the soul and body, but also emphasizes the distance between the soul and the deity. Speaking of the process of introspection, Hilton writes:

A soul that wants to have knowledge of spiritual things needs first to have knowledge of itself. For it cannot have knowledge of a nature above itself unless it has knowledge of itself; and that is when the soul is so gathered into itself, separated from the consideration of all earthly things and from the use of the bodily senses, that it feels itself as it is in its own nature, without a body. (II.38.252)

These underlying assumptions about the incompatibility of the spirit and body are betrayed by the optical metaphors that Hilton chooses to refer to the relationship between the soul and God, its object of desire in the contemplative process. He describes the soul as a mirror in which the *imago Dei* is occluded by sin and sensuality. "For your soul is only a mirror in which you shall see God spiritually. Therefore, you shall first find your mirror and keep it bright and clean from fleshly filth and worldly vanity, and hold it well up from the earth so that you can see it, and in it likewise our Lord" (II.38.252). Like a mirror the soul reflects God, but its image is a distortion of the original object. Metaphors of distorted sight pervade Book II of the *Scale*. In Chapter 32, for example, the different spiritual states are compared to degrees of sightedness: the unreformed sinners are analogous to the blind; those reformed in faith, to the sighted who keep their eyes closed; and those reformed in feeling metaphorically glimpse the full sun with open eyes (II.32.260).

Throughout Book II Hilton figuratively construes this highest state of perfection, contemplation, in terms of sight and illumination, or as he phrases it, "the opening of heaven to the eye of a pure soul" (II.32.261). Contemplation is like the act of staring on the desired object from a distance without hope of achieving complete comprehension in this life.

As [Jesus] illuminates the reason through the touch and shining of his blessed light he opens the inner eyes of the soul. . . . He [the soul] does not see *what* he [God] is, for no created being can do that in heaven or earth; and he [the soul] does not see him *as* he is, for that sight is only in the glory of heaven. But he sees *that* he is: an unchangeable being; a supreme power, supreme truth, supreme goodness; a blessed life, an endless beatitude. (II.32.259)

Like the male lover in the courtly tradition, the soul gazes on its desired object from afar and comes to recognize its own inferiority and insignificance as well as the incomprehensible brilliance of the deity.

> That is, Lord Jesus, the sight of your blessed uncreated substance and your infinite being shows me clearly that my substance--and the being of my soul--is as nothing beside you. . . . That is, compared with the eternal being and unchangeable nature of God, mankind is as nothing, for it is made from nothing and to nothing it shall return, unless he who made it from nothing holds it in existence. (II.37.272-73)

Although Hilton here approaches Julian's concept of the soul as a substance, enlivened and sustained by God,[31] his emphasis is on the disparity between the two, not their indivisible bond. For Hilton, the idea of the sensuality as the ground of sin has far more force than that of the soul's substance or ground of being in God.

Julian of Norwich, on the other hand, does not regard the sensuality as the ground of sin nor does she concentrate on the displacement of the *imago Dei* by the image of sin. Rather, she claims that the substance of the soul inextricably rests in God as the ground of being on which its existence depends just as the *imago Dei* resides in the soul.

> A hye vnderstandyng it is inwardly to se and to know that god, whych is oure maker, dwellyth in oure soule, and a hygher vnderstandyng it is and more, inwardly to se and to know oure soule that is made dwellyth in god in substance, of whych substance by god we be that we be. (54.562)

> [It is a great understanding to see and know inwardly that God, who is our Creator, dwells in our soul, and it is a far greater understanding to see and know inwardly that our soul, which is created, dwells in God in substance, of which substance, through God, we are what we are. (285)]

According to Julian God and the soul permeate each other in reciprocal enclosure.[32] Because of these existential entanglements, she claims that the contemplative must know the self to know God, and conversely, know God to know the self. The two kinds of knowledge are complementary, simultaneous, and bidirectional because, as Julian insists, the *imago Dei* is enclosed within the individual soul at the same time that the individual soul is enclosed within God.

Julian's conception thus exactly reverses Hilton's; instead of stressing the intractable ground of sin on which the soul rests and the distance between it and God, she emphasizes its situation in God as the ground of being and its inextricable connection with a divinity that invigorates both substance and sensuality. And rather than focusing on the ascetic discipline that results from the contemplative's self-loathing as her introspection brings her to recognize the deformation of the *imago Dei*, Julian stresses the self-confidence that comes from her revelation's assurance that in the elect the soul and God as well as the substance and the sensuality will inevitability be fully integrated.

Julian's metaphoric language reveals the striking difference between her idea of union and Hilton's. In contrast to the metaphors of the mirror and the gaze that he uses for the soul's separation from God, she employs throughout Revelation 14 metaphors of enclosure and interlacing to refer not only to contemplative union, the highest state of perfection, but also to the ontological union that binds those who will be saved to the deity. She interprets the theological commonplace of the soul's creation out of nothing not, like Hilton, as evidence of the incommensurable difference between it and its maker, but rather as proof of their indivisible bond.

> And thus I vnderstode that mannes soule is made of nought, that is to sey it is made but of nought that is made, as thus: whan god shulde make mannes body, he toke the slyme of the erth. . . . But to the makyng of mannys soule he wolde take ryght nought, but made it. And thus is the kynde made ryghtfully onyd to the maker, whych is substanncyall kynde vnmade, þat is god. And therfor it is that ther may ne shall be ryght nought betwene god and mannis soule. (53.558-59)

> [And so I understood that man's soul is made of nothing, that is to say that it is made of nothing that is made, in this way: When God was to make man's body, he took the slime of the earth. . . . But to the making of man's soul he would accept nothing at all,

all, but made it. And so is created nature rightfully united to the maker, who is substantial uncreated nature, that is God. And so it is that there may and will be nothing at all between God and man's soul. (284)]

Julian develops the metaphor of the knot to signify this ontological connection of the elect to the deity and to each other as they have been predestined for glory in the mind of God for all eternity.

And ferthermore he wyll we wytt that this deerwurthy soule was preciously knytt to hym in the makyng, whych knott is so suttell and so myghty that it is onyd in to god. In whych onyng it is made endlesly holy. Farthermore he wyll we wytt that all the soulys þat shalle be savyd in hevyn with out ende be knytt in this knott, and onyd in this oonyng, and made holy in this holynesse. (53.560)

[And furthermore, he wants us to know that this beloved soul was preciously knitted to him in its making, by a knot so subtle and so mighty that it is united in God. In this uniting it is made endlessly holy. Furthermore, he wants us to know that all the souls which will be saved in heaven without end are knit in this knot, and united in this union, and made holy in this holiness. (284)]

Julian calls this entanglement of the divine and human substances "a godly wylle that nevyr assentyd to synne ne nevyr shall, whych wyll is so good that it may nevyr wylle evyll, but evyr more contynn(u)ly it wyllyth good and werkyth good in the syght of god" (53.555); ["a godly will which never assents to sin and never will, which will is so good that it can never will evil, but always constantly it wills good and it does good in the sight of God" (283)]. She bases her idea of the godly will on the concept of predestination in Christ and describes it as the intersection or overlap between the souls of the elect and the second Person of the Trinity:

ech kynde that hevyn shall be fulfyllyd with behovyd nedys of goddys rygh(t)fulnes so to be knytt and onyd in hym that there in were kepte a substannce whych myght nevyr nor shulde be partyd from hym, and that thorow his awne good wyll in his endlesse forse(ing) purpose. (53.556)

[every nature with which heaven will be filled had of necessity and of God's rightfulness to be so joined and united in [Jesus] that in it a substance was kept which could never and should never be parted from him, and that through his own good will in his endless prescient purpose. (283)]

Not only does the *imago Dei* reside within the soul as the soul rests within the Being of God, but this reciprocal enclosure is enhanced by the godly will of those predestined for salvation. Like a complex and intricate knot, by which two distinct objects are bound together so tightly that they cannot be separated, so the elect and God are ontologically intertwined in a union that cannot be severed by mortal sin. Julian develops this concept of the godly will precisely to counteract the tradition of identifying the sensuality, as Hilton does, with the bestial part of the soul. "Ryght as there is a bestely wylle in the lower party that may wylle no good, ryght so there is a godly wyll in the hygher party, whych wylle is so good that it may nevyr wylle evylle, but evyr good" (37.443); ["Just as there is an animal will in the lower part which cannot will any good, so there is a godly will in the higher part, which will is so good that it cannot ever will any evil, but always good" (242)]. Because of their godly will, Julian is confident that for the elect "alle shalle be wele."

What accounts for the striking divergence between Walter Hilton's and Julian of Norwich's development of their common Augustinian model of the soul? Is Hilton's emphasis on the conflict within the soul, its separation from God, and the need to discipline the sensuality and body typically masculine? Is Julian's concentration on the complementarity of the two parts of the soul, its enclosure of and in God, and her assurance that despite human failings "alle shalle be wele" characteristically feminine? It is indeed tempting to conclude that these two contemporaries, both drawing on the same theological tradition, provide such startlingly disparate analyses because of their different genders. Such a generalization, however, based on only two examples and informed by an assumption of essentialism, is neither warranted nor necessary. Certainly, a comparison between Hilton and one of the other male writers of mystical discourse such as Rolle or the *Cloud* author would reveal significant disagreement. Likewise, Julian's theology is distinct from that of Margery Kempe even though these two women met in 1413. While there are undoubtedly important distinctions between the writings of male and female mystics in the Middle Ages, these can be explained as plausibly by the social construction of gender as by the premise that there are essential psychological differences between men and women.[33]

It may be more legitimate, though ultimately unprovable, to attribute the disparity between Hilton's and Julian's perspectives to her claim that she received revelations from God. As a cleric and spiritual advisor, Hilton has a position of authority based on his learning rather than on a personal experience; what he knows about contemplation comes from his study of authoritative texts. Throughout both books of *The Scale of Perfection*, he intermittently acknowledges that his reader's spiritual experience may well be superior to his own intellectual understanding; at the end of Book II, for example, he writes: "for a soul that is pure, stirred by grace to the practice of this work, can see more of such spiritual matter in an hour than could be written in a great book" (II.46.302).[34] On the other hand, whatever the cause of the visionary experience that Julian had in May 1373, it exercised a profound influence over her subsequent life. It undoubtedly compelled her to become the first English woman known as an author. Not only was she incited to record the event in the short text of her *Showings*, but she also reflected on its meaning for twenty years before she achieved sufficient understanding to compose the innovative long version of her book. Though the cause of her revelations remains open to speculation, the two versions of the *Showings* attest to their consequences for her. While Hilton, a priest and scholar, transmits the Augustinian model of the soul to his readers, Julian, a mystic and theologian, transforms this paradigm to express her own unique vision.

NOTES

1. I am grateful to Judith Ferster, Charlotte Gross, Megan Matchinske, Sol Miguel-Prendes, Claire Schen, and Olga Valbuena for their valuable comments on a draft of this essay.

2. Jonathan Hughes, *Pastors and Visionaries: Religion and Secular Life in Late Medieval Yorkshire* (Woodbridge: Boydell, 1988) 213; John P. H. Clark, Introduction, *Walter Hilton: The Scale of Perfection,* trans. John P. H. Clark and Rosemary Dorward, Classics of Western Spirituality (New York: Paulist, 1991) 33.

3. Nicholas Watson, "Censorship and Cultural Change in Late Medieval England: Vernacular Theology, the Oxford Translation Debate and Arundel's *Constitutions,*" *Speculum* 70 (1995): 822-64.

4. Bernard McGinn surveys modern studies of mysticism in the appendix to *The Presence of God: A History of Western Christian Mysticism,* vol. 1 of *The Foundations of Mysticism* (New York: Crossroads, 1992) 265-343. For a critique of ahistorical analyses of medieval mysticism, see Grace M. Jantzen, *Power, Gender and Christian Mysticism,* Cambridge Studies in Ideology and Religion 8 (Cambridge: Cambridge UP, 1995) Chapters 8 and 9.

5. The phrase is from David Aers and Lynn Staley, *The Powers of the Holy: Religion, Politics, and Gender in Late Medieval English Culture* (University Park, PA: Pennsylvania State UP, 1996) 1; see also Grace Jantzen, *Power, Gender and Christian Mysticism.*

6. Grace M. Jantzen evaluates the documentary evidence and various theories about Julian's life in Chapter 2 of *Julian of Norwich: Mystic and Theologian* (New York: Paulist, 1988) 15-27.

7. Clark, Introduction, *Walter Hilton* 14; Hughes, *Pastors and Visionaries,* 180-81, suggests that Hilton might have studied for his degree in Civil Law while he was still an undergraduate and therefore would have been born a few years later.

8. In his Introduction, *Walter Hilton* 15, Clark indicates that sometime after 1383 Hilton lived briefly as a solitary but his location at this time is not known.

9. In "The Composition of Julian of Norwich's *Revelation of Love,*" *Speculum* 68 (1993): 637-683, Nicholas Watson argues that the short text was written after 1382 and perhaps as late as 1388 and that the long text was completed early in the fifteenth century. Most scholars, however, continue to believe that the long text was finished soon after 1393; see Staley's response to Watson's argument in *Powers of the Holy,* 110-12.

10. Quotations in Middle English are from *A Book of Showings to the Anchoress Julian of Norwich,* ed. Edmund Colledge, O.S.A., and James Walsh, S.J., 2 vols., Studies and Texts 35 (Toronto: Pontifical Institute of Mediaeval Studies, 1978); quotations in Modern English are from *Julian of Norwich: Showings,* trans. Edmund Colledge, O.S.A., and James Walsh, S.J., Classics of Western Spirituality (New

York: Paulist, 1978). Quotations are documented parenthetically by chapter and page.

11. *The Book of Margery Kempe*, ed. Sanford B. Meech and Hope Emily Allen, Early English Text Society, o.s., 212 (London: Early English Text Society, 1940) 42; *The Book of Margery Kempe,* trans. B. A. Windeatt (Harmondsworth: Penguin, 1985) 77.

12. Vincent Gillespie, "Vernacular Books of Religion," in *Book Production and Publishing in Britain, 1375-1475,* ed. Jeremy Griffiths and Derek Pearsall, Cambridge Studies in Publishing and Printing History (Cambridge: Cambridge UP, 1989) 322.

13. For an introduction to the theology of the *imago Dei*, see Bernard McGinn, "The Human Person as Image of God II: Western Christianity," in *Christian Spirituality: Origins to the Twelfth Century*, vol. 16 of *World Spirituality: An Encyclopedic History of the Religious Quest*, ed. Bernard McGinn and John Meyendorff (New York: Crossroads, 1985) 312-30.

14. Saint Augustine, *The Trinity*, trans. Stephen McKenna, C.SS.R., The Fathers of the Church 45 (Washington, D. C.: Catholic U of America P, 1963) 14.8.11:426; subsequent citations from this translation will be documented parenthetically in the text.

15. Andrew Louth, *The Origins of the Christian Mystical Tradition* (Oxford: Clarendon, 1981) 147.

16. Wolfgang Riehle, *The Middle English Mystics,* trans. Bernard Standring (London: Routledge, 1981) discusses Hilton's and Julian's development of the *imago Dei* in Chapter 11.

17. *Walter Hilton: The Scale of Perfection*, trans. John P. H. Clark and Rosemary Dorward, Classics of Western Spirituality (New York: Paulist, 1991) I.43:114. Since a Middle English edition is not available, all quotations are from this translation and will be documented parenthetically in the text.

18. Peter Lombard, *Sententiae*, in *Patrologiae Latinae*, ed. J. P. Migne (Turnholt: Brepols, 1844-1864) 192:702-706. D. W. Robertson, Jr., *A Preface to Chaucer: Studies in Medieval Perspectives* (Princeton, NJ: Princeton UP, 1962) 74-75, demonstrates the misogynist implications of this tripartite model and points out that Lombard even conflates the lower reason with the sensuality.

19. For a more extended discussion see Denise N. Baker, *Julian of Norwich's Showings: From Vision to Book* (Princeton, N. J.: Princeton UP, 1994) Chapter 5. Among the critics who consider Julian's model of the soul are Jantzen, *Power,*

Gender and Christian Mysticism, 146-56; Joan Nuth, *Wisdom's Daughter: The Theology of Julian of Norwich* (New York: Crossroads, 1991) 104-16; and Nicholas Watson, "'Yf wommen be double naturelly': Remaking 'Woman' in Julian of Norwich's Revelation of Love," *Exemplaria* 8 (1996): 1-34, who argues that medieval misogyny informs Julian's representation of sensuality. Trajei Park contrasts Julian's and Hilton's views on the sensuality in "Reflecting Christ: The Role of Flesh in Walter Hilton and Julian of Norwich," in *The Medieval Mystical Tradition in England: Exeter Symposium V*, ed. Marion Glasscoe (Cambridge: Brewer, 1992) 17-37.

20. At the end of his discussion in *Sententiae* 2.24.11, Lombard says that sensuality can also refer to the lower reason; see Migne, *PL* 192:705-706. Julian uses the term with this denotation, but with a very different connotation from Lombard's or Hilton's.

21. Riehle, *Middle English Mystics* 130-31, regards this respect for sensuality as Julian's most important contribution to the theology of the *imago Dei* and as evidence of her great familiarity with Latin theology.

22. See Baker, *Julian of Norwich's Showings* 118-22.

23. See Baker, *Julian of Norwich's Showings* 74-82.

24. For a discussion of the differences between the Augustinian and the scholastic conceptions of the soul, see Heinz Heimsoeth, *The Six Great Themes of Western Metaphysics and the End of the Middle Ages,* trans. Ramon J. Betanzos (1987; repr. Detroit: Wayne State UP, 1994) 110-38. Anton Charles Pegis, *St. Thomas and the Problem of the Soul in the Thirteenth Century* (1934; repr. Toronto: Pontifical Institute of Mediaeval Studies, 1976), explains the challenge that Aristotle's notion of substance posed for Bonaventure, Albert the Great, and Thomas Aquinas. Influenced by Thomas Aquinas, Eckhart often used this common scholastic term; see *substantia* in the Latin Glossary of *Meister Eckhart: Teacher and Preacher,* ed. Bernard McGinn with Frank Tobin and Elvira Borgstadt, Classics of Western Spirituality (New York: Paulist, 1986) 398.

25. Michael Hearn, *Medieval Thought: The Western Intellectual Tradition from Antiquity to the Thirteenth Century* (New York: St. Martin's, 1985) 84.

26. *Oxford Latin Dictionary*, ed. P. G. W. Glare (Oxford: Clarendon, 1982).

27. David N. Bell, *The Image and Likeness: The Augustinian Spirituality of William of St Thierry* (Kalamazoo, MI: Cistercian, 1984) 23. See also J. F. Anderson, *St. Augustine and Being: A Metaphysical Essay* (The Hague: Martinus Nijhoff, 1965). The idea of God as the ground of the soul is one Julian shares with the Rhineland mystics. According to McGinn et al., *Meister Eckhart: Teacher and*

Preacher 402, Eckhart uses the German word *grunt* to indicate the "'ground' or 'innermost depths,' referring both to God and the deepest level of the soul where it is identical with God." See also Oliver Davies, *God Within: The Mystical Tradition of Northern Europe* (New York: Paulist, 1988), for discussion of Eckhart's (47-55) and Tauler's (78-84) developments of this concept. There is no evidence, however, that Julian knew their texts.

28. Augustine, *The City of God* 12.2, trans. M. Dods with G. Wilson and J. J. Smith, *Basic Writings of Saint Augustine*, ed. Whitney J. Oates (New York: Random, 1948) 2:180.

29. For a discussion of Eckhart's concept of indistinct union and its connection with the idea of God as the ground of the soul, see Bernard McGinn, "Love, Knowledge, and Unio Mystica in the Western Christian Tradition," in *Mystical Union and Monotheistic Faith: An Ecumenical Dialogue*, ed. Moshe Idel and Bernard McGinn (New York: Macmillan, 1989) 75-78.

30. For a discussion of this *imago peccati*, see Vincent Gillespie, "Idols and Images: Pastoral Adaptations of *The Scale of Perfection*," in *Langland, the Mystics and the Medieval English Religious Tradition: Essays in Honour of S. S. Hussey*, ed. Helen Phillips (Cambridge: Brewer, 1990) 97-123.

31. Hilton expresses an understanding similar to Julian's when he warns his reader not to regard God's immanence literally, as he implies Richard Rolle has done. "This word *within* is to be understood [spiritually]. It is commonly said that a soul shall see our Lord within all things, and within itself. It is true that our Lord is within all creatures, but not in the way that a kernel is hidden inside the shell of a nut, or as a little bodily thing is held inside another big one. But he is within all creatures as holding and keeping them in their being, through the subtlety and power of his own blessed nature and invisible purity" (II.33.262). While Hilton acknowledges that a divine principle of life resides in the soul, he does not claim, as Julian does, that the soul resides in divine Being.

32. I am grateful to Charlotte Gross for this phrase.

33. For such an analysis, see Jantzen, *Power, Gender and Christian Mysticism*.

34. Staley contrasts the difference in Hilton's and Julian's claims to authority in *Powers of the Holy*, 134-44.

The Trinitarian Hermeneutic in Julian of Norwich's *Revelation of Love*[1]

Nicholas Watson

If we want to reach a more elevated understanding of the mind intelligently, a useful preliminary task is to take note of the ways in which we generally arrive at our knowledge of things. So: unless I am mistaken, we arrive at knowledge of things in three ways. For some things we discover by experience, others we acquire by reasoning, and a belief in yet others we hold by faith. Thus, for example, we come to know temporal things by experiencing them, but we rise to knowledge of the eternal by way of reasoning or by way of faith. (Richard of St Victor)[2]

Be iii things man stondith in this life, be which iii God is worshipped and we be spedid, kept and savid. The ist is use of manys [kyndly reson]; the ii is commen teching of holy church; the thred is inward gracious werking of the Holy Gost. And these iii ben all of one God: God is the ground of our kindly reason, and God the teaching of holy church, and God is the Holy Gost. And all ben sundry gifts, to which he will we have gret regard and attenden us therto. For these werkyn in us continualy all to God. And [thoo] ben grete thyngs, of which gret things he will we have knowing here as it were in one ABC: that is to seyn, that we have a litill knoweing whereof we shall have fullhede in hevyn, and that is for to spede us. (Julian of Norwich)[3]

[Humanity is supported by three things in this life, through which God is worshipped and we are helped, nurtured and saved.

The first is the use of humanity's natural reason; the second is the common teaching of the holy church; the third is the inner, grace-inspired work of the Holy Spirit. And these three are all from one God: God is the ground of our natural reason, and God the teaching of holy church, and God is the Holy Spirit. And all these are different gifts, which he desires us to have great respect towards and attend to closely. For these work within us continually, always towards God. And there are great things, about which great things he desires that we have knowing in this life in the way we know an ABC: that is to say, that we have a little knowing of the things we will know fully in heaven, and that is to help us.]

I

How does the *Revelation of Love* describe and interpret the experience that forms its starting-point? In what ways does it claim to be a true account of that experience, and in what ways does it treat the experience itself as truth-bearing? What principles govern the relationships between Julian's memory of her revelation, her subsequent meditations on it, and the written accounts that attempt to articulate it? In spite of the fact that these hermeneutic questions, and the host of others which they bring to mind, are of obvious importance and difficulty, they have received oddly little by way of detailed attention.4 Indeed, Julian scholarship--which, when it is not singing its subject's praises, is still often perceptibly apologetic in its tone--has, I think, been guilty of a kind of fundamentalism in its treatment of such questions. Perhaps this is because most scholarly work on Julian since the turn of the century has been motivated at least in part by the desire to confirm that her vision of an all-unifying cosmic love is in some final sense right;5 under these circumstances, it may have seemed to be in everyone's interests to protect the *Revelation of Love* from the fissuring process that hermeneutic enquiry tends to initiate.

The present paper is written in the belief that any such protection, for two reasons, is inappropriate. The first reason is that a fundamentalist reading of the work--which insists upon, for example, an absolutely literal meaning for phrases like "I saw," or "I understood," or "these iii come to my [mynde] in the tyme6--finally provides as partial and misleading an understanding of the work as do fundamentalist readings of anything. The second reason is that, as so often elsewhere, Julian proves to have thought things out more clearly than her readers, and at a number of points in the revised version of the *Revelation of Love* displays a hermeneutic awareness that is at once sophisticated, individual, and impressively of a piece with the rest of her theology. The purpose of this paper is in fact to argue that hermeneutic enquiry is basic to Julian's enterprise in something of the sense it is to Chaucer's project in *The Canterbury Tales* or Langland's in *Piers Plowman*.7 In different ways, all three writers find themselves concerned almost as closely with the question of how truth can be known and interpreted as they do with the nature of truth. As the passage from Chapter 80 of the *Revelation of Love* quoted above makes clear, such a concern is of course integral to any spirituality that takes seriously Paul's dictum, *"nunc cognosco ex parte,"*8 an acceptable paraphrase of which would be "in this life all knowledge is contingent": a dictum which we can also see in operation in the babbling heterogeneity of Chaucer's Canterbury pilgrims, and which is perhaps the only immovable truth uncovered by Will in all of his wanderings. Yet these same parallels also suggest something distinctively late medieval about Julian's belief that no knowledge beyond the merest "ABC" can be obtained in this life. Between her remarks and the superficially similar ones, likewise quoted above, with which Richard of St. Victor begins his wonderfully confident speculations on the Trinity lie all that separate the middle of the twelfth century from the last years of the fourteenth: the age of scholasticism, the rise of nominalism, the decline of the crusading ideal, the growth of ever more successful heresies, the advent of the Great Schism. Where Julian is apparently closer to Richard than to either Langland or Chaucer is in the assurance with which she can incorporate into her vision of life the second half of Paul's dictum: *"tunc autem cognoscam sicut et cognitus sum"*--"but then I shall know even as I am known" (I Corinthians 13:12b). It is this optimistic and intimate expectation of knowledge that is to come that distinguishes the *Revelation of Love* from most other products of the late medieval "age of anxiety," and which enables Julian to resolve--and to do so with a remarkable intellectual coherence--most of the hermeneutic difficulties in which her long life's labor involved her.

II

The essence of the hermeneutic problem which any reader of Julian faces, and which she faced in recording her experience, lies in the impossibility of distinguishing clearly between the revelation itself and the responses and reflections it provoked.9 Very many years--certainly more than twenty and perhaps as many as forty--separate Julian's experiences in May, 1373 from the final account given in the Long Text. These years were presumably spent in meditation on those experiences, but this is not an altogether reassuring fact to the literal-minded reader; after all, intense thought on a single set of themes over a sustained period is hardly the best way to preserve those themes in their original form. Nor does the earlier Short Text (which I will not on the whole be considering here) provide as much help as we might like. Even if it really is the freshly immediate response to revelation that it has generally been taken to be--and I will argue elsewhere that it is not10--it differs so markedly and in so many respects from Julian's revision as to raise more difficulties than it settles. For example, most of the imagistic precision for which Julian has become famous--as when she likens the blood flowing down from Christ's forehead to pellets, herring-scales and rain falling off a roof, explaining gravely why each image is appropriate--is absent from the Short Text, even though she frequently states or implies in the Long Text that such images "came to her mind" at the time of the revelation.11 Is this absence because Julian for some reason suppressed material, perhaps because it seemed too trivial and non-symbolic? Or has her memory of her "mind" at the time of the revelation undergone that drift towards greater vividness that occurs when we tell an important dream many times, gradually fusing our sense of what we experienced with our understanding of what it meant and our desire to convey some of the force as well as the bare bones of the experience to our listeners? These may seem the tiresomely unanswerable questions of a precisionist--literary and theological scholars alike have tended to hop over them with little more than a backward glance--but their importance is real enough if we take Julian's own precision seriously. The passing of time is not an incidental feature of the Long Text; on the contrary, dates, numbers of years, Julian's own age, are carefully brought before us at the work's most crucial moments, as though they are of thematic significance.[12]

I will return later to consider the problem of time from Julian's own perspective and to discuss the passage in the Long Text which effectively cuts the Gordian knot I am attempting here to tie. But the inseparability of divine revelation from human reflection and the hermeneutic tangles this inseparability creates are not, of course, the products merely of Julian's failure to record her experiences sooner than she did or to do so with complete consistency on two different occasions. They are integral, rather, to the very qualities of the revelation itself which made it at once so time-consuming and so important to comprehend, assess and at last write down: to its experiential elusiveness and its structural complexity, its apparently endless profundity and its disconcerting, potentially perhaps even dangerous, theological optimism. I clearly cannot hope to discuss any of these qualities adequately in a paper of this size (and I will be giving Julian's theology in particular only a peripheral treatment). Nonetheless, something must now be said about the nature of Julian's revelation, about the exegetical framework that she evolves in order to deal with it, and about how that framework is in practice applied.

III

Whether or not she knew much or anything about mystical predecessors such as Bridget of Sweden, Mechthild of Hackeborn or Elizabeth of Schönau, the form of Julian's revelation presented her with an interpretive task which would have rendered their examples of limited usefulness.[13] As they have come down to us and conceivably came down to Julian, the experiences of these women seem to have been of a fairly direct kind: a succession of visions, often accompanied by celestial conversations, and sometimes also affecting the senses of smell, touch and taste, which in bald outline at least would not have been difficult to understand or record.[14] It is clear that Julian's experience was radically different: a disparate series of glimpses of Christ's Passion, strung like beads along her life-saving gaze at a crucifix, and interspersed with other, more abstract sights, as well as with a few pregnant words passed from Christ to her and sometimes back again. The power of this revelation must have lain more in its sense of latency than in any of its unspectacular external manifestations: in the way that it seemed to offer (as it still seemed to offer decades later) no more than as it were the begynnyng of an ABC "of our lordis menyng"--as though the entire revelation corresponded to the introductory *aleph* which some Cabbalists averred was all that God actually said to Moses on Mount Sinai.[15] In my own view, though many will not agree, the lack of visual detail in the Short Text perhaps indicates that even the Passion scenes themselves originally had little of the mesmerising clarity that so colors their presentation in Julian's revision; after all, her youthful request for more "feleing in the passion of Christ," which she describes at the beginning of the work, surely implies that her imagination was not of the kind that found easy the sympathetic absorption in the events of Christ's death that Passion meditation demands.[16] This may, of course, be quite wrong. But even if it is, Julian's revelation has an imagistic sparseness and at least a surface fragmentariness to it that is largely untypical of the experiences of medieval women visionaries, and which must initially have been deeply confusing to its recipient. It is not surprising that her own earliest interpretation of her experience was that it was an attack of madness: "Then cam a religious person to me and askid me how I ferid. And I seyd I had ravid today, and he leuhe loud and inderly" (66.81) ["then a member of a religious order came to me and asked me how I was. And I said I had been raving that day, and he laughed loud and long"].

The basic exegetical strategy which both versions of the *Revelation of Love* describe and apply in an attempt to articulate and circumscribe the complexities of Julian's experience is the familiar tripartite division of the "shewings" into "bodily sight," "word formyd in my understonding" and "ghostly sight": a division which is occasionally complicated by further categories, such as "gostly in bodily lyknes" and "more gostly without bodyly lyknes," but which by and large provides a serviceable framework.[17] Two of the three main terms, "bodily sight" and "ghostly sight," occur in other Middle English religious writings (for example, Walter Hilton's *Scale of Perfection),* where they characteristically derive (albeit indirectly) from Augustine's distinctions (in his commentary *De Genesi ad Litteram)* between "corporeal," "imaginative" and "intellective" vision--his three categories sometimes being reduced to two under the influence, presumably, of the better known distinction between the corporeal and spiritual senses.[18] I know of no other women visionaries who use this Augustinian terminology,[19] and no other visionary material which combines "bodily" and "ghostly sight" with any of the almost polyphonic complexity of Julian's revelation (it is more common for them to be contrasted, as they are by Hilton, than to occur together in an integrated act of divine communication).[20] Nonetheless, by employing them Julian evidently intends to suggest the continuity between her revelation and visionary tradition and to lessen both our and perhaps her own sense of the revelation's essential elusiveness and strangeness.[21]

The "Augustinian" hermeneutic thus creates some basic categories which have the added benefit of being sanctioned by tradition. Yet as soon as we look in detail at the interpretive problems posed by Julian's revelation, it becomes clear how inadequate this exegetical device, taken on its own, must prove to be. For in practice Julian finds herself describing almost as many kinds of "sight" and other divinely-inspired experiences, and invoking almost as many kinds of exegesis with which to interpret them, as her revelation can be separated into distinguishable visionary moments. The flexibility with which she deploys words depicting her apprehension of the revelation--words such as "understood," "showed," "took," "conceived" and especially "saw"-- indeed renders her own (or any other) system of categorization virtually useless for the purposes of detailed analysis. Nor does Julian seem to resist this flexibility; on the contrary, she seems determined to use the language of revelation in as wide a variety of ways as possible, almost as though she is deliberately working against the restrictions of her own circumscribing hermeneutic structure.

IV

Consider first, for example, the opening of one of Julian's exegetical showpieces, the famous passage with which the series of revelations begins:

> In this sodenly I saw the rede blode trekelyn downe fro under the garlande, hote and freisly and ryth plenteously, as it were in the time of his passion that the garlande of thornys was pressid on his blissid hede. Ryte so, both God and man, the same that sufferd thus for me, I conceived treuly and mightily that it was himselfe

shewed it me, without ony mene. And, in the same sheweing, sodenly the Trinite fullfilled the herte most of ioy. And so I understood it shall be in hevyn withoute end to all that shall come there. For the Trinite is God, God is the Trinite; the Trinite is our maker and keeper, the Trinite is our everlasting lover, everlasting ioy and blisse, be our lord Iesus Christ. And this was shewed in the first and in all; for where Iesus appereith the blissid Trinite is understond, as to my sight. (LT 4.4)

[In this I suddenly saw the red blood trickling down from under the garland, hot and freshly and very plentifully, as though it was the time of his Passion, when the garland of thorns was pressed on his blessed head. In just this way, both God and human, the same who suffered like this for me--it was borne upon me, truthfully and powerfully, that it was he himself showing it to me, without anything in between. And, in this same moment of vision, suddenly the Trinity filled up the heart with the most joy. And so I understood it shall be in heaven without end for everyone who will come there. For the Trinity is God, God is the Trinity; the Trinity is our maker and keeper, the Trinity is our everlasting lover, everlasting joy and bliss, by our lord Jesus Christ. For where Jesus appears, the blessed Trinity is to be understood, according to my view of things.]

This passage moves from the phrase "I saw," which apparently signifies in a wholly literal sense that "there appeared before my eyes," to the phrase "as to my sight," in which the image of seeing is equally wholly figurative, meaning something like "according to my divinely inspired interpretation." Between these points there is a development from Julian's "conceiving" what it is she is seeing and who it is that is showing it to her, to the joy she feels, to her understanding of an eternal theological truth about that joy, and to her generalizing of that truth-- on the basis both of this showing and of those that follow--into the interpretive principle that "where Iesus appereith the blissid Trinite is understond." This principle is described as "shewed," that is, "manifested," in the revelation as a whole--although the physical sight of the blood has also been called a "sheweing"--and the phrase "as to my sight" which rounds the passage off is clearly intended to intensify, not qualify, one's sense that the revelatory process is still at work even as Julian sets out to record an experience that is far in her past.[22] Thus although the vision begins with the simple miracle of a sight of Christ's blood, every moment of this progression towards abstraction and generalization continues to be suffused with the language of revelation, and both Julian's original response to what she saw and, indeed, her *present* response prove to form as vital a part of the whole picture as the vision of the blood itself. After all, it is her "true and mighty" acceptance of the vision as it begins, and her much later identification of its deepest source as the Trinity rather than Christ alone, that renders the process of interpretation--of "seeing" in a figurative as well as a visual sense--possible.[23] A term as crude as "bodily sight" is hardly an adequate or accurate way of describing the delicate interaction of eye and mind, of memory, thought and feeling, of God and Julian, which blossoms upwards and outwards from a single visionary moment in the text.

It is true that once this "blossoming" process is established, the more analytic parts of Julian's account are attributed to the visionary faculty of "ghostly sight." Yet even in the first revelation, the terminology associated with "ghostly sight" is already used still more creatively, and more inconsistently, than that associated with "bodily sight." The term enters the work in an indirect and somewhat mysterious fashion. Looking at the "bodily sight" of the Passion, Julian "knew wele that it was strength enow to me, ya and to all creturers leving, ageyn all the fends of hell and ghostly temptation" (LT 4.4) ["knew well that it was enough strength for me, yes, and to all living creatures, against all the devils of hell and all spiritual temptation"]. Then, "in this" (that is, either "in" the Passion or "within" Julian's knowledge of its efficacy), God "browght our blissid lady to my understonding," where she is seen "in the stature that she was wan she conceived with child" ["at the age she was when she conceived a child"], in a mode which is called "ghostly in bodily likeness." This expression, which is suggestive of a visual experience in a less concrete form than the vision of the blood, perhaps evocative of Augustinian "imaginative vision," is made redundant after only a sentence by a shift to a more abstract kind of showing, a partial intuition of "the wisedam and the trueth of hir soule" which "caused hir sey full mekely to Gabriel: 'Lo me, Gods handmayd'" (LT 4.5) ["which made her say very meekly to Gabriel: behold, me, God's maidservant"]. This would seem close to the category of "intellectual vision." So likewise would the next visionary moment, which occurs "in this same time," when Christ shows "a ghostly sight of his homely loveing" (LT 5.5) in which Julian says she "saw" (that is, more or less, "realized") "that he is to us everything that is good and comfortable for us." At this point, we appear to have reached the terminus of another such process of abstraction from the visual to the theological of the kind we saw growing out of the vision of the blood. But now, from "in this" apparently wholly non-visual realization, Christ shows a new, partly visual image of "a littil thing, the quantitye of an hesil nutt in the palme of my hand" ["a little thing, the weight of a hazel-nut in the palm of my hand"], which a "general" voice tells Julian is "all that is made," and which she considers "with eye of my understondyng," seeing in it "iii propertes"--that God makes it, loves it and keeps it. Here, Julian claims to "see" the properties of the Trinity reflected in an image of the creation that is seemingly also "seen," in a quasi-physical sense, lying in her hand. Evidently the process we are now involved with is not one of abstraction from images but of theological thinking through images; the line of development runs from Mary's "wisedam and trueth" in anticipation of the Incarnation, through Julian's intuition of God's love for humankind, to her recognition that this love encompasses the whole of creation. Yet a further surprise is in store, for the long argument which follows from the vision of the "littil thing," and which focusses now on the human response to God, instead of the divine response to humanity--on the need to approach God "nakidly," turning away from the created order in an act of apophatic forgetting--is actually a meditation not on the "litill thing" itself but on Julian's immediate reaction to it: "methowte it might suddenly have fallen to nowte for littil" ["I thought it might suddenly have collapsed into nothingness, it was so small"]. Indeed, Julian treats this statement with much the intensity of attention she will later bestow on the words Christ "forms in her understanding," returning to the words "nowte" and "littil" (for example, "it needyth us to have knoweing of the littlehede of creatures and to nowtyn all things" (LT 5.5) ["we need to have knowledge of the smallness of created things and to deny all things"]) as though they form part of the divinely inspired "text" of her revelation. Rather as in the account of the "bodily sight," the revelation here expands to incorporate, perhaps even to become, Julian's response to it, which as she writes she further elaborates into a speech spoken by the soul to God ("God of thy goodnesse give me thyselfe") that is also treated as part of the revelation--it is written "as be the understonding that I have in this sheweing" (LT 5.6).[24] It seems that the term "ghostly sight" encompasses the entirety of words, thoughts and feelings that she associates with this complex succession of insights.

In the first revelation, the terminology associated with "bodily" and "ghostly sight" is thus already being stretched beyond its limits both by the complexity of the visionary experience itself and by Julian's desire to articulate that complexity as fully as possible. Yet the exposition of the first revelation is more systematic than most of what follows, in which an ever-increasing variety of phenomena are assimilated into the categories of sight and showing. For example, at several points and in various ways, Julian finds revelatory material in what she *does not* see. The main significance of the second revelation develops from her initial inability to decide whether it really is a revelation or not; here, her disappointment at seeing Christ's bleeding head on the point of turning back into a mere figure on a crucifix becomes a lesson about God's necessary absences, in spite of which "he wille that we levyn that we se him continually" ["he desires it that we believe we see him continually"], holding on by faith to the vision we cannot always keep in sight. This is a vision about the limitations of vision.[25] The third revelation centres attention on what is not therein a more radical way. After seeing "God in a point" ("by which sight I saw that he is in al things"), Julian proceeds to the generalization, "here I saw sothly that synne is no dede, for in al this was not synne shewid" ["here I saw truly that sin is not an action, for in all this sin was not shown"]. Here, Julian explicitly "sees" an insight (and one which comes to be of considerable importance to her theology) *as a result* of its not being "showyd" (LT 11.13-14). Yet another kind of showing based on the absence of vision is revelation XI, in which Christ first offers Julian sight of his mother (in the words, "wilt thou se her?" ["do you want to see her?"]), then fails to bestow this sight on her when she accepts it. "Oftentymes I prayd this ['ya, good lord, if it be thy will'], and I wend a seen hir in bodily presens, but I saw hir not so" ["I often prayed this, 'yes, good lord, if it is your will,' and I hoped to have seen her in her bodily actuality, but I did not see her like this"], comments Julian, only to insist at once that "Iesus *in that word* ['wilt thou se her'] shewid me a gostly sigte of hir" ["Jesus, in that very saying 'do you want to see her?'

showed me a spiritual sight of her"], saving the revelation by retreating from a literal to a figurative reading of Christ's offer (LT 25.27-28).

In the later stages of the *Revelation of Love,* these "apophatic" and oxymoronic ways of understanding visionary material develop into Julian's marvellously subtle discussions of the partiality of all earthly knowledge, such as the one from Chapter 80 with which this paper is prefaced. Yet by the time we have reached revelation XI we have also encountered other uses of the language of vision that are almost as unexpected. Revelation VII, for example, is called both a "showing" and a "vision," but consists only of a sensation: a "soveren gostly lekyng in my soule" ["a high, spiritual pleasure in my soul"], which is alternately bestowed on Julian and withdrawn.[26] Revelation III contains a speech by God which Julian does not hear, but somehow extrapolates merely from seeing him "in a point": "And al this shewid he ful blisfully, meneing thus: 'Se, I am God. Se, I am in althing'" (LT 11.14) ["and all of this he showed very happily, meaning this: 'see, I am God. See, I am in everything'"].[27] An integral part of the visionary content of revelation V is a speech made, apparently out loud, by Julian herself about the things she is "seeing" in Christ's Passion, "game, scorne and arneste."[28] Revelation VIII even contains a curious passage in which a sentence from her own Short Text is seemingly treated in the same way, as visionary material requiring explication.[29] In later chapters of the Long Text, especially in the major digression between revelations XIV and XV (Chapters 44-63) and the lengthy conclusion after revelation XVI (Chapters 73-86), there are yet more new applications for the terms "ghostly sight" and "showing," this time to indicate things Julian has learned from the entirety of the revelation: for example, that "I saw that God may done all that us nedith" ["I saw that God can do everything that is necessary for us"], or "I had in parte touching, sight and feling in iii propertes of God, in which the strength and effect of all the revelation stondith" (LT 75.90; 83.100) ["I had in some measure awareness, insight and feeling about three characteristics of God, on which the power and the outcome of the whole revelation is based"]. Indeed, the whole concluding movement of fourteen chapters is announced as a sustained exposition of "ghostly sight": "for the gostly syght, I have seyd sumdele, but I may never full tellen it. And therefore of this syght I am sterrid to sey more as God will give me grace" (LT 73.88) ["and I have said some things about the spiritual vision, but I cannot tell it all. And so I am moved to say more about this mode of vision, as God will give me grace"]. This grandly general application of the terminology of revelation finally moves it to a place where its original basis in an Augustinian conception of imaginative and intellectual vision is apparently almost forgotten.[30]

V

Faced with a revelation which it took her a lifetime to begin to plumb and whose divine source made it by definition inexhaustible, Julian evidently felt it both appropriate and necessary to wield her basic exegetical tools in a comparably inexhaustible variety of ways. Medieval biblical exegetes formalized their interpretive terminology into the celebrated "four senses of Scripture," but nonetheless often pointed out the extraordinary capacity of God's word to exceed all attempts so to circumscribe it. For example, Gilbert of Stanford exclaims with awestruck poetry over the way that:

> Imitating the action of the swiftest of rivers, Holy Scripture fills up the depths of the human mind and yet always overflows, quenches the thirsty and yet remains inexhaustible. Bountiful streams of spiritual senses gush out from it and, merging into others, make still others spring up--or rather (since "wisdom is undying"), they do not merge but *emerge* and, showing their beauty to others, cause these others not to replace them as they fail but to succeed them as they remain.[31]

If Julian continues to use her threefold exegetical system, it is with a similar belief in its final inadequacy and a similarly loving intention of letting her revelation "fill up the depths of the human mind" by employing whatever means she can to make it speak. Indeed, the flexibility of her exposition, the variety of its strategies, and the rapidity with which it shuttles between particular moral points and far-reaching theological ones all suggest the influence of biblical exegesis--mediated, perhaps, mainly through preaching--on her writing and thought. It would even be possible, I think, to interpret many of her own interpretations using the framework of the tropological, allegorical and anagogical senses, and thus to regard the whole of the *Revelation of Love* as an intensely meditative commentary, rather along the lines of Bernard's *Sermones super Cantica Canticorum*.

Yet while the analogy between Julian's practice as an interpreter and those of a biblical exegete is a real one, it must not be allowed to blind us to a fundamental difference: that the revelation that constitutes the "text" which Julian expounds is not a fixed entity--an immutable set of propositions or simple pictorial visions--but rather an interaction between a number of profoundly mysterious and (in their way) highly intellectual visionary moments and their actively-engaged recipient, the boundaries of which are by their very nature so fluid as to be impossible to chart. The consequences of this fluidity we have seen to be far-reaching indeed. For precisely the most distinctive and surprising thing about Julian's use of the language of revelation is her tendency to apply it so broadly that all her comments on the "text" of her showings--both her brief responses and remarks as an actor in the drama and even her vastly extended meditations as its narrator--turn into further "sights" and "showings," thus in effect becoming "text" themselves. Indeed, if we take all Julian's references to "sight," "showing," "understonding" and so on seriously, it is hard to find any passage of the *Revelation of Love* which is not implicitly or explicitly treated as actually constituting (as distinct from merely commenting on) part of the revelation. It is as though the biblical text in the centre of its manuscript page were literally to "overflow" and to merge with the surrounding apparatus; or, to put the same point the other way around, as though the apparatus were to merge with the text, annexing its divinely-inspired status and authority, and forming a layered, composite text which engages in its own exegesis. It is true that Julian emphasises that her book is provisional and impossible to finish in this life, stating as she closes that "this book is begunne be Gods gift and his grace, but it is not yet performid, as to my syte" (LT 86.102) ["this book has been begun by God's gift and his grace, but it is not yet carried through, according to my view"].[32] Yet as I have pointed out, the *Revelation of Love* views such contingency as a condition of all earthly understanding whatever; one of the most theologically daring aspects of the work is its insistence that even the truth God revealed to the Church is provisional in very much the same way.[33] Within the limitations imposed by the present life, the words with which the Long Text opens are apparently meant to be applied literally not merely to the original "showings," narrowly defined, but rather to the work as a whole: "*this* is a revelation of love" (LT 1.1).

VI

At this point, I anticipate the objection that, after laying grave charges of fundamentalism against readings of Julian which ignore the hermeneutic complexities of her work, I am merely compounding the offence in my own way, by insisting with dogged persistence on a literalistic reading of her visionary language. Am I not pressing her uses of "see," "sight," even "showing" and especially "understanding" too hard by claiming that, taken *in toto,* they obliterate the distinction between revelation and commentary? After all, what purpose could it serve Julian to present her work in this audacious way, as though it were a direct equivalent of--rather than merely a vehicle for--the word of God? And how, in any case, could she justify such a presentation when she is writing at so many years remove from her original, authenticating experience? Further, if the *Revelation of Love* is indeed intended to be as well as merely to contain a revelation, why is it that Julian nonetheless maintains so much of the format of a "text" with accompanying commentary, rather than fusing the two into a work that is overtly visionary in nature throughout?[34] I wish to end by considering some of the issues raised by these important questions.

First, Julian's purpose in presenting her work as somehow constituting an equivalent of her original revelation has to do with her fundamental understanding of the revelation's significance: that through it, God is announcing his nature anew not only to her but to Christian humanity as a whole. This understanding takes various forms during the course of the *Revelation of Love.* It is at its most daring in the chapters following the exposition of revelation XIII, in which Julian learns that "al manner of thyng shal be wele" (LT 27.28-29): a statement that opens up a gulf, which the rest of the work concludes is finally unbridgeable in this life, between what is at one point called the "heyer dome" ["higher understanding"] of the revelation and the "lower dome" (LT 45.48) (or "dome of holy church") of received Christian orthodoxy.[35] From this revelation on, indeed, the tension between the two "domes" provides one of Julian's most fertile sources of "ghostly sight"--for she assures us earlier that she was aware, throughout her experience, of "the feith of holy church" which "stode continualy in my sight" (a hermeneutic principle garbed like a personification out of *Piers Plowman*), "willing and meneing never to receive onything that might be contrary therunto" (LT 9.10) ["the holy church's faith which was continually present to my sight, willing and intending that I never accept anything that might be incompatible with it"]. Such tension can only be meaningful or productive, however, if Julian's experience can be regarded as being embodied in an authoritative and definitive form, accessible to all in the same way as the "feith of holy church" itself. This, I believe, is one of the motivating forces behind the vital passage of hermeneutic reflection which occurs at the end of the first revelation and which is far more than the prolonged gesture of humility it appears to be. Chapter 8 of the Long Text, a kind of coda to revelation I, describes Julian's immediate response to it (a response that makes her say to those around her, "it is today domysday with me") by recalling how "I was mekil sterid in charite to mine even cristen, that thei might seen and knowyn the same that I saw" (LT 8.9) ["I was much moved with love towards my fellow Christians, that they should see and know the same things I saw"]. Julian expounds this reminiscence (which, interestingly, she explicitly calls "the gostly shewing of our lord God") in a celebrated passage where she states that "all that I say of me I sey in the person of al myn even cristen" ["all that I say about myself I say as a representative of all my fellow Christians"], and counsels readers to:

> levyn the beholding of a wretch that it was shewid to, and mightily, wisely and mekely behold God, that of his curtes love and endles godenes wolde shewyn it generally in comfort of us al . . . For it is Gods will that ye take it with gret ioy and likyng as Iesus had shewid it on to you all. (LT 8.10)

> [stop gazing at a wretch to whom it was shown, and powerfully, wisely and meekly gaze on God, who in his gracious love and endless goodness wanted to reveal it universally, to comfort all of us. For it is God's will that you receive it with as great joy and pleasure as if Jesus had shown it to you.]

Here we are given two different hermeneutic instructions. First, we are to read every reference to Julian as indicating Christian humanity as a whole--the phrase "in the person of," which derives from the technical language of biblical exegesis, suggesting the formal nature of this instruction.[36] Second, it is God's will that we should "take"--that is, appropriate--the revelation as though it is each of us who receives it, individually and affectively as well as in a merely representative sense. Chapter 9 elaborates the theological basis of these instructions and concludes with a practical admission that readers will still need divine inspiration to "take" Julian's exposition of her "ghostly sight" in a manner "more gostly and more swetely than I can or may telle it" (LT 9.11). Yet even bearing this qualification in mind, Julian's belief in the universality of her revelation makes logically inevitable the view of her own written account that she here implies. For if the showing was indeed made for all, it must be possible for her readers to appropriate it "as Iesus had shewid it on to you all." Moreover, through God's inspiration and her own lifetime of thought and prayer, her account of her experience must potentially have the same relation to her readers as the experience itself has to her. For the slow, deliberative and prayerful reader, the written *Revelation of Love* must be, or be meant to become, the showing.

The hermeneutic instructions given in this passage thus raise to the level of a principle what we have already seen to be Julian's practice both in revelation I and throughout her work. If God is described as "showing" or Julian as "seeing" many difficult and daring ideas that derive only in a convoluted way from the original revelation, we (I am using this word to designate the kind of reader Julian had in mind) are still obliged to "take" such ideas to ourselves with as much of the force of revelation as we can. According to Chapter 9, moreover, our success will even be a measure of our love for God: "in as much as ye love God the better, it is more to you than to me" (LT 9.10) ["in as much as you love God more than I do, it means more to you than to me"]. Yet on what basis can we as readers, or could Julian as a writer, have confidence that everything the *Revelation of Love* treats as revealed actually is so? On the face of it, after all, the work is obviously no more (and no less) than a movingly personal elaboration of a series of divinely-inspired but still inchoate ideas and images: an elaboration which it is tempting to assume (especially when we refer back to the Short Text) could as easily have been taken in quite different directions. Is there not even the danger that Julian's ubiquitous use of the terminology of revelation at such distant removes from her original experience will have the unintended effect of dissipating its power and authority, by making all references to "sight" and "showing" seem merely ornamental? With these questions we suddenly find ourselves back somewhere near our starting-point: the hermeneutic problem confronting readers who think of the *Revelation of Love* as a product not only of divine inspiration but of time and of human fallibility. Let us at last see, then, what Julian has to say that bears on this problem.

VII

Julian's defence of the authenticity of her interpretation occurs at the hinge of Chapter 51 of the Long Text, where she recounts her long failure to penetrate the "misty example" [enigmatic parable] of the lord and the servant, and the three "propertes" which eventually in part alleviated her frustration, allowing her to comprehend at least "the begynnyng of an ABC." While the passage is familiar, the breadth of its application has not always been understood:37

> And thus in that tyme I stode mekyl in onknowyng. For the full vnderstondyng of this mervelous example was not goven me in that tyme--in which mystye example [the privities] of the revelation be yet mekyl hidde; and notwithstondyng this I saw and understode that every shewing is full of privities. And therfore me behovith now to tellen iii propertes in which I am sumdele esyd. The frest is the begynnyng of techyng that I understod therein in the same tyme. The ii is the inward lernyng that I have vnderstodyn therein sithen. The iii, al the hole revelation from the begynnyng to the end (that is to sey, of this boke), which our lord God of his goodnes bryngeth offentymes frely to the syte of myn vnderstondyng. And these iii arn so onyd, as to my vnderstondyng, that I cannot, ner may, depart them. And be these iii as on I have techyng wherby I owe to leyvyn and trostyn in our lord God, that of the same godenes that he shewed it, and for the same end, ryth so of the same goodnes and for the same end he shal declaryn it to us whan it is his wille. For xx yeres atter the tyme of the shewing, save iii monethis, I had techyng inwardly, as I shal seyen: "it longyth to the to taken hede

to all the propertes and condition that weryn shewed in the example, thow thou thynke that they ben mysty and indifferent to thy syte." I assend wilfully with grete desire, [seeing] inwardly with avisement al the poynts and propertes that wer shewid in the same tyme, as ferforth as my witt and vnderstondyng wold servyn. (LT 51.55-56)[38]

[And so in that time I remained very much in the dark. For the whole understanding of this wonderful parable was not given to me at that time--in which enigmatic parable the secrets of the revelation are still much concealed; and for all this I saw and understood that each showing is full of secrets. And so I must now explain three features of the vision by which I am partly satisfied. The first is the beginning of teaching, the things I understood in the vision at the time it happened. The second is the inner learning I have understood from it since then. The third, the whole revelation from beginning to end (that is to say, of this book), which our lord God, in his goodness, often brings freely to the sight of my understanding. And these three are so unified, to my understanding, that I cannot and may not separate them. And by these three as one, I am taught how I ought to believe and trust in our lord God, that by the same goodness because of which he revealed it, and to the same end, he will expound it to us when it is his will. For twenty years after the revelation, save three months, I had inner teaching, as I shall say: "you must take notice of all the characteristics and conditions that were revealed in the parable, even though you find them enigmatic and meaningless." I agree to this, wanting it with great desire, seeing inwardly with concentration all the details and characteristics that were revealed at the time of the revelation, as far as my wit and understanding could manage it.]

The immediate context of this passage is limited. Three "propertes"--Julian's memory of the "example" as she originally saw it, her subsequent reflections on it, and her understanding of it in relation to the rest of her revelation--all combine, emboldened by her "inward techyng," into the synthetic account that follows in the rest of the chapter. Although this account attempts to distinguish these "propertes," the passage admits it to be an impossibility, seeming rather to shelter behind the "inward techyng" Julian receives from God, as though this provided a fresh authentication of her thoughts, in spite of the confusion into which they have fallen. Yet there is more to the passage than this. First, Julian makes it clear that the hermeneutic "propertes" she describes here are those she has brought not only to the key parable of the lord and servant but to the whole of her revelation; "*every* shewing," not merely this "misty example," is described as "full of privities"--as the lengthy digression on "the hole revelation" of which Chapter 51 forms a part is indeed in the process of demonstrating. Second, these "propertes" are far from being a casual grouping of modes of understanding. It is often noted that the Long Text constantly alludes to two triads: those of the human memory, reason and will on the one hand, and of the traditional attributes of the persons of the Trinity--respectively might, wisdom and love--on the other.39 Julian uses such allusions--which operate within a cognitive framework most famously defined by Augustine's *De Trinitate*--to bring out her view that "where Iesus appereith the blissid Trinite is understond," and also to insist on the intimacy of the image and likeness that unites God with the human soul. Chapter 44 of the Long Text, for example, states explicitly that God is: "endles soverain trueth, endles severeyn wisdam, endles sovereyn love, onmade, and mans soule is a creature in God which hath the same propertyes made. . . it seith God, it beholdyth God and it lovyth God" (LT 44.47) ["endless high truth, endless high wisdom, endless high love, unmade; and the human soul is a created being, in God, which has the same characteristics in a created sense: it sees God, it beholds God and it loves God"]. What has gone unnoticed (or, at least, undiscussed) is the deliberate way that the "made" and "unmade" trinities parallel (and thereby implicitly correspond to) the hermeneutic "propertes" that Julian describes in the present passage--the correspondences being as follows:

> *the begynnyng of techyng*/ Julian's memory/ Father/ might-truth
> *inward lernyng*/ Julian's reason/ Son/ wisdom
> *the hole revelation*/ Julian's will/ Holy Spirit/ love

These correspondences considerably enlarge the implications of what Julian is saying in this passage about the interpretation of her revelation. For if the process by which Julian experienced her revelation, reflected on it, and analyzed its various parts in the light of the whole finds a parallel at each stage with the dynamic inner structure of the Trinity, it follows that the Trinity has been present at each of these stages. It also follows that the divine inspiration which produced her revelation has continued to aid her as she reflects on it and writes it down. Thus whatever relation in literal terms the written *Revelation of Love* has to the experience from which it grew, it can legitimately claim to be an authentic and inspired account of that experience. What proves this last conclusion for Julian is the very thing that seemed initially to cast doubt on the authenticity of her account: the fact that after twenty years and more it is impossible to distinguish between original experience and subsequent interpretation: "these iii arn so onyd, as to my vnderstondyng, that I cannot, ner may, depart them" (LT 51.56). For rather than reading this situation as a sign of her own confusion, she sees it as evidence of the underlying unity inherent in each stage of her experience of the revelation, which both corresponds to and is a product of the unity that inheres in the Trinity itself. Just as the Trinity consists of three persons whose activities are ultimately indistinguishable, since they are united in a single godhead, so her revelation, and the book in which she embodies it, consist of three "propertes" which are indistinguishably united in one showing. In other words, her written account of the "revelation of love" is authentic not in spite of the fact that, but *because,* revelation and interpretation are impossible to disentangle.

This, then, is the "trinitarian hermeneutic" which underpins Julian's interpretation of her revelation, allowing her to pronounce on it with confidence, and allowing her intended readers to treat her pronouncements as the constituent parts of God's "showing" that she claims them to be. The thoroughness with which she reflects on all aspects of her experience here bears remarkable fruit, in a sophisticated analysis of the problem of time and human memory that turns what was at first sight a serious hermeneutic difficulty into her most important argument for the authority of her work. Nor is this argument in any sense merely a clever evasion of the problem; it is far too carefully integrated into both the structure and the theology of the *Revelation of Love* for that. By this point in the work, after all, we have encountered both the distinction between these three hermeneutic "propertes" and the fact of their inseparability many times. For example, the passage at the beginning of the first revelation describing the "bodily sight" of the blood quoted above proves to move schematically from Julian's memory of this sight ("the begynnyng of techyng"), to her understanding of it ("inward lernyng"), to her sense of its significance in relation to "the hole revelation"; at the same time, the difficulty of separating experience and reflection even in this passage, especially in the subtle shift from "I saw" to "as to my sight," already implies the fact that "these iii arn so onyd, as to my vnderstondyng, that I cannot, ner may, depart them." This combination--of a format that always seems *about* to be that of text and accompanying commentary, with slippages between the two that continually undo this distinction--is indeed, as we have seen, a virtual hallmark of Julian's exegetical practice. In the light of the "trinitarian hermeneutic" such a combination takes on a thematic importance. On the one hand, it corresponds to the paradoxically triune nature of the godhead: in which, for example, the Father "gives birth" to the Son as his Word, and the procession of the Spirit acts as a further "stage" in the divine self-articulation, but in which all the persons are to be seen as constituting a single essence. On the other hand, it corresponds to the triadic structure of Julian's soul, which, until it is united with God in heaven, can only experience the truth partially, not as accomplished and completed revelation but as *process*. What Julian learns in Chapter 51 is nothing like a full understanding of the "misty example" (which is why attempts to show how this chapter resolves the tension between revelation and Christian orthodoxy not only fail but miss the point). Julian is only "sumdele esyd" because at last she has learnt "to leyvyn and trostyn in our lord God, that . . . he shal declaryn [his full meaning] whan it is his wille" (LT 51.56). She has learnt, in short, how to live *without* the full knowledge that even after her revelation she can only long for, never attain, in this life.

VIII

If the whole of the *Revelation of Love is* meant to be read as a species of divinely inspired text, a revelation in its own right to the properly attentive reader, the truth it imparts turns out to be of an interestingly self-reflexive and provisional kind. As with *Piers Plowman,* which leaves us with the simple injunction "lerne to love . . . and leef alle othere" ["learn to love and abandon everything else"], the work can conclude by asserting a single, unifying meaning to all God has revealed through it:

"woldst thou wetten thi Lord's mening in this thing? Wete it wele: love was his mening" (LT 86.102) ["do you want to know your lord's meaning in this matter? Know it well: love was his meaning"].40 But also as with *Piers Plowman,* in which even the injunction to love must lead to the initiation of still one more pilgrimage, as Conscience walks "as wide as the world lasteth" ["as far as the world's end"] in search of Piers,41 the end of the *Revelation of Love* asserts simultaneously that full knowledge of that meaning is always in the future: "this booke is begunne . . . but it is not yet performid" (LT 86.102). Indeed, in a certain way this prolonged deferral proves ultimately to be a condition not only of life but of love itself. "Ere God made us, he loved us", says Julian, and plays with the idea of closure as she insists on its impossibility: "which love was never slakid, no never shall" ["before God made us, he loved us; and this love was never sated, no, nor will it be"]. *Tunc autem cognoscam sicut et cognitus sum:* (1 Cor 13:126) even this lasting fullness, it seems, finally emerges not as a state but as a never-satiated process.

NOTES

1. This essay was first published in 1991, in *The Medieval Mystical Tradition in England: Exeter Symposium V*, ed. Marion Glasscoe (Brewer: Cambridge, 1991) 79-100. I am grateful to Boydell and Brewer for permission to reprint it. I have made no changes except in format and to add approximate translations--exact ones being impossible, given the nature and density of Julian's prose--and to add a very few bibliographic items in square brackets in the notes.

2. *Si ad sublimium scientiam mentis sagacitate ascendere volumus, opere practium est primo nosse quibus rerum modis notitiam apprehendere solemus. Rerum itaque notitiam, ni fallor, modo triplici apprehendimus. Nam alia experiendo probamus, alia ratiocinando colligimus, aliorum certitudinem credendo tenemus. Et temporalium quidem notitia per ipsam experientiam apprehendimus; ad aeternorum vero notitiam, modo ratiocinando, modo credendo assurgimus.* Richard of St Victor, *De Trinitate,* Book I, ch.l, in Migne, Patrologia Latina (PL) 196, col.1891; the translation is my own.

3. *A Revelation of Love*, Long Text (LT), Ch. 80, from MS Bl Sloane 2499 (S1), edited by Marion Glasscoe (Exeter: Exeter University Press, 1976; rptd. 1986) 97, although punctuation in this and all other quotations from medieval sources is my own. Unless otherwise indicated, readings in square brackets are taken from MS Paris, BN fonds anglais 40 (P), edited by Edmund Colledge and

James Walsh, *A Book of Showings to the Anchoress Julian of Norwich*, 2 vols. (Toronto: Pontifical Institute of Mediaeval Studies, 1978) cited as Colledge and Walsh. (Citations from Julian's Short Text [ST] are from volume I of this edition.) Here, S1 reads "reason naturall" for "kyndly reson," and "these" for "thoo" (which seems wrong, since the "common teching of holy church" *can* be understood in this life, for Julian). It is tempting to think that Julian originally wrote "And *there* ben grete thyngs," pointing forward to the rest of the chapter, which lists some of them.

4. A number of studies touch on hermeneutic issues. See especially: B. A. Windeatt, "Julian of Norwich and Her Audience," *Review of English Studies*, n.s., 28 (1977): 1-17, a comparison between ST and LT which *is* most suggestive but does not explicitly discuss Julian's hermeneutics; Paul Molinari, *Julian of Norwich* (London: Burns and Oates, 1958) which deals at length with Julian's classification of her visions (see further note 18), and with the question of their authenticity; and the lengthy introduction to Colledge and Walsh's edition, especially 67-71, which outlines their own hermeneutic assumptions, and 71-198, a richly controversial account of Julian's exegesis of her revelation.

5. Such a desire is most obvious in the many studies which emphasize either the authenticity of Julian's revelation or the orthodoxy of her book (for example, Molinari, Colledge and Walsh), but is also evident in what we might call the "appreciations" of Julian that make up the bulk of writing on her. See Valerie Lagorio and Ritamary Bradley, *The Fourteenth-Century English Mystics: A Comprehensive Annotated Bibliography* (New York: Garland, 1981) most of items 530-619. It needs to be remembered that Julian studies have developed in proximity to a religious controversy about the worth of mysticism as a whole, and that the caution and occasional defensiveness of some writing on Julian is a response to real attacks on her authenticity and value--for which see, most recently, Andrew Ryder, "A Note on Julian's Vision," *Downside Review*, 96 (1978): 299-304.

6. LT, ch.7.8; S1 omits "mynde"; BL Sloane 3705 (S2), which seems to share an immediate ancestor with S1, reads "enderstanding."

7. For hermeneutic enquiry in Chaucer, see, most recently, Carolyn Dinshaw, *Chaucer's Sexual Poetics* (Madison: U of Wisconsin P, 1989). The most thorough-going analysis of Langland in these terms is still Mary Carruthers, *The Search for St Truth: A Study of Meaning in Piers Plowman* (Evanston: U of Northern Illinois P, 1973).

8. 1 Corinthians 13:12a, from *Biblia sacra iuxta vulgatam versionem,* ed. Bonifatio Fischer *et al.,* 2 vols (Stuttgart, 1983).

9. This is also the view of Roger Ellis in "Revelation and the Life of Faith: The Vision of Julian of Norwich," *Christian,* 6 (1980): 61-71, (especially 70), and of

Marion Glasscoe in "Means of Showing: An Approach to Reading Julian of Norwich," *Analecta Cartusiana* 106 (Salzburg, 1983): 151-77, especially 151-52). Contrast the opposite view of Colledge and Walsh, e.g. note to LT, Chapter 51, line 80 (520), which holds that revelation and reflection are always carefully distinguished; see further section 4 below.

10. See "The Composition of Julian of Norwich's *Revelation of Love*" [*Speculum* 68 (1993) 637-83], which presents evidence that ST dates from the first half of the 1380s at the earliest, and may have been completed after 1388: an argument that of course has a considerable impact on our dating of LT. The article is based on a paper given at the conference, 'A wyf ther was': Women in Middle English Literature, Liège, December 1990.

11. LT, 7.8: "These iii come to my [mynde] in the tyme: pellots, for roundhede in the comynge out of the blode; the scale of heryng, [for roundhede] in the spreadeing in the forehede; the dropys of evese, for the plentioushede inumerable." (Compare ST. Chs 3 and 5, 210-11, 217-18). Another example of the passage which is far more detailed visually in LT is provided by the description of the dying and drying of Christ in Chs 16 and 17, 18-20, with which compare ST, Ch 10 (233-35). See especially LT, 19: "And ferthermore, I saw that the swete skyn and the tender flesh, with the heere and the blode, was al rasyd and losyd abov from the bone with the thornys, where thowe it were daggyd on many pecys, as a clith that were saggand, as it wold hastely have fallen of for hevy and lose while it had kynde moysture. And that was grete sorrow and drede to me, for methowte I wold not for my life a sen it fallen. . . . And than . . . it began to dreyen and stynte a party of the weyte and sette abute the garland. And thus it envyrouyd al aboute, as it were garland upon garland. . . ." This passage is instructive in another sense also, since S1 here differs importantly from P (see Colledge and Walsh, vol.2, 362-63), as though the scribes of the two manuscripts, or of their ancestors, have felt free to develop this Passion meditation in their own directions. See Windeatt for further examples of the relation between LT and ST.

12. References to the passing of time are introduced in the first chapter of exposition (2.2), in the key Chapter 51, almost at the centre of the work (56), and again in the last chapter (86.102).

13. The works of all three writers were available in England by the fifteenth century. In view of Margery Kempe's intense awareness of Bridget, Julian probably knew at least of her, although not until some time after 1373. For Bridget, see Roger Ellis, "'Flores ad Fabricandum . . . Coronam': An Investigation into the Uses of the Revelations of St Bridget of Sweden in Fifteenth-Century England," *Medium Aevum* 51 (1982): 163-86. For Mechtild, see *The Booke of Gostlye Grace of Mechtild of Hackeborn,* ed. Theresa A. Halligan (Toronto: Pontifical Institute of

Medieaval Studies, 1979) 47-59. For Elizabeth, see Ruth J. Dean, "Manuscripts of St Elizabeth of Schönau in England," *Modern Language Review* 32 (1937): 62-71.

14. Bridget's visions, for example, were set down immediately by her scribes, although the process of editing and organizing them into the structure that became the *Liber Celestis* was not completed until after her death. See Ellis, "'Flores ad Fabricandum.'"

15. See LT 51.59. For the radical Cabbalist view of the handing down of the Ten Commandments (held, e.g., by Rabbi Mendel of Rymanow), see Gershom Scholem, *On The Kabbalah and Its Symbolism* (New York: Schocken, 1961) 30, who remarks: "In Hebrew the consonant *aleph* represents nothing more than the position taken by the larynx when a word begins with a vowel. Thus the *aleph* may be said to denote the source of all articulate sound. . . . To hear the *aleph* is to hear next to nothing; it is the preparation for all audible language. . . ." Similarly, to call one's own mature understanding of a revelation merely the 'begennynge of an ABC' involves a recognition that the revelation itself is still only a tiny part not of truth as such but of the preparation for knowing a truth that it can no more than dimly foreshadow.

16. Compare LT 51.54-61 (part of which is discussed at length below), in which Julian confessedly extrapolates her vision with details she cannot be sure were originally there. With the exception of a few famous passages, the *Revelation of Love* is not rich in visual imagery.

17. The basic tripartite distinction is made in LT 9. 11 (compare ST 7.224), and reiterated in 73.88 (compare ST 23.272-73); the category "gostly in bodily lyknes" is introduced in LT 4.5, to describe Julian's first vision of Mary, and is mentioned again, with "more gostly without bodily Iyknes," at the beginning of LT 51.54, at the beginning of the parable of the lord and servant.

18. See Augustine, *De Genesi at Litteram,* Book XII, Ch. 6 ff. In PL 34, cols. 458ff. For discussions of the medieval influence of Augustine's distinctions, see J.-P. Torrell, *Theorie de la prophetie et philosophie de la conaissance aux environs 1230: La Contribution d'Hughes de Saint-Cher,* Spicilegium Sacrum Lovaniense, Etudes et documents, 40 (Louvain, 1977). For Hilton's use of "bodily" and "ghostly" sight, see *Scale of Perfection* (e.g., in the modernization of Evelyn Underhill, London: Burns and Oates, 1923), Book I, Ch 10-11, and Book II, Ch 43-46, where the terms undoubtedly correspond to Augustinian "corporeal" and "intellectual" vision. The phrase "gastelich sihthe" is also used in Book II of *Ancrene Wisse* (ed. J.R.R. Tolkien, Early English Text Society, O.S., 249, London: Oxford University Press, 1962, f.24a, 7) to describe contemplation by the spiritual senses, in a passage indebted to Gregory's *Moralia in Iob* and Book X of Augustine's *Confessions;* see *Anchoritic Spirituality: "Ancrene Wisse" and Associated Works,* trans. Anne Savage and Nicholas Watson, The Classics of Western Spirituality (Mahwah: Paulist Press,

1991) 355-56, notes 58 and 63-66. In *The Chastizing of God's Children* (ed. Joyce Bazire and Eric Colledge, Oxford: Blackwell, 1957, 169.12-171.17), the term "bodily" sight again has a strictly Augustinian sense, this time transmitted via Alphonse of Pecha's *Epistola Solitarii,* the source of this part of the *Chastizing.* In the light of these parallels, the insistence by both Molinari (60-70) and Colledge and Walsh (87) that Julian's use of the term "bodily sight" corresponds to Augustinian *intellectual* vision is unacceptable-- especially if we recall that Julian's first "bodily sight" of the bleeding head, and all subsequent sights in this mode, develop from her continuing gaze at a crucifix which is physically present throughout. Nor is Molinari likely to be right in assuming that Julian's terminology is subjectively descriptive rather than formally analytic; on the contrary, her careful attempts to distinguish different modes of vision using the accepted Middle English terminology suggests that she is almost certainly aware on some level of the Augustinian categories.

19. Note, however, that if Julian encountered Bridget's *Liber Celestis* (or *The Chastizing of God's Children),* she would have met this terminology in *relation* to Bridget's visions, albeit not in the visions themselves, in Alphonse of Pechats *Epistola Solitarii.* For the circulation of this work with the second edition of the *Liber,* see Roger Ellis, *The Liber Celestis of St Bridget of Sweden,* Early English Text Society, O.S., 291 (London: Oxford University Press, 1988) x-xii.

20. See, e.g., *Scale of Perfection,* Book I, Chapters 10-12, which admit the existence of genuine "bodily sight," but focus the reader's attention on the capacity of such sensual visions to lead one away from true contemplation.

21. I will not mostly be concerned here with Julian's other category of revelatory modes, "word formyd in my understonding," but it too can be linked to traditional mystical terminology. For example, Alphonse of Pecha (and after him *The Chastizing of God's Children,* 172.9-173.4, see notes 19 and 20) discusses the various kinds of mystical locutions, drawing on Book XVIII of Gregory's *Moralia in Iob.*

22. While Middle English "as to my sight" was doubtless sometimes used with the vague generality of the modern English "in my view," the instances of similar phrases given in the *Middle English Dictionary* article on "sight" mostly give the term real weight, as though it is more closely equivalent to "in my *judgement"* (see especially definition 8 (b), where "as to my sight" itself is not recorded). For obvious reasons, Julian's use of the term is likely to have been especially conscious and serious.

23. Contrast the equivalent passage in ST 3.210-11, which omits everything from "And, in the same showeing," presenting us with an incident and its immediate response ("I conseyvede treuly and myghttyllye that itt was hym selfe that schewyd it me") rather as the B and C texts of *Piers Plowman* builds on the A

text's relatively simple notion of Dowel, Dobet and Dobest, turning them into no more than what John Alford calls "primarily a rhetorical scheme for amplification." *A Companion to "Piers Plowman,"* ed. John A. Alford (Berkeley: U of California P, 1988), 46.

24. The immediate context makes the "revelatory" status of this speech clearer: "Also our lord God shewed that it is full gret plesance to him that a sily soule corne to him nakidly and pleynly and homely. For this is the kinde yernings of the soule by the touching of the Holy Ghost, as be the understondyng that I have in this sheweing: 'God, of thy goodnesse, give me thyselfe' . . ." (LT 5.6). Logically, the word "for" suggests that rather than being a meditative extrapolation of the "showing" described in the first sentence, the speech actually is that "showing"--as becomes clear if one substitutes "so," "thus" or even "and."

25. See LT 10.11-13. In her account of this revelation, Julian also amplifies an "answer, made in her reason" to her desire for more light: "If God wil shew thee more, he shal by thy light. Thee nedith none but him." Like the "general voice" which identifies the nut-like "thing" in revelation I, the source of this speech is not specifically identified as God.

26. LT 15.17-18: "And after this he shewid a soveren gostly lekyng in my soule . . . then the peyne shewid ageyn to my feling, and than the ioy and the lekyng, and now that one, and now that other. . . . This vision was shewid me, after myn vnderstondyng, that it *is* spedeful to some soulis to fele on this wise." Contrast the *Scale of Perfection,* Book I, ch. 10, which distinguishes between "bodily appearing" and "any other feeling in bodily wits . . . in sounding of ear, or savouring in the mouth, or smelling at the nose. . . ."

27. After the speech, Julian concludes the chapter, "Thus migtily, wisely and lovinly was the soule examynyd in this vision. Than saw I sothly that me behovyd nedis to assenten with gret reverens, enioyand in God." That is, the speech is a fictional dramatization of the effect of the "vision" on the soul, at the end of which it "sees" the truth.

28. LT 13.16. Julian explicates part of her own speech ("I se scorne that God scornith him and he shal be scornyd") rather as if it were a locution spoken by Christ [italics mine]: "And I seid 'He is scornid', I mene that God scornith him-- that is to sey, for he seeth him now as he shall done withoute end. For in this God shewid that the fend is dampnid. And this ment I when I seid, 'He *shall be* scornyd': at domysday generally of all that shal be savyd, to hose consolation he hath gret invye. . . ."

29. "Thus I saw the swete fleshe dey, in semyng be party after party, dryande with mervelous peynys. And as longe as any spirit had life in Crists fleshe, so longe sufferid he peyne. This longe pynyng semyd to me as if he had bene seven night

ded, deyand, at the poynt of out passing away, sufferand the last peyne. And than I said [P reads 'say'] it semyd to me as if he had bene seven night ded, it menyth that the swete body was so discoloryd, so drye, so clongen, so dedely and so petevous as he had be seven night dede, continuly deyand" (LT 16.18-19). The third sentence here ("This longe pynyng" etc.) is an expansion of a passage of ST (10.233) which is then explicated (somewhat clumsily) by means of further expansion in the next sentence. The formula "that I said . . . it menyth" is most suggestive of the process of meditative amplification by which the sparseness of ST's accounts of Julian's "bodily sights" acquire the far greater detail they possess in LT.

30. It would be possible, perhaps, to defend Julian's extremely broad use of "ghostly sight" as a specialized development of the category of "intellectual vision" as this is described in, for example, the last chapters of Book II of *The Scale of Perfection,* in which the soul "sees" the truths of the Scriptures by intuition (see Book II, Ch 43), and then, presumably through the Scriptures, learns to contemplate the major doctrines of the Christian faith, "seeing" the natures of souls (Ch 45), of angels (Ch 46), of the humanity and divinity of Christ (Ch 46), and finally of the Trinity (Ch 46). My point is that Julian's use of the terminology of revelation is so flexible that such parallels are likely to be almost accidental; she uses the terms as it suits her to, not according to any disciplined or learned idea of their meanings.

31. *"Scriptura Sancta, morem rapidissimi fluminis tenens, sic humanarum mentiumprofunda repla, ut semper exundet; sic haurientes satiat, ut inexhausta permaneat. Profluunt ex ea spiritualium sensuum gurgites abundantes, et transeuatibus aliis, alia surgunt-immo, non transeuntibus (quia 'sapientia immortalis est'* [see Wisdom 1.15], *sed emergentibus, et decorem saum ostendentibus aliis, alii non deficientibus succedant sed manentes subsequuntur."* Gilbert of Stanford, *In Cant.* 20.225, quoted in Umberto Eco, *Semiotics and the Philosophy of Language* (Bloomington: U of Indiana P, 1984) 150; the translation is my own. I am grateful to Anne Savage for drawing my attention to this passage, and to Eco's useful accompanying discussion.

32. Note again how much more pointed is Julian's use of the phrase "as to my sight" than first appears.

33. The provisional and temporary nature of the "feith of holy church" is stressed throughout chs. 44-47, where this faith is described as the "lower dome" (the "heyer dome" being the revelation), necessary only on account of the fallen state of human sensuality, which demands that we know ourselves sinners and worthy of wrath *even though* God is not in fact capable of such wrath (see especially LT 45.47-48). For an analysis, see Grace Jantzen, *Julian of Norwich* (London: SPCK, 1987) 177-80.

34. Compare, for example, Hildegard of Bingen's *Scivias,* a series of visions, prophecies and expositions, all of which are presented as divine in their immediate origin, and as having been given in a timeless visionary moment, but which clearly incorporate the author's thought and reading during the ten years the work took to write. Ed. Angela Carlevaris and Adelgundis Führkötter, *Corpus Christianorum, Continuatio Medievalis,* volumes 43-43a. (Turnhout: Brepols, 1978).

35. As I understand Julian's argument, she clearly articulates the continuing *necessity* for both "domes'" but is unable to reconcile their truth, that is, how God views both. See especially LT 45.48: "Than was this my desire: that I myte sen in God in what manner that the dome of holy church herin techyth is trew in his syte . . . wherby thei myte both be savid. . . . And to al this I had non other answere but a mervelous example of a lord and of a servant--as I shal seyn after-- and that full [mystely] shewid. And yet I stond in desire, and will into my end, that I myte be grace knowen these ii domys as it longyth to me. . . ." Instead of reconciling this opposition in a systematic theological way, as Colledge and Walsh's notes and summaries persistently suggest, the rest of the *Revelation of Love* seems to me, rather, to make theology out of the fully acknowledged impossibility of doing so.

36. In medieval biblical exegesis, the phrase *in persona is* a standard way of identifying the category of individual to whom a biblical passage refers, or is being made to refer--sometimes a biblical *auctor* being deemed to speak *in propria persona,* sometimes *in persona aliorum.* For discussion, see A. J. Minnis, *Medieval Theory of Authorship* (London: Scholar, 1983) Ch.3.

37. My analysis takes its own direction, but is somewhat parallel to those of Glasscoe 168-69, and Colledge and Walsh, notes to Ch. 51, 11.76 and 80 (519-20).

38. S1 and S2 read "iii propertes" for P's "the privities," which is possible (as an early expression of the extent to which the meaning of the revelation is still latent), but lacks the clarity of P. P omits "that is to sey of this boke" of S1 and S2 which resembles an unhelpful scribal gloss, and reads "thre knowyages" for "onknowyng" of S1 and S2; this makes very poor sense and is surely a nervous scribal emendation, rather than the "clear example of P's superiority" to S1 and S2 that Colledge and Walsh claim it to be (51.519 n. 70).

39. See, for example, Jantzen Ch. 7. For a succinct account of the theological background, see J. P. H. Clark, "*Fiducia* in Julian of Norwich, II," *Downside Review,* 95 (1979): 214-29, especially 225.

40. *Piers Plowman,* ed. A. V. C. Schmidt (London: Everyman, 1978) B XX, 1.208.

41. *Piers Plowman* B XX, 1.382

St. Cecilia and St. John of Beverly: Julian of Norwich's Early Model and Late Affirmation

Susan K. Hagen

Early in the short version of her *Showings*, Julian of Norwich explains that, moved by a story she heard in Church, she had prayed for three wounds just as St. Cecilia, "hadde thre wonndys with a swerde in the nekke, with the whilke sche pynede to the dede" ["received three wounds in the neck from a sword, through which she suffered death"].[1] Rarely commented upon in criticism,[2] there is no further mention of this virgin martyr in Julian's writing. About mid-way through the long version, Julian adds St. John of Beverly to a list of saints previously mentioned in the short version as she enumerates persons brought to mind in the understanding that there is no lasting shame in sin, "then god brought merely to my mynde David and other in the olde lawe with hym wyth ouȝt number; and in the new lawe he brought to my mynde furst Magdaleyne, Peter and Paule, Thomas of Inde, sent John of Beverly, and other also with ouȝt number" (LT 38.446; cf. ST 255) ["then God brought joyfully to my mind David and innumerable others with him in the Old Law; and in the New Law he brought to my mind first Magdalen, Peter and Paul, Thomas of India, St. John of Beverly and others too without number" (242-43; cf. 154)]. As with the reference to St. Cecilia, the addition of St. John is seldom commented upon,[3] and Julian, herself, says little more of him other than that his fall into sin and return to grace is an example "to make vs glad and mery in loue" (LT 39.448) ["to make us glad and happy in [God's] love" (243)].

Since the references to these saints are rather incidental to the theological--even to the literary--import of the *Showings*, the title of this essay might suggest that it focuses on something akin to Julian of Norwich trivia. But I turn to Sts. Cecilia and John of Beverly less as topics themselves than as emblems for, or reflections of, a tonal and intentional difference between the two texts of Julian's revelations. The omission of a female martyr sentenced to die for her refusal to stop evangelizing and renounce Christ and the addition of a beloved local preacher reflect a change in Julian's own self-assurance as a recipient of Christ's truth--and as a teacher. Moreover, it is that confidence in her hard-fought understanding of her visions and her desire to communicate that intelligence to others that result in the considerably longer revision of the initial recounting of Christ's revelations to her.

At the initial recording of the visions of the day-long experience, Julian did not have the confidence in the import of her visions that would come with years of thoughtful consideration, additional divine instruction,4 and practical experience as a counselor and spiritual advisor. The voice of the first writing is the voice of the uncertain woman still shamed by telling the "religiouse personn" ["man of religion"] who came to visit her that she "hadde raued þat daye" (ST 266) ["had been raving" (162)]; it is far from the voice of the theologically mature woman who summarily claims in the final chapter of the Long Text, "Thus was I lernyd, þat loue is oure lordes menyng" (LT 86.733) ["So I was taught that love is our Lord's meaning" (342)]. Remembrance of an early Christian woman who trusted her conversations with angels and believed in the validity of her own evangelical mission--even at the cost of death--might well provide comfort for a devout, yet common, fourteenth-century woman embarking on the disclosure of her intimate exchanges with Christ and her smoky, vile-smelling visitation by the devil (ST 163, 165-66).5 St. Cecilia might well not appear in the Long Text because Julian's own focus is no longer on recording personal experience but on teaching others what she has learned from that experience. That meant concern not for creating a context for the validity of the events the 13th of May 1373 but for devising a way to communicate to average women and men of her time the difficult and often elusive theological concepts that took her nearly twenty years to understand and articulate; furthermore, it meant communicating them in a way that was both easily comprehended and recollected.

Turning her attention away from self-validation and toward instruction, Julian might feel more kinship with her compatriot John of Beverly who entered St. Hilda's double monastery at Whitby, who served as a bishop, who ordained Bede as a priest in 703, and who, though little remembered today, once was greatly honored in England as a blessed man and teacher.[6] Guided by her instructional intent then, the methodology Julian decided upon to teach her "fellow Christians"--as well as the fact that she could now better explicate her visions--accounts for more than the absence of one saint and the appearance of another; it also accounts for the extraordinary differences in length and visual detail in the shorter and longer texts.

Many others have written about the differences between the two versions of the revelations in terms of Julian's maturing theological understanding of those revelations or, as she refers to them, her showings.[7] Certainly none has done so as thoroughly as Denise Baker in *Julian of Norwich's Showings: From Vision to Book*, who argues that "Julian explores the implications of these showings with a thoughtfulness and precision that transforms the primarily devotional Short Text into the theologically sophisticated Long Text."[8] Similarly, numerous scholars have commented upon the Franciscan devotional methodology that lies behind the milieu of affective piety that infuses the nature of her visions.[9] Although both James Walsh[10] and Baker note that Julian seems scrupulously to omit personal details in the Long Text "in order to universalize her experience" (54) making it more clearly applicable to her "fellow Christians," scholars interested in either Julian's theological development or the affective visual detail of the longer text make virtually no connection between an overt desire to teach to others what she has come to understand and the increased length and visual detail of the showings of that longer version. Yet that connection does exist in her mnemonic--rather than the affective--use of images. To that end, Julian vivifies and expands the recollections of the showings more with the purpose of making them evocatively memorable and clear in their import than of moving her audience to ardent devotional responses.

This is not to say that the affective spirituality and its foundation in Franciscan devotion cited by so many is not to the point here, for surely it is. But in and of itself it does not account for the extensively developed visual detail of the Long Text. Nonetheless, it would be worthwhile to review the traditions of affective devotion that were so popular at the close of the fourteenth century in order to clarify the distinction in intention I am claiming for Julian. Based on the Franciscan premise that one could move toward identification with Christ by focusing on and attempting to experience vicariously those moments in his life that are shared by all humans--birth, and suffering and death--the meditative process invariably leads the meditator to a recognition of the all encompassing love of his birth as human and to the unparalleled innocence of his Passion and death. Faced with the absolute goodness of Christ's life and the comparative meanness of his or her own life, the devotee quickly becomes a penitent, affectively moved to tears of contrition and avowals of correction of sin.[11] A brief lyric from the thirteenth century exemplifies this process with touching simplicity,[12]

> The minde of thi passiun, suete Ihesu,
> The teres it tollid,
> The eyes it bolled,
> The neb it wetth
> In herte sueteth.[13]

[The mind of your Passion, sweet Jesus, the tears it draws forth, the eyes it makes swollen, the face it wets, in heart [it] sweetens]

Simply remembering Jesus' suffering and death brings one to tearful compassion and softening of heart. But we must consider the importance of the fact that that remembrance comes forth embodied in the visual image of the suffering Christ. We should note as well that in medieval science and psychology sight was the most immaterial, and therefore most perfect, universal, and intellectual, of the senses. Not as dependent on biology as the pleasures of the other senses, the pleasures of sight were considered more aesthetic and greater; they were, however, also far more seductive, for as both Chaucer's Palamon and Troilus know, the pleasures of the eye almost invariably lodge in the heart.[14] Is it any wonder then that the remembrance of Christ's Passion would "in [human] heart sueteth"? With simple--yet powerfully evocative--detail, another brief Passion lyric, dating about 1300, illustrates the capability of the visual image to move one to contrition in the face of Jesus' love for humankind.

> Whan I on the rode see
> Faste nayled to the tree
> Jhesu my lemman,

I-bounde blak and blody,
And his moder stonde him by
Wepyng and Iohan;

His bak wyth scourge i-swongen,
His side depe i-stongen
For synne and love of man:
Wel oghte I synne lete
And neb wyth teres wete,
If I of love can.[15]

[When I see our loving Jesus nailed to the cross, blackened and bloody, his Blessed Mother and St. John standing weeping at this feet, his back broken and scared by lashings, his side deeply wounded by Longinus' spear—all for the love of humankind—how can I but eschew sin and wet my face with tears if I know anything of love?]

Such is the question the speaking "I" of the poem shares with the reader/meditator emotionally touched by the poignantly horrific details of Jesus' anguish. Quoting another version of this same poem as representative of "an established meditational scheme that all Franciscan meditation ultimately shared," Denise Despres, in *Ghostly Sights: Visual Meditation in Late-Medieval Literature*, cites Elizabeth Salter's description of "the three principal stages of Christocentric meditation as (1) sensible recollection, (2) emotional reflection, and (3) moral application" (6). It is the issue of "sensible recollection" that has further implications for Julian of Norwich's revision of her text as her images become more detailed, more striking, and more memorable.

In *Themes and Images in Medieval Religious Lyrics*, Douglas Gray cites the former poem to underscore how important "the *memoria* of Christ incarnate" was to affective devotion, concluding that "it is not surprising that images--whether visual images made by artists or craftsman or mental images made by the words of writers--have such an important function in medieval devotion" (41).[16] Adding the caveat that many late medieval mystics shun the use of images of any sort in preference for contemplation upon the pure essence of God, Gray points out that few nonetheless "despise material images at earlier stages of the mystic's 'work'," in fact the "vision" becomes the characteristic form which the mystic's writing takes (41).[17] In an endnote to this observation, Gray directs readers to Julian of Norwich, stating "Among the English visionaries Julian of Norwich is especially interesting for the way in which she discusses her images" (239, n. 41). Unfortunately, other than giving an example of Julian likening blood from Christ's head to three things (round pellets, herring scales, and raindrops off eaves), Gray does not explain what he means by "interesting." However, it is an observation to which I will return a little later.

Undeniably, as Gray's note suggests, Julian of Norwich's *A Book of Showings* differs from the apophatic tradition of works such as the *Cloud of Unknowing*, but we should be cautious not to assume that the strikingly visual quality of Julian's images in the Long Text are the result purely of a cultural climate thick with the figures of affective devotion. Baker comes all too close to this when she suggests that the eidetic quality of Julian's recounted showings "results from a sensitivity to concrete detail gained by frequent concentration on devotional art, particularly paintings, and through repeated practice of the imaginative visualization required for meditation" (48).[18] Certainly Julian was familiar with devotional art. Norwich of her day was a commercial art center, and she was hardly a woman ignorant of either popular or learned religious culture. In fact, in the short version of her *Showings*, she herself refers to the suffering and pain that "the payntyngys of crucyfexes that er made be the grace of god aftere the techynge of haly kyrke to the lyknes of Crystes passyonn, als farfurthe as man ys witte maye reche" (ST 202) ["paintings of the Crucifixion represent, which are made by God's grace, according to Holy Church's teaching, to resemble Christ's Passion, so far as human understanding can attain" (125-26)].

This reference to devotional art Julian omits from the longer text, offering evidence, I believe, that for her the expanded visual details of the later renderings find their impetus in something other than the tradition of affective piety--however much that tradition may have acclimated her to the richness and emotive power visual images might possess. Again, in her own words she tells us at the outset of even the Short Text that she already had "grete felynge in the passyonn of Cryste" (ST 201) ["great feeling for the Passion of Christ" (125)], but she desired "the more trewe mynde in the passionn of Cryste" (ST 203) ["a truer recollection of Christ's Passion" (126)].

I desyrede to haue mare be the grace of god. Me thought I wolde
haue bene that tyme with Mary Mawdeleyne and with othere that
were Crystes loverse, that I myght have sene bodylye the passionn
of oure lorde that he sufferede for me, that I myght have sufferede
with hym as othere dyd that lovyd hym, not withstandynge that I
leevyd sadlye alle the peynes of Cryste as halye kyrke schewys and
techys, and also the payntyngys of crucyfexes that er made be the
grace of god aftere the techynge of haly kyrke to the lyknes of
Crystes passyonn, als farfurthe as man ys witte maye reche. Nouȝt
withstondynge alle this trewe be leve I desyrede a bodylye syght,
whare yn y myght have more knawynge of bodelye paynes of oure
lorde oure savyoure, and of the compassyonn of oure ladye and of
alle his trewe loverse that were be levande his paynes that tyme
and sythene; for I wolde have beene one of thame and suffrede
with thame. (ST 201-202)

[I desired to have more by the grace of God. I thought that I
wished that I had been at that time with Mary Magdalen and
with the others who were Christ's lovers, so that I might have
seen with my own eyes our Lord's Passion which he suffered for
me, so that I might have suffered with him as others did who
loved him, even though I believed firmly in all Christ's pains, as
Holy Church shows and teaches, and as paintings of the
Crucifixion represent, which are made by God's grace, according
to Holy Church's teaching, to resemble Christ's Passion, so far as
human understanding can attain. But despite all my true faith I
desired a bodily sight, through which I might have more
knowledge of our Lord and saviour's bodily pains, and of the
compassion of our Lady and all of his true lovers who were living
at that time and afterwards, for I would have been one of them
and have suffered with them. (125-26; see n. 1)]

Julian's insistence on seeing with her own eyes, on having bodily sight,
and more knowledge of the actual suffering of the crucifixion, suggests
that she seeks no mere memorial image, but a mystical first-hand
experience. Note, too, that this wished for scene has no penitential
dimension for her. It comes from a pre-existing longing to better
understand her god; it does not elicit a new found awareness of her

sinful distance from her god. In other words, her yearning comes out of a visionary impulse rather than a devotional one.[19]

Once that understanding is achieved by Julian after years of reflection and additional revelation, her desire becomes to communicate it to her "fellow Christians," and here is where the visual details of the longer version of her showings become so instrumental to her purpose. As Despres points out, Franciscans considered "meditations on Christ's humanity that provided moral illumination and elicited compassion . . . the best ways to teach the unlearned and laity to prepare for penance" (7), but detailed visual images served another useful purpose for the learned and unlearned alike in the Middle Ages; they made the images far more memorable and they provided a way to make essential yet intellectually difficult concepts clear through extended metaphor. As Bonaventure explains in the *Lignum vitae*, a meditative biography of Christ, "since imagination [i.e., the imaging of sensible objects or the recollection of images] aids understanding, I have arranged in the form of an imaginary tree the few items I have collected from among many" (quoted in Despres 29, my emendation).[20]

Bonaventure understood that sensible things could be used as similitudes for otherwise elusive moral and theological concepts, as did his contemporary Albertus Magnus, who considered images helpful to memory because through only a few of them many details could be remembered, and--even though those details relate most immediately to the image itself--as metaphors they nonetheless can affect the soul and consequently help memory (Hagen, *Allegorical Remembrance* 61). Defining a *sign* much as St. Augustine did in *On Christian Doctrine* as "a thing which causes us to think of something beyond the impression the thing itself makes upon the senses,"[21] Bonaventure concludes that corporeal images can communicate noncorporeal concepts as signs communicate "what is signified" (quoted in Despres 33).

This utilization of visual images as memorial devices is hardly unique to Bonaventure and Albertus Magnus; much less is it original to the Middle Ages. Quite the contrary, as Frances Yates notes in *The Art of Memory*,[22] medieval scholastics based their methods for better placing elusive concepts in understanding and holding them in memory on classical rhetorical techniques (61).[23] Noting that "artificial memory begins to appear as a lay devotional discipline, fostered and recommended by the friars . . . [and that it] was a creator of imagery which must surely have flowed out into creative works of art and literature" (91). Yates provides us with a propitious statement that beautifully joins the topic of artificial memory as we have been discussing it with our other topic of affective devotion. It is, I believe, out of both the traditions of affective piety and out of a desire to make the lessons of her showings both accessible and memorable to lay persons, that Julian of Norwich composes the second version of her showings, a second version that is more detailed in both its moving visual exactitude and its resonant explanatory narrative.

In a series of four rules for improving memory, St. Thomas Aquinas directs that anyone who would remember something, especially something of spiritual intention, should link it to some "corporeal similitude" which is easier held in human cognition. But, he warns, that similitude "should not be too familiar, because we wonder more at unfamiliar things and the soul is more strongly and vehemently held by them" (quoted in Yates 74). Here lies the rationale for the striking visual accuracy of Julian's visions. And here, too, lies the key to the memorable quality of many of her metaphors, as she creates striking similes out of comparisons of common occurrences of daily life with the most uncommon occurrences of divine experience. Blood dripping from the wounded head of Christ becomes raindrops or herring scales; the dehydrating of his crucified flesh becomes a cloth drying in the wind; our god becomes our mother; and all creation becomes a simple, brown hazelnut. It is the very familiarity of the vehicle for these metaphors that makes the tenor so striking--and memorable.

If we look at a couple of examples of changes Julian made to descriptions and explanations of her showings in the two versions, we can easily see the techniques of artificial memory at work. Since Gray had commented on the interesting way Julian handles visual images, but never expounded on how it is all so interesting, we may do well to begin with the pellets, herring scales, and raindrops he mentions. Notice how the brief, unadorned four lines of the first version become the highly eidetic and glossed image of the longer text.

And in that tyme that oure lorde schewyd this that I haue nowe saydene gastelye syght, I saye the bodylye syght lastande of the plentyuouse bledynge of the hede, and als longe as y sawe that syght y sayde oftynn tymes: Benedicite dominus. In this fyrste schewynge of oure lorde I sawe sex thynges in myne vndyrstandynge. (ST 217)

[And during the time that our Lord showed me this spiritual vision which I have now described, I saw the bodily vision of the copious bleeding of the head persist, and as long as I saw it I said, many times: Blessed be the Lord! In this first revelation of our Lord I saw in my understanding six things. (132)]

And in alle þat tyme that he schewd thys that I haue now seyde in gostely syght, I saw the bodely syght lastyng of the pletuous bledyng of the hede. The grett droppes of blode felle downe fro vnder the garlonde lyke pelottes, semyng as it had comynn ou3te of the veynes. And in the comyng ou3te they were browne rede, for the blode was full thycke; and in the spredyng abrode they were bryght rede. And whan it camme at the browes, ther they vanysschyd; and not wythstonding the bledyng contynued tylle many thynges were sene and vnderstondyd. Nevertheles the feyerhede and the lyuelyhede continued in the same bewty and lyuelynes.

The plentuoushede is lyke to the droppes of water that falle of the evesyng of an howse after a grete shower of reyne, that falle so thycke that no man may nomber them with no bodely wyt. And for the roundnesse they were lyke to the scale of heryng in the spredyng of the forehede.

And thre thynges cam to my mynde in the tyme: pelettes for the roundhede in the comyng ou3te of the blode, the scale of heryng for the roundhede in the spredyng, the droppes of the evesyng of a howse for the plentuoushede vnnumerable. Thys shewyng was quyck and lyuely and hidows and dredfulle and swete and louely; and of all the syght that I saw this was most comfort to me, that oure good lorde, that is so reverent and dredfulle, is so homely and so curteyse, and this most fulfyllyd me lykyng and syckernes in soule.

[Here follow another 32 lines of development of Christ's courtesy, which Colledge and Walsh see as anticipating the allegory of the lord and the servant, also new to the Long Text.]

And as longe as I saw thys syght of the plentuousnesse of bledyng of the heed, I myght never stynte of these wordes: Benedicite dominus. In which shewyng I vnderstodd vj thynges. (LT 7-8.311-17)

[And during all the time that our Lord showed me this spiritual vision which I have now described, I saw the bodily vision of the copious bleeding of the head persist. The great drops of blood fell from beneath the crown like pellets, looking as if they came from the veins, and as they issued they were a brownish red, for the blood was very thick, and as they spread they turned bright red. And as they reached the brows they vanished; and even so the bleeding continued until I had seen and understood many things. Nevertheless, the beauty and the vivacity persisted, beautiful and vivid without diminution.

The copiousness resembles the drops of water which fall from the eaves of a house after a great shower of rain, falling so thick that no human ingenuity can count them. And in their roundness as they spread over the forehead they were like herring scales.

At the time three things occurred to me: the drops were round like pellets as the blood issued, they were round like herring scales as they spread, they were like raindrops off a house's eaves so many that they could not be counted. This vision was living and vivid and hideous and fearful and sweet and lovely; and in all this vision which I saw, what gave me most strength was that our good Lord, who is so to be revered and feared, is so familiar and so courteous, and most of all this filled me full of delight and certainty in my soul. . . .

And as long as I saw this vision of the copious bleeding of the head, I could not stop saying these words: Blessed be the Lord! In this revelation I understood six things. (187-90)]

Julian transforms a simple statement of fact from her initial account, "I saw the bodily vision of the copious bleeding of the head persist" into, in her own words, a "living and vivid and hideous and fearful and sweet and lovely"--and moving and memorable--image of the suffering Christ. The added details change the force of the remembrance from one of simple narrative incident to one of richly textured visual recreation. We feel the almost sticky texture of the drops of blood as heavy, thick, coagulating pellets. We hear their near pouring persistence as waterfalls of raindrops running off the roof in a great shower. We see their abundance as rounded, overlapping herring scales. By increasing the visual impact of the image, and by doing so with similes at once both homely in their familiarity and striking in the disparity between their commonality and the singularity of god incarnate, Julian increases the imaginative effect of the text, thereby implanting it more firmly in both the mind and the heart of her reader. But she also increases the intellectual effect of the text as that disparity just noted leads the reader to a startling realization of the love and courtesy displayed by the Lord so deserving of awe and reverence.

Simple recall of the bleeding head, recall made easier because we know what pellets and fish scales and water drops running off eaves in a heavy rain look like, then, elicits recall of Christ's courtesy, which Julian then explicates in six clearly enumerated points of understanding: his Passion, his virgin mother, the divinity, all creation, the love of the creator, and "the goodnesse that alle thyng hath, it is he" (LT 8.318) ["the goodness which everything has is God" (190)]. In both texts, Julian follows this vision of the bleeding head with an emphatic statement that she was shown the vision to share it with her fellow Christians, and she encourages them to contemplate upon God who presented this vision "in comfort of vs alle" (ST 219; LT 8.320) ["to the comfort of us all" (133; 191)].

Throughout the longer version of the *Showings*, Julian augments remembrances of her visions with similar sensual details and explanatory glosses. Especially vivid are the recounting of the second revelation of the changing color of Christ's face and the eighth revelation of the drying of his flesh. At the risk of overquotation, I offer a portion of the eighth showing below, taken from the Long Text, but with material having no parallel in the shorter version in bold type.

> After thys Crist shewde a parte of hys passyon nere his dyeng. I saw the swete face as it were drye and blodeles with pale dyeng and deede pale, langhuryng and than turned more deede in to blew, and after in browne blew, as the flessch turned more depe dede. For his passion shewde to me most propyrly in his blessyd face, and namely in hys lyppes. Ther in saw I these iiij colours:

tho þat were be fore fressch and rody, lyuely and lykyng to my syght. This was a peinfulle chaungyng, to se this depe dying, and also hys nose clongyn to geder and dryed to my syght; **and the swete body waxid browne and blacke, alle chaungyd ouȝte of þe feyer fressch and lyuely coloure of hym selfe in to drye dyeng. For that same tyme that oure blessyd sauyour dyed vppon the rode, it was a dry sharp wynd, wonder colde as to my syght; and what tyme that þe precyous blode was bled out of the swete body that myght passe ther fro, yet ther was a moyster in the swete flessch of Crist as it was shewde. Blodlessehed and payne dryed with in, and blowyng of the wynde and colde comyng from with out, mett to geder in the swete body of Christ; and these iiij dryed the flessch of Crist by prosses of tyme. And thowe this peyne was bitter and sharp, yet it was fulle longe lastyng, as to my syght. And the payne dryede vppe alle the lyuely spyrites of Cristes flessh. Thus I saw the swete flessch dry in my syght, parte after perte dryeng with mervelous payne.** And as long as any spryte had lyffe in Cristes flessch, so longe sufferde he. This long peyne semyde to me as if he had be sennyght deede, dyeng at þe poynt of out passyng, alwey sufferyng the gret peyne. **And ther I say it semyd as he had bene sennyght deed, it specyfyeth that the swet body was so dyscolouryd, so drye, so clongyn, so dedly and so pytuous as he had bene sennyght deed, contynually dyeng.** And me thought the dryeng of Cristes flessch was the most peyne and the last of his passion. (LT 16.357-59)

[After this Christ showed me part of his Passion, close to his death. I saw his sweet face as it were dry and bloodless with the pallor of dying, and then deadly pale, languishing, and then the pallor turning blue and then the blue turning brown, as death took more hold upon his flesh. For his passion appeared to me most vividly in his blessed face, and especially in the lips. I saw there what had become of these four colors, which had appeared to me before as fresh and ruddy, vital and beautiful. This was a painful change to watch, this deep dying, and his nose shrivelled and dried up as I saw: **and the sweet body turned brown and black, completely changed and transformed from his naturally beautiful, fresh and vivid complexion into a shrivelled image of death.** For **at the time when our blessed saviour died upon the Cross, there was a dry, bitter wind, I saw; and when all the precious blood that might had flowed out of his sweet body, still there was some moisture in the sweet flesh as it was revealed.** It **was dried up from within by bloodlessness and anguish, from without by the blowing of the wind and the cold, all concentrated upon Christ's sweet body; and as the** hours passed these four circumstances dried up Christ's flesh. **And though this pain was bitter and piercing, still it lasted a very long time. And this pain dried up all the vital fluids in Christ's flesh.** Then I saw the sweet flesh **drying before my eyes, part after part drying up with astonishing pain. And as long as there was any vital fluid in Christ's flesh, he went on suffering.** The long torment impressed me as if he had been dead for a week, dying and on the point of death, always suffering this great pain. **And when I say that it seemed as if he had been dead for a week, that means, as I have explained, that the sweet body was so discoloured, so dry, so shrivelled, so deathly and so pitiful that he might have been dead for a week, though he went on dying.** And it seemed to me as if the greatest and the last pain of his Passion was when his flesh dried up. (206-207)]

The supplementary details make the image of the dying body of Christ notably more visceral and animated. The reiterated liquid images of blood, moisture, and fluids juxtaposed to the images of desiccation heighten the pathos of the vision, while the references to the dehydrating bitter, cold wind infuse it with a tactile, yet again, homely, quality. Painting with artistically grotesque precision, Julian continues the description of the eighth revelation with new details about the sagging weight of Christ's body and the hardness of the nails in his hands and feet widening the wounds in his flesh as the pressure of the crown of thorns widens the wounds in his forehead and the sharp individual thorns scrape and loosen his dried flesh. Then, as if the vividness of the image itself were not sufficient to make it memorable, she offers two similes so common to the everyday lives of her "fellow Christians" that they cannot help but linger at the fringes of memory. The skin of Christ's face and body, she says was "smalle rympylde with a tawny coloure, lyke a drye bord when it is agyd" ["covered with fine wrinkles, and of a tawny color, like a dry board which has aged"] and his body was "hangyng vppe in the eyer as men hang a cloth for to drye" (LT 17.363) ["hanging in the air as people hang up a cloth to dry" (208)]. A weathered board and a cloth drying in the wind, striking and memorable images for the dying body of Christ.

Not all of Julian's homely metaphors are striking in their vivid detail, however. At least one--probably the most memorable, or at least most popular of her work--achieves its status through wonderful simplicity.

And in this he shewed a little thing, the quantitie of an haselnott, lying in þe palme of my hand, as me semide, and it was as rounde as a ball. *I looked theran with the eye of my vnderstanding, and thought: What may this be?* And it was answered generaelly thus: It is all that is made. I marvayled how it might laste, for me thought it might sodenly haue fallen to nawght for littlenes. And I was answered in my vnderstanding: It lasteth and ever shall, for god loueth it; and so hath all thing being by the loue of god.

In this little thing I saw iij propreties. The first is þat god made it, the secund that god loueth it, the thirde that god kepyth it. But what behyld I ther in? Verely, the maker, the keper, the louer. (LT 5.299-300; emphasis added; cf. ST 212-13)

[And in this he showed me something small, no bigger than a hazelnut, lying in the palm of my hand, as it seemed to me, and it was as round as a ball. *I looked at it with the eye of my understanding and thought: What can this be?* [sic]24 I was amazed that it could last, for I thought that because of its littleness it would suddenly have fallen into nothing. *And I was answered in my understanding:* It lasts and always will, because God loves it; and thus everything has being through the love of God.

In this little thing I saw three properties. The first is that God made it, the second is that God loves it, the third is that God preserves it. But what did I see in it? It is that God is the Creator and the protector and the lover. (183; emphasis added; cf. 130-31)]

I quote this passage not only because it shows the range of Julian's everyday images, but also because it provides an illustration of exactly how the mnemonic method functions in her work. Perception of the physical thing with the bodily eye leads Julian to contemplation of the thing with "the eye of [her] understanding,"[25] and from there to discovery of three points of wisdom to be associated with the thing. She must, in effect, learn to read the image to discover what it signifies, to see it twice, once with the physical eye then with the eye of intellect. Whenever that image is called to mind in the future, it will now bring with it the three associated points of wisdom--an effective and efficient mnemonic device for the remembrance of God's creative, loving, and sustaining power. Now, in Julian's case we must not overlook the phrase, "And I was answered in my understanding," for this passive verbal construction reminds us that she came to her understanding through a visionary experience, through direct instruction through Christ's grace rather than through her own powers of discernment. Nonetheless, through her presentation of the vision of the hazelnut and her recounting of how she came to understand its significance, early in her *Showings* Julian presents her audience with a highly effective memory aid that her readers continue to use today.[26]

At this point, it is worth noting an observation made by Baker. She points out that unlike authors of devotional works on the Passion coming out of the meditative tradition, Julian does not tell the story of the Crucifixion; rather she concentrates on moments in the story, focusing on Christ's pain, yet making no reference to those who inflected that pain. Baker concludes, "Julian reads her vision like a picture rather than a story" (48-49). If Julian is embellishing her descriptions to transform them from mere recollections or reportage into mnemonic devices, then her explanations of what she understood or of what Christ taught her to understand from her showings stand as the noncorporeal concepts Bonaventure, Albertus Magnus, or St. Thomas Aquinas would have communicated by the corporeal (or sensible) image or sign.[27] The later rendition of *Showings* then, goes beyond the reporting of the original version to evolve into an intentional teaching tool by which all her "fellow Christians" can both grasp and remember the understandings she received from Christ and through numerous years of contemplation, recollection, and "reading" of her sixteen showings.[28]

By the writing of the Long Text, Julian had gained an intellectual resolve and confidence that rendered no longer appropriate the self-demeaning denial of aspirations to teach offered in the Short Text via a gender specific humility *topos* so common to the writings of medieval women.[29] Claiming, "Alle that I sawe of my selfe, I meene in the persone of alle myne evynn cristene" ["Everything that I say about myself I mean   to apply to all my fellow Christians"], Julian admonishes all to "leve the behaldynge of the wrechid worme, synfulle creature, that it was schewyd vnto" (ST 219) ["disregard the wretched worm, the sinful creature to whom it was shown" (133)], later adding this caveat: "Botte god for bede that ȝe schulde saye or take it so that I am a techere for I meene nouȝt soo, no I mente nevere so; for I am a womann, leued, febille and freylle" (ST 222) ["But God forbid that you should say or assume that I am a teacher, for that is not and never was my intention; for I am a woman, ignorant, weak and frail" (135)]. She immediately follows this self-effacement with a series of three additional *buts* that belie any claims to meekness, if not to ignorance and frailty.

Botte I wate wele, this that I saye, I hafe it of the schewynge of hym that es souerayne techare. *Botte* sothelye charyte styrres me to telle ȝowe it, for I wolde god ware knawenn, and mynn evynn crystene spede, as I wolde be my selfe to the mare hatynge of synne and lovynge of god. *Botte* for I am a womann, schulde I therfore leve that I schulde nouȝt telle ȝowe the goodenes of god, syne that I sawe in that same tyme that is his wille, that it be knawenn? (ST 222; emphasis added)

[*But* I know very well that what I am saying I have received by the revelation of him who is the sovereign teacher. *But* it is truly love which moves me to tell it to you, for I want God to be known and my fellow Christians to prosper, as I hope to prosper myself, by hating sin more and loving God more. *But* because I am a woman, ought I therefore to believe that I should not tell you of the goodness of God, when I saw at the same time that it is his will that it be known? (135; emphasis added)]

What we see in this series of sentences is a tension between a culturally imposed doubt about her own worth and aptitude[30] and a mystically validated self-confidence that marshals the boldness needed to record her showings. St. Cecilia, noted for her temerity before the Roman officials, provides Julian with historical affirmation of woman's value as a voice for Christian wisdom in the face of skeptics and nay-sayers. The apprehension that turns to the martyred saint for mystic inspiration and rhetorical affirmation in the short version of her showings no longer plagues Julian by the writing of the longer text. Compare the gendered tone of the sentences above to the parallel passage from the Long Text:

Alle that I say of me I mene in person of alle my evyn cristen, for I am lernyd in the gostely shewyng of our lord god that he meneth so. And therfore I pray yow alle for gods sake, and counceyle yow for yowre awne profyght, þat ye leue the beholdyng of a wrech that it was schewde to, and myghtely, wysely and mekely beholde in god, that of hys curteyse loue and endlesse goodnesse wolld shew it generally in comfort of vs alle. (LT 8.319-20)

[Everything that I say about me I mean to apply to all my fellow Christians, for I am taught that this is what our Lord intends in this spiritual revelation. And therefore I pray you all for God's sake, and I counsel you for your own profit, that you disregard the wretch to whom it was shown, and that mightily, wisely and meekly you contemplate upon God, who out of his courteous love and his endless goodness was willing to show it generally, to the comfort of us all. (191)]

While a touch of the humility *topos* remains in the word *wretch*, gone are the gendered apology and the self-abasing word *worm*. Julian no longer requires the protection of the virgin martyr's palm. Instead, in the moderated humility of a sinful human, rather than "a woman, ignorant, weak and frail," she turns to a local English bishop noted for his teaching and penchant for solitude (*Dictionary of Saints* 193). By adding John of Beverly to a procession of beloved Christian penitents, Julian reminds her audience that blessed individuals close to them in heritage and geography were known to teach the wisdom of God, thereby suggesting and historically validating her own worth as an anchorite and teacher. By alluding to an apparently lost legend of this late seventh-century saint's straying away from God and recovery by grace,[31] Julian may also release herself of the shame for her brief moment of doubting the authenticity of her showings,[32] a shame which shadowed her in the closing chapters of the Short Text. Debra Scott Panichelli argues that Julian comes to terms in the revision of the *Showings* with the doubting of her visions expressed in the Short Text; if correct, this argument offers additional support for the "penitent's" rationale behind John of Beverly's appearance in the Long Text.

As well as drawing attention to the prospect of inspired teachers of God's love historically closer to Julian and her "fellow Christians" than the biblical penitents named in the Short Text (154), St. John, then, may well represent Julian's own universalized fall and recovery. In the maturity of Julian's theological understanding and mystic's perspicacity, he can step forward to relieve St. Cecilia of her duty to provide inspiration (and justification) for an English religious woman's voicing of revelations shown to her by Christ, and the ancient Roman visionary and evangelist may retire to the company of martyrs. It is the change in self-perception and confidence suggested by the omission of St. Cecilia and the inclusion of St. John of Beverly that characterizes intentional, and consequently tonal, differences between the two versions of the *Showings* of Julian of Norwich. Years of contemplation and additional revelation from Christ had brought Julian to the point of trust in her own experience and perspicacity. At the writing of the long version she is finally ready and able to communicate to all what was shown for all in a way that all can understand and remember. And so her writing becomes strikingly detailed, richly painted and richly glossed. With metaphors comforting in their familiarity but striking in their application to Christ's Passion, Julian of Norwich renders her visions with animated intensity and then reads their message with clear, coherent, and universalizing application.

NOTES

1. All Middle English quotations of Julian are from the two-volume edition *A Book of Showings to the Anchoress Julian of Norwich,* edited by Edmund Colledge and James Walsh (Toronto: Pontifical Institute of Mediaeval Studies, 1978) ST 205. All modern English translations are from *Julian of Norwich: Showings*, translated and edited by Edmund Colledge and James Walsh (New York: Paulist Press, 1978) 127. Subsequent citations will be parenthtically provided in the text.

2. The most extensive comment I have found to Julian's mention of St. Cecilia appears in Nicholas Watson's "The Composition of Julian of Norwich's *Revelations of Love*," *Speculum* 68 (1993): 651-52 and is more to the point of Chaucer's "Second Nun's Tale" and fourteenth-century attitudes toward women preaching than to the intention behind Julian's reference.

3. According to Walsh, Julian "accepts the introduction of the popular English saint into the procession of saintly penitents as yet another example of God's homely dealings with his creatures—his readiness to 'come down to the least part of our need'" (3).

4. "And from the time that it was revealed, I desired many times to know in what was our Lord's meaning. And fifteen years after and more, I was answered in spiritual understanding" (LT 342).

5. For a discussion of St. Cecilia as an important Roman woman of the early church, rather than as a virgin martyr, see Susan K. Hagen, "Feminist Theology and 'The Second Nun's Tale': Or St. Cecilia Laughs at the Judge," *Medieval Perspectives* 4-5 (1989-90): 42-52.

6. *A Dictionary of Saints*, ed. Donald Attwater (Middlesex: Penguin, 1965) 193.

7. On the dating and differences between the two versions, see Watson and the Introduction to Colledge and Walsh's edition of *Showings*.

8. Denise Baker, *Julian of Norwich's Showings: From Vision to Book* (Princeton: Princeton UP: 1994) 62.

9. See in particular Chapter 1, "Affective Spirituality and the Genesis of *A Book of Showings*" in Baker, and Robert E. Wright's "The 'Boke Performyd': Affective Technique and Reader Response in the *Showings* of Julian of Norwich" in *Christianity and Literature* 36 (1987.4): 13-32. For background on Franciscan meditation method see Denise Despres, *Ghostly Sights: Visual Mediation in Late-Medieval Literature* (Norman, Oklahoma: Pilgrim, 1989).

10. James Walsh, trans. *The Revelations of Divine Love of Julian of Norwich*. (Wheathampstead: Clarke Books, 1973) 2-3.

11. See Despres: "The purpose of affective devotion, as developed by Bonaventure in Franciscan theology and implemented by the Preaching Friars in penitential programs, was to arouse feelings of remorse in the penitent that would move the will to contrition. . . . Franciscan meditation on Christ's humanity enabled the penitent, educated or uneducated, male or female to experience the Passion personally and to scrutinize his or her individual response" (5, 7).

12. Citing a slightly different version of this poem, Rosemary Woolf (*English Religious Lyric in the Middle Ages*. Oxford: Oxford UP, 1968) claims that the idea it contains stands as "the cornerstone of the Middle English Passion lyrics and of the Latin tradition of meditation lying behind them" (21, cf. 371).
Loverd þi passion,
Who þe þenchet arist þaron,
teres hit tollet,
and eyen hit bollet,
nebbes hit wetet,
ant hertes hit swetet. (20)

13. Theodore Silverstein, ed. *English Lyrics before 1500,* York Medieval Texts (Evanston: Northwestern UP, 1971) 20; Douglas Gray, *Themes and Images in Medieval English Religious Lyric* (London: Routledge, 1972) 41.

14. See Susan K. Hagen, *Allegorical Remembrance: A Study of* The Pilgrimage of the Life of Man *as a Medieval Treatise on Seeing and Remembering* (Athens: U of Georgia P, 1990) 17-20.

15. Robert D. Stevick, ed, *One Hundred Middle English Lyrics* (Indianapolis, IN: Bobbs-Merrill, 1964) 23.

16. In a rich discussion of the function of images in late medieval monastic devotion, Jeffrey M. Hamburger concludes: "late medieval devotional imagery should be seen as a response to a new set of religious aspirations in which the image plays a central role. These aspirations are manifested in the monastic as well as in the secular sphere." "The Visual and the Visionary: The Image in Late Medieval Monastic Devotions," *Viator* 20 (1989): 182.

17. See Hamburger, "The ties between devotional and visionary imagery fly in the face of the theoretical prescriptions that art and mysticism should have nothing to do with one another" (167).

18. In *Visual Sources in the Visions of Julian of Norwich* (MA thesis, Northern Illinois University, 1993), Annette Lermack argues that the compositional patterns in East Anglian manuscript illumination provide the visual sources for Julian's visions. While the thesis fails to take fully into account a number of other possible influences, especially literary influences connected with devotional lyrics, it nonetheless makes a convincing case for Norwich as a center for art commerce and for the prevalence of affective images in the fourteenth century.

19. Speaking of this same passage, Watson concludes "I take it that although Julian's desire actually to attend the Passion. . . is related to the practice of Passion meditation. . . , the first chapter of S[T] deliberately draws a distinction between the practice and its literal realization in the visionary experience which Julian craves " (649 n. 30).

20. See Despres: "In the *Lignum vitae*, Bonaventure reconstructs episodes of the Gospels to imprint (*imprimere*) them on the penitent's memory (*memoria*) for future recollection. Each scene is an abbreviated narrative, a summary rather than an extract from the Gospels phrased simply but vividly to call images to memory" (29).

21. Augustine, *On Christian Doctrine*, trans. D. W. Robertson (Indianapolis: Bobbs-Merrill, 1958) 34.

22. Frances A. Yates, *The Art of Memory* (London: Routledge, 1966; Chicago: U of Chicago P, 1968).

23. For further discussions of the mnemonic and allegorical use of images in the Middle Ages, see Rosemund Tuve, *Allegorical Imagery: Some Medieval Books and Their Posterity,* (Princeton: Princeton UP, 1966); Hagen, *Allegorical Remembrance*; and Mary J. Carruthers, *The Book of Memory: A Study of Memory in Medieval Culture* (Cambridge: Cambridge UP, 1990).

24. In their modern English translation of the Long Text, Colledge and Walsh omit the phrase "And I was answered in a general way, thus: It is all that is made." The sentence does appear, however, in Walsh's translation (53).

25. This phrase is added in the longer text, indicating, I believe, Julian's deliberate intention of modeling her mnemonic method so that it will be of use to her audience. See ST 130-31.

26. Over ten years ago I attended a one-woman show on Julian of Norwich performed by Roberta Nobleman at St. Andrew's Episcopal Church, Birmingham, Alabama; all members of the audience were given a hazelnut, our own gift of a mnemonic device to remember Julian and the wisdom embodied in her showings.

27. Asserting that "The importance of the body as a non-rational vehicle of divine perception has not usually been seen in Julian's work" (12), Maria R. Lichtmann makes a point that is well worth remembering when we discuss the matured theology of Julian's Long Text: "The key to Julian's hermeneutics of this vision [the head of Christ] and of all her visions is that all the theology found in the Long Text is contained first in the visions." "'I Desyrede a Bodylye Syght': Julian of Norwich and the Body," *Mystics Quarterly* 17 (1991): 15.

28. In an extended discussion arguing for a dating of the Long Text as late as the early fifteenth century, Watson comments that "when Julian wrote L, parts of S had in some respects come to substitute for her original revelation--to act, at least, as an essential aide mémoire in recalling that revelation" (679). Although his concern is not with mnemonic devices, his discussion of Julian's "deliberate and controlled" pattern in the Long Text "of treating the account in S as effectively corresponding to the original divine message, which now requires to be interpreted in its spiritual as well as literal senses" (679) supports my general argument.

29. See Gerda Lerner, *The Creation of Feminist Consciousness: From the Middle Ages to Eighteen-seventy* (Oxford: Oxford UP, 1993) 51-52, who notes that both female and male mystics used the humility *topos* "to heighten the power and effect of their miraculous inspiration," which certainly may be true of the Long Text; nonetheless, Julian uses the trope in the Short Text in such a gender specific way as to have more in common with forthright apologies almost always used by medieval women writers, apologies Lerner characterizes as "pathetic remnants of what must have been agonizing struggles each woman had to conduct within her own soul and mind." For a less gender-specific reading, see Ritamary Bradley, "Christ, the Teacher, in Julian's Showings: The Biblical and Patristic Traditions," *The Medieval Mystical Tradition in England*. (Exeter: Exeter: U of Exeter P, 1982) 127-42.

30. Arguing that an essential difference between the first and second versions of the *Showings* is Julian's coming to terms with her doubting of the authenticity of her visions at one point, Debra Scott Panichelli claims, "One important thing which happens through the re-writing is that the centre of the short version, which is the area of human doubt and denial, eventually dissolves as the centre of

the conflict." To the point of our discussion here, Panichelli writes, "Julian cannot make her confession, for she fears that the priest cannot believe her. More importantly, she fears *her* inability to believe anything after disbelieving God. Here, then is a voice on the margins of its abilities--how is it to be believed? How does the voice avoid a mere mouthing of unbelievable language? Julian's, at the end of the short version of the text, is a voice afraid to go forward." "Finding God in the Memory: Julian and the Loss of the Visions" *The Downside Review* 104 (1986): 302, 303.

31. ". . .in his youth and in his tender years he was a beloved servant of God, greatly loving and fearing him. And nevertheless God allowed him to fall, mercifully protecting him so that he did not perish or lose any time; and afterwards God raised him to many times more grace, and for the contrition and the meekness that he had loved, God has given him in heaven manifold joys, exceeding what he would have had if he had not sinned or fallen. And God shows on earth that this is true by constantly working many miracles about his body. And all this was to make us glad and happy in love" (LT 243).

32. "Then a man of religion came to me and asked me how I did, and I said that during the day I had been raving. And he laughed aloud and heartily. And I said: The cross that stood at the foot of my bed bled profusely; and when I said this, the religious I was speaking to became very serious and surprised. And at once I was very ashamed of my imprudence, and I thought: This man takes seriously every word I could say, and he says nothing in reply. And when I saw that he treated it so seriously and so respectfully, I was greatly ashamed, and wanted to make my confession. But I could not tell it to any priest for I thought: How could a priest believe me? I did not believe our Lord God. I believed this truly at the time I saw him, and it was then my will and intention to do so forever. But like a fool I let it pass from my mind" (ST 162).

A Genre Approach to Julian of Norwich's Epistemology

Brad Peters

I. Genre as Ideology

Julian of Norwich's *Book of Showings* has become known to a wider audience of readers than ever she might have imagined during her years of anchoritic enclosure. Yet Alexandra Barratt feels that much work in editing and translation remains to be done, because Julian's surviving manuscripts are "of obscure and uncertain history" which may or may not accurately preserve Julian's original telling.[1] A host of other tasks remains to be done as well. Perhaps one of the most basic and important of these tasks is to decide to what genre the *Showings* belongs. The manuscripts are usually categorized amorphously as exploratory, autobiographical accounts.

Julian herself claimed that of the *Showings'* two texts, her short, earlier version is "a visionn . . . in the whilke . . . er fulle many comfortabylle wordes" ["a vision in which are many comforting words"], and her long, revised version is "a reuelacion of loue that Jhesu Christ . . . made in xvi shewynges" ["a revelation of love that Jesus Christ . . . made in sixteen showings"].[2] Julian's instinct to elude categories of genre may represent her wish that readers replicate her own experience of a God "whose absolutely just and responsive understanding" is not metaphysically distant, but intimately in touch with the reflective operations of the human mind.[3]

As a producer of a text, Julian was far from naive. She knew the *Showings* had to meet certain cultural conventions or expectations, so that her readers would study the book in its entirety, rather than take "on thing after thy affection and liking and leve another" (86.734)["take what you prefer and disregard what you dislike"]. Yet I will propose that Julian did not meet these cultural conventions and expectations uncritically, as is evident in the *many* genres that we find in her text.

Indeed, Mikhail Bakhtin observes that "The vast majority of literary genres are . . . complex . . . composed of various transformed primary genres (the rejoinder in dialogue, everyday stories . . . and so forth)."[4] Primary genres include what Bakhtin calls the "speech genre"--forms that recur so commonly in written or conversational discourse that often, the speaker may not be fully aware of their "lexical composition and grammatical structure," even while she uses them (78). When we identify and analyze such speech genres in a text we learn more about how the writer wishes to present herself, what effect she seeks upon her audience, how her audience affects her, and what social constraints exist in these rhetorical dynamics.

For example, early in her Short Text, Julian writes:

> Alle that I sawe of my selfe, I meene in the persone of alle myne evynn cristene. . . . And therfore I praye ȝowe alle for goddys sake, and cownsayles ȝowe for ȝowre awne profyt, that ȝe leve the behaldynge of the wrechid wor(m)e,/ synfulle creature, that it was schewyd vnto. . . . god for bede that ȝe schulde saye or take it so that I am a techere, for I mene nouȝt soo . . . for I am a womann, leued, febille and freyle. Botte I wate wele, this that I saye, I hafe it of the schewynge of hym tha(t) es souerayne techare. . . . Botte for I am a womann, schulde I therfore leve that I schulde nouȝt telle ȝowe the goodness of god, syn that I sawe in that same tyme that is his wille, that it be knawenn?. . . Thane schalle ȝe sone forgette me that am a wrecche, and dose so that I lette ȝowe nought, and behalde Jhesu that ys techare of alle. . . . bot in alle thynge I lyeve as haly kyrke techis, for . . . this blyssede schewynge of oure lorde, I be helde it as ane in god syght, and I vndyrstode neuer nathynge þer yn that stoneȝ me ne lettes me of the trewe techynge of halye kyrke. (219; 222-23)

> [All that I saw of myself, I mean in the person of all my even Christians. . . . And therefore I pray you all for God's sake, and counsel you for your own profit, that you believe the beholding of the wretched worm, sinful creature, that it was showed unto. . . .

God forbid that you should say or take it so that I am a teacher, for I mean not so . . . for I am a woman, common, feeble and frail. But I know well, this that I say, I have it of the showing of him that is sovereign teacher. . . . But for I am a woman, should I therefore believe that I should not tell you the goodness of God, since what I saw in that same time that it is his will, that it be known?. . . Then shall you soon forget me that am a wretch, and do so that I impede you not, and behold Jesus that is teacher of all. . . . But in all things I believe as Holy Church teaches, for . . . this blessed showing of our Lord, I beheld it as one in God's sight, and I understood never nothing therein that astonished me nor obstructed me from the true teaching of Holy Church.]

In this instance, the speech genre--a *captatio benevolentiae*---consists of more than lexicon and structure. Julian's marginalized position according to her gender transforms the speech genre's "grammar" of humility and good will to her readers into a grammar of resistance, when she says: "But for I am a woman, should I therefore believe that I should not tell you?" The passage's displacement is also surprising. It appears in Chapter 6 instead of the beginning of Chapter 1, where convention would normally situate it. Even more surprising, Julian's *captatio benevolentiae* follows--rather than leads--the account and analysis of her first vision of Christ's humanity, creation's smallness, and Mary's maidenhood.

This unusual use of a *captatio benevolentiae* enables Julian to establish *auctoritas* not merely on the basis of her own experience, but on the authority of Jesus and Holy Church.[5] She thereby de-emphasizes her startling originality so that her readers will focus instead upon the importance of what she feels her Lord means to say through her. But such a revision of the speech genre reifies medieval women's power relations to the church--and to their "even Christians"--in the explicit terms of weakness, feebleness, and frailty. At the same time, it suggests that Julian challenges the fourteenth-century patriarchal construction of women only so she may "participate in the religious hegemony," without revolutionary intent.[6] Genre theory reveals that all too often, "what a text says and how it says it cannot be separated," because genres conventionally reproduce the ideologies of those in power, positioning readers--and writers--in compliance with "the dominant social/ideological formation."7 Perhaps this tenet explains why Julian chooses to excise both her "grammar of resistance" and her authorial de-emphasis in the above passage, when she more fully develops her long text.

Medieval genres tended to be prescriptive and utilitarian. Derived primarily from Ciceronian models, they focused on *ars dictiminis* (the art of letter writing), *ars grammatica* (the art of analyzing and applying tropes), and *ars praedicandi* (the art of sermonizing). The forensic elements of the Ciceronian models probably helped to "naturalize" the misgynistic elements of medieval patristic attitudes, producing genres that were inherently predisposed to an objectification of women and to a moralistic reduction of their subjective experience. Medieval genres would thus contribute significantly toward structuring what Jacques Lacan calls the mind's unconscious Other(A)--a "secondary unconscious created by subjugation to the social order of symbols, rules, and language"--so that even in the work of resistant women writers, some indication of subjugation seems inevitable.8

However, Andrea Lunsford asserts that the Middle Ages seldom recognized women's discursive forms, strategies, or aims as rhetorical.9 Thanks to this ironic cultural lacuna women writers became free to produce texts that reformulated the conventions of genres and constructed "a new, different consciousness; a consciousness which . . . inevitably become[s] a source of questioning, interrogation and further contradiction, which produce[s] a new, different social subject" (Cranny-Francis III-12). But to take advantage of this freedom, a writer like Julian needed a method that empowered her, on the one hand, to compose without becoming unwittingly subjugated by the ideologies of medieval genre conventions even while she reformulated them. On the other hand, she needed a method that enabled her to articulate and authenticate her own subject position, without which the production of a text such as the *Showings* might single her out as a heretic. Interesting enough, Augustine--whose gendered notion of the essential self, with the lower reason as female and the higher as male--provided women with precisely the theory they required for freedom of textual production. His "law of love" endorsed the private interpretation of scripture, stating that:

rhetors do not persuade, but that hearers move themselves; that teachers do not teach, but instead that learners learn. Ultimately this is a denial of the preceptive theories implicit in [Ciceronian-based] education; its corollary is increased reliance on imitatio as a learning process, encouraging individual activity by a student or reader.[10]

A method so-described was often practiced in religious houses and in the pulpits of churches such as the one where Julian was enclosed. She could easily have heard religious speakers use it. The method was known as *lectio divina*.

This essay investigates how Julian constructs a woman-positive epistemology in three ways. First, Julian negotiates a dialectics with Christ, which derives from her desire to experience the suffering he experienced on the cross. Second, when a major tension on the question of sin arises, she uses the *lectio divina* to invoke--and reformulate--other speech genres as rejoinders to her dialectics, so she can preserve the internal consistency of her epistemology (see Bakhtin 98). Finally, Julian's mariology and her construction of Jesus as mother enables her to articulate the embodiment of divine love without being male-centered or exclusionary.

Concurrently, Lacanian theory sheds light upon Julian because it is anchored in orality, language philosophy, and poetics. Lacan recognizes that mystics have a special knowledge of pleasure and suffering that goes beyond the language of human logic or need.[11] Therefore he finds that mystical epistemology is deeply imbricated in the mystic's *being*; it is discovered in a game of words, a *jouissance*, that remains "at odds with what we call knowledge," because it defies the dangerous myth that all mysteries of human existence can be resolved (65).

II. Dialectics: The Genre of Desire

Julian's epistemology emerges from a matrix of intensely focused desire. As Julian seeks to articulate that desire and point to its origins, her language engenders what, for her, is the ur-genre of her two texts: dialectics. But to say that desire engenders dialectics in the *Showings* is to say *a priori* that Julian reformulates a speech genre, whose prescriptiveness Bakhtin excoriates when he says: "remove the voices (the partition of voices), remove the intonations (emotional and individualizing ones), carve out abstract concepts and judgments from living words and responses, cram everything into one abstract consciousness--and that's how you get dialectics" (147).

Julian's desire-driven epistemology leads her to invent the dialectical "grammar" afresh vis-á-vis the relationship between her, the one who desires, and Christ, the one desired. She reinvents medieval conventions of lexicon, structure, and ideology, because such male-centered rhetoric remains extrinsic to the relational nature of her visions. Yet we cannot claim that Julian was formally educated in dialectics. Rather Jean Leclerq observes that in medieval culture, dialectics was pervasive not only among the monastics and schoolmen, but among many folk; literary genres such as debate poetry attest to its wide secular dissemination--and perhaps, degradation.[12] As with the *captatio benevolentiae*, Julian is accordingly able to appropriate dialectics for her own purposes.

But how *and why* did Julian appropriate a basically agonistic speech genre, to convey the meaning of her visionary experience? She discovered the necessity of doing so in the process of writing the Short Text, where she struggles rhetorically to position herself in relation to the church, her culture, her readers, and her Lord.

When Julian describes her original desire for Christ, she creates a broadly Christian context for transmitting her visionary experience, saying:

> Here es a visionn . . . gretly styrrande to all thaye that desires to be Crystes looverse.
> I desyrede thre graces be the gyfte of god. The fyrst was to have mynde of Cryste es passionn. The seconnde was bodelye syeknes, and the thryd was to haue of goddys gyfte thre wonndys. For the fyrste . . . I hadde grete felynge in the passyonn of Cryste, botte ȝitte I desyrede . . . that I myght have sufferede with hym as othere dyd that lovyd hym. . . . For the seconnde . . . a wylfulle desyre to hafe of goddys gyfte a bodelye syekenes . . . alle the dredes and tempestes of feyndys, and alle manere of (oþere) paynes, safe of the owȝte passynge of the sawlle, for I hoped that it myȝt be to me a spede whenn I schulde dye. . . . For the thirde, I harde . . . That [St Cecelia] hade thre wonndys

with a swerde in the nekke, with the whilke sche pynede to the dede. By the styrrynge of this I conseyvede a myghty desyre . . . thre wonndys in my lyfe tyme . . . the wonnd(e) of contricyoun, the wonnde of compassyoun and the wonnde of wylfulle langgynge to god. (201-206)

[Here is a vision . . . greatly stirring to all them that desire to be Christ's lovers.

I desired three graces by the gift of God. The first was to have mind of Christ's Passion. The second was bodily sickness, and third was to have of God's gift three wounds. For the first . . . I had great feeling in the Passion of Christ, but yet I desired . . . that I might have suffered with him as others did that loved him . . . . For the second . . . a willful desire to have of God's gift a bodily sickness . . . all the dreads and trials of fiends, and all manner of other pains, save the out-passing of the soul, for I hoped that it might be to me a quickening when I should die. . . . For the third, I heard . . . That [St. Cecelia] had three wounds with a sword in the neck, with which she suffered to the death. By the stirring of this I conceived a mighty desire [for] . . . three wounds in my lifetime . . . the wound of contrition, the wound of compassion, and the wound of willful longing to God.]

This passage is Julian's analysis of her prayer, rather than the prayer itself. She deeply identifies with her Lord's and others' suffering at the scene of the crucifixion. As Gregory Clark says, "It is within this [dialectical] process of identifying ourselves with others that we . . . define our common ground and articulate the way it might be extended."[13] The origins of Julian's dialectical process seem fairly orthodox, if unusual. Her devotion to the crucifixion scene extends the spectacular--what she has clearly witnessed in images of scripture and religious art--and she desires to become an ahistorical participant. Her hagiographical source extends the crucifixion as an image of lived Christian experience. She does not literally seek martyrdom but desires to internalize abstract, spiritual principles.

But in this passage, Lacanian theory might stipulate that Julian's language obscures, or even downplays, the extent to which her desire, if realized, will redefine who and what she is. She wants to become hyperconsciously engaged in what Lacan calls the "dialectical nature of being," where the self is dynamically constructed through its asymmetrical communion with the Other; the Other thus speaks her into being and compels her to come to voice (Ragland-Sullivan, *Philosophy* 231). That is why Julian's second expression of desire becomes so interesting. It opens up to, and receives, that which crosses the boundaries between rational and extra-rational, conscious and unconscious, for she says it "come to my mynde . . . Frelye with outen any sekynge" ["came to my mind . . . freely without any seeking"]. Desire for bodily sickness like unto death imaginatively puts Julian's body in a communion with the flesh of Christ's body, and analogously permits her to imagine being crucified with her Lord. Just so, Julian's representation of her previsionary self allows her to establish a multi-valent ethos--an ethos that positions her not only in a dialectics with Christ, but also with her readers, with her sociocultural milieu, and with her own unconscious.

Lacan's theory of dialectical thinking would also posit that Julian's analysis of her prayer puts her "unconscious into circular motion, unwittingly emitting messages from the Other," that may, in the very least, provide less convention-bound ways for her--and her readers--to reconstruct their understanding of how God operates upon, or how God communes with, a human soul (Ragland-Sullivan, *Philosophy* 161). A good, rudimentary example of such dialectical thinking occurs when Julian recounts the onset of illness in her thirtieth year, saying:

> And sodeynly comme vnto my mynde that I schulde desyre the seconnde wonnde of oure lordes gyfte . . . that he walde fulfylle my bodye with mynde of felynge of his blessede passyonn as I hadde before prayede, for I wolde that his paynes ware my paynes. . . . Thus thou3t me that I myght with his grace have his wonndys that y hadde before desyrede; but in this I deseyrede neuere ne bodely syght ne no manere schewynge of god, botte compassyonn . . . with oure lorde Jhesu, that for love wolde be come man dedlye. With hym y desyrede to suffere, lyevande in dedlye bodye. . . . (210)

> [And suddenly it came into my mind that I should desire the second wound of our Lord's gift . . . that he would fulfill my

body with mind of feeling of his blessed Passion as I had before prayed, for I would [desire] that his pains were my pains. . . . Thus thought I that I might with his grace have his wounds that I had before desired; but in this I desired never any bodily sight nor any manner of showing of God but compassion . . . with our Lord Jesus, that for love would become mortally human. With him I desired to suffer, living in mortal body. . . .]

This more precise articulation of desire calls for Christ's dying body to become affectively inscribed upon Julian's. But her desire for union with Christ--through the miraculous granting of metonymical signs that fulfill her body and mind--also seems to invoke the gendered language of sexual submission, of men wounding women in carnally deadly ways. Grace intervenes and grants her a bodily sight instead of an experience comparable to physical/sexual contact in the tradition of the *brautmystik*. Julian's dialectics of desire thus opens the imagination of her readers--especially her women readers--to the possibility of an incarnate, but not carnal and deadly, love. Perhaps, from the Lacanian perspective, there is "woven into her speech as an implicit tension or pressure which asks for love and recognition, a *demande* that has very little to do, in fact, with the real objects that are requested"--so an untraditional (read: non-masculine) revelation of God was indeed part of what she sought in the first place (Ragland-Sullivan, *Philosophy* 161).

When a crucifix is placed at the foot of Julian's bed and the vision of Christ himself occurs, the purpose for composing a dialectics with him becomes more salient. She sees only a part of her Lord's Passion--the bruises, wounds, and indignities caused by human spite, and the terrible changes in Christ's face as his increased suffering discolors his complexion. "This I sawe bodylye and hevelye," she says, "and I desyred mare bodelye lyght to hafe sene more clerelye. And I was annswerde in my resone that 3yf god walde schewe me mare he schulde, botte me nedyd na lyght botte hym" (225) ["This I saw bodily and heavily and darkly; and I desired more bodily light to have seen more clearly. And I was answered in my reason that if God would show me more he should, but I needed no light but him"]. In the Long Text, Julian embellishes upon this answer, saying, "And thus I saw him and sought him, and I had hym and wantyd hym; and this is and should be our comyn workyng in this life, as to my syght" (10.326) ["And thus I saw him and sought him, and I had him and wanted him; and this is and should be our common working in this life, as to my sight"]. Sight only sharpens the lack, or the void, that exists between her desire and the object of her desire. She needs more than sight; she needs verbal exchange.

At the same time, Julian realizes that her body has been released from pain. It is *almost* an about-face of her request: the suffering of a woman's body having been imposed upon her Lord's human male body. And yet, by gazing upon him, she feels pains that are no pains but his. What is this suffering that is not hers, but is? Sight leads her to comprehend the role that language must play. Seeking is not a *visual* but a *verbal* activity, even though the image of Christ is absolutely central to that activity and provides "a perceptual basis to which to apply language" (Ragland-Sullivan, *Philosophy* 143). Thus, quest becomes question, and desire, from the Lacanian point of view, serves as a dialectical motivation "to speak for the purpose of being recognized as . . . a subject, and in this way serves to create a future," or at least an argument that accounts for what is happening to her (161).

All the same, the mature manifestation of dialectic does not spontaneously spring from the verbalization of Christ's suffering. Instead, Christ establishes a question/answer pattern and poses questions of identity that translate Julian's desire into language that is tenderly relational. He thanks her for the travail she has experienced for his sake and asks her, "Arte thou wele payde that I suffyrde for the?" (239) ["Are you well paid that I suffered for you?"]. She answers him directly, saying, "3a, goode lorde . . . Gramercy . . . blissyd mut thowe be" ["Yes, good Lord . . . grant mercy . . . blessed might you be."] He goes on to say "3yf thowe be payede . . . I am payede. It is a ioye and a blysse and ane endlesse lykynge to me that euer y sufferde passyonn for the, for 3yf I myght suffyr mare, I walde suffyr" (239) ["If you be paid. . . I am paid. It is a joy and a bliss and an endless liking to me that ever I suffered Passion for you, for if I might suffer more I would suffer"]. Looking at the spear wound in his side, he says, "Loo how I lovyd the"--and in recording this locution, Julian adds the rejoinder, "as 3yf he hadde sayde: My child, yif thow kan nought loke in my godhede, see heere how I lette opyn my syde and my herte be clovene in twa and lette oute blude and watere, alle þat was thare yn; and this lykes me and so wille I that it do the" (242) ["as if he had said: My child, if you cannot look in my godhead, see here how I let open my side and my heart be cloven in two and let out blood and water, all that was therein; and this pleases me and so will I that it do you"]. Elizabeth Petroff observes that among many women mystics, "Images of wounding . . . are central to the presentation of desire and body," and usually representative of "yearning and openness with the female."[14] But Julian's developmental appropriation of dialectics feminizes *Christ's* words--not with the grammar of abstract concepts, judgments, and one-sided rhetorical manipulation but with a grammar of embodiment, negotiation, and semiotic union, suggesting that a woman may speak for Christ as the wounded Other.

Because Julian directly engages with Christ in the question/answer pattern at this point, she also begins to reformulate the genre of dialectic--its context, its ethos, its participants, its purpose, and its grammar--along guidelines that are not male-centered, but which value mutual exchange over authority. This reformulation confirms her desire as fully christocentric when Julian recounts the locution in which the suffering Christ is transformed into a blissful and radiant Christ, who tells her: "I it am that þou luffes. . . . I it am that þowe desyres" (243) ["I it am that you love. . . . I it am that you desire"]. Julian's language has constructed Christ at the same time Christ's direct questions have constructed her. Hence, "desire derived from lack . . . elicits desire as exchange," and her subjectivity is thus transformed into intersubjectivity--as demonstrated in what becomes Julian's tendency to amplify the syntactic pattern of Christ's locutions with her own rejoinder: "he said/ *as if he said*" (Ragland-Sullivan, *Philosophy* 40-41). The effect is that Christ begins to "speak" with a woman's voice: hers.

The intersubjective dynamic which transforms dialectics in the *Showings* heightens Julian's recognition that she would have her desire--which she sees as ontological wholeness in Christ--if only sin did not hold her back from it. But in the epistemology that has so far emerged, Julian has not seen sin. Unsatisfied desire causes her to recover the "repressed text" of a question she has asked earlier: "Whate es synne?" ["What is sin?" (226)]. She has seen that God "es in alle thynge" ["is in all things"] and "dose alle that es done" ["does all that is done"], yet God is not present in sin. Nonetheless, sin causes the pain she has experienced in her own body and the pain she witnesses in Christ's--"And this payne, it is sumthynge" ["And this pain, it is something"]; it has ontological status, even if the sin which causes it is not of God, "has na manere of substannce, na partye of beynge"(245) ["has no manner of substance, nor part of being"]. So what is sin? Such a question does not have a place in any tradition of systematic logic, where all quandaries have rational solutions. Nor does it belong to the realm of apophatic logic, where mysteries are simply taken as indicators of the limits of human intellect. Such a question can only invoke the pre-philosophical, pre-scientific, extra-rational impulse of interrogative wonder, which Hans Robert Jauss identifies as "the origin of thought."[15] Julian reiterates and extends her interrogative wonder after the "I it am" locution, and this is where, in turn, true dialectic emerges:

> I wondrede why, be the grete forseande wysdome of god, syn was not lettede; for than thought me that alle schulde hafe bene wele . . . . He annswerde be this worde and sayde: Synne is behouelye . . . . Botte alle schalle be wele, and all maner of thynge schalle be wele. . . . Bot in this I schalle studye, behaldande generallye, drerelye and mournande, sayande thus to oure lorde . . . Ah, goode lorde, howe myght alle be wele for the grete harme that is comonn by synn to thy creatures? And I desired as I durste to hafe sum mare open declarynge whare with I myght be hesyd in this. (244-47)

> [I wondered why, by the great foreseeing wisdom of God, sin was not prevented; for then, thought I that all should have been well. . . . He answered by this word and said: Sin is behovable . . . . But all shall be well, and all manner of thing shall be well . . . . But in this I shall study, beholding generally, drearily, and mourning, saying thus to our Lord . . . Ah, good Lord, how might all be well for the great harm that is come by sin to your creatures? And I desired as I dared to have some more open declaring wherewith I might be eased in this.]

Here we find the most convincing evidence as to why dialectics rather than some other speech genre prevails at the core of the *Showings*. With Julian's challenge to God's "great foreseeing wisdom," she summons up the rhetorical technique of *audacitas*, which at this sensitive moment rhetorically empowers her in a way that parallels Christ's transformation during the "I it am" locution. The result is not nearly so blissful or radiant a one for her. Yet Julian is now able to represent herself as worshipfully respectful of her Lord, submissive to Holy Church, and in conformity with her "even Christians," even while she assumes a position of resistance to the orthodox teaching of sin and penance, and its corollary oppressions, confinements, and punishments of the human body (which medieval theology constructs as inferior, as *feminine*, regardless of sex).

Julian no longer acquiesces meekly to a question and answer pattern, because Christ's response to her question is an answer that is not one--to say that "sin is behovable, but all shall be well" does not define sin any more than it explains its function. Julian must therefore lead her readers in the search for his meaning. She finds herself in a "place from which to produce, rather than merely to repeat, language."[16] Her reformulation of dialectics also allows her as a woman to signify on the body of Christ the devastating effects of the sociocultural conventions that would erase or silence her, saying: "Here yn I sawe anynge be twyx Criste and vs; for when he was in payne we ware in payne. . . . For I am sekyr, ȝif thare hadde nane benn bot I that schulde be safe, god wolde hafe done alle that he hase done for me. And so schulde ilke saule thynke. . . ." (235; 264-65) ["Here I saw a great unity between Christ and us; for when he was in pain, we were in pain. . . . I am sure, if there had been no one but I that should be saved, God would have done all he has done for me. And so should each soul think. . ."]. But those effects cannot exert their influence upon her, because Christ simultaneously occupies the place of her material suffering and endorses her speaking forth. Thus, dialectics provides the discursive environment in which Julian's subject position as a woman can not only emerge, but participate in the real speech communication that the *Showings* as a whole participates and is communicated (see Finke 14; Bakhtin 116).

In such an environment, knowledge of salvation is no longer finite, nor can it be transmitted in linear, temporal, continuous, or progressive methods (see Finke 16). Instead, such knowledge has become unfixed, open to infinite methods of interpretation, incapable of being reduced to essentials--like Christ's body, for instance, which is ultimately neither masculine nor feminine, but transformed by language into a manifestation of God's love. Julian will also discover how language can transform the painfully fragmented states of the human mind and human existence. However, as the transformation occurs, what her visions tell her about sin places a large conceptual obstruction before her. How can she deal with it?

III. *Lectio Divina*: The Counter-Genre of Law

If sin is behovable but has no substance or part of being, Julian realizes that major shifts must occur in her grasp of the laws of Christian ontology. Dialectics remains at the very core of her text, because the dialectical principle accommodates "the continual . . . constructing and reconstructing [of] the knowledge that supports our collective life" (Clark 26-27). But as Julian grows increasingly aware that collective human knowledge changes and must be reconstructed, the implications destabilize much more than the composition of her text. Lacanian theory posits that when disjunctures occur in the discourse structures that represent some pre-existing attitude in the human drive for unity and certainty, it "parallels the dialectical disunity within one's own being" (see Ragland-Sullivan, *Philosophy* 155-57).

What is Julian's response? First, it is necessary to look at the many impasses Julian runs up against. When she wants to know how all shall be well, given the great harm sin causes, Christ answers that he will/shall/may/can make all things well, and she shall see so for herself (249). When she desires to know if a certain person dear to her will be redeemed--proof that all shall be well--an answer comes to her as a friendly man speaking: "Take it generally, and be halde the curtayssy of thy lorde god as he schewes it to the, for it is mare worschippe to god to be halde hym in alle than in any specyalle thynge" (252) ["Take it generally, and behold the courtesy of your Lord God as he shows it to you, for it is more worship to God to behold him in all than in any special thing"]. When she sees that neither she, nor anyone dear to her, nor any of the saints can avoid sin, she desires simply to die, so she might be released from sin and the pain it inflicts. Christ tells her: "Sudanly thowe schalle be takene fra alle thy payne, fra alle thy dissese and fra alle thy waa. . . . Whate schulde it than greve the to suffyr a while, senn it is my wille and my wirschippe?" (263) ["Suddenly you shall be taken from all your pain, from all your disease, and from all your woe. . . . What should it grieve you to suffer a while, since it is my will and my worship?"].

It is God Incarnate's direct but open-ended statements that accordingly force Julian's dialectics to evolve into what Bakhtin calls a complex genre, "composed of various . . . primary [speech] genres" (98). The speech genre that emerges most often at first is the rejoinder. Julian adds many rejoinders to Christ's locutions, usually prefacing them with the phrase *as if he said*, to interpret his meaning. In turn, these rejoinders lead Julian to use the *lectio divina*. The *lectio* remains faithfully rooted in the dialectical principle and helps Julian systematically to expand the rejoinders, allowing her to explore ever more profoundly the knowledge that Christ imparts to her.

Jean Leclercq asserts that the *lectio* requires full mental concentration and physical engagement, similar to the movement from chant to meditation: the mouth pronounces the text, the memory fixes it in mind, the intelligence sorts through its meaning, and the will seeks to enact it (15-17). The *lectio's* grammar of association draws not only upon the text being read, but on other texts as well. Moreover, the *lectio* draws upon images, art, ordinary events, trends in current discourse, or other material which may emerge from the unconscious or the superconscious, rendering unexpectedly rich (and sometimes, highly idiosyncratic) forms of personal insight. But the method does not invite solipsism. The *lectio divina*--practiced mostly in the controlled environments of religious houses and the pulpit--was modelled by those in authority to convert even the most unruly reader, so that in the process of producing his own interpretation, he became aligned with the dominant, orthodox ideologies of the text being read (143).

All the same, Julian does not use the *lectio* to read texts, but to read her three modes of visionary instruction: bodily sight, words formed in her understanding, and spiritual sight (see Baker 159; SV 224). For her, it thus becomes a method of synthesis which deconstructs the underlying cultural principles that cause dialectical disunity. For example, in response to Christ's two locutions that assure Julian all shall be well, the following series of rejoinders appear:

> . . . oure blyssede lorde . . . schewed me that Adammes synne was the maste harme that euer was done . . . this is opynnly knawyn, in alle haly kyrke. . . . þanne/ menes oure blyssede lorde: . . . senn I hafe made wele the maste harme . . . knawe

þerby that I schalle make wele alle that is the lesse. . . . This blyssed party is opynn and clere. . . . The tother parte is spared fra vs and hidde . . . alle that is besyde oure saluacionn. For this is oure lordys prive consayles . . . and it langes to his seruanntys . . . nought to wille witte his councelle. . . . And than schalle we nathynge wille ne desyre botte the wille of oure lorde. . . . And in thies same fyve wordes before sayde: I make alle thynge wele, I vndyrstande a myghtty comforthe of alle the werkys of oure lorde that ere for to comme; for ryght as the blissyd trinyte made alle thynge of nought, ryght soo the same blyssed trinyte schalle make wele alle that es nought wele. . . . and þat schewyd he me . . . that alle manere of thynge schalle be wele. . . . It is goddys wille that we witte that alle schalle be wele in generalle, botte it is nought goddys wille that we schulde witte it nowe . . . and þat is the techynge of haly kyrke. (247-51)

[. . . our blessed Lord . . . showed me that Adam's sin was the most harm that ever was done . . . this is openly known in all Holy Church. . . . Then means our blessed Lord: . . . since I have made well the most harm . . . know thereby that I shall make well all that is the least. . . . This blessed part is open and clear. . . . The other part is closed from us and hidden . . . all that is beside our salvation. For this is our Lord's private counsels . . . and it belongs to his servants . . . not to wish to know his counsels. . . . And then shall we nothing will nor desire but the will of our Lord. . . . And in these same five words before said: I make all things well, I understand a mighty comfort of all the works of our Lord that are to come; for right as the blessed Trinity made all things of nought, right so the same blessed Trinity shall make well all that is not well. . . . and that showed he to me . . . that all manner of things shall be well. . . . It is God's will that we know that all shall be well in general, but it is not God's will that we should know it now . . . and that is the teaching of Holy Church.]

In the passage above, the only immediate sense Julian can make of the showing is to reconcile it to Holy Church's position: we were born in the condition of sin, but the salvation of Jesus Christ redeems that condition absolutely. Any question of why Adam's sin was the most harm, or why that harm wasn't prevented, or why Adam's sin seems to elide all other human folly and misdeeds, defies human logic and remains hidden from it. Rather than express resistance outright, Julian ostensibly explains that Christ's promise that "all shall be well" is a super-rational construct, a "private counsel." Moreover she opts for a more subtle resistance because in revelation, as Lacan mentions, "something of Real originary determination" may threaten to tear apart the veil of socially constructed knowledge (Ragland-Sullivan, *Philosophy* 193).

Just so, she uses the *lectio* to posit the limits of human intellect as nought in the presence of the Trinity, whose mind is only to be revealed in its perpetual work of making all things well. Julian's repetition and permutations of the phrase "all shall be well" imitates the Trinity's perpetual work in creation, semiotically overwhelming a humanly limited notion of sin with a verbal excess that makes things well. Lacanian theory would suggest that this verbal excess causes the "curious structure" of the *lectio* to reveal "the dialectical unconscious at the level of conscious life" (Ragland-Sullivan, *Philosophy* 112). The structures of Julian's verbal excess become much like the beneficial flow of menses--"effective beyond any of the analogues attributed to men"--but in harmony with a vision Julian has had earlier of Christ's plenteous blood which redemptively washes over hell, earth, and heaven (227). [17] In a Lacanian sense, Julian's repetition is thus a means of asserting a non-traditional, feminine perspective which "is not of independent terms or analogous themes," but "a structure of differential interrelationships" between a God who keeps his privy counsels and a writer who does not try to force that God or his counsels into a system of logic that schoolmen have devised (Ragland-Sullivan 111). Is it coincidental, then, that the verbal excess in this particular *lectio* springs from Julian's ruminations on Adam, not Eve? Cultural associations between women and the origin of sin do not appear in her visions, so they do not appear in her text.

As a result, Julian's problem with the vision of Adam, which specifically has to do with the problem of sin, causes three genres to emerge in her compostion process: a sermon on sin, an apostrophe to sin, and her celebrated parable of the lord and servant. I shall argue that she is able to use the *lectio* to reformulate these three genres, to "explore the institutional ideology within which [women] work, and deconstruct its positioning of them," so that she as a writer, or other women as readers, might gain "access to knowledges and to power from which they are otherwise socially excluded" (Cranny-Francis 108).

The sermon on sin appears shortly after Julian is shown that no souls escape sin or its painful effects. Although she conceives a dread of this inevitability, Christ assures her that he keeps her securely and that sin is no shame, but is turned into a kind of worship, or honor. Immediately, she says:

> Synn is the scharpyste scourge that any chosenn saule maye be
> bette with, whilke scourge it alle for bettes mann and womann,
> and alle for brekes thamm, and noughteþ hym selfe in thare awne
> syght. . . . The haly gaste leddes hymm to confessyonn, wilfully
> to schewe . . . that he hase swa defowled the fayre ymage of god.
> Than he takes pennannce. . . that is growndyd in haly kyrke. . . .
> Be this medycynn behoues euer ilke synfulle sawlle be heled. . . .
> And so . . . as it es punysched here with sorowe and with
> penannce, it schalle be rewarded in heuen be the curtayse loue of
> oure lorde god. . . .
>
> Bot ȝif thowe be styrred to saye or to thynke: Senn this is
> sothe, þan were it goode for to synn for to hafe the mare mede,
> be ware of this styrrynge and dispice it, for it is of the enmy. . . .
> For synne is so vyle and so mykille for to hate that it maye be
> likened to na payne whilke payne es nought synn. For . . . synn
> es nowthere deed no lykynge, botte when a saule cheses wilfully
> synne, that is payne, as fore his god, atte the ende he hase ryght
> nought. . . .
>
> For Criste hym selfe is grownde of alle the lawe . . . for he
> wille that we . . . hate synne and endelesslye love the saule as god
> love it. (256-57)

> [Sin is the sharpest scourge than any chosen soul may be beaten
> with, which scourge it altogether beats man and woman, and
> altogether breaks them, and reduces themselves to nought in their
> own sight. . . . The Holy Ghost leads him to confession,
> willfully to show . . . that he has so befouled the fair image of
> God. Then he takes penance . . . that is grounded in Holy

Church. . . . By this medicine behoves every like sinful soul to be healed. . . . And so . . . as it is punished here with sorrow and with penance, it shall be rewarded in heaven by the courteous love of our Lord God. . . .

But if you be stirred to say or think: Since this is true, then were it good to sin for to have the more reward, beware of this stirring and despise it, for it is of the enemy. . . . For sin is so vile and so much for to hate that it may be likened to no pain which pain is not sin. For . . . [s]in is neither deed nor pleasure, but when a soul chooses sin willfully, that is pain, as before his God, at the end, he has right nought. . . .

For Christ himself is ground of all the law . . . for he wills that we . . . hate sin and endlessly love the soul as God loves it.]

Julian's medieval readers would have immediately recognized this excerpt as a sermon (see Murphy 347-55). Authority for what she says rests again on the combined teachings of Holy Church and Christ as the ground of all law. The division of the theme is in two parts: 1. sin is a scourge; 2. sin is vile. In the first division, her prosecution consists of a series of cause and effect relationships in the sin/confession/penance continuum. Her second division exemplifies how the devil tries to turn that continuum toward evil ends. Her conclusion directs the minds of her readers toward the Incarnate God and God the Father.

Why might this speech genre emerge, given Julian's sensitivity to the Pauline injunction against women teaching or preaching and given the materiality it confers on sin? In her dialectical context, Julian must explain how sin becomes a "worship." Lacanian theory would indicate that Christ's showing appears to subvert "Symbolic order contracts, pacts, laws," as his definition of sin changes the law code from the stratum of culture to the stratum of the visionary, "leaving doubt about appropriate behavior" in the everyday world (Ragland-Sullivan, *Philosophy* 179). Thus, Julian is obliged to warn her readers directly that they cannot sin merely to earn more reward in repentance. The sermon, with its prescriptive and fixed grammar, labels and names sin, bridging the gap that Christ's language has opened between "a structural defect in being [in this instance, sin] and the demands of society" for laws which rationally explain how to deal with that defect (281).

But sermonic discourse also replicates an ideology of asymmetrical power relations, in this case subjecting the body to punishment for what it is, because punishment on earth leads to rewards in heaven. The sermonic lexicon of sin--scourging, beating, breaking, and reducing the soul--derives from the vision of Christ on the cross, but can become an emblem of acceptable abuse or persecution of the body, an essentially feminine construct. With the dangers of ascetic extremism or social quietism on the one end, and institutionalized violence on the other, women may be especially vulnerable to getting crushed in the middle of such an ideology.

Julian's revision of the sermon in the Long Text significantly reformulates and feminizes the genre. Her amplification does not extend the sermon's ideology of punishment or bodily mortification. Instead, she uses the *lectio* to foreground the relational aspect between God's will and the will of the human soul, embedded in the continuum of sin, confession, and penance. She represents Christ as one who "Fulle preciously . . . kepyth vs whan it semyth to vs that we be neer forsaken and cast away for oure synne and for we se þat we haue deservyd it" (39.451) ["Fully preciously . . . keeps us when it seems to us that we be near forsaken and cast away for our sin because we see that we deserve it"]. She addresses the psychological dangers of sin, saying: "oure curtesse lorde wylle nott that hys seruantys despeyer for ofte fallynge ne for grevous fallynge; for oure fallynge lettyth nott hym to loue vs" (39.453) ["our courteous Lord wills not that his servants despair for often falling nor for grievous falling; for our falling does not prevent him from loving us"]. Most important, she deconstructs mundane hierarchies by reinventing the lord/servant relationship, saying, "than shewyth oure curtesse lorde hym selfe . . . seyeng thus: My dere darlyng I am glad thou arte come to me in alle thy woe. I haue evyr ben with the, and now seest thou me louyng, and we be onyd in blysse" 40.454-55) ["then our courteous Lord shows himself . . . saying thus: My dear darling, I am glad you are come to me in all your woe. I have ever been with you, and now you see me loving you, and we be made one in bliss"]. In Lacanian theory, this reformulation of the sermon reverses the structural drama of the child's separation from its mother's feminine body. Julian transforms the "signifier of the social or Symbolic order," God the Father who speaks the Law, into a feminized Christ, whose nurturing provides a sense of reconciling triumph over "cultural self-alienation and allusive Desire, which are both born of Law" (see Ragland-Sullivan, *Philosophy* 281-82).

The revised sermon's reconciliation between soul and body is enacted--and has its genesis--in the short text of the *Showings*. After fifteen visions, Julian "comes back" to her ill but recovering body. A religious person visits. She tells him she hallucinated that the cross "bled fast" at the foot of her bed. The religious takes her seriously and she is ashamed that she has denied her visions' divine origin to him. But she does not confess it. To her, this is a heinous sin, but she adds, "here in walde nought oure curtayse lorde leue me" (267) ["herein would not our courteous Lord leave me"]. Then she falls asleep and dreams that the devil attempts to assault her body. He cannot. But the dream is so real, she awakens in horror, still smelling the demonic stench, feeling the intense heat of hellfire, and detecting a little smoke. No one in her attendance senses anything. Presently, the sixteenth vision comes to her. Christ appears in the city of her soul. He tells her, "Witte it welle, it was na rauynge that thowe saw to day, botte take it and leue it and kepe þe ther to, and þou schalle nought be ouercomenn" (269) ["Know it well, it was no raving that you saw today, but take it and believe it and keep yourself thereto, and you shall not be overcome"]. Afterwards, the devil returns, bothering her with jangling speech, but she occupies herself by speaking of Christ's Passion.

Two details are particularly important in this dramatic enactment. First, the sin/confession/penance continuum is *not* preserved. She commits the worst sin she can imagine: denying her Lord. Yet she does not confess. Even so, the assault on her body--which is also an assault on the social construct of the feminized body--is not a punishment. Such punishment has no place in the economy of salvation because Christ's crucifixion has intervened, as Julian's painful descriptions of him have earlier shown. The violence comes from outside, from the evil one. And he cannot harm her, notwithstanding that fact that she has sinned and has not gone through the offices of Holy Church to atone for that sin.

The true message of the demonic confrontation is revealed in the second detail. The image of the crucified Christ, so central to the development of her epistemology, has transformed into a strangely maternal construct: he sits in the city of her soul, in the midst of her human, bodily heart, as if she bears him in her spiritual womb. Yet it is his presence within her that preserves her and keeps her, a construct of *écriture féminine* that Roger Corless calls "coinherently placental."[18] The significance of this transformation of christocentric images cannot be underestimated. It is the pivot upon which Julian's entire epistemological development turns.

But before Julian can fully recognize what the image of the indwelling Christ means, she worries about the subversive potential of the narrative that enacts the demonic confrontation. Her apostrophe to sin emerges at this time:

> A wriched synne, whate ert þou? Thowe er nought. For I sawe that god is alle thynge; I sawe nought the. And when I sawe that god hase made alle thynge, I sawe the nought. And when I sawe that god is in alle thynge, I sawe the nought. And whenn I sawe that god does alle thynge þat is done, lesse and mare, I sawe the nought. And when I sawe oure lorde Jhesu sitt in oure saule so wyrschipfully, and luff and lyke and rewle and ȝeme all that he has made, I sawe nouȝt the. And thus I am sekyr þat þou erte nouȝt, and alle þa that luffeþ the and lykes the and folowes the and wilfully endes in the, I am sekyr thay schalle be brought to nought with the and endleslye confownded. God schelde vs alle fra the. Amen pour charyte. (271)

> [Ah, wretched sin, what are you? You are nought. For I saw that God is all things; I saw not you. And when I saw that God has made all things, I saw you not. And when I saw that God is in all things, I saw you not. And when I saw that God does everything that is done, less and more, I saw you not. And when I saw our Lord Jesus sit in our soul so worshipfully, and love and like and rule and guard all that he has made, I saw not you. And thus I am sure that you are nought, and all they that love you and please you and follow you and willfully end in you, I am sure they shall be brought to nought with you and endlessly confounded. God shield us all from you. Amen, for charity.]

Nicholas Watson observes that this passage is informed by Julian's "dissatisfaction with the emphasis on sin and the 'confounding' of sinners" that Christ's pronouncement has led her to.[19] Yet why an apostrophe? The main grammatical convention of this genre is digression, a turning away from that which is present to address something that is absent. As such, apostrophe becomes what Lacan calls the "empty" word, a kind of social cliche, through which the soul might misrecognize or even "deny the unconscious and thus eschew truth" (Ragland-Sullivan, *Philosophy* 161). Repetition in the passage seems to confirm it: "You are nought. . . . I saw you not. . . . all they that love you . . . shall be brought to nought." Repetition constitutes a sort of paean to nothingness, projected into an abyss that sends back echoes of sin's insubstantiality, from which, nonsensically, God must shield us. The apostrophe, from this perspective, seems little more than the demon's "jangling," that divides itself to confound the unwary soul. However, the guilt and consequent terror that Julian's own sin precipitated, are very substantial.

Just so, the image of Christ seated in the city of Julian's soul causes her to reformulate the apostrophe in the long text. As the Christ moves dialectically from the margins into the center of the passage, the apostrophe becomes an address to him as an internalized other. Julian says:

> Goode lorde, I see the that thou arte very truth, and I know truly þat we syn grevously all day and be moch blame wurthy; and I may neyther leue the knowyng of this sooth, nor I se nott the shewyng to vs no manner of blame. How may this be? . . . And yf it be tru that we be synners and blame wurthy, good lorde, how may it than be that I can nott see this truth in the, whych arte my god, my maker in whom I desyer to se alle truth? . . . A, lorde Jhesu, kyng of blysse, how shall I be esyd, who shall tell me and tech me that me nedyth to wytt, if I may nott at this tyme se it in the? (50.510-12)

> [Good Lord, I see you, that you are the veritable truth, and I know that we sin grievously all day and be much blameworthy; and I may neither leave the knowing of this truth, nor I see not the showing to us no manner of blame. How may this be?. . . And if it be true that we be sinners and blameworthy, good Lord, how may it then be that I cannot see this truth in you, which are my God, my maker in whom I desire to see all truth? . . . Ah, Lord Jesus, king of bliss, how shall I be eased, who shall

tell me and teach me what I need to know, if I may not see it in you?"]

Julian's revised apostrophe accordingly underscores Lacan's dictum that "language is more than a mouthpiece for the Imaginary"; for her, language can only yield the truth if she directs it toward the Person, the resurrected Christ, seated in the city of the human soul, who has vanquished death and healed the "primordial split" between the "nought" of human sinfulness and spiritual being (Ragland-Sullivan, *Philosophy* 160). Contrary to the grammatical convention of the original apostrophe, then, Julian's revision does not address an ellipsis in her knowledge. Instead, it acknowledges that the indwelling Christ is a real presence and has the capacity for response, which in turn affirms her own being materially as well as spiritually, because she finds him enclosed in her soul, heart, and body. Thus, she says: "for in the same poynt that oure soule is made sensuall, in the same poynt is the cytte of god . . . oure soule with oure body and oure body with oure soule" (55.567) ["for in the same point that our soul is made sensual, in the same point is the city of God . . . our soul with our body and our body with our soul"]. Accordingly, Julian's reformulated apostrophe dialectically displaces the medieval sociomedical construct of the womb as the empty, active sexual organ whose appetitive faculty dominates and controls women's desire (see Cadden 178). In its stead, the maternal construct of the soul as city of God becomes the womb transformed, and women's capacity for pregnancy becomes women's capacity to know the God who dwells within them.

The same kind of reformulation occurs in Julian's parable of the lord and servant. But here, her task is far more daunting. She is recounting a new version of the Genesis fall from grace, which text is the very cornerstone of medieval misogyny. This is probably why Julian explains that the parable is a showing she repressed, even though "the marveylyng of þe example went nevyr fro me; for me thoght it was gevyn me for answere to my desyer. And yet culde I nott take there in full vnderstandyng . . . for [it] . . . was not gevyn me in that tyme" (51.519) ["the marvelling of the example went never from me, for I thought it was given me for an answer to my desire. Yet could I not take therein full understanding . . . for [it] . . . was not given me in that time"]. She goes on to say:

I sawe two persons in bodely lycknesse . . . a lorde and a
servannt. . . . The lorde syttyth solempnely. . . . The servannt
stondyth before his lorde, reverently redy to do his lordes wylle.
The lorde . . . sendyth hym in to a certeyne place to do his wyll.
The servannt nott onely he goyth, but sodenly he stertyth and
rynnyth in grett hast for loue. . . . And anon he fallyth in a slade
. . . and than he gronyth . . . and wryeth, but he may nott ryse
nor helpe hym selfe . . . for he culde nott turne his face to loke
vppe on his lovynge lorde, whych was to hym full nere. . . . I
behelde [this servant] with avysement to wytt yf I culde perceyve
in hym ony defau3te, or yf the lorde shuld assigne in hym ony
maner of blame; and verely there was none seen, for oonly hys
good wyll and his grett desyr was cause of his fallyng. And he
was . . . as good inwardly as he was when he stode before his
lorde. . . .

And ryght thus contynuantly his loueyng lorde full tenderly
beholdyth hym: and now wyth a doubyll chere, oone owtwarde
. . . with grett rewth and pytte . . . another inward . . . which I
sawe hym hyely enjoy for the wurschypfull restyng and noble that
he wyll and shall bryng his seruannt to by his plentuous grace.
(51.514-15)

[I saw two persons in bodily likeness. . . a lord and a servant. . . .
The lord sits solemnly. . . . The servant stands before his lord,
reverently ready to do his lord's will. The lord . . . sends him
into a certain place to do his will. The servant not only . . .
goes, but suddenly he starts and runs in great haste for love. . . .
And so he falls in a gully . . . and then he groans . . . and
writhes, but he may not rise nor help himself . . . for he could
not turn his face to look up on his loving lord, which was to him
fully nearby. . . . I beheld [this servant] with advisement, to
know if I could perceive in him any fault, or if the lord should
assign him any manner of blame; and verily there was none seen,
for only his good will and his great desire was cause of his
falling. And he was . . . as good inwardly as he was when he
stood before his lord. . . .

And right thus, continuously, his loving lord full tenderly beheld him, and now with double countenance, one outward . . . with great ruth and pity . . . another inward . . . which I saw him highly enjoy for the worshipful resting and nobility that he will and shall bring his servant to by plenteous grace.]

Hearkening back to her *lectio* on Adam, whose sin was the most harm ever done, Julian explains, "For in the servannt, that was shewed for Adam . . . I sawe many dyuerse properteys that myght by no manner be derecte to syngell Adam" (51.519) ["For in the servant that was showed for Adam . . . I saw many diverse properties that might by no manner be directed to Adam alone"]. After years of meditation, she has come to realize that the image of the servant represents not only all of humanity, but also the new Adam, Christ, in whom humankind is refashioned, and in whom all is made well.

As Lacanian theory might assert, the problem of sin is "enigmatic to conscious life, but decipherable through the laws of . . . metaphor and metonymy . . . when taken in dialectical relationship" with what Julian's Lord has taught her (see Ragland-Sullivan, *Philosophy* 169). As such, the grammatical conventions of the parable provide Julian and her readers access to this enigmatic part of her visions through analogies from ordinary human experience, a spiritual or moral lesson, and the likelihood of multiple interpretations (see Murphy 279-80). We cannot overlook the biblical evidence that Christ used this genre to subvert a number of culturally-entrenched maladies: religious hypocrisy, abuses of the poor, inept or evil education, misappropriation of civic power, unfair or foolish customs of inheritance, bad stewardship, and the like. The counter-ideological and prophetic elements of the genre lend themselves to Julian's necessity.

Most significant for Julian, the lord/servant parable is a New Testament-inspired revision that subverts the male-centeredness of the Genesis account. Instead of advocating creation as an earthly hierarchy that places Adam above all creatures, Julian re-orders the cosmos in respect of the mutual love existing between lord and servant. Instead of representing human toil as a curse, Julian sees it as means by which the servant may do his lord's will. Instead of portraying a figurative fall as a result of demonic temptation and womanly weakness, Julian depicts a literal fall resulting from the servant's eagerness to serve. Instead of pronouncing divine anger and exile and punishment, Julian emphasizes divine tenderness and pity and the promise of ennoblement.

At this point, some recapitulation might be useful. Taken together, Julian's revised sermon, her reformulated apostrophe, and her lord/servant parable provide the last part of a powerful critique of her culture's accepted teachings about sin. Her anxiety is that those teachings seem to be the root system of a negative theology that alienates her and her "even Christians" from the very God who wants them to know him. Her accomplishment is that she reconceptualizes sin and explains precisely why it is so destructive to the soul, without succumbing to moral relativism or universalism. Yet she remains faithful as well to her puzzling revelation that sin is behovable, but that Christ makes all things well. With her insistence upon a synthesis of parts--that "the hole revelation fro the begynnyng to the ende . . . be so onyd, as to my vnderstondyng, that I can nott nor may deperte them" (51.520) ["the whole revelation from the beginning to the end . . . be so united, as to my understanding, that I cannot nor may separate them"], Julian brings to mind Bakhtin's assertion about speech genres and how they function. Within a larger, complex genre such as the *Showings*, primary speech genres "are not indifferent to one another, and are not self-sufficient. . . . [They] must be regarded primarily as a *response* to preceding utterances of the given sphere. . . . Each . . . refutes, affirms, supplements, and relies on the others . . . but they can also be re-accentuated . . . [or] repeated with varying degrees of reinterpretation" (91).

Lacan teaches that "it is the words which culture imposes on the [person] . . . that create the human subject as a specificity," clarifying Julian's initial impulse to find specific human examples to illustrate how all shall be well (Ragland-Sullivan, *Philosophy* 145). Yet in the epistemologies of Lacan and Julian alike, there exists a doctrine that subverts the more general cultural pre-determination of the human subject, a doctrine "that the unconscious text can be rewritten, that the relationship between signifiers and signifieds can be altered; and that the Real has nothing to do with [sociocultural] fixities" (289-90). It follows that Julian's gloss on the lord/servant parable underscores an entirely different dimension to the teachings of Holy Church on sin, which Lacan would identify as "a feminine side aligned with a 'beyond' in law and culture" (Ragland-Sullivan, "Masquerade" 63). This different dimension not only deconstructs a patriarchal ideology of inflexible world order, gender construction, and judgment. It also opens up a discursive space that will permit the reconstruction and resituation of woman--a new Eve, as it were--whose revised role in the plan of salvation, consonant with the dialectical principle, is to provide an architectonic parallelism--a *reply*--to Jesus as the new Adam. The allegory of Jesus as mother emerges as a result.

IV. Jesus as (m)Other: Allegory as the Genre of Embodied Knowledge

The allegory of Jesus as mother is the most interesting of the primary speech genres that emerge in her two texts, because it resists the topos of the *brautmystik*, in which so many female and male mystics use sexually-charged language to explicate the relationship between the soul and God (e.g. Bernard of Clairvaux, Richard Rolle, Margery Kempe, Catherine of Siena). The accretive images of Julian's mariology help to explain why, once the concept of sin is reconceptualized, the allegory emerges.[20]

The bedrock of Julian's mariology is the participatory role that the Mother of Christ fulfills in the salvific plan. However, Julian's interpretation of this role does not remain static. For example, in the short text she portrays Mary as mediatrix, saying, "ilke saule contemplatyfe to whilke es gyffenn to luke and seke god schalle se hire and passe vnto god by contemplacionn" (243) ["each contemplative soul to which is given to look for and seek God shall see her and pass unto God by contemplation"]. In the Long Text, Julian reworks the idea with far greater precision and knowledge, indicating that of "the meanes that the goodnes of god hath ordeineth to helpe vs . . . the chiefe and principall meane he toke of the maiden" (6.305) ["the means that the goodness of God has ordained to help us . . . the chief and principal means is the blessed humanity that [Jesus] took from the maiden"].

It becomes clearer how and why Julian's mariology evolves, if it is examined in light of Lacan's comments on the development of identity, from the primordial mother to the internalized (m)Other, which reveal "the whole of the 'lived' experience of the mother, in part forgotten, in part integrated into conscious memories . . . in relation to . . . the necessity of verifying one's place in a widening [social] sphere" (Ragland-Sullivan, *Philosophy* 116).

Julian's first mention of Mary is brief. In her prayer of petition, she says, "I desyrede a bodylye syght, whare yn y myght have more knawynge of bodelye paynes of oure lorde oure savyoure, and of the compassyonn of oure ladye" (202) ["I desired a bodily sight, wherein I might have more knowing of bodily pains of our Lord our saviour, and of the compassion of our Lady"]. Lacan indicates that the mother is the anchor in identity formation, "the primordial pivot of Desire of one's unconscious," the "self's double" through whom feelings of unity outside one's fragmented self are first known (26-27). Although this description pertains to an infant, Lacan notes that "adults will always be caught up in the spatial lures of identification with their *semblables*" (27). The image of the mother as a bridge to others occurs because of bodily identification, as Julian's use of the word "compassion" illustrates; she seeks to know her Lord's bodily pains through the empathetic suffering of his mother. Mary becomes a kind of *subjective* correlative.

The next reference to Mary comes rather incongruously, when Julian is shown a little thing the size of a hazelnut, which, as she learns from words formed in her understanding, represents the smallness of all creation and the enormity of God. Mary is drawn in as an image that facilitates the dialectical process. Julian says:

I sawe hir gastelye in bodilye lyekenes, a sympille maydene and a meeke, 3onge of age, in the stature that scho was when scho conceyvede . . . whare yn I vndyrstode . . . þat sche behelde hyre god, that ys hir makere, mervelande with grete reuerence that he wolde be borne of hir. . . . I sawe sothfastlye that scho ys mare than alle þat god made benethe hir in worthynes. . . . For abovene hir ys nothynge that is made botte the blyssede manhede of Criste. This lytille thynge that es made that es benethe oure ladye saynte Marye--god schewyd it vnto me als litille as it hadde beene a hasylle notte . . . it myght hafe fallene. (213-14)

[I saw her spiritually in bodily likeness, a simple maiden and a meek, young of age, in the stature she was when she conceived... wherein I understood . . . that she beheld her God, that is her maker, marvelling with great reverence that he would be born of her. . . . I saw truthfully that she is more than all that God made beneath her in worthiness. . . . For above her is nothing that is made but the blessed manhood of Christ. This little thing that is made that is beneath our Lady Saint Mary--. . . as little as it had been a hazelnut . . . it might have fallen.]

A concatenation of seeing/beholding is immediately noteworthy: Julian is gazing on Mary, who is gazing on God. The vision constructs Mary as a bodily "other," who links Julian (and her "even Christians") to God. This gazing does not entirely replicate the trauma of individuation and separation from the mother, because Mary serves as the model of contemplation, and more significantly, as a model for women. Consequently, Julian becomes more aware of her own worth by formulating Mary as (m)Other (see Ragland-Sullivan, *Philosophy* 16). That is, if Mary is above all creation in her worthiness, then the hazelnut-sized object placed in *Julian's* hand, not Mary's, emphasizes Julian's similarly enlarged state of grace. On an unconscious level, three elements--the voice of the locution, Mary's gaze upon her God, and the void into which all of creation could fall for its littleness--heighten Julian's awareness of her human dependency on, and desire for, God. These elements serve as "structuring principles of human identity" (80).

But the temporary formulation of Mary as (m)Other is supplanted at one of the most ironic points in Julian's visionary experience. Julian is gazing intently upon the crucified Christ just at the time his body is ready to die. Julian seems to be ready to die as well, and *her own mother*, "that stode emangys othere and behelde me lyftyd vppe hir hande before m(y) face to lokke mynn eyenn, for sche wenyd I had bene dede . . . and this encresyd mekille my sorowe, for . . . I wolde nouȝt hafe benn lettyd for loove that I hadde in hym" (234) ["that stood among others . . . lifted up her hand before my face to close my eyes, for she thought I had been dead . . . and this increased much my sorrow, for . . . I would not have been prevented from seeing for love I had of him"]. Julian's mother enters the visionary experience as what Lacan would call a "phallic signifier": she separates Julian from her radical bodily identification with Christ, individuating Julian as a "self" when "[she] felyd no payne, botte for Cristes paynes; þan thouȝt [she, she] knewe ful lytylle whate payne it was that [she] askyd" (234-35) ["[she] felt no pain but for Christ's pain; then [she] thought how little what pain it was that [she] asked for"] (Ragland-Sullivan, *Philosophy* 216). A phallic signifier--usually masculine and usually the father, but here not--creates the necessary identificatory boundaries between a self's body and its mother's. Therefore, here, if Julian's abjection in Christ is at first "a straying into unstable territories where the limits of the self are not clearly defined," it becomes a very unusual case of transference which ties back again to Mary.[21]

When Julian goes on to wonder if there is any pain like Christ's pain, she receives an answer in her reason that despair is more painful. Mary re-enters her thoughts as a symbol of compassion. Julian says: "Here yn I sawe in partye the compassyonn of oure ladye saynte Marye; for Criste and scho ware so anede in loove that þe gretnesse of hir loove was the cause of the mykille hede of hir payne. For so mykille as scho lovyd hym mare than alle othere, her payne passed alle othere" (235) ["Herein I saw in part the compassion of our Lady Saint Mary, for Christ and she were so united in love that the greatness of her love was the cause of the immensity of her pain. For so much as she loved him more than all others did, her pain passed all others"]. The pain with which Julian has so intensely identified is now transferred to a representation of Mary's capacity for suffering. This is a phenomenon that Lacan labels a "secondary repression . . . [also] essential to psychic health, individuation and social functioning," because it relegates fragments and images to the unconscious that might otherwise push the conscious beyond its capacity to cope (Ragland-Sullivan, *Philosophy* 116).

A continuation of this transference and secondary repression happens shortly after Christ begins to address direct questions to Julian. When he looks down to the spear wound in his side and says, "Loo how I lovyd the" ["Lo, how I loved you"], Julian recalls that he "brought to my mynde whare oure ladye stode in the tyme of his passionn, and sayde: Wille thowe see hir?" (242) ["brought to my mind where our Lady stood in the time of his Passion and said, Will you see her?"]. Julian is surprised by a spiritual showing of Mary as Queen of Heaven. This is not a bodily showing at all, as she later clarifies: "I [am] nott lernyd to long to see her bodely presens whyle I am here, but the vertuse of her blyssydfulle soule, her truth, her wysdom, her cheryte, wher by I am leern(yd) to know my self, and reuerently drede my god" (25.399) ["I was not taught to long to see her bodily presence . . . but the virtues of her blessed soul, her truth, her wisdom, her charity, whereby I am taught to know myself and reverently fear my God"].

Why this progressive separation from, and eventual disappearance of, Mary's feminine body in Julian's mariology? For one thing, we have seen, in Lacanian terms, Julian's "psychic fusion and corporeal identification with [Christ's] human form" (Ragland-Sullivan, *Philosophy* 134). For another, Mary's spiritual glorification insures a necessary separation, an "exchange of mother fusion for . . . otherness" (270). Julian cannot articulate these psychosomatic impulses--they remain repressed--until she sorts through the lord/servant parable and explicates it in the long text, where the *lectio divina* enables her, by means of her mariology, to recover Mary's feminine body through Christ. This act of bodily recovery begins when Julian describes how the servant rushes off to do his lord's will.

She writes:

His stertyng was þe godhede, and the rennyng was þe manhede; for the godhed sterte fro þe fader in to þe maydyns wombe, fallyng in to the takyng of oure/ kynde. . . . The flessch was rent fro the head panne, fallyng on pecys vnto the tyme þe bledynge feylyd. . . . And by . . . Wrythyng . . . and monyng, is vndyrstonde that he myght nevyr ryse all myghtly fro that tyme þat he was fallyn in to the maydyns wombe, tyll his body was sleyne . . . yeldyng the soule to the fadyrs hand. . . . (51.539-42)

[His starting was the godhead, and the running was the manhood; for the godhead starts from the father into the maiden's womb, falling into the taking of our humanity. . . . The flesh was rent from the skull, falling in pieces until the time the bleeding stopped. . . . And by the . . . Writhing . . . and moaning, is understood that he might never rise all mightily from that time that he was fallen into the maiden's womb, till his body was slain. . .yielding the soul to the father's hand. . . .]

By means of the *lectio*, Julian invokes Mary metonymically through her womb, writing the feminine body into a scene where it is absent. But the invocation of Mary's womb would be little more than gratuitous, if the substitutive powers of language, as Lacan calls them, did not consequently move Julian toward the stunning, semiotic transformation of Christ's horribly mutilated body into Mary's whole, unviolated one (see 298-99). The transformation occurs as follows:

> For in that same tyme that god knytt hym to oure body in the meydens wombe, he toke oure sensuall soule, in whych takyng, he vs all having beclosyd in hym, he onyd it to oure substance. . . .
>
> Thus oure lady is oure moder, in whome we be all beclosyd and of hyr borne in Crist, for she that is moder of oure savyoure is moder of all þat ben savyd in our savyour; and oure savyoure is oure very moder, in whome we be endlesly borne and nevyr shall come out of hym. (57.579-81)

> [For in that same time that God knit himself to our body in the maiden's womb, he took our sensual soul, in which taking, he us having enclosed in him, he united it to our substance. . . .
>
> Thus our Lady is our mother, in whom we be all enclosed and of her born in Christ, for she that is mother of our saviour is mother of all that be saved in our saviour; and our saviour is our true mother, in whom we be endlessly born . . . we be all in him enclosed, and he is enclosed in us. And that is spoken of in the sixteenth showing, where he says he sits in our soul.]

This *lectio* supports Lacan's assertion that just as language has its laws-- upon which conventions such as lexicon and grammar impose an order-- just "so the unconscious has its own syntax and transforms images and language through analogous procedures of combination, condensation, referentiality, substitution, and displacement" (Ragland-Sullivan, *Philosophy* 267). In Julian's fully developing epistemology, the sociocultural ideologies of gender construction do not constrict her. Rather, her gendered knowledge, in Lacanian terms, represents a "logical, symbolic, representational, and transformational drama" that situates a woman's body in a place where it can modify "the fixity of the Symbolic order by redefining the meaning of gender and by reshaping the relationship between signifier and signified" (268; 299). Thus, Julian's text engages in what Karma Lochrie calls "incarnating discourse, signifying 'that which suffers in the soul' through words and the return of the body through discourse" (74). And in returning the body through discourse, Julian's mariology makes Christ's word and flesh spiritually regenerative, nurturing, vital.

A basis for new feminine identity thus emerges in the allegory of Jesus as (m)Other. This development remains in harmony with the conventions of the genre. According to one fourteenth-century grammarian, the primary grammatical principle of allegory is permutation, in which "the signification of the term itself is not changed; rather, some new other thing is given to be understood by it" (Murphy 238). The following excerpt bears witness:

> Thus in oure very moder Jhesu oure lyfe is groundyd in the forseeyng wysdom of hym selfe fro with out begynnyng, with þe hye myght of the fader and þe souereyne goodnesse of the holy gost. And in the takyng of oure kynde he quyckyd vs, and in his blessyd dyeng vppon the crosse he bare vs to endlesse lyfe. and fro þat tyme . . . to domysday, he fedyth vs and fordreth vs, ryght as þe hye souereyne kyndnesse of moderhed wylle, and as þe kyndly nede of chyldhed askyth. Feyer and swete is our hevenly moder in þe syght of oure soule, precyous and louely be þe gracyous chyldren in þe syght of oure hevynly moder,/ with myldnesse and mekenesse and alle þe feyer vertuse that long to chyldren in kynde. . . . And I vndyrstode none hygher stature in this lyfe than chyldehode . . . in to þe tyme þat oure gracious moder hath brought vs vpp to oure fadyrs blysse. (63.616-18)

> [Thus in our true mother Jesus our life is grounded in the foreseeing wisdom of himself from without beginning, with the high might of the father and the sovereign goodness of the Holy Ghost. And taking on our humanity he restored us, and in his blessed dying upon the cross he bore us to endless life. And from that time . . . to doomsday, he feeds us and nurtures us, right as the high sovereign nature of motherhood wills, and as the natural need of childhood asks. Fair and sweet is our heavenly mother in the sight of our soul, precious and loving be the gracious children in the sight of our heavenly mother, with mildness and meekness and all the fair virtues that belong to children naturally. . . . And I understood no higher stature in this life than childhood . . .

until the time that our gracious mother has brought us up to our father's bliss.]

In this allegory, Jesus, as second person of the Trinity, retains the biological markers of his Incarnation in masculine pronouns. But Julian's mariology has reached its inevitable culmination. The *brautmystik* has been subverted by something else: *jouissance.* Julian portrays it as Lacan does. It is a unity between child and (m)Other that has come about "through substitution and displacements" which sustain the loss of Mary's body through secondary repression, but which in turn provide the new body that conflates Mary's and Christ's combined humanity (Ragland-Sullivan, *Philosophy* 139).

Julian's image of Jesus as (m)Other revises the subject position of the feminine body, so that women do not have to imagine finding their spiritual fulfillment in submission to a celestial, masculine lover. And because the sentiment of bliss in Julian's allegory derives from excruciating suffering--Christ's feminized suffering--she conveys an implicit message that "sexual identities are sociostructural constructs and not natural ones" (303). What *is a* natural construct to Julian, in the words of Hélène Cixous, is a divine love that does not collude "with the old story of death," but brings to fruition a desire of the child for the mother and the mother for the child, whose dialectical destiny rises gloriously above "the debasement of one by the other."[22]

V. Notes on a Text "of obscure and uncertain history"

Women's bodies, as Laurie Finke asserts, are the sites of contested discourse in the Middle Ages, and that in part is because they have so little recourse to other kinds of power to express their subject positions. Thus, when women mystics write the body, they manifest "cultural and ideological constructs that both share in and subvert orthodox religious institutions."[23] Just so, Julian's prayer that God visit a near-death illness upon her body leads to the powerful exercise of inscribing the maternal body on that of Christ, as he encloses her illness in his Passion. Julian's text renders the human body androgynous. Denise Baker finds that this androgyny is even detectable on the structural level in the *Showings*; Chapters 53 through 63 are arranged according to the Pauline chronology of election found in Romans 8:30, at the same time that Julian integrates in these chapters an organizational principle based upon "ontological bonds [of motherhood and family] among the Persons of the Trinity and humankind" (112).

A genre approach to the *Showings* extends these findings and suggests that remarkable consistencies exist in Julian's patterns of development and revision. A genre approach also suggests that no ultimate genre classification for the *Showings* is possible, because Julian's purpose appears to have been to evade such classification. Evidence supports the supposition that she deeply distrusted the implicit ideologies which accompany genres and that she made concerted efforts to deconstruct those ideologies wherever she found them in her work. Further studies of the existent manuscripts may bear this assessment out.

I share Barratt's hope that more accessible versions of the existent Julian manuscripts eventually *will* appear, so as to make such investigation easier and more reliable--although I am not so quick to aver that Julian remains "a shadowy figure of whom we know practically nothing except that she wrote at least two accounts of a series of visions . . . the exact meaning of which we often do not understand" (39).

Maybe, from a genre approach that incorporates a Lacanian perspective, we can understand that the *Showings* illuminates an archetypal struggle within the fragmentary human consciousness, where the (m)Other is regarded as "either a dark-faced and absent part of oneself which one must flee or a mysterious force which one renders divine and proceeds to worship" (Ragland-Sullivan, *Philosophy* 297). And maybe, as Julian's and Lacan's epistemologies seem to concur, the resolution of that struggle, which entails the discovery of the (m)Other who resides in the city of the soul for Julian and the discovery of the unconscious for Lacan, "leads not to death, but to life" (300).

NOTES

1. Alexandra Barratt, "How Many Children Had Julian of Norwich?" *Vox Mystica: Essays on Medieval Mysticism.* Ed. Anne Clark Bartlett. (Cambridge: Brewer, 1995) 38-39.

2. Quotations in Middle English are from *A Book of Showings to the Anchoress Julian of Norwich,* ed. Edmund Colledge and James Walsh, 2 vols., (Toronto:

Pontifical Institute of Mediaeval Studies, 1978) 201; 281. Translations into modern English are mine. Wherever possible, I have preserved syntax and lexicon. Subsequent references are provided parenthetically within the text.

3. Caryl Emerson and Michael Holquist, eds., Introduction, *Speech Genres and Other Late Essays* (Austin: U of Texas P, 1986), xviii. Also see Denise Baker, *Julian of Norwich's Showings* (Princeton: Princeton UP, 1994) 147.

4. Bakhtin, *Speech Genres* 98.

5. See Nicholas Watson, *Richard Rolle and the Invention of Authority* (New York: Cambridge UP, 1991) 4-5.

6. Elizabeth Robertson, "Medieval Medical Views of Women and Female Spirituality," *Feminist Approaches to the Body in Medieval Literature*, ed. Linda Lomperis and Sarah Stanbury (U of Pennsylvania P, 1993) 161.

7. Anne Cranny-Francis, "Gender and Genre: Feminist Subversion of Genre Fiction," *The Powers of Literacy*, ed. Bill Cope and Mary Kalantzis (Pittburgh: U of Pittsburgh P, 1993) 113; 94.

8. Ellie Ragland-Sullivan, *Jacques Lacan and the Philosophy of Pychoanalysis* (Chicago: U of Illinois P, 1986) 16.

9. Andrea Lunsford, "On Reclaiming Rhetorica," *Reclaiming Rhetorica*, ed. Andrea Lunsford (Pittsburgh: U of Pittsburgh P, 1995) 6.

10. James Murphy, *Rhetoric in the Middle Ages* (Berkeley: U of California P, 1974) 289. Also see St. Augustine, *Concerning the Teacher* and *On Christian Doctrine*.

11. Ellie Ragland-Sullivan, "The Sexual Masquerade," *Lacan and the Subject of Language*, ed. Ellie Ragland-Sullivan and Mark Bracher (New York: Routledge, 1991) 65.

12. Jean Leclercq, *The Love of Learning and the Desire for God*, trans. Catharine Misrahi (New York: Fordham UP, 1982) 202.

13. Gregory Clark, *Dialogue, Dialectic, and Conversation* (Carbondale: S. Illinois UP, 1990) 29.

14. Elizabeth Petroff, *Body and Soul* (New York: Oxford UP, 1994) 192-93.

15. Hans Robert Jauss, *Question and Answer*, trans. Michael Hays (Minneapolis: U of Minnesota P, 1989) 68.

16. See Laurie Finke, "Knowledge as Bait: Feminism, Voice, and the Pedagogical Unconscious," *CE* 55 (1993): 20.

17. See Joan Cadden, *Meanings of Sex Difference in the Middle Ages* (New York: Cambridge UP, 1993) 175.

18. Roger Corless coined this term in delivering the paper "Comparing Cataphatic Mystics," 29th International Congress on Medieval Studies, W Michigan U, May 5-9, 1994. The term does not show up in his later article with the same title in *Mystics Quarterly* XXI.

19. Nicholas Watson, "The Composition of Julian of Norwich's *Revelations of Love*," *Speculum* 68 (1993): 669.

20. In this section of the essay, I owe a great debt to Valerie Lagorio for our numerous conversations on Julian's mariology.

21. See Karma Lochrie, *Margery Kempe and Translations of the Flesh* (Philadelphia: U of Pennsylvania P, 1991) 38.

22. Hélène Cixous, "Sorties," Hélène Cixous and Catherine Clément, *The Newly Born Woman*, trans. Betsy Wing (Minneapolis: U of Minnesota P, 1986) 78.

23. Laurie Finke, "Mystical Bodies and the Dialogics of Vision," *Maps of Flesh and Light*, ed. Ulrike Wiethaus (Syracuse: Syracuse UP, 1993) 29.

The Point of Coincidence: Rhetoric and the Apophatic in Julian of Norwich's *Showings*

Cynthea Masson

According to theories of negative theology and apophatic language, God in his essence cannot be known or spoken about at all.[1] As one commentator on the pseudo-Dionysius argues, "Ultimately, theology is not only wordless but even thoughtless. . . . God transcends every human word or concept, dwells on a plane above them all, and yet is revealed to those who leave behind every perceptible light, every voice, every conceptual word from heaven" (Rorem 189). Likewise, the anonymous author of the *Cloud of Unknowing* suggests to those seeking God, "put a cloud of forgetting beneath you and all creation"; indeed, "everything must be hidden under this cloud of forgetting."[2] Although Julian of Norwich does not directly speak of such a cloud in her *Showings*, she does refer to a moment of forgetting prior to receiving her revelations.[3] After Julian describes her initial desire for "thre gyftes by the grace of god," she explains that two of them, the desire for a bodily sight of the Passion and a bodily sickness, "passid from my mynd."[4] In this manner, Chapter 2 of the Long Text ends with Julian's acknowledgment of having forgotten her desire for bodily sickness; then, apparently in juxtaposition to this, Chapter 3 opens with a description of the bodily sickness sent to her by God--the sickness during which she experiences her showings. Julian's desires for sickness and for showings of the Passion are realized only after she has forgotten those very desires.

By juxtaposing the desires with the lack thereof, that is, with the forgetting of the desires, Julian opens the possibility for the showings on which her text is based. Vincent Gillespie and Maggie Ross claim that such a juxtaposition is a necessary part of the apophatic experience:

To enter apophatic consciousness, the seeker must simultaneously desire it intensely and give up all desire. This paradox is deliberately subversive. . . . It is a sign of contradiction, allowing the creative tension between its conflicting significations to generate a precious stillness, a chink in the defensive wall of reason that allows slippage into apophatic consciousness.[5]

Through her forgotten desire Julian opens such an apophatic "chink in the wall" as the moment of origin for her *Showings*. Julian is, moreover, on the threshold of death during her bodily sickness: "I weenied often tymes to haue passed, and so wenyd thei that were with me" (3.289) ["I often thought that I was on the point of death, and those who were with me often thought so" (179)]. As Gillespie contends, "Mystical writing can only ever be about thresholds."[6] Here, in terms of the *Showings*, the placement of the narrator/Julian at the brink of death reinforces the idea that the origin of the text lies at the threshold to the apophatic. Indeed, since Julian's revelations begin to occur during a near-death experience when her body is "dead from the miedes downward" (3.290) ["dead from the middle downwards" (179)], the *Showings* evolve from the chasm between life and death, between physical death and spiritual awakening.

In a discussion of Julian of Norwich and the continental mystic Mechthild of Magdeburg, Oliver Davies suggests that "the origin of their writings lies in an *excessus*, which is to say a transformational state located between ordinary and extraordinary perception."[7] This "excessus" or chasm, as I have referred to it, is the theoretical point of crossing between opposites--the ineffable coincidence of unity and difference.[8] Post-modern scholarship on mysticism abounds with references to such oppositional relationships. Karma Lochrie, for example, continually uses the words "fissure" and "between" to point to the place (or space) in which the mystical experience occurs.[9] She submits that the mystical text "is always fissured at the juncture between its oral and written texts" and that the mystic "returns again and again to this location between silence and utterance, doubt and presumption" (69, 71). Likewise, along with their theories of paradox and the "creative tension" therein, Gillespie and Ross speak of the mystics' longing to become the word of God which, in turn, "becomes the bridge between voice and silence" (55). David Thomson in "Deconstruction and Meaning in Medieval Mysticism" discusses techniques of affirmation and negation in mysticism and concludes that "meaning is situated neither in the aggregate of assertions nor in the void consequent to deletion but in the dialectical exchange which involves each."[10] Although Thomson bases his argument on theories of deconstruction, similar ideas can be found in Paul Rorem's commentary on the pseudo-Dionysius's *The Mystical Theology* where he argues that "affirmation and negation are not separate enterprises applied to separate lists of characterizations, but the two complementary facets of the same interpretive process" (203). Finally, Michael Sells, in his "Principles of Apophatic Language," contends, "The meaningfulness of the apophatic moment of discourse is unstable, residing in the momentary tension between two propositions" (207). I offer these quotations as a starting point for the analysis of mystical texts and, in particular, for the *Showings* of Julian of Norwich.

This paper brings together such theories of negative theology with rhetorical theory to argue that Julian of Norwich rhetorically structures her *Showings* to gesture toward an unknown, ineffable God.[11] In particular, the rhetorical figures of *contentio* and *chiasmus* are examined for their ability to represent the paradox associated with the apophatic moment or point of exchange between the human and the divine.[12] Within this discussion, I examine Julian's use of the word "poynt(e)" in its various contexts. Julian's "poynt(e)," like the rhetorical figures, can be understood to represent the point of crossing between opposites. Throughout the *Showings*, Julian asserts the necessity of opposites in her mystical experiences. Although this assertion is not always direct, Julian arguably builds her theology on a coincidence of opposites.

Theories on the coincidence of opposites were formally put forth in the fifteenth century by Nicholas of Cusa. I am not suggesting that Julian had access to Cusa's work; I am, however, going to suggest that she structures many of her ideas on the premise of coincidence of opposites before it was formally outlined by Cusa.[13] In his discussion of Cusa's "appeal to Christology, the paradox of Christ's person, as the norm for theological method," H. Lawrence Bond paraphrases Cusa's thoughts as follows: "Discourse about God inevitably fails because God is unnameable, indescribable, indefinable, while language is naming, enclosing, defining, that is, giving limitations. This dilemma is solved only by Christ, the divine mediator of opposites."[14] In other words, Christ is the link between the human and the divine or between human language and the ineffable divinity. As a solution to the "radical gulf between divine wisdom and the finite ways of knowing," Cusa maintains that "[t]he only valid dialectic is the coincidence of opposites" manifest in the "paradox of the Christ-maximum" or the "nexus" that is Christ (Bond 84, 85).[15] Bond explains, moreover, that the Incarnation provides "the gross metaphor for all coincidences, including the coincidence of finite language with the ineffable God. And the icon of icons is the incarnate Christ; the hypostatic union of his person is the prime and model coincident" (88). I refer to Bond's article on Nicholas of Cusa only to illustrate some of the theories behind coincidence of opposites, a concept that Julian appears to have understood (whether or not she named it as such) and integrated into her own work.

Julian's well-known edict that "alle shalle be wele" (Chapter 27) has as its base her faith in the transformational power of divine love and grace. That is, Julian believes that God has, among other things, the power to turn human suffering into its apparent opposite, everlasting bliss. When discussing God's mercy and related qualities, Julian describes the human relationship with divine grace as follows: "And this is of þe habundannce of loue, for grace werkyth oure dredfull faylyng in to plentuouse and endlesse solace; and grace werkyth oure shamefull fallyng in to hye wurschyppefull rysyng; and grace werkyth oure sorowfull dyeng in to holy blyssyd lyffe" (48.503) ["And this is from the abundance of love, for grace transforms our dreadful failing into plentiful and endless solace; and grace transforms our shameful falling into high and honourable rising; and grace transforms our sorrowful dying into holy, blessed life" (263)]. Julian's perception of God's grace and its transformative power is not evidence of a theology grounded in coincidence of opposites; that is, although this passage deals with transformation from one state to its opposite, it does not directly address the paradox of the Incarnation. However, both the passage just quoted and the following quotation (the former's immediate continuation) do illustrate Julian's use of rhetorical opposition and suggest (at least in the latter) a system of belief that gives priority to opposition as a necessary component in humanity's relationship with God and God's grace:

> For I saw full truly that evyr as oure *contraryousnes* werkyth to vs here in erth payne, shame and sorow, ryght so on the *contrary wyse* grace werkyth to vs in hevyn solace, wurschyp and blysse, ovyr passyng so forth that when we come vppe and receyve that swete reward whych grace hath wrought to vs, there we shall thanke and blysse oure lorde, *endlessly enjoyeng that evyr we sufferyd woo*; and that shalle

be for a properte of blessyd loue that we shalle know in god, *whych we myght nevyr haue knowen withou3te wo goyng before.* (48.503-4; emphasis added)

[For I saw most truly that always, as our *contrariness* makes for us here on earth pain, shame and sorrow, just so in *contrary manner* grace makes for us in heaven solace, honour and bliss, so superabundant that when we come up and receive that sweet reward which grace has made for us, there we shall thank and bless our Lord, *endlessly rejoicing that we ever suffered woe*; and that will be because of a property of the blessed love which we shall know in God *which we might never have known without woe preceding it.* (263; emphasis added)]

This passage exemplifies her theology of the necessity of opposites existing together. Indeed, she admits that love in God could never be known without woe preceding it. Julian's faith that "we shall . . . endlessly [rejoice] that we ever suffered woe" suggests that she has the ability to see one thing in terms of its opposite. If earthly suffering is what will bring everlasting bliss, then suffering can be equated with (attaining) bliss, at least according to Julian's faith in the necessity of opposites and the transformative power of grace.

With regard to the long passage quoted above, Colledge and Walsh note Julian's use of the terms "contraryousnes" and "contrary wyse" and suggest that in doing so she implies the rhetorical figure *oppositio contrariorum*.[16] Whether or not Julian directly refers to a rhetorical figure here, she nonetheless infers that contrariness or antithesis is an integral part of humanity's relationship with the divinity. Indeed, Julian stresses such opposition elsewhere in the text in terms of her own spiritual growth and understanding. When, for example, Julian recognizes that domination of the flesh caused her to regret the pain she had prayed for, she concludes, "Repentyng and wylfulle choyse be two contrarytes, whych I felt both at that time; and tho be two partes, that oon outward, that other inwarde" (19. 372) ["Reluctance and deliberate choice are in opposition to one another, and I experienced them both at the same time; and these are two parts, one exterior, the other interior" (212)]. As Julian herself explains, the outward part "is our dedely flessh, whych is now in payne and now in woo, and shalle be in this lyfe" ["is our mortal flesh, which is sometimes in pain, sometimes in sorrow, and will be so during this life"]; whereas the inward part "is a hygh and a blessydfulle lyfe, whych is alle in peece and in loue, and this is more pryvely felte" (19.372) ["is an exalted and blessed life which is all peace and love; and this is more secretly experienced" (212)].[17] What must be noted in the first quotation is the simultaneity of the two contraries; she feels both contraries at the same time. Thus, at the point in her visions where Julian, through her inward part, says "I chose Jhesu to my hevyn" ["I chose Jesus for my heaven"], she clearly outlines the coincidental opposition between the inward and the outward. Moreover, with regard to this opposition of parts, she declares shortly thereafter that "both shalle be onyd in blysse without ende by the vertu of Christ" (19.373) ["both will be eternally united in bliss through the power of Christ" (213)]. That which she feels simultaneously here and now will be united through Christ later.

The spiritual goal does not appear to be that of ignoring or eliminating one part in lieu of the other, but for both parts to be "onyd" ["united"] in eternity. In the meantime, while Julian is still on earth, the two parts will work together toward the goal of oneness—a oneness only possible through the "vertu of Christ," the perfect coincidence of opposites. As Ewert Cousins suggests in his article on Bonaventure and the coincidence of opposites, there are three classes of coincidence. One involves "unity" which eliminates the original opposition, one involves "difference" or an ongoing juxtaposition, and one involves both unity and difference: "In the third framework, that of unity and difference, opposites genuinely coincide while at the same time continuing to exist as opposites. They join in a real union, but one that does not obliterate differences; rather it is precisely the union that intensifies the difference" (180). This "third framework" is the type on which Julian appears to structure her argument. In light of her faith in Christ and, specifically, in the Incarnation and hypostatic union, Julian's "unity and difference" approach is certainly not unfounded.[18] The structural framework and theological focus grounded in the coincidence of opposites is, however, extended to topics beyond those on Christ Himself.

For example, Julian describes human nature as having two parts in Christ, "the heyer and þe lower, whych is but one soule" (55.569) ["the higher and the lower, which are only one soul" (288)].[19] She neither negates nor subsumes either part; instead she insists on two distinct parts which, together and simultaneously, form one whole. Likewise, in a discussion of substantial and sensual nature (again, related to the higher and lowers parts of human existence), Julian insists that God "in his endlesse wysdom wolde that we were doubyll" (56.575) ["in his endless wisdom willed that we should be double" (290)].[20] She then extends her discussion of this double nature into the following chapter and concludes, "oure kynde is in god hoole" ["our nature is wholly in God"] and, likewise, "in Crist oure two kyndys be onyd" (57.577, 78) ["in Christ our two natures are united" (291)]. Ideas that may at first appear to promote or suggest a theology of difference are then subsumed into an overall theology of unity and difference or a coincidence of opposites. She speaks of two different natures, but these two are united.

Bond contends that "[t]he theologian can speak of the divine only in the language of paradox, of the reconciliation of opposites, which exceeds logical discourse" (94). This precept could undoubtedly be extended to mystics. Julian, as theologian and mystic, consistently uses the language of paradox and rhetorical opposition to represent her theology of coincidence. She describes her first revelation--a vision of Christ's blood--as "quyck and lyuely and hidows and dredfulle and swete and louely" (7.313) ["living and vivid and hideous and fearful and sweet and lovely" (188)]. She then expands on these oppositions when she describes Christ as "so reverent and dredfulle" ["revered and feared"] and "so homely and so curteyse" ["so familiar and so courteous"]. Colledge and Walsh comment on the rhetorical structure: "It is significant that to convey these paradoxes, [Julian] uses her favourite figure, *oppositio*" (313, n. 30). They appear to have based this observation on Julian's frequent use of opposition; whether or not the figure is Julian's "favourite" is perhaps questionable. Nonetheless, in this first revelation, Julian experiences the paradox that will become central to her visionary experience. The frequent antithetical experience "of wele and of wooe" (1.282) ["of well-being and of woe" (176)] that, according to her outline in the first chapter, forms the teaching of her seventh revelation, finds its root in Julian's initial reaction to Christ's blood as quoted from the first revelation.

Julian further situates her body between rhetorical opposites in the seventh revelation when she emphasizes the continual fluctuation between pain and joy: "And than the payne sheweth ayeenn to my felyng, and than the joy and the lykyng, and now that oonn and now that other, dyuerse tymes, I suppose about twenty tymes" (15.355) ["And then again I felt the pain, and then afterwards the delight and the joy, now the one and now the other, again and again, I suppose about twenty times" (205)]. According to Julian's understanding, this showing was meant to teach her that "some tyme to be in comfort, and some tyme for to fayle" (15.355) ["to be comforted at one time, and at another to fail" (205)] is advantageous to the soul. Moreover, Julian states that it is God's will that people do not focus on the woe "but sodaynly passe ovyr and holde vs in the endlesse lykyng that is god" (15.356) ["but that suddenly we should pass it over, and preserve ourselves in the endless delight which is God" (205)]. The fluctuation or exchange between opposites actually forms the means by which Julian can suddenly pass over into eternal life with God. The tension itself opens the "chink in the defensive wall of reason" and thereby allows access to the apophatic realm (Gillespie and Ross 56).

Given the dynamic of exchange just presented, Julian's statement, "Man is channgeabyll," can be seen in a new light. Man *is* changeable; that is, mimetic to Julian's rhetorical representation of exchange within the *Showings* (through *contentio*), her theological belief insists that people exist in a perpetual state of change or exchange. However, once union is achieved--that is, once a person has crossed over the point of exchange into eternal oneness with the divinity--God will make us "vnchaungeable" (49.509). This, as is stressed in Julian's theology, is only possible because of the "vnchanngeabylte of [God's] love" (79.703) ["unchangeability of [God's] love" (334)]. In other words, Julian sets up another opposition that involves the changeable and the unchangeable. God, in His divine nature, does not change; people, in their humanity, do change in order finally to reach the unchangeable divine. Julian explains in terms of contrariness:

> And thus I saw whan we be alle in peas and in loue, we fynde no contraryousnes in no manner of lettyng, and that contraryousnes whych is now in vs, oure lorde god of hys goodnes makyth it to vs fulle profytable. For contraryousnes is cause of alle oure tribulation and alle oure woo; and oure lorde Jhesu takyth them and sendyth them vppe to hevyn, and then they are made more swete and delectable than hart may thyngke or tonge can tell. (49.509)

> [And so I saw that when we are wholly in peace and in love, we find no contrariness in any kind of hindrance, and our Lord God in his goodness makes the contrariness which is in us now very profitable for us. For contrariness is the cause of all our tribulation and all our woe; and our Lord Jesus takes them and sends them up

to heaven, and then they are made more sweet and delectable than heart can think or tongue can tell. (265)]

Two key points are brought together in this passage. First, Julian emphasizes her belief that opposition is positive or "fulle profytable" and will eventually lead us into the lack or absence of opposition (change or contrariness) that is God. Second, Julian admits that this transformation is beyond what the heart can think or tongue can tell. She resorts to *adynaton* at the point where her theory leaves the realm of exchange and enters the unknowable, hidden union with the divine.[21]

Opposition is central to the teaching Julian receives inwardly and outwardly. She claims to be taught inwardly by the Holy Spirit and outwardly by the Holy Church. Julian does not shun the preaching and teaching of the Church; indeed, she maintains, during a discussion of her belief in the Church's teaching, that she wishes "never to receyve ony thyng that myght be contrary ther to" (9.323) ["never to accept anything which might be contrary to it" (192)]. Evidently, Julian does not see the inward teaching as contrary to the outward; each method of teaching (although perceived in apparently opposite manners) is merely one part of her whole body of spiritual education. In addition, Julian maintains that these two methods--that of the Church and that of the Holy Spirit--together form one part of human understanding and describes the other part as follows:

That other is hyd and sparryd fro vs, that is to sey alle that is besyde oure saluacion; for that is oure lordes prevy conncelle, and it longyth to the ryalle lordschyppe of god to haue hys pryvy connceyles in pees, and it longyth to his saruanntes for obedyence and reverence nott wylle to know hys connceyles. (30.415)

[The other portion is hidden from us and closed, that is to say all which is additional to our salvation; for this is our Lord's privy counsel, and it is fitting to God's royal dominion to keep his privy counsel in peace, and it is fitting to his servants out of obedience and respect not to wish to know his counsel. (228)]

Once again, the knowable is paired with the unknowable. Not only does Julian stress both outward (Church) and inward (Holy Spirit) methods of learning, but she also reiterates her belief in a hidden God.[22] In doing so,

Julian justifies that which she cannot explain. When Christ says, "That þat is vnpossible to the is nott vnpossible to me" (32.426) ["What is impossible to you is not impossible to me" (233)], Julian (and all her "even Christians") must have faith in these words rather than attempt to understand how this can be.

For Julian, such faith is the bridge between the human and the divine; indeed, faith is the quality that allows for the conception of an unknowable divinity at all. That which can neither be known nor spoken of can, through faith, be *believed* in. Julian separates conscious knowledge of the self from knowledge of the *true* self through faith: "But oure passyng lyvyng þat we haue here in oure sensualyte knowyth nott what oure selfe is but in our feyth" (46.490) ["But our passing life which we have here does not know in our senses what our self is, but we know in our faith" (258)]. However, just as a person can never completely know God, s/he can never completely know his/her true self. Faith apparently allows only for the possibility of a higher self; it does not provide direct access to that self. According to Julian, "we may nevyr fulle know oure selfe in to the last poynt, in which poynte thys passyng life and alle manner of woo and payne shalle haue ane ende" (46.491) ["we may never fully know ourselves until the last moment, at which moment this passing life and every kind of woe and pain will have an end" (258)].

Several key concepts can be found in these two quotations from Chapter 46. First, faith acts as a bridge between the human and the divine; that is, it allows for a connection between what the mind consciously knows and what the mind conjectures about the divine. Second, life is transitory, passing onward to an end point. Third, once this point is attained, woeful life ends and, one assumes, perpetual bliss begins. What, then, is this point? Colledge and Walsh translate "poynt(e)" as "moment"; likewise, in the passage where Julian claims, "I saw god in a poynte" (11.336), they translate "poynte" as "an instant of time."[23] In the footnote to the latter quotation, Colledge and Walsh admit that Julian may have "meant that she saw God as the centre of a circle," but maintain that "it seems more probable that she meant 'in an instant of time'" (336).[24] Neither one nor the other translation succeeds at interpreting *how* the term works within Julian's faith.

Gillespie and Ross suggest, "God in a point may be deliberately enigmatic: it is certainly non-figural and non-referential. It is apophatic in that one can imagine what she means without being able to represent it in terms of imagery" (72). However, no one (as far as I know) compares Julian's use of the word "poynte" in the "god in a poynte" quotation to her use of the same word elsewhere. Later in the same chapter, for example, Julian claims that God "is in the myd poynt of all thynges" (11.338) ["is at the centre of everything" (197)]. Both of these uses must be taken in conjunction with her concept of "the last poynt." In the case of "the last poynt," Julian suggests a point of transition between life and death; that is, she explains that this "last poynt" is the point at which "thys passyng life and alle manner of woo and payne shalle haue ane ende" (46.491) ["this passing life and every kind of woe and pain will have an end" (258)].25 In the case of God being in the "myd poynt" of all things, Julian suggests a space within the created where the Creator resides; likewise, in the case of seeing "god in a poynte," Julian suggests a space in which she, a human being, can locate God, the divinity. In each instance, Julian's "poynt(e)" acts as a point of access to the divine--whether that point be the last point of earthly life (and, thus, the first point of everlasting life with God) or the point in which God Himself resides. As will be emphasized below, Julian's "poynt(e)" can be understood as a point of access to the apophatic realm.

Julian's use of "poynt(e)" must also be examined in connection with her use of the expression "in a touch." As with their translation of "poynt(e)," Colledge and Walsh translate Julian's use of the expression, "in a touch," as "in an instant" or "in a brief moment."26 Their translation suggests that Julian's use of "in a poynte" is synonymous with her use of "in a touch." However, as I will illustrate, a distinction can and should be made between the two. Whereas "in a poynte" indicates a space (albeit a liminal and abstract space) beyond which one can only conjecture the ineffable, "in a touch" indicates a rift in temporal knowledge. When Julian claims to understand Christ's Passion "for the most payn and ovyr passyng" ["for the greatest and surpassing pain"], she immediately notes, "thys was shewde in a touch, redely passyd ovyr in to comfort" (27.406) ["this was shown to me in an instant, and it quickly turned into consolation" (225)]. The "touch" collapses time in that Julian feels only Christ's pain before it and His comfort after it; she does not indicate an extended period of transition between the pain and the comfort. As opposed to the way Julian uses "in a poynt(e)"--that is, as a nexus between opposites--she uses "in a touch" more distinctly as a temporal shift.27

This distinction is especially important when considering Julian's conception of our space and/or time on earth. Julian's use of "poynte" later in the text acts to collapse the distinction between space and time. In Chapter 64, Julian discusses the pain of this world and repeats three times (in close proximity) the Lord's promise, "Sodeynly thou shalte be taken from all thy payne" (64.620) ["Suddenly you will be taken out of all your pain" (306)]. Julian's repetition of the word "suddenly" emphasizes the instantaneousness of the transformation from pain to well-being and suggests a preoccupation with the time frame in which the transformation will occur.[28] Indeed, the conception of a lack of time begins to surface. This concept is likewise emphasized when Julian then discusses human patience over the "vnknowyng" of the time of death. Whereas each person has a conscious awareness of life, s/he has a complete lack of awareness--an unknowing--of the time of death. In other words, Julian again acknowledges an aspect of God's plan that remains hidden or unknown until the point of crossing.

Establishing the sudden and unknowable nature of the time of death is an essential step in establishing a similar chasm of unknowing within life itself. Immediately following her discussion of patience (over the time of living) and unknowing (over the time of passing), Julian discusses a further relationship between life and death: "And also god wylle that whyle the soule is in the body, it seeme to it selfe þat it is evyr *at þe poynte* to be takyn. For alle this lyfe and thys longyng that we haue here is *but a poynt*, and when we be takyn *sodeynly* out of payne in to blesse, than payn shall be *nought*." (64.622; emphasis added) ["Then, too, it is God's will that so long as the soul is in the body it should seem to a man that he is always *on the point* of being taken. For all this life and this longing we have here is *only an instant of time*, and when we are *suddenly* taken into bliss out of pain, then pain will be *nothing*" (306; emphasis added)]. Colledge and Walsh translate the first "poynte" simply as "point" and the second "poynt" as "instant of time" (306). However, given Julian's use of "poynt(e)" elsewhere in her *Showings*, the two examples here do not necessarily refer only to time. The first example--"at þe poynte" of being taken--can imply both time and space. That is, at any time or place a person may be taken; at any time or place, a person may enter the "poynte" between the pain of life and the bliss of the afterlife. Note, however, that the sentence has a qualifier: so long as the soul is in the body. In other words, the body itself is not "at þe poynte"; only the soul will be taken and, therefore, only the soul in its relationship with the body is ever (and always) "at þe poynte." Thus, even this example of "poynt" occurs rhetorically amidst the apparent opposites of body and soul.

The second example, in which Julian claims that all life and longing "is but a poynt," also needs examination. Certainly, "poynt" in this case could mean an "instant in time," but what would that imply? How, moreover, does that relate to Julian's other uses of "poynt(e)"? If, to begin with the last question, a "poynt(e)" is something situated between two other (and opposite) things, then this "poynt" is situated between pain and bliss (or life and death). Remember, moreover, that Julian speaks of life and longing--meaning, presumably, a longing for God or, more specifically, a reference back to the beginning of the chapter where Julian speaks of the "grete longyng and desyer of goddys gyfte to be delyuerde of this worlde" (64.619) ["great longing and desire of God's gift to be delivered from this world" (305)]. The life and longing to be with God is "but a poynt" from which we are "takyn sodeynly" and at which pain will become "nought." Thus, the "poynt" is both the crossing point between the life of pain and the "nought" thereafter.

Much earlier in the text, Julian makes reference to a similar (and perhaps identical) idea while discussing Christ's appearance on the cross. She emphasizes the change in His appearance (implying that the change is from one of suffering to one of joy) and then continues, "Sodeynly he shalle channge hys chere to vs, and we shal be with hym in hevyn. Betwene that one and that other shalle alle be one tyme" (21.380) ["Suddenly he will change his appearance for us, and we shall be with him in heaven. Between the one and the other all will be a single era" (215)]. Immediately prior to these comments, Julian notes that people will suffer pain with Christ "in to the last poynt." As in the passage from Chapter 64, Julian here combines a temporal reference ("suddenly") with a reference to "poynt(e)." Once again, we find reference to the point between life and death (pain and bliss/suffering and joy), followed by a reference to a sudden change which, in turn, results in an apparent melding or deletion of space and/or time. That is, in Chapter 64 the sudden change between pain and bliss results in "nought" and in Chapter 21 the sudden change between suffering and joy results in "one tyme" (or, potentially, "no tyme")[29] and, thus, is consistent with the idea of coincidence--as the point where suffering and joy coincide.

A potential meaning of "poynt" as a reference to life itself still remains to be considered. Julian claims, as quoted above, that "lyfe . . . is but a poynt" (64.622); but to understand this, we must take into account an aspect of Julian's theology not directly referred to in these passages. Two chapters prior to her comment that life is "but a poynt," Julian discusses how nature (or "kynd") flows in and out of God: "God is kynd in his being. . . . And alle kyndes that he hath made to flowe out of hym to werke his wylle, it shulde be restoryd and brought agayne in to hym by saluacion of man throw the werkyng of grace" (62.611-12) ["God is essence in his very nature. . . . And all natures which he has made to flow out of him to work his will, they will be restored and brought back into him by the salvation of man through the operation of grace" (302-3)]. The idea that all nature flows out of God and that all shall be restored in Him again suggests that human nature (life, as we know it) exists between the emanation and return. In this sense, Julian's "poynt" could be a reference to the space and time filled by life itself as it exists between a coming from and returning to God. As will be discussed further, this space and time appears to be negligible, as if reduced or even deleted when witnessed from the (theoretical) perspective beyond the point of death. In other words, from a certain point of view, life is merely a "poynt(e)."

Given Julian's belief in an emanation from and return to God, given her belief in "one tyme" (or "no tyme") between life and death, and given her use of "poynt(e)" as a *place/space* (albeit an abstract one) throughout the text, her concept that this life and the longing that people have here is "but a poynt" can be taken both temporally and spatially. If, however, life is merely a temporal and spatial point of crossing, Julian's point of view appears to be from a time and place beyond life. Julian cannot actually witness and write about life from a time and place beyond life; however, as a matter of faith, she can imagine life from God's point of view. She does, after all, claim to envision the entire world, or "all that is made" (5.300)[30] from such a perspective in the "hazelnut" passage. Yet a complex dynamic arises in Julian's theological thought when the life is "but a poynt" quotation is considered in conjunction with the claims that she "saw god in a poynte" and that God "is in the myd poynt of all thynges" (11.336, 338). If God is a point and life is a point, is God (by syllogism) life?

Elsewhere, Julian does indeed make statements that, when taken together, suggest the possibility of God being the source for life. That is, she makes numerous references to the idea that God is, in one way or another, within humankind. She discusses, for example, the concept that the soul is united with and resides in God and, shortly thereafter, concludes: "God is more nerer to vs than oure owne soule" (56.571). Moreover, she claims that God is "more nere to vs than tonge may telle or harte may thyngke" (72.662) ["nearer to us than tongue can tell or heart can think" (320)]. Both of these quotations suggest that God resides extremely near or within each person. Julian also contends that "in man is god, and in god is alle" (9.322).[31] This last quotation brings together the idea of God as a mid-point of creation with the apparently opposite concept that "we, soule and body, [are] cladde and enclosydde in the goodnes of god" (6.307) ["we, soul and body, [are] clad and enclosed in the goodness of God" (186)]; that is, not only is humankind enclosed in God, but He is also enclosed in humankind.

The rhetorical structure of these thoughts is *chiastic*.[32] Julian thereby emphasizes a reciprocal relationship between God and humanity. The "in man is god, and in god is alle" statement is also paradoxical in that it suggests a God who resides both inside and outside of His creation. This belief is not synonymous with the concept of God's omnipresence. Julian does not simply say, "God is everywhere"; instead she makes a deliberately paradoxical statement. If the statement is taken as such and is not glossed over with a "God is everywhere" explanation, this paradox can be understood to open the way (or "chink in the wall" as it were) to the apophatic realm. Conceivably, it is at the point of crossing between the inside and the outside (or, as represented rhetorically, between the crossing of the two halves of the "in man is god/in god is alle" *chiasm*) where Julian can be said to have glimpsed "god in a poynte."

Life as a "poynt," moreover, can be seen as the temporal counterpart to the eternal "myd poynt" that is God. Whereas Julian glimpses "god in a poynte" from her temporal-bound position, she gains an apparently eternal point of view when she sees that "lyfe . . . is but a poynt."[33] Julian cannot gain access to an eternal point of view; however, the repetition of "poynt(e)" throughout the *Showings* helps her to suggest that very possibility. In addition to "all that is made" "lying in þe palme of [her] hand" (5.299),[34] Julian sees both God and human life as a point. Through rhetorical manipulation of one word, Julian subtly gives herself, as narrator, an omniscient point of view.

Julian also manipulates space through the rhetorical construction of dwellings. That is, Julian creates metaphorical dwellings in which she locates the divinity; as will be seen, the dwelling place is also connected with the "poynt." Most of these dwellings are centered in the soul and, thereby, reinforce the "in man is god" passage quoted above. She explains, for example, that God "made mannes soule to be his owne cytte and his dwellyng place" (51.525) ["made man's soul to be his own city and his dwelling place" (272)] and that "in vs is [Jesus's] homelyest home and his endlesse dwellyng" (68.641) ["in us is [Jesus's] home of homes and his everlasting dwelling" (313)]). Julian also recaptures the reciprocity of such human/divine indwelling:

> For I saw full suerly that oure substannce is in god, and also I saw that in oure sensualyte god is, for in the same *poynt* that oure soule is made sensuall, in the same *poynt* is the cytte of god, ordeyned to hym fro without begynnyng. In whych cytte he comyth, and nevyr shall remeve it, for god is nevyr out of the soule, in whych he shalle dwell blessydly without end. (55.566-7; emphasis added)

> [For I saw very surely that our substance is in God, and I also saw that God is in our sensuality, for in the same instant and place in which our soul is made sensual, in that same instant and place exists the city of God, ordained for him from without beginning. He comes into this city and will never depart from it, for God is never out of the soul, in which he will dwell blessedly without end. (287)]

Julian again uses the word "poynt" to refer to something both temporal and spatial; indeed, Colledge and Walsh translate "poynt" in this instance as "instant and place." Arguably, the first "poynt" refers to the temporal moment at which "our soul is made sensual" and the second "poynt" refers to the spatial location of "the city of God." Julian's use of the same word in reference to two separate incidents supports the possibility that her use of "poynt(e)" elsewhere also implies both time and space. Moreover, she speaks here of the soul becoming sensual or entering the body and, simultaneously, suggests a link between the human (soul and body) and the divinity in the capacity of the city of God. Once again the "poynt" is the nexus between opposites--in this case, between the human and the divine-- and, therefore, again represents the apophatic moment of exchange.

Besides her belief that God dwells within humankind, Julian also discusses the possibility of human entrance into the divine realm. In one such passage, Julian describes Christ looking into the wound in His side and explaining that this wound will be occupied by people: "[W]ith hys swete lokyng he led forth the vnderstandyng of hys creature by the same wound in to hys syd with in; and ther he shewyd a feyer and delectable place, and large jnow for alle mankynde that shalle be savyd and rest in pees and in loue" (24.394-5) ["[W]ith his sweet regard he drew his creature's understanding into his side by the same wound; and there he revealed a fair and delectable place, large enough for all mankind that will be saved and will rest in peace and in love" (220)]. Julian's description of Christ's offer of a dwelling place can be seen to reciprocate her often-repeated notion of the human soul as God's dwelling. However, this example not only speaks of a space in Christ but also describes that space in terms of an apophatic image: the chasm of the wound.[35] All the people who shall be saved will enter the chasm and, thereafter, will rest in peace and love.

This idea of entering into Christ is reiterated in another passage about emanation and return: "þe myd person wolde be grounde and hed of this feyer kynde out of whom we be all come, in whom we be alle enclosyd, in to whom we shall all goo, in hym fyndyng oure full hevyn in everlastyng joy" (53.557-8) ["the mediator wanted to be the foundation and the head of this fair nature, out of whom we have all come, in whom we are all enclosed, into whom we shall all go, finding in him our full heaven in everlasting joy" (283)]. By the "myd person," Julian refers to Christ. In their footnotes to the Middle English edition, Colledge and Walsh further suggest that Julian refers to Christ as such "because he is the second of the three Persons." More notable is their suggestion that the term "myd person" "may well be of Julian's own coining" (557). Given everything discussed thus far in terms of points, crossing points, and God as "the myd poynt of all thynges" (11.338), Julian's use of the expression "myd person" could well imply that Christ is the ultimate mid-point, the point of crossing or the coincidence of opposites, the epitome of the potential of human union with the divine. She also reiterates the idea of human life being a point between emanation and return when she explains how people come out of, are enclosed in, and, finally, return to the divine. Presumably, the "in whom we are all enclosed" clause--being rhetorically situated between "out of whom we have all come" (birth) and "into whom we shall all go" (death)--refers to our human lifetime, the point between birth and death.

Throughout her *Showings*, Julian maintains not only that the divine dwells within humankind but also that humankind dwells within the divine. Although these two ideas are not always presented together, they nonetheless combine over the course of the text to present a theology of mutual exchange. Julian frequently uses the rhetorical figure of *chiasmus* as a structural parallel to this aspect of her theology. Before elaborating on Julian's use of *chiasmus*, I submit a brief explanation on the theories of this particular figure in order to emphasize its significance to apophatic language in general.

In his discussion of the "word" (as a left brain phenomenon) and the "image" (as a right brain phenomenon), Max Nänny claims that *chiasmus* "as a pattern of words or textual elements partakes of these two dimensions: it can be experienced only verbally in time but its chiastic arrangement must be seen as a simultaneous, quasi-spatial pattern."[36] *Chiasmus*, thereby, is a figure that can be said to physically re-present an image on the page. However, in its rhetorical structure or "movement," *chiasmus* is associated with reversal. As Nänny explains,

> As a temporal or dynamic sequence, the chiastic series *abba* may be construed as reversing its movement or inverting its development. Hence, chiasmus may be used as an 'emblem' or icon of reversal or inversion generally. But the return to the initial element *a* at the end of the chiastic sequence may also suggest circularity and, ultimately, a form of closure or non-progressive stasis. Furthermore, *abba* may be seen as an emblem of two contrary movements, either towards each other, or away from each other. (53)

Thus, *chiasmus* can represent both inversion and circularity, opposition and wholeness. Furthermore, although the circular structure of *chiasmus* can represent closure, as Nänny states, it can also represent infinity in the sense that a return to "A" would necessitate a return to "B," then eventually a return to "A" and again a return to "B," ad infinitum. Clearly, the importance of *chiasmus* is not merely in its literal representation on the page, but in its figural representation of movement--in the continual turning and re-turning between opposites. Thomas Mermall claims that the structure of *chiasmus* is "symbolic of the fusion of opposites."[37] The figure is one in which opposites merge, where beginnings and endings become indistinguishable within a continuum. Hence, *chiasmus*, as it has been outlined thus far, is a figure of paradox and coincidence.

Nänny concludes that *chiasmus*, in its iconic sense, is "an important structural device which fuses word and image" (58). John Welch believes that *chiasmus* holds the ability to order thoughts and argues that "the form itself merges with the message and meaning of the passage. Indeed what is said is often no more than how it is said."[38] Rodolphe Gasché describes *chiasmus* as "a decisive ordering principle employed on all levels of complexity, that is, with respect not only to sounds but to thoughts as well."[39] Indeed, Gasché goes as far as to say that *chiasmus* is "an originary form of thought" which "as *the* form of thought . . . is what allows oppositions to be bound into unity in the first place. It is a form that makes it possible to determine differences with respect to an underlying totality" (xvii).

The concepts which begin to emerge from these theories on *chiasmus* are strikingly similar to those associated with the *verbum Dei*. As the Word is "the perfect coincidence of sign and signified" (Thomson 107), the figure of *chiasmus* is the perfect fusion of "word and image" (Nänny 58). Both are thought of as originary--an original state of totality to which one aims to return. I am not suggesting that *chiasmus is* the Word; however, the figure can act as a rhetorical representation that gestures toward the Word. The figure is paradoxical in its nature and perhaps, like all paradoxes, cannot be completely understood except at the apophatic moment of crossing (and here, not to be remembered consciously) where the opposites coincide.

The concept of this apophatic moment of crossing (within the chasm) is indeed part of the theory of *chiasmus*. Ralf Norrman acknowledges that between any two bilaterally symmetrical halves "is also a dividing-element which the chiasticist perceives as constituting a third entity."[40] Sanford Budick, moreover, "emphasize[s] that chiasmus creates a species of absences between its binary terms."[41] This notion of an absence or gap in *chiasmus* is crucial to the figure's ability to function; as Gasché explains,

> At the core of the chiasm one sees either an absence of contact
> between infinitely distant terms or terms contaminated by each other
> to such an extent that all attempt to distinguish between them
> corresponds to an arbitrary decision or an act of violence. This
> excessive gap or excessive opacity allows the chiasmic reversals of
> interpretation to take place, insofar as they provide the space for
> interpretative (mis)reading. (xxvi)

As may be ascertained from these few quotations, post-modern theories of *chiasmus* are (and perhaps unnecessarily so for our purposes) extremely complex. However, I feel it is necessary at least to acknowledge these theories in order to examine the possibility of the "chasm in the chiasm" which they put forth.[42]

Obviously, Julian of Norwich would not have been thinking of *chiasmus* in the terms of Gasché. However, she may very well have been thinking about it in terms of a representation of the crossing point between opposites. At the very least, Julian would have had exposure to the figure as it is used in the bible.[43] Modern research into the rhetorical structure of the bible has yielded numerous articles on the prevalence and importance of *chiasmus* in its structure. Yehuda T. Radday claims that *chiasmus* in biblical narrative is a "key to meaning" and that "[n]ot paying sufficient attention to it may result in failure to grasp the true theme" (51);[44] John Welch refers to *chiasmus* as "a basic aspect of the literary structure of the texts of the New Testament."[45] Furthermore, in his *Poetria Nova*, a text written in the early thirteenth century and used throughout the Middle Ages to teach rhetoric, Geoffrey of Vinsauf illustrates *chiasmus* in the section on "Easy Ornament" where "a mode of expression both easy and adorned is desired."[46] This section, a virtual sermon on sin and redemption, "succinctly summarizes the whole of Christian doctrine."[47] The specific example of *chiasmus* involves Christ: "O how holy the grace of Christ! How gracious the holiness!" (58.1174-75).[48] Julian would not have needed formal training in rhetoric to have heard *chiasmus* used in sermons as a means of "easy ornament."

Julian's use of *chiasmus* is remarkably extensive.[49] Along with the "in man is god, and in god is alle" example (as quoted above from 9.322), many of her chiastically structured sentences embody her theological concept of unity. For example, during her telling of the lord and servant allegory, Julian discusses how the servant stands for all men: "For in the syghte of god alle man is oone man, and oone man is alle man" (51.522) ["For in the sight of God all men are one man, and one man is all men" (270)]. Not only does Julian claim an understanding of God's all-encompassing point of view, but she also emphasizes the idea that opposites coincide in God's view by structuring the sentence with *chiasmus*, a figure of mutual exchange between opposites. In and of itself, this example does not contribute much to our understanding of Julian's theology. However, this is but one of several chiastically structured sentences within her explication on the lord and the servant.

Of particular interest is a thirteen-line passage in Chapter 51 in which *chiasmus* occurs three times. This passage spans over two paragraphs dealing with two distinct subjects; however, I quote the paragraphs together in order to examine the *chiastic* thought underlying both:

And all that be vnder hevyn, whych shall come theder, ther way is by *longyng and desyeryng*; whych *desyeryng and longyng* was shewed in the seruant stondyng before the lorde. . . . For the *longyng and desyer* of all mankynd that shall be safe aperyd in Jhesu. *For Jhesu is in all that shall be safe, and all that shall be safe is in Jhesu.* . . .
Also in thys merveylous example I haue techyng with in me, as it were the begynnyng of an A B C, wher by I may haue some vnderstondyng of oure lordys menyng, for the *pryvytes* of the *reuelacion* be hyd ther in, not withstondyng that alle þe *shewyng* be full of *prevytes.* (51.538, 539; emphasis added)

[And all who are under heaven and will come there, their way is by *longing and desiring*, which *desiring and longing* was shown in the servant standing before the Lord. . . . For the *longing and desire* of all mankind which will be saved appeared in Jesus, *for Jesus is in all who will be saved, and all who will be saved are in Jesus.* . . .
Also in this marvellous example I have teaching within me, as it were the beginning of an ABC, whereby I may have some understanding of our Lord's Meaning, for the *mysteries* of the *revelation* are hidden in it, even though all the *showings* are full of *mysteries.* (276; emphasis added)]

If the theoretical implications of *chiasmus* are applied to this passage, three points of crossing occur in this section of *Showings*. Prior to the first *chiasm*, Julian is discussing how humanity will be saved by Christ and enter a state of everlasting joy. She then explains that the way in which they will come there is through longing and desire. However, as discussed above in relation to apophatic theology, longing and desire must be given up in order for one to reach that which is longed for/desired. Within the structure of the *chiasm*, the words "longyng and desyeryng" are literally reversed; indeed, they are reversed again further along in the passage (as "longyng and desyer").[50] Yet the *chiasm* itself also creates an absence (or chasm) of longing and desire at the theoretical point of crossing. Julian may well be suggesting here that the way into heaven is through a coincidence of opposites or, more precisely, through the opening created at the point of crossing or (ex)change between opposites. This point of crossing is suggested rhetorically through the *chiasm* and theologically through the invocation of Christ (the embodiment of coincidence) both prior to and within the section quoted. Julian's statement that all will be saved in Jesus is also structured with *chiasmus*; thus, Julian once again reinforces her faith in the power of Christ and the coincidence of opposites.

This is especially relevant with respect to the mysteries/revelation/ showings/mysteries *chiasm*. Here, Julian juxtaposes that which is shown with that which is hidden. The tension between these two opposites is necessarily carried throughout the *Showings*; indeed, such tension between the seen and the unseen would be at the heart of any mystical text that attempts to verbalize the ineffable. How can the hidden be shown? How can the unsayable be said? For Julian, "this marvellous example" of the lord and the servant represents a pinnacle of her thought between the short and long texts.[51] Through it she has gained, as quoted above, "some vnderstondyng of oure lordys menyng" and it is this understanding that she structures on *chiasmus*. The final *chiasm* in the cited passage emphasizes the mysteries that must remain hidden despite the numerous revelations and the chasm that must remain void despite the numerous gestures toward it.

The *chiasm* is a single unit with two apparently opposite parts; it must remain as a single unit and cannot, without changing its very nature, lose one of its two "sides." It is in this way that Julian sees her personal relationship with the divine--reciprocal and everlasting. She writes near the end of her *Showings* in the context of Christ's promise of protection, "*I loue the and thou lovyst me*, and oure loue shall nevyr be depertyd on two" (82.719) ["*I love you and you love me,* and our love will never be divided in two" (338)] (emphasis added). The rhetoric of opposites remains, from beginning to end, a crucial structuring device of the *Showings*. Julian cannot fully represent God; she can, however, rhetorically reconstruct the coincidence of opposites--a concept rooted in Christ, the embodiment of coincidence between the human and the divine. Although she has not consciously reached the "poynt(e)" of union with the divinity, she can nonetheless reveal her faith in its existence, rooted in Christ's love. Indeed, Julian claims her book "is nott yett performyd" (86.731); performance of the ineffable mystical union with the divinity is beyond all words and all discussion of what each vision, each representation, and each rhetorical figure may or may not have meant.

NOTES

1. Space constraints do not allow for a lengthy discussion of negative theology and apophatic language. For the purposes of this essay, "apophatic" refers to that which is beyond all knowing. For a more thorough understanding, see Paul Rorem, *Pseudo-Dionysius: A Commentary on the Texts and an Introduction to Their Influence* (Oxford: Oxford UP, 1993), and Michael Sells, *Mystical Languages of Unsaying* (Chicago: U of Chicago P, 1994).

2. Clifton Wolters, trans., *The Cloud of Unknowing and Other Works* (London: Penguin, 1978) 66, 67. For the Middle English text, see Phyllis Hodgson, ed., *The Cloud of Unknowing*. EETS 218 (London: Oxford UP, 1944) 24.

3. I am not suggesting in this section that Julian necessarily had knowledge of the *Cloud*; I am suggesting that she describes an apophatic moment similar to the type outlined in the *Cloud*.

4. Edmund Colledge and James Walsh, eds., *A Book of Showings to the Anchoress Julian of Norwich*. Studies and Texts, vol. 35 (Toronto: Pontifical Institute of Mediaeval Studies, 1978) 2. 288. Edmund Colledge and James Walsh, trans., *Julian of Norwich: Showings* (New York: Paulist Press, 1978) 179. All Middle English quotations are taken from *A Book of Showings*; all modern English quotations are taken from *Julian of Norwich: Showings*. Subsequent references to these works appear in parentheses after the text.

5. Vincent Gillespie and Maggie Ross, "The Apophatic Image: The Poetics of Effacement in Julian of Norwich," *The Medieval Mystical Tradition in England*, ed. Marion Glasscoe (Cambridge: Brewer, 1992) 56.

6. Vincent Gillespie, "Postcards from the Edge: Interpreting the Ineffable in the Middle English Mystics," *Interpretation: Medieval and Modern*, eds. Piero Boitani and Anna Torti (Cambridge: Brewer, 1993) 140.

7. Oliver Davies, "Transformational Process in the Work of Julian of Norwich and Mechthild of Magdeburg," *The Medieval Mystical Tradition in England*, ed. Marion Glasscoe (Cambridge: Brewer, 1992) 39.

8. See Ewert H. Cousins's interpretative models in "Bonaventure, The Coincidence of Opposites and Nicholas of Cusa," *Studies Honoring Ignatius Charles Brady*, eds. Romano Stephen Almagno and Conrad L. Harkins (St. Bonaventure,

NY: Franciscan Institute, 1976) 177-197. Cousins outlines three basic models for the *coincidence of opposites*: 1) unity, 2) difference, and 3) unity and difference.

9. Karma Lochrie, *Margery Kempe and Translations of the Flesh* (Philadelphia: U of Pennsylvania P, 1991).

10. David Thomson, "Deconstruction and Meaning in Medieval Mysticism," *Christianity and Literature* 40.2 (1991): 114.

11. This essay is based on a chapter of my Ph.D. dissertation, *Crossing the Chasm: The Rhetoric of the Ineffable in Margery Kempe and Julian of Norwich* (McMaster University, 1995). In the dissertation, I argue that both Julian and Margery Kempe structure their writing with rhetorical icons that gesture toward an ineffable God.

12. *Contentio* is defined as "Contrary and contrasting words or sentences placed together" in Lee A. Sonnino, *A Handbook to Sixteenth-Century Rhetoric* (London: Routledge, 1968) 251. *Chiasmus* in its most basic definition "is derived from the Greek letter X (chi) whose shape, if the two halves of the construction are rendered in separate verses, it resembles." See Richard A. Lanham, *A Handlist of Rhetorical Terms* (Berkeley: U of California P, 1968) 22. Written linearly, the pattern of repetition in *chiasmus* can be charted as "A-B-B-A."

13. Julian may have had access to Bonaventure's ideas and, as Ewert Cousins argues, Bonaventure's work is structured on the coincidence of opposites.

14. H. Lawrence Bond, "Nicholas of Cusa and the Reconstruction of Theology: The Centrality of Christology in the Coincidence of Opposites," *Contemporary Reflections on the Medieval Christian Tradition*, ed. George H. Shriver (Durham, N.C.: Duke UP, 1974) 82.

15. See also: "Christ is the mediator of knowledge by being simultaneously the limited and absolute Maximum, that is, Creator and creature. He is the nexus both in the coincidence of the Infinite and the finite and in the coincidence of knowledge and ignorance" (Bond 85).

16. See the Colledge and Walsh edition footnote at 503.40 and its references to 372.25 and 500.11. Colledge and Walsh define *oppositio contrariorum* in their appendix of rhetorical figures by quoting Arbusow: "Combining a litotes with a corresponding positive affirmation" (744). Colledge and Walsh's definition differs from other sources; Sonnino, for example, defines *contrarium* (also listed as *oppositio*) as follows: "A *sententia* or pithy saying drawn from contraries" (251). My intention here is merely to point out Julian's use of antithetical rhetoric. The antithesis in the quoted passage can therefore fit under the general definition of *contentio*: "Contrary or contrasting words or sentences placed together" (Sonnino 251).

17. In their note to 19.372.25, Colledge and Walsh explain that the "two partes" allude to what Julian later calls "substance and sensuality" (for example, see 55.566-67). In general, "substance" refers to the divine quality of the soul, whereas "sensuality" refers to the "body informed by [the] soul" (footnote to 566.23).

18. Cousins's argument focuses briefly on how each of the interpretive models of coincidence of opposites relates to the "great religions." For example, he links Hinduism with the "unity" model and Judaism with the "difference" model. He then asserts, "Christianity is more difficult to place. . . . While sharing the Semitic affirmation of the difference between God and the world, its doctrine of the Incarnation necessarily places it at least partially within the third class: of unity and difference; for Christ is both God and man, joined through the hypostatic union" (181).

19. As with the inward and outward parts, Julian distinguishes the higher and lower parts as follows: "The hyer perty was evyr in pees with god in full joy and blysse. The lower perty, whych is sensualyte, sufferyd for the saluacion of mankynd" (55.569) ["The higher part was always at peace with God in full joy and bliss. The lower part, which is sensuality, suffered for the salvation of mankind" (288)].

20. As Colledge and Walsh note in their footnote to 575.59, "doubyll" implies "substantial and sensual"; that is, Julian here again makes reference to the higher and lower parts of human nature.

21. *Adynaton*: "To admit that one's message is beyond the power of words to convey" (Sonnino 248).

22. In Chapter 4 of my Ph.D. dissertation, I discuss Julian's numerous references to a "hidden" God in the "long text" version of the *Showings*. I use this observation as part of my argument that Julian moves from "a cataphatic exposition of her experiences in the short text to an apophatic representation of them in the long" (137).

23. Compare Middle English (11.336.3) with modern English (197). See also 52.549.38 vs. 280 and 81.714.5-6 vs. 337.

24. Colledge and Walsh do not provide much of an explanation for this "probability" in Julian's text. They merely cite a few references to the word as it is used in other medieval texts.

25. Throughout the *Showings* Julian makes clear her belief that the end of pain in life marks the beginning of joy in afterlife. For example, Christ explains to her: "Sodeynly thou shalte be taken from all thy payne, from alle thy sycknesse, from alle thy dyseses and fro alle thy woo. And thou shalte come vp abone, and thou schalt haue me to thy mede, and thou shalte be fulfyllyd of joye and blysse, and thou shalte

nevyr more haue no manner of paynne, no manner of sycknes, no manner mysselykyng, no wantyng of wylle, but evyr joy and blysse withoute end" (44.620-21) ["Suddenly you will be taken out of all your pain, all your sickness, all your unrest and all your woe. And you will come up above, and you will have me for your reward, and you will be filled full of joy and bliss, and you will never again have any kind of pain, any kind of sickness, any kind of displeasure, no lack of will, but always joy and bliss without end" (306)]. As will be discussed shortly, Julian also explains that between one state and the other of sudden transformation "shalle alle be one tyme" (21.380) ["all will be a single era" (215)]--that is, instantaneous. Thus, the "last poynt" at which pain ends simultaneously represents the point at which joy begins.

26. Compare "thys was shewde in a touch" (27.406) to "this was shown to me in an instant" (225). Compare "and this was shewed in a touch" (51.527) to "and this was shown in a brief moment" (272).

27. Similarly, during the lord and the servant allegory, Julian explains that the amplitude of the lord's clothing, "betokenyth þat he hath beclosyd in hym all hevyns and all endlesse joy and blysse; and this was shewed in a touch, wher I saw that my vnderstandyng was led in to the lorde" (51.527) ["signifies that he has enclosed within himself all heavens and all endless joy and bliss; and this was shown in a brief moment, when I perceived that my understanding was directed to the lord" (272)]. Here the "touch" again represents a temporal event after which Julian's understanding is changed.

28. "Sodeynly thou shalte be taken" is repeated at 64.621.22 and then varied slightly at 64.622.29-30 as "we be takyn sodeynly out of payne in to blesse." See also the following examples from other chapters: "we shuld sodeynly be takyn from all oure payne" (2.284), "sodenly all my paine was taken from me" (3.292), "they be sodeynly delyverde of synne and of payne" (39.451), and Julian's reference to the exchange between her body's pain and ease as "sodeyn change" (3.292).

29. I suggest a reading of "no tyme" here since, according to the textual notes in Colledge and Walsh's edition, the Sloane manuscripts (as distinct from the Paris manuscript on which the Colledge and Walsh edition is based) record "no tyme" instead of "one tyme." Certainly, "no tyme" would be consistent with Julian's theology as it has been discussed thus far; that is, "no tyme" posits a chasm of time resulting from (ex)change between opposites. I give this alternative reading of "no tyme" merely as a point of interest. Colledge and Walsh defend their choice of the Paris manuscript at length in the introduction to their edition. They criticize the Sloane manuscript(s) for mixing "archaic forms and modernizations" and for being "marred throughout by the persistent omission of words and phrases which the scribe--or his copy--had deemed superfluous to the sense, but which destroys Julian's rhetorical figures, which are integral to her thought" (26).

30. In what appears to be an editorial error on page 183 of the Colledge and Walsh modern English translation, the words "all that is made" are left out.

31. The modern English translation, "For God is in man and in God is all" (192) does not retain the *chiasmus*.

32. Wolfgang Riehle, in his discussion of Julian's concept of God's "indwelling," emphasizes her frequent use of *commutatio* (a form of *chiasmus*): "[Julian] tells us that God dwells in the soul, and consequently the soul dwells in God. . . . Such an antithetical mode of expression *which is formed along the lines of the rhetorical figure of commutatio* and which illustrates the indissolubility of the union between the soul and God, is *highly characteristic of the style of her mystical language*. It does not, however, detract from the individuality of her dialectically skilful style if we observe that similar linguistic formulations can occasionally be found in German mysticism. . . . And there cannot be really any question of an influence from German mysticism here. The parallelism would seem rather to be the result of both going back to the same source, namely the words of Christ in John 6:56, where there is already a hint of this antithesis." See Wolfgang Riehle, *The Middle English Mystics*, trans. Bernard Standring (London: Routledge, 1981) 130-31; emphasis added.

33. Although Julian's use of "poynt(e)" has never (to my knowledge) been discussed in the way I have brought forth here, Joan Nuth does make a suggestion along these lines: "When Julian 'saw God in a point' in the third revelation, she received a fleeting glimpse of God's point of view. The basic difference between God's perspective and ours lies in the fact that God is eternal Being and we are temporal beings." See Joan M. Nuth, *Wisdom's Daughter: The Theology of Julian of Norwich*. (New York: Crossroad, 1991) 100.

34. These quotations refer to the object she describes as having "the quantitie of an haselnott" (5.299).

35. In their article on "The Apophatic Image," Vincent Gillespie and Maggie Ross never directly define "apophatic image." However, they do imply by examples throughout the article that such images are associated with absence or emptiness. Indeed, they begin their discussion with a description of "empty spaces" in the bible. One such space is the empty tomb in the New Testament which they refer to as being "eloquent in its absence of presence" (53). They later refer to the crown of thorns as having an "apophatic centre surrounded by the signs of human suffering" (59). The emptiness of the apophatic image is, in theory, "non-figural" and, because of this absence of figural significance, causes the mind's "usual interpretative strategies" to be "temporarily suspended" (57). Thus, through the suspension of such conscious strategies, the mind moves from "the world of signs to the world of the apophatic" (55).

36. Max Nänny, "Chiasmus in Literature: Ornament or Function?" *Word and Image: A Journal of Verbal Visual Enquiry* 4.1 (1988): 51.

37. Thomas Mermall, "The Chiasmus: Unamuno's Master Trope," *PMLA* 105.2 (1990): 251.

38. John W. Welch, Introduction, *Chiasmus in Antiquity: Structures, Analyses, Exegesis, ed.* John W. Welch (Hildesheim: Gerstenberg, 1981) 11.

39. Rodolphe Gasché, Introduction, *Readings in Interpretation: Hölderlin, Hegel, Heidegger*, ed. Andrzej Warminski (Minneapolis: U of Minnesota P, 1987) xvi.

40. Ralf Norrman, *Samuel Butler and the Meaning of Chiasmus* (London: Macmillan, 1986) 21.

41. Sanford Budick, "Chiasmus and the Making of Literary Tradition: The Case of Wordsworth and 'The Days of Dryden and Pope'," *English Literary History* 60 (1993): 964.

42. The term "chasm in the chiasm" is used by Gasché in reference to Warminski's work (xxv). I have adopted the term to refer to the apophatic space where opposites merge--the moment of suspended self-consciousness.

43. As Colledge and Walsh indicate in footnotes throughout their editions of the *Showings*, Julian makes continual references and allusions to the bible. Julian would have had access to biblical material through sermons, other texts, and conversations with priests.

44. Yehuda T. Radday, "Chiasmus in Hebrew Biblical Narrative," *Chiasmus in Antiquity: Structures, Analyses, Exegesis*, ed. John W. Welch. (Hildesheim, Germany: Gerstenberg, 1981) 51. It is not possible to go into detail regarding the use of *chiasmus* in the bible. For more information, see further Wilfred G. E. Watson,"Further Examples of Semantic-Sonant Chiasmus," *The Catholic Biblical Quarterly* 46 (1984): 31-33; Antti Laato, "The Composition of Isaiah 40-55," *Journal of Biblical Literature* 109.2 (1990): 207-228.

45. John W. Welch, "Chiasmus in the New Testament," *Chiasmus in Atniquity: Structures, Analyses, Exegesis*, ed. John W. Welch (Hildesheim: Gerstenberg, 1981) 211.

46. Geoffrey of Vinsauf, *Poetria Nova of Geoffrey of Vinsauf*, trans. Margaret F. Nims (Toronto: Pontifical Institute of Mediaeval Studies, 1967) 56.1094-95. See also Chapter IV: "Ars poetriae: Preceptive Grammar, or the Rhetoric of Verse Writing" in James Murphy, *Rhetoric in the Middle Ages: A History of Rhetorical Theory from Saint Augustine to the Renaissance* (Berkeley: U of California P, 1974).

47. Laurence K. Shook, Foreword, *Poetria Nova of Geoffrey of Vinsauf*, trans. Margaret F. Nims (Toronto: Pontifical Institute of Mediaeval Studies, 1967) 7-8.

48. In *Poetria Nova, chiasmus* is referred to as *commutatio* (the Latin term referring to the same rhetorical pattern). I have used the term *chiasmus* rather than *commutatio* throughout this paper simply because of my reliance on material by contemporary theorists who refer to it as such.

49. Other examples of *chiasmus* include those at 4.295.11, 6.308.57-8, 17.361.13-15, 44.484.15-16, 57.577.17-18, 57.580.48-9, 62.611.13-14, 64.624.40-1, 65.627.3-4, and 72.661.18-20.

50. This double reversal forms an **ABBA**AB pattern.

51. The allegory of the lord and the servant does not appear in the short text.

"I wolde for thy loue dye": Julian, Romance Discourse, and the Masculine

Jay Ruud

Studies of Julian of Norwich dealing with gender have naturally focused on Julian and femininity because, as the first known woman writing in the English language, her female-engendered discourse is important and engaging, and secondly, the elaborate feminization of God in her "Christ as Mother" passages profoundly interests those concerned about a feminist theology. Accordingly, Julian's treatment of masculinity has received relatively little critical attention heretofore. But Julian's representation of the masculine bears exploring because, first, despite her striking "Christ as Mother" language, the majority of her imagery surrounding God is masculine, so that to understand Julian's theology, a reader should understand the masculine aspect of her God and Christ. Secondly, Julian makes another important figure in the *Showings*--the Fiend--unmistakably male and a figure engaged in a masculine competition with Julian's God. Like many medieval mystics, Julian owes much to the masculine imagery of romance literature, but her use of romance discourse in her portrayal of God, herself, and the Fiend goes beyond the merely conventional in its treatment of male- and female-gendered qualities.

To begin with, how typically male is Julian's God? What, in fact, would be expected of a representative male in Julian's day? Vern L. Bullough generalizes that acting like a man (for non-clerical males at any rate) meant protecting one's dependents, serving as a provider for one's family, and impregnating women. Failing at any of these might lead others to challenge one's masculinity, or to label one as showing feminine weakness.[1] Julian's God vividly displays all but the last of these characteristics.

When Julian speaks of her Lord, which sometimes means God the Father and sometimes Christ in his human incarnation, she speaks of him, first, as the protector of his vast human family; "he is oure evyrlastyng keper, and myghtely defendyth vs aȝenst alle oure enmys that be full felle and full fers vpon vs" ["he is our everlasting protector, and mightily defends us against all our enemies, who are very cruel and fierce towards us"][2] she says at one point, and later "he kepyth vs myghtly and mercyfully, in þe tyme that we are in oure synne, among alle oure enmys that are fulle felle vppon vs; and so moch we are in the more parell for we geve them occasyon therto, and know not oure awne nede" (78.697) ["he protects us mightily and mercifully, during the time that we are in our sin, among all our enemies who are so fierce against us; and we are in so much more peril because we give them occasion for this, and we do not know our own need" (332)].

Bullough's second criterion, that a man be a provider, applies equally well to Julian's God. Not only does Julian call him "the grownde, of whom we haue alle oure lyfe and oure beyng" (78.697) ["the foundation from whom we have our life and our being" (332)], but she emphasizes that he has made all of creation for human happiness: God loves his children, and "in this loue he hath done alle his werkes, and in this loue he hath made alle thynges profytable to vs" (86.733-34) ["in this love he has done all his works, and in this love he has made all things profitable to us" (342)]. Ultimately, God has furnished heaven for humankind, which will provide complete satisfaction eternally. In Julian's vision, God presides over heaven like the male head of a household:

And in thys my vnderstondyn was lyftyd vppe in to hevyn, wher I saw our lorde god as a lorde in his owne howse, whych lorde hayth callyd alle hys derewurthy frendes to a solempne fest. Than I saw the lorde takyng no place in hys awne howse; but I saw hym ryally reigne in hys howse, and all fulfyllyth it with joy and myrth. (14.351)

[And in this my understanding was lifted up into heaven, where I saw our Lord God as a lord in his own house, who has called all his friends to a splendid feast. Then I did not see him seated anywhere in his own house; but I saw him reign in his house as a king and fill it all full of joy and mirth. (203)]

God as ideal male is protector and provider. However, Bullough's third criterion, "impregnating women," hardly seems appropriate. Nevertheless, as Creator, God has sired the entire human race; and further, while not explicitly presented in a sexual way, God is very clearly portrayed as a lover in Julian's *Showings,* and one who keeps his beloved (Julian herself, as representative of the human soul) perpetually satisfied.

While the image of Christ as mother dominates the second half of Julian's visions, the first half relentlessly develops the image of Christ/God as the lover of humanity, and this love as the motive for his protecting and providing for his people. Often, in a way that might satisfy the spirit of Bullough's third criterion, Julian describes this love in terms that would apply to a physically human, masculine lover:

> our good lord shewed a gostly sight of his homely louyng. I saw that he is to vs all thing that is good and comfortable to our helpe. He is oure clothing, that for loue wrappeth vs and wyndeth vs, halseth vs and all becloseth vs, hangeth about vs for tender loue, þat he may never leeue vs. (5.299)

> [our good Lord showed a spiritual sight of his familiar love. I saw that he is to us everything which is good and comforting for our help. He is our clothing, who wraps and enfolds us for love, embraces us and shelters us, surrounds us for his love, which is so tender that he may never desert us. (183)]

The love that "wrappeth" and "becloseth" the beloved may have clear secular connotations. But God's love is purely true and honorable, its ultimate aim an eternal union with the one he loves: "And in the knyttyng and in the onyng he is oure very tru spouse and we his lovyd wyfe and his feyer meydyn, with whych wyfe he was nevyr displesyd; for he seyeth: I loue the and thou louyst me, and oure loue shall nevyr parte in two" (58.583) ["And in the joining and the union he is our very true spouse and we his beloved wife and his fair maiden, with which wife he was never displeased; for he says: I love you and you love me, and our love will never divide in two" (293)]. Certainly Julian does not invent the "God as lover" image. It was part and parcel of the affective piety movement of the later Middle Ages, culminating most strikingly with

St. Bernard's commentary on the *Song of Songs*.³ This new affective piety naturally lay behind much late medieval devotional literature, in which the presentation of God as lover is particularly commonplace. Nor, as Bernard's example makes clear, is employment of the image necessarily limited to women writers like Julian.⁴ What Julian does with the imagery, however, makes hers particularly effective.

Expanding from the basic presentation of God-as-lover, Julian develops that lover into a sort of knight or romance hero. This, indeed, was also traditional. The move toward affective piety paralleled the development of the romance genre, the popularity of which influenced religious imagery. Rosemary Woolf notes how, beginning in the twelfth century, "The theme of Christ's redemption of faithless Israel was . . . most commonly transformed . . . from the story of a husband reclaiming in his charity a lapsed and fickle wife to that of a king or knight fighting to save a lady and win her love."⁵

Perhaps what is most noteworthy in Julian's representation of the male Christ/knight is the consistency with which she develops and sustains the masculine "courtly love" imagery relating to God, and how she transforms the female narrator into a romance heroine in the process. The narrator as romance heroine responds to the male lover/God in conventional courtly fashion. As Marie Collins describes it, "For the women of medieval romance fiction, response to masculine attractiveness is governed not so much by personal beauty, . . . as by general 'personality', the sum of various moral and social qualities, and by awareness that a certain amount of careful thought must be devoted to the matter before commitment."⁶ Julian devotes a good deal of time to concrete descriptions of Christ's broken body, apparently chiefly as a meditative device; but she makes it clear that those torments which rent his flesh obscured what was in fact the most beautiful of physical bodies: "so feyer a man was never none but he, tylle what tyme that his feyer coloure was changyd with traveyle and sorow, passion and dyeng" (10.330-31) ["there was never so beautiful a man as he, until the time when his lovely complexion was changed by labour and grief, suffering and dying" (195)]. And when she pictures him in bliss with her "gostely eye," she sees "oure lorde Jhesu, very god and very man, a feyer person and of large stature" (68.639-40) ["our Lord Jesus, true God and true man, a handsome person and tall" (313)]. Most concretely, when she pictures the Lord in her allegory of the servant, he is described thus:

His clothyng was wyde and syde and full semely, as fallyth to a lorde. The colour of the clothyng was blew as asure, most sad and feyer. His chere was mercifull, the colour of his face was feyer brown why3t with full semely countenannce, his eyen were blake, most feyer and semely, shewyng full of louely pytte. (51.523)

[His clothing was wide and ample and very handsome, as befits a lord. The colour of the clothing was azure blue, most dignified and beautiful. His demeanour was merciful, his face was a lovely pale brown with a very seemly countenance, his eyes were black, most beautiful and seemly. (271)]

Julian's God, then, is undeniably physically attractive. But to be worthy of his lady's love, the romance hero must possess, as Collins asserts, more attractive moral and social qualities. First, he should have qualities that would define masculinity in that age: power and authority, courage, strength, action, and honor. Julian's Lord displays these in abundance. She calls him "hyghest and myghtyest, noblyest and wurthyest" (7.314) ["highest and mightiest, noblest and most honourable" (188-89)]. None dare question God's manhood, as he remains in complete control even in the face of the wiles of the Fiend, from whom he protects humankind: "hys myght is alle lokked in gods hande" (13.347) ["His power is all locked in God's hands" (201)].

Sin, however, challenges God's authority and honor, and hence his manhood. God is righteous and therefore bound to punish evil, and in so punishing to avenge his honor as any man must. Yet God is merciful, and Julian sees this as a problem. How can God forgive sin and still maintain his honor as a man? In Chapter 32, Julian describes how her visions provide her with a solution to this dilemma, a solution that preserves God's honor and, in fact, underscores his manhood: God will perform a great deed (one might read, a great feat of arms) at the end of history that will save those whose damnation had seemed inescapable. Julian had worried that sinners and heathens "shall be dampnyd to helle withou3t ende, as holy chyrch techyth me to beleue" ["will be eternally condemned to hell, as Holy Church teaches me to believe"], and so she feared "it was vnpossible that alle maner of thyng shuld be wele, as oure lorde shewde in thys tyme" (32.425) ["it was impossible that every kind of thing should be well, as our Lord revealed at this time" (233)]. But her answer comes in God's promise to perform the great feat: "There is a deed the whych the blessydfulle trynyte shalle do in the last day. . . . This is the grett deed ordeyned of oure lorde god fro withou3t begynnyng, tresured and hyd in hys blessyd brest, only knowyn to hym selfe, by whych deed he shalle make all thyng wele" (32.423-24) ["There is a deed which the blessed Trinity will perform on the last day. . . . This is the great deed ordained by our Lord God from without beginning, treasured and hidden in his blessed breast, known only to himself, through which deed he will make all things well" (232-33)]. Thus the challenge to God's manhood is met "so as," as Julian says, "it ware wurschypfulle to god" (45.488) ["as might be glory to God" (257)].

The aforementioned mercy suggests another aspect of the romance hero. For the heroine to grant him her love, he must possess not only generalized masculine virtues but courtly virtues as well. The most important of these virtues is courtesy. Julian calls her Lord "courteous" no less than nineteen times in the *Showings*. In courtly romance, "courtesy" implies more than simply polite behavior and speech. It is the chief characteristic of the knight/lover and is generally both the result of his love and the quality that makes him most worthy of being loved. D. S. Brewer calls it "an ideal of personal integrity, . . . but its quality can only be realized in benevolent *actions* or at least speech towards other people."[7] When Julian describes the courtesy of God, she consistently uses the term to speak of something the Lord has done for her or those he loves; in her vision of heaven as God's house, she says he fills his house with joy "hym selfe endlesly to glad and solace hys derewurthy frendes fulle homely and fulle curtesly" (14.351-52) ["gladdening and consoling his dear friends with himself, very familiarly and courteously" (203); later, she tells us that "by þe curtesy of god he forgetyth oure synne after the tyme that we repent vs" (73.670) ["by God's courtesy he forgets our sin from the time that we repent" (323)], and, on a personal level, "oure curteyse lorde answeryd for comfort and pacyens" (64.620) ["our courteous Lord answered,to give me comfort and patience" (306)].

The Lord's courtesy establishes him as a romance hero, but he also manifests other moral and social qualities expected of the knight/lover: Julian calls him "lowest and mekest, hamlyest and curtysest" (7.314) ["lowest and humblest, most familiar and courteous" (189)]. He is characterized by "hye plentuousnesse, largesse" (48.503) ["vast plenty and generosity" (263)] as every lover must be. He is peaceful and controlled, not quick to anger-- "where oure lorde aperyth, pees is takyn and hath no stede" (49.506) ["where our Lord appears, peace is received and wrath has no place" (264)]. And he is possessed of "kynde compassion . . . with charyte" as well as "ruth and pytte" (28.410-11) ["pity and compassion" (227)], so that he "comfortyth redely and swetly"(27.407) ["comforts readily and sweetly" (225)]. It might be noted that these latter virtues--peace, compassion, pity, the ability to comfort--are feminine-gendered qualities that have been coopted by the masculine romance hero. Such qualities, however, do not diminish the masculinity of the hero. As Susan Crane asserts in discussing Chaucer's *Knight's Tale,* when men coopt feminine qualities like pity, "the complications of masculine behavior that femininity figures contribute to enlarging and universalizing rather than feminizing the masculine experience."[8]

Indeed, it could be argued that all of the strictly courtly virtues-- pity, generosity, courtesy --are feminine-gendered, and that the feminine softening of male aggressive behavior is, in the romances, the work of love, which itself was often seen as a "feminine" quality. Bullough notes that Isadore of Seville, in defining *femina,* called love beyond measure "womanly" love. A man in love, therefore, acted like a woman (38). In romances, "acting like a woman" by acting courteously becomes the ideal of masculinity. Thus in Julian the Lord acts as the ideal masculine romance hero, whose gendered character encompasses both masculine and feminine virtues.

But speech is important to the romance hero as well, for by courtly speech he wins the heroine's love. And the courtly heroine could easily go astray at this point.[9] In the courtly tradition, since the manner in which the lover declared his love for the lady always followed the same conventions (he will be true to her forever, he will serve her, he suffers pain for love of her, he will die of his love, only she can cure his pain and bring him bliss), it was impossible to tell the false lover from the true.

Not so with Julian's God. To be sure, his language displays many of the clichés of the romance lover. The lady's perfect servant, "he hath made alle thynges profytable to vs" (86.734) ["he has made all things profitable to us" (342)]. The lady's *daunger* makes him wait, but he longs for her like an unrequited lover: "this is his thurste and loue longyng of vs, all to geder here in hym" (31.418) ["this is his thirst and

his longing in love for us, to gather us in all here into him" (230)].
Even when his lady is unfaithful, his truth remains steadfast, for like the
true lover he can never stop loving. He says to his beloved "Lett me
aloone, my derwurdy chylde, intende to me. I am inogh to þe" (36.439)
["Leave me alone, my beloved child, attend to me. I am enough for
you" (240)].

The striking difference between God and other romance heroes is
that the soul knows it can trust the Lord, because all of God's claims are
true, for he already has suffered and died for love of humanity. Julian's
God says "I loue the and thou lovyst me, and oure loue shall nevyr be
depertyd on two; and for thy profyte I suffer" (82.719) ["I love you and
you love me, and our love will never be divided in two; it is for your
profit that I suffer" (338)], and the narrator must needs believe him.
"Endlesse loue made hym to suffer" (52.550) ["endless love made him
suffer" (280)], she says. When he says he will die for her love, he really
means it: "How shulde it than be that I shulde nott for thy loue do all
that I myght? Whych deed grevyth me nought, sethyn that I wolde for
thy loue dye so oftyn, havyng no regard to my harde paynes" (22.386)
["How could it be that I should not do for love of you all that I was
able? To do this does not grieve me, since I would for love of you die
so often, paying no heed to my cruel pains" (217)]. The generosity of his
love knows no bounds:

> behold and see that I louyd thee so much, or that I dyed for thee,
> that I wolde dye for the. And now I haue dyed for the, and
> sufferd wyllingfully that I may. And now is all my bitter payne
> and alle my harde traveyle turnyd to evyrlastyng joy and blysse to
> me and to the. How shulde it now be that thou schuldest any
> thyng pray me that lykyd me, but yf I shulde fulle gladly grannte
> it the? For my lykyng is thyne holynesse and thy endlesse joy and
> blysse with me. (24.396)

> [Behold and see that I loved you so much, before I died for you,
> that I wanted to die for you. And now I have died for you, and
> have willingly suffered what I could. And now all my bitter pain
> and hard labour is turned into everlasting joy and bliss for me and
> for you. How could it now be that you would pray to me for
> anything pleasing to me which I would not very gladly grant to

you? For my delight is in your holiness and in your endless joy and bliss in me. (221)]

Like any other romance hero, the Lord considers it his duty to accomplish great deeds for his lady to approve. His suffering and death are only the beginning of the deeds he intends to accomplish for his beloved. That great ultimate future deed of salvation alluded to above is described in Chapter 36 of the *Showings*, where Julian says that God "shewde that a deed shalle be done and hym selfe shalle do it. . . . This dede shalle be begon here, and it shalle be wurschypfulle to god and plentuously profetable to alle hys lovers" (36.436-37) ["revealed that a deed will be done, and he himself will do it. . . . This deed will be begun here, and it will be honour to God and to the plentiful profit of all his lovers on earth" (238)]; and this mighty deed will win his beloved from the thought of any other lover, for surely it will be the "hyghest joy that may be beholdyn of þe dede, þat god hym selfe shalle do it, and man shall do ryght nought but synne" (36.438) ["the highest joy which can be contemplated in the deed, that God himself will do it, and that man will do nothing at all but sin" (239)].

Julian's God possesses all of the ideal masculine traits of the romance hero--attractive features, social and moral virtues, and courtly speech and actions. In her response, and her decision to love him, Julian's language places her in the role of romance heroine. She cannot abide being separated from her lover; "yet maye we nevyr stynte of mornyng ne of wepyng nor of sekyng nor of longyng, tyll whan we se hym clere in his blessydfulle chere" (72.662) ["we can never cease from mourning and weeping, seeking and longing, until we see him clearly face to his blessed face" (320)], she says. As the romance heroine has pity on her lover because he suffers so for the sake of her love, so Julian's pity in the face of God's suffering is the clearest sign of her love. As in the psychomachia which characteristically depicted the Lady's inner thoughts while she contemplated giving in to the Lover, Julian's Reason says to her: "But of alle peyne þat leed to saluacion, thys is the most, to se the louer so suffer. How myght ony peyne be more then to se hym that is alle my lyfe, alle my blysse and alle my joy suffer? Here felt I stedfastly that I louyd Crist so much aboue myselfe" (17.365) ["But of all the pains that lead to salvation this is the greatest, to see the lover suffer. How could any pain be greater than to see him who is all my life, all my bliss and all my joy suffer? Here I felt unshakably that I loved Christ so much more than myself" (209)].

Julian uses imagery for her own love of God that echoes traditional imagery used in courtly love poetry.[10] Qualities like courtesy, honor, generosity, nobility, and intelligence make the male worthy of love; only a lack of truth makes the lady turn from him. The perfect knight/lover Christ has all of these virtues, and Julian concentrates on other traditional images to describe her love. For example, the suffering of love-longing is like being in a prison: "And than shewyth oure curtesse lorde hym selfe to the soule merely and of fulle glad chere, with frendfully wellcomyng, as if it had ben in payne and in preson" (40.454-55) ["our courteous Lord shows himself to the soul, happily and with the gladdest countenance, welcoming it as a friend, as if it had been in pain and in prison " (246)].

A second example borrows another traditional image of the love poets. Here God is like the beloved who heals the lover of her deadly wound or lovesickness: in the spiritual sense, the longing to be united with God is a kind of lovesickness, and the pain of separation, the wound, is caused by consciousness of sin. But God will heal the wound. We must first feel contrition, Julian says, "and than shalle oure blessyd savyour perfetely cure vs and oone [unite] vs to hym" (78.698-99); and later, "we sorow and morne dyscretly, . . . seeyng that he is oure medycyne, wyttyng that we do but synne" (82.718) ["we sorrow and moan discreetly, . . . seeing that he is our medicine, knowing that we only sin" (338)].

Julian's greatest desire, because of her deep love, is to be joined to God completely. In language that suggests physical union, she says "till I am substantially vnyted to him I may never haue full reste ne verie blisse; þat is to say that I be so fastned to him that ther be right nought that is made betweene my god and me" (5.300) ["until I am substantially united to him, I can never have perfect rest or true happiness, until, that is, I am so attached to him that there can be no created thing between my God and me" (183)]. Even more physical is the later description of what it would mean to "possess" God "completely"--an experience that involves all of her bodily senses: "we endlesly be alle hyd in god, verely seyeng and fulsomly felyng, and hym gostely heryng, and hym delectably smellyng, and hym swetly swelwyng" (43.481) ["we shall all be endlessly hidden in God, truly seeing and wholly feeling, and hearing him spiritually and delectably smelling him and sweetly tasting him" (255)].

Finally, then, God is presented as ideally masculine in every way, and more specifically as the ideal lover in the courtly sense; he is, therefore, the fitting object of Lady Julian's love. But one of the chief determinants of masculinity, according to Bullough, is the ability to satisfy a woman as lover. Indeed, a husband's sexual impotency was ground for annulment or divorce (Bullough 41). Clearly God does not satisfy in this merely mundane way; instead, his lovers' satisfaction goes beyond anything earthly. The physical satisfaction the Lord creates in his lovers is the ultimate proof of his masculinity: "Arte thou welle apayde?" ["Are you well satisfied?"] God asks his lovers. "Yf thou arte welle apayd, I am welle apayde, as yf he had sayde, it is joy and lykyng enough to me, and I aske not elles of the of my travayle but that I myght apaye the" (23.392) ["If you are well satisfied, I am well satisfied; it was as if he had said: This is joy and delight enough for me, and I ask nothing else from you for my labour but that I may satisfy you" (219)].

If God is the perfect romance hero, then Julian is the ideal romance lady. But she is more than that. While God is clearly the male lover of romance, he is in the *Showings* the object of desire, and Julian herself is the subject. This reverses the most conventional roles of the courtly romance. As defined by Susan Crane, "Intrinsic to masculine identity in romance is the concept of a fundamental difference between self and other. In the dominant paradigm of courtships, women attest to their suitors' deeds and reflect back to them an image of their worth" (13). Thus, in romance, "The social position occupied by those gendered male becomes conflated with that of humanity at large, exiling those gendered female to the position of difference, otherness, and objectification. The process is central to romance's depiction of masculine maturation and courtship" (13).

In objectifying the romance hero God and making herself as romance heroine the subject, Julian redefines women--specifically herself as a woman--as human, while the masculine becomes the other. Julian the narrator repeatedly assures us that Julian the woman is only an individual representative of all those to be saved. At first she wants to share her visions with the Christian community: "In alle this I was much steryde in cheryte to myne evyn christen, that they myght alle see and know the same that I sawe, for I wolde that it were comfort to them" (8.319) ["In all this I was greatly moved in love towards my fellow Christians, that they might all see and know the same as I saw, for I wished it to be a comfort to them" (190)]. Later she becomes convinced that the revelations are not only about her and for her, but for all: "this shewyng I toke syngulary to my selfe. But by alle the gracious comfort that folowyth, as ye shalle see, I was lernyd to take it to alle myn evyn cristen, alle in generalle and nothyng in specialle" (37.442) ["I applied this revelation particularly to myself. But by all the consolations of grace which follow, as you will see, I was taught to apply it to all my fellow Christians, to all in general and not to any in particular" (241)]. As if to underscore the fact that Julian has coopted for women the designation "human," she has God show her another representative example of humanity--his Mother: "And also to more vnderstandyng thys swete word oure good lorde spekyth in loue to al mankynd that shall be savyd, as it were alle to one person, as yf he sayde, wylt thou se in her how thou art louyd?" (25.399) ["And for greater understanding of these sweet words our good Lord speaks in love to all mankind who will be saved, addressing them all as one person, as if he said, do you wish to see in her how you are loved?" (222)]. Thus in a reversal of the norm, by identifying herself and the Virgin as representatives of humanity, and also by insisting that those to be saved must all be designated "lovers" of Christ, Julian insists in the *Showings* that to be gendered female is to be human. God, the masculine, is the ideal, but also the "other."

But the masculine as "other" is not always positive in Julian. While descriptions of the masculine Lord fill the pages of the *Showings* in the first forty chapters, another clearly male figure dominates certain pages of the text, and that of course is the Fiend who torments her. In a description much expanded from the Short Text, and so one which Julian clearly spent considerable time carefully revising, Julian in the Long Text depicts her tempestuous encounter with the Fiend in some of her most vivid and concrete language.[11] The devil appears clearly masculine, clearly physical, and implicitly sexual:

> Ande in my slepe at the begynnyng, me thought the fend sett hym in my throte, puttyng forth a vysage fulle nere my face lyke a yonge man, and it was longe and wonder leen. I saw nevyr none such; the coloure was reed, lyke þe tylle stone whan it is new

brent, with blacke spottes there in lyke frakylles, fouler than þe tyle stone. His here was rede as rust, not scoryd afore, with syde lockes hangyng on þe thonwonges. He grynnyd vpon me with a shrewde loke, shewde me whyt teth and so mekylle me thought it the more vgly. Body ne handes had he none shaply, but with hys pawes he held me in the throte, and woulde a stoppyd my breth and kylde me, but he myght not. (67.635-36)

[As soon as I fell asleep, it seemed to me that the devil set himself at my throat, thrusting his face, like that of a young man, long and strangely lean, close to mine. I never saw anything like him; his colour was red, like a newly baked tile, with black spots like freckles, uglier than a tile. His hair was red as rust, not cut short in front, with side-locks hanging at his temples. He grinned at me with a vicious look, showing me white teeth so big that it all seemed the uglier to me. His body and his hands were misshapen, but he held me by the throat with his paws, and wanted to stop my breath and kill me, but he could not. (311-12)]

The details of this description bear close examination. The Fiend's aggressive physical assault on Julian with an attempt to throttle her is a blatant display of raw masculine power. Two details of Julian's description in particular emphasize the strength, power, and aggressive virility of the Fiend: his coloring and his hairiness. Although most commonly the devil was pictured as black, the red color of Julian's Fiend is not unusual. Jeffrey Burton Russell notes that although he may be associated with the colors blue or green (as he is in Chaucer's *Friar's Tale*), next to black the Fiend's second most common color is red, the color of blood and the flames of hell (Russell 69). The violence thus associated with the color underscores the power and aggression of the Fiend. But while the red of the newly fired tilestone is conventional, the dark spots in Fiend's coloring are not. Crampton suggests that these spots have their source in contemporary representations, or even personal memories, of the bubonic plague (197), and the association of the Fiend with death and pestilence, particularly in Julian's mind as she lay ill and, for all she knows, dying, would not be inappropriate--the ability to kill suggested in the allusion to the pestilence would further emphasize the aggressive violence of the Fiend.

This aggressive violence implies the Fiend's masculinity, but his hairiness in particular may denote as well his hyper-virility in a sexual sense. Julian's Fiend does not seem to have a hairy body, but has a very unusual coif, which will be considered below, and his head is especially shaggy. Hairiness was common in depictions of the medieval devil, and seems to have owed something to earlier fertility spirits who, while surviving in the later Middle Ages in depictions of the Green Man or Wild Man, according to Russell "lent their greenness and their hairiness as well as their unbridled sexuality to the Devil and his demons" (78). Considering Bullough's characteristics of medieval masculinity, this kind of virility certainly underscores the male-gendered qualities of the Fiend.

Thus Julian's devil displays the aggressive, violent qualities associated with the male, but without the refinements of courtly behavior displayed by the knight/lover Christ. But the sexual virility of the Fiend implies something more important for the *Showings* as a whole. In the first place, Julian's portrayal of the Fiend in human shape is a fairly unusual choice iconographically. Typically, the devil was pictured after the eleventh century in animal-like or monstrous shape. In folklore, when the devil assumed human shape (male or female), it was to entice a member of the opposite sex to sin, usually through lust. I suggest that the Fiend is presented in the context of Julian's romance discourse as God's rival for Julian's love: as Palamon must have his Arcite and Troilus his Diomede, as Lancelot must defeat Meliagaunt and Nicholas Absalon, so in romance discourse or its parody God must have his rival for Julian as well. The way he holds his face close to hers, puts his hands on her and throttles her all suggest that the Fiend is a contender for Julian's love in a physical sense. Just as her vision of united bliss with her Lord involved all of her physical senses, Julian's vivid memory of the "heet and . . . stynch" (69.648) associated with the devil's assault emphasize the sensual nature of the encounter. The stench itself in particular may be associated with lust: David F. Tinsley, in his essay in this volume, goes so far as to suggest that the smell connotes the danger of Julian's own lust, a sin which could clearly sever her from her relationship with God as her lover. Tinsley bases his interpretation on the meaning of such a stench in Gregory's dialogues. According to Tinsley, "it is entirely possible that Julian's readers might have associated the darkness and stench she describes with 'thoughts of the delights of the flesh.' According to this reading, Julian's fall into blindness is the supremely painful sin of turning away from God, her outer enemy is Lucifer, and her inner enemy is the deadly sin of lust" (215).

More than presenting Julian with a passive temptation, however, this highly virile Fiend holds her tightly, his face close to hers so that she can feel his breath and smell his body. It is a rape-like situation, but Julian the true lover resists the aggression of the masculine rival, and must remember that the ideal male God will protect her from her enemies. The situation puts the knight/lover Christ into direct masculine competition with the Fiend for the female Julian, the female "Everyman." Julian clearly recognized that "honor" as depicted in romance narrative was associated with male assertiveness and competition with other males, that the heart of romance discourse depended on a definition of masculinity that made possession of a woman a chief characteristic of manhood, and that therefore the woman of the romance could easily become the locus and excuse for male competitiveness. As Anne Laskaya says, in describing the genre as characterized by Chaucer:

Women, the focus of men's amorous desire, are presented as goals to be attained or as sexual territories to be conquered or resisted. It is common for them to be jealously possessed and/or protected by men, not adored. Women usually become the site of a struggle between men so that at the heart of Chaucer's depiction of men in love . . . is homosocial competition, rather than a courtly code praising the devotion of men to women. (78)[12]

Clearly the Fiend doesn't love Julian but only wants to dominate and possess her. Like Meliagaunt in the Lancelot story, he is the false lover who cannot keep faith. Like the false lover, he lies to Julian. He says to her:

Thou wottest wele thou arte a wrech, a synner and also vntrew, for thou kepyst nott thy cou(en)annt. Thou promysse oftyn tymes oure lorde þat thou schallt do better, and anon þou fallest agayne in þe same. . . . And this makyth vs a dred to appere afore oure curteyse lorde.

Than it is oure enmye þat wylle put vs aback with his false drede of oure wrechydnesse, for payne that he thretyth vs by. (76.687-88)

[You know well that you are a wretch, a sinner and also unfaithful, because you do not keep your covenant. Often you promise our Lord that you will do better, and then you fall again into the same state. . . . And this makes us afraid to appear before our courteous Lord.

Thus it is our enemy who wants to retard us with his false suggestions of fear about our wretchedness because of the pain which he threatens us with. (329)]

But his words turn out to be lies. Through God the lover of the human soul, "þe bytternesse of douȝte be turned in to swetnes of kynde loue by grace" (74.673) ["the bitterness of doubt be turned into the sweetness of gentle love by grace" (324)]. Things turn out quite different from what the devil has claimed, and in the end Julian can trust and rely on the Lord. Thus, unlike the words of the true lover Christ, the Fiend's words deceive and cannot be trusted.

Beyond the tendency to lie, the Fiend also displays a number of male-gendered qualities which in Julian's value system are conceived of as negative--aggressiveness, anger, a need to control, subdue, dominate-- those that in the ideal knight/lover are superseded by female-gendered qualities like peace and pity. As Julian depicts them, these negative masculine-gendered qualities make the Fiend not more of a man, but more of a beast. Certainly, as already noted, bestiality was typical of late medieval pictures of the devil in any case. As Russell summarizes, "among the common bestial characteristics given [devils] were tails, animal ears, goatees, claws, and paws (horns, not so common earlier, became standard by the eleventh century)" (131). This certainly explains the "paws" of Julian's Fiend, and goes far in explaining the teeth which frighten her so much. Her Fiend has no horns, or even beard, or any other animal-like facial feature, but it may be that the prominent white teeth are intended to be fang- or even tusk-like--the only bestial characteristic of a face otherwise human, like a young man's face. Thus Julian's Fiend, posing as a young man, physically displays his bestiality in subtle ways, as his male-gendered aggressive tendencies seem manlike but only make him more bestial.

In one sense, then, the Fiend comes up short in the competition with the masculine God by proving to be less than a man in being more like a beast. In another sense, the Fiend proves less than a man in being more like a woman. That is, in his ultimate impotence, Julian's Fiend is portrayed as effeminate. In the first place, the Fiend is impotent in his inability to make good on his threats or his designs; in this respect, he lacks the masculine qualities of real power and control that make Christ the ideal. As Julian says: "also sore he traveyleth, and as contynually he seeth that all sowles of saluacion eskape hym worshyppfully by the vertue of his precious passion. . . . hys myght is alle lokked in gods hande" (13.347) ["he works as hard, and he sees as constantly as he did before that all souls who will be saved escape him to God's glory by the power of our Lord's precious Passion. . . . His power is all locked in God's hands" (201)]. The Lord cannot lose the competition. The Fiend consistently challenges God's position of power, but just as consistently is defeated in the competition by God as the lover/knight.

The ultimate weakness and impotence of the Fiend who seems at first so virile may be implied particularly by some of the other details of Julian's description. First consider this: with regard to genuine masculine competitiveness, embodied in warfare, the most appropriate opponent for the Christian knight in fourteenth-century Europe might be the Saracen--foreigner and "other"--against whom he might test his prowess in a spiritually sanctioned setting. It might be noted that the dark skin of Julian's Fiend and his strange hair suggest a wholly other kind of male--one who, like a Muslim (the dark skin?) or a Jew (the side locks?) may figure a being outside the scope of God's love. The very specific detail that Julian's Fiend has long side locks hanging from his "thonwonges," which literally means *temples,* is highly unusual and invites interpretation. Why would Julian choose to emphasize this very specific and curious detail? One possible explanation is that the description owes something to the widespread tendency in the late Middle Ages to demonize the image of the Jew. Russell notes a tendency to depict devils with long, hooked noses, a trait "invidiously combined with racial stereotypes to demonize Jews in later medieval art" (132). Léon Poliakov goes further. He lists the chief attributes of the medieval devil as follows: "He had horns, talons, a tail, wore a goat's beard, and he was black. He gave off a strong odor. All these were symbols of lewdness and extreme virility" (141). What, then, in legends accepted throughout Europe in the late Middle Ages, were characteristics of Jews? "The Jews are horned. They are tricked out with a tail and the beard of a goat . . . the mephitic odors attributed to them are so violent that they have persisted down through the ages . . ." (142). Other than the odor already discussed, Julian's Fiend has none of these stereotyped attributes, but where else might the detail of the side locks come from?

The biblical injunction of Leviticus 19.27 forbade the removal or shaving of hair at the *peot* or "corners" of the head. The Talmud interpreted this regulation to mean that a man may not "level the growth of hair on the temple from the back of the ears to the forehead" (Mak. 20b). The extreme version practiced by Hassidic Jews today may not have been as widely practiced in the Middle Ages, but Maimonides gives specific instructions that "a minimum of 40 hairs must be left" in the temples ("Pe'ot" 270). There is no definitive proof that the Fiend's side locks owe something to images of the demonic Jew, but it is hard to account for them in any other way.[13]

This relates particularly to the fact that, in his weakness and impotence, Julian's Fiend shows *undesirable* "feminine" qualities. In this respect, Julian's representation of the Fiend parallels the depiction of "other" males, particularly Muslims and Jews, in late medieval folklore and literature. Louise Mirrer, for example, describes the effeminacy of "other" males in Castilian literature. She notes that, in the epics and the ballads, a connection between masculinity and militarism is made through enforced "feminization" of enemies.[14] In these texts, Christians often speak with threats and imperatives, and Muslims with polite expressions, flattery, and self-effacing utterances (Mirrer 175). Jews in the *Cid* speak with flattering epithets or, at times, empty threats, and engage in a great deal of fawning hand kissing. Their locus of activity, like that of a woman, is the home and not the battlefield (Mirrer 180-81). But the feminization of non-Christian males, particularly Jews, goes beyond these specific literary examples. Referring to folklore, Leon Poliakov asserts that in their association with the demonic hairiness, bestiality and stench, from one point of view "the Jews are hypervirile . . . but at the same time they are weak and sickly, suffering from a thousand malignant afflictions that only Christian blood can cure."[15] In particular, it was believed that among Jews "men as well as women, [were] afflicted with menses." Poliakov quotes the late fifteenth century Anton Bonfin, who in *Rerum Hungaricum Decades*, Dec. 5, Book 4, writes "suffering from menstruation, both men and women alike, they have noted that the blood of a Christian constitutes an excellent remedy" (143).

The point is that depictions of the medieval devil in general, and Julian's image of the Fiend in particular, depending as they do on stereotypical images of the pagan, Muslim, or particularly Jewish "other," suggest the effeminate characteristics associated with the "other" males as well. Thus Julian's Fiend, like Julian's God, is androgynous, but unlike the God that combines male- and female-gendered positive qualities, the Fiend embodies negative characteristics of both genders. And the effeminate and powerless demonic rival for Julian's love, therefore, becomes merely laughable in his defeat and impotence.

Thus Julian's rising from his attempt to throw her into despair torments the Fiend, a fact that merely amuses her:

and this glorious rysyng, it is to hym so great sorow and payne, for the hate þat he hath to oure soule, that he brynneth contynually in envy. And alle this sorow þat he would make vs to haue, it shall turne in to hym selfe, and for this it was þat oure lorde skornyd hym, and shewed þat he shalle be skornyd; and this made me myghtely to lawgh. (77.690)

[and this glorious rising is to him such great sorrow and pain, because of the hatred which he has for our souls, that he burns constantly in envy. And all this sorrow which he would make us have will come back to him, and this is why our Lord scorned him, and revealed that he will be scorned; and this made me to laugh greatly. (330)].

Jeffrey Burton Russell cites laughter as one of the chief means of negating the devil's power: "Protected by God's grace, we fend off the Devil with faith, humility, obedience, love and hilarity. Many of the mystics recommended laughter and hilarity as effective defenses against the Evil One, who longs to terrify us into despair."[16] In terms of the masculine competition characteristic of Julian's romance discourse, the effeminate male, raging impotently but powerless as a woman, is laughable--particularly to the lady who loves the true hero and spurns the advances of the weak "other."

Ultimately, in Julian's text, in the most ideal male (Julian's God), male-gendered qualities like power and aggression must be tempered with female-gendered qualities, like compassion and love. The romance hero, tempered by female love, is, like Julian's God, androgynous, possessing the ideal qualities of both genders. Furthermore, Julian the female speaker and lover of God, who addresses her visions to all those "that will be his faithfull lovers" (734n), uses her discourse to reclaim for women the role of "human." But there are certain negative characteristics which traditionally accrue to each gender; in Julian's text, all of these, masculine or feminine, belong to the false lover and uncourtly masculine rival--the Fiend--by way of contrast to the perfect knight/lover, Christ, and with his completely human partner, the female-gendered lover.

NOTES

1. Vern L. Bullough, "On Being a Male in the Middle Ages" *Medieval Masculinities: Regarding Men in the Middle Ages*, ed. Clare A. Lees, et al. Medieval Cultures, vol. 7 (Minneapolis: U of Minnesota P, 1994) 34.

2. *A Book of Showings to the Anchoress Julian of Norwich,* Eds. Edmund Colledge and James Walsh (Toronto: Pontifical Institute of Mediaeval Studies, 1978) 39.453. Translation is from *Julian of Norwich.: Showings,* Edmund Colledge and James Walsh, trans. (New York: Paulist, 1978) 245. Subsequent quotations will be parenthetically included in the text.

3. For a good discussion of affective piety, medieval images of Christ as lover, and Julian's knowledge of the affective piety movement, see Denise Baker, *Julian of Norwich's Showings: From Vision to Book* (Princeton: Princeton UP, 1994).

4. Richard Rolle, for example, writes of his love of Christ in clearly physical terms:
My sange es in sihting,
My life es in langinge,
Till I thee se, my king,
so faire in thy shining,
So faire in they fairehede. (ll. 1-5)
And later in the same poem, in terms clearly borrowed from the tradition of romantic love, Rolle writes:
Now wax I pale and wan
For luve of my lemman.
Jesu, bath God and man,

Thy luve thou lerd me than
When I to thee fast ran;
Forthy now I luve can.

("A Song of Love for Jesus," *Medieval English Lyrics: A Critical Anthology,* Ed. R.T.
Davies [Evanston, IL: Northwestern UP, 1964] no. 36, ll. 31-36)

It could be argued that in accepting the traditional Christ as lover/husband
motif, Julian is doing precisely what the patriarchal Church hierarchy would
encourage her to do. As Jo Ann McNamara describes it, "The imagery associated
with celibate women as brides of Christ was revived in male rhetoric [after the
eleventh century], where it firmly placed even the most resolute virgin in the
gender system as a structural wife" ("The *Herrenfrage*: The Restructuring of the
Gender System, 1050-1150," *Medieval Masculinities: Regarding Men in the Middle
Ages,* ed. Clare A. Lees, et al., Medieval Cultures, vol. 7 [Minneapolis: U of
Minnesota P, 1994) 21. But the image does not seem to work this way in Julian.
In reviving the Christ as Lover image, Julian effectively challenges the
exaggerated definition of masculinity that had grown among celibate males after
the new emphasis on male celibacy that effectively shut women out of positions
of power or, even, of personhood. But by reasserting Christ as lover, Julian
undercuts clerical celibacy that insisted on masculine superiority and creates a
situation where, metaphorically, the female must be part of the salvation
equation.

5. *The English Religious Lyric in the Middle Ages* (Oxford: Clarendon, 1968) 47.
Julian's Christ/knight as lover is traditional and has its roots in the affective piety
of the late Middle Ages and can be seen in English male contemplatives and
mystics of the earlier fourteenth century.

6. "Feminine Response to Masculine Attractiveness in Middle English
Literature," *Essays and Studies* 38 (1985): 28.

7. "Courtesy and the *Gawain*-Poet," *Patterns of Love and Courtesy,* ed. John
Lawlor (Evanston, IL: Northwestern UP, 1966) 85.

8. *Gender and Romance in Chaucer's Canterbury Tales* (Princeton: Princeton
UP, 1994) 21.

9. Marie Collins, for instance, cites the wife of the Knight of Tour-Landry,
who warned her daughters to be careful of smooth-talking men (18). But this is
only practical advice stemming from an all-too-obvious problem; the heroines of
Chaucer's *Legend of Good Women,* for example, consistently lament their
foolishness at believing deceiving men.

10. Lest it be argued that the conventional poetry of romantic love was
typically in the masculine voice, let me assert that when women wrote courtly

verse, they played on most of the same clichés as the male speakers. The
Countess of Dia gives this advice to other women:

> The lady who knows about valor
> should place her affection
> in a courteous and worthy knight
> as soon as she has seen his worth,
> and she should dare to love him face to face;
> for courteous and worthy men
> can only speak with great esteem
> of a lady who loves openly.

> I've picked a fine and noble man,
> in whom merit shines and ripens--
> generous, upright and wise,
> with intelligence and common sense.
> I pray him to believe my words
> and not let anyone persuade him
> that I ever would betray him,
> except I found myself betrayed.

("Ab joi et ab joven m'apais," *The Women Troubadours*, ed. Meg Bogin [New
York and London: Paddington P, 1976] 82-85)

11. For the suggestion that the detailed and visual nature of Julian's visions
was inspired in part by her familiarity with the school of manuscript illumination
centered in late fourteenth-century Norwich, see Catherine Jones, "The English
Mystic Julian of Norwich," *Medieval Women Writers*, ed. Katharina M. Wilson
(Athens: U of Georgia P, 1984) 272; see also Baker 42ff. Such a claim is, of
course, hard to substantiate specifically. But familiarity with the visual arts may
help to explain some specific aspects of her depiction of the Fiend, particularly the
side locks, as suggested below.

12. *Chaucer's Approach to Gender in the* Canterbury Tales (Cambridge: D.S.
Brewer, 1995) 78. These aspects of masculinity in romance discourse are deemed
typical of fourteenth-century society in general by many readers. See especially
Anne Laskaya 30. See also Monica McAlpine, *The Genre of Troilus and Criseyde*
(Ithaca and London: Cornell UP, 1978) 174; David Aers, *Community, Gender, and
Individual Identity: English Writing 1360-1430* (London and New York: Routledge,
1988) 126-27; and Stephen Knight, *Geoffrey Chaucer* (Oxford: Blackwell, 1986) 84.

13. Whether Julian would have associated devils with Jews is certainly a
debatable question. But the widespread medieval Christian identification of Jew
and devil is well documented, and an old but still valuable study by Joshua
Trachtenberg is a good review of the attitudes and their sources: *The Devil and
the Jews: The Medieval Conception of the Jew and Its Relation to Modern Antisemitism*
(New Haven: Yale UP, 1943) especially 11-52. Thus the atmosphere of Julian's

society may have made such an identification inevitable, as it was for Chaucer. In addition to this general anti-semitic atmosphere, it should be pointed out that Julian lived in Norwich, site of one of the most notorious ritual killings attributed to Jews--that of William of Norwich in 1144. Norwich, in fact, has been suggested as the model for Chaucer's city in *The Prioress's Tale*, both because of its association with a ritual child-murder, and because it had in the past had a Jewish ghetto like the one in Chaucer's tale. See Beverly Boyd, ed., *A Variorum Edition of the Works of Geoffrey Chaucer, Volume II: The Canterbury Tales, Part Twenty: The Prioress's Tale* (Norman, OK: U of Oklahoma P, 1987) 128).

14. "Representing 'Other' Men: Muslims, Jews, and Masculine Ideals in Medieval Castilian Epic and Ballad," *Medieval Masculinities: Regarding Men in the Middle Ages*, ed. Clare Lees, et al., Medieval Cultures, vol. 7 (Minneapolis: U of Minnesota P, 1994) 172.

15. Leon Poliakov, *The History of Anti-Semitism,* trans. Richard Howard (New York: Vanguard, 1965) 142-42.

16. *Lucifer: The Devil in the Middle Ages* (Ithaca: Cornell UP, 1984) 292.

Julian's Diabology

David F. Tinsley

Affective spirituality constitutes perhaps the single most influential aspect of religious experience in the later Middle Ages.[1] Best understood in the context of contemplative piety, affective spirituality was practiced by believers who wished to "stand alone before God" and remained "fundamentally private, unofficial and unstructured," thereby differentiating itself from liturgical exercises, which are "public and official" and largely shaped by "the Mass and the Divine Office."[2] Its practitioners, predominately but not exclusively religious women, immersed themselves in mysticism or in devotional exercises shaped by "penitential asceticism, particularly self-inflicted suffering, extreme fasting and illness borne with patience." Susceptible to spiritual phenomena such as trances, levitation, and stigmata, these charismatics were frequently forced to seek authenticity outside of the Book of God's Word, often in "visions and supernatural signs" (Kieckhefer 76). Central to affective spirituality was not just the experience of the Divine but also the call to communicate one's experiences to others, which explains in part the number of convents and religious houses in which "collections of the sisters' lives and visions were often read as a form of spiritual instruction" (Bynum 131).

The roots of affective spirituality stretch from Flanders to Teutonia, from northern France to northern Italy, and from Spain to Sweden.[3] Such broad proliferation and rich cross-fertilization gave rise to a remarkable range of spiritual experiences, two extremes of which are exemplified in the writings of Julian of Norwich, the "first English woman identified as an author" and Elsbeth von Oye, whose Zurich revelations comprise the oldest extant autograph-manuscript in the German vernacular.[4] Julian, the inclusa of East Anglia, describes visions in which the sharpest scourge is sin, and the inherently divine "higher soul" of the elect is assured of ultimate consolation at the breast of Jesus the loving mother. Living a rigorous, cloistered existence at the heart of the European continent, Elsbeth von Oye recounts years of bloody self-mortification in which her cross of nails awakens in God the desire to re-experience the suffering of His son. Her destiny is a total self-abnegation which brings God spiritual satiation; His joy begins with her despair. Each numbers herself among the elect, but for the anchoress of Norwich, suffering comes from sin and is ultimately transcended, while for the Dominican nun of Ötenbach, suffering defines all spiritual experience and only ends in death.

These two compelling and seemingly incompatible spiritual journeys both feature encounters with a sinister figure apparently made superfluous by what has come before. Enter the devil!5 Following scores of *auditiones,* in which spiritual experience is reduced to blood exchange and where no temptation is described beyond the desire to lay aside her cross, Elsbeth confides: "Whatever I have suffered from the cross that I wear outside myself, as is described in this little book, this seems insignificant in comparison to the real cross I wear inside myself."6 This real cross is the fiend. The suffering and despair that characterize her revelations--"In such deadly fear and terminal want, my heart never ceases to strive day and night"7--, are, in one brief and powerful moment, displaced by her terror of Lucifer: "and at these times it seems as if the fiend never ceases to occupy me and to strive to rend my limbs, and this brings such unspeakable pain that I cannot describe it in words."8 In a similar reversal, Julian devotes an entire revelation, the fifth of her long text, to celebrating the devil's impotence and the inevitable victory of the elect.9 She subsequently rewrites Genesis into a parable of the lord and the servant (Baker 83-106), in which the servant falls into the pit--with no help from the fiend's outstretched cloven hoof!--only because he is so eager to serve (Baker 107-134). The comforting image of Jesus as mother seems to ensure that "alle shalle be wele," no matter what the devil does (Baker 63-82). Yet Julian still finds it necessary to bring her readers face to face with Lucifer in the sixteenth revelation. Indeed no account of medieval diabology is complete without her unforgettably demonic portrait:

Ande in my slepe at the begynnyng me thought the fende sett hym in my throte, puttyng forth a vysage fulle nere my face lyke a yonge man, and it was longe and wonder leen. I saw nevyr none such; the coloure was reed, lyke þe tylle stone whan it is new brent, with blacke spottes there in lyke frakylles, fouler than þe tyle stone. His here was rede as rust, not scoryd afore, with syde lockes hangyng on þe thonwonges. He grynnyd vpon me with a shrewde loke, shewde me whyt teth and so mekylle me thought it the more vgly. Body ne handes had he none shaply, but with hys pawes he helde me in the throte, and woulde a stoppyd my breth and kylde me, but he myght not. (67.635-6)

[And as soon as I fell asleep, it seemed to me that the devil set himself at my throat, thrusting his face, like that of a young man, long and strangely lean, close to mine. I never saw anything like him; his colour was red, like a newly baked tile, with black spots like freckles, uglier than a tile. His hair was red as rust, not cut short in front, with side-locks hanging at his temples. He grinned at me with a vicious look, showing me white teeth so big that it all seemed the uglier to me. His body and his hands were misshapen, but he held me by the throat with his paws, and wanted to stop my breath and kill me, but he could not. (311-312)]

The prominence of Julian's "vgly shewyng" in studies of medieval diabology is matched only by the insignificance accorded it in Julian scholarship. By stressing the conventional nature of Julian's diabolical rhetoric, Colledge and Walsh hope to exorcise the devil from the body of Julian showings, reassuring us that "Julian's belief in the devil is firmly rooted in Scripture;" and that "all that she writes on the theology of the devil and temptation is of impeccable orthodoxy and is a model of restraint" (*Showings* 99-100).[10] Essentially they say that we have seen it all before. They are correct. No one would deny the conventional nature of the motifs Julian employs in her portrait of Lucifer.[11] While one cannot take issue with her editors' answer, this study will explore a different question: what *use* that Julian makes of convention, that is, what the choices she makes from the treasury of anecdotes, scenarios, and diabolical qualities attributed to the devil in medieval lore might have signified for her readers. For this one looks to texts which must have been as readily available to Julian, in whatever form, as the writings of Augustine and Anselm, for example, legends similar to those of the *Legenda aurea* and accounts of diabolical interventions such as are found in Gregory's dialogues.[12]

When measured against the theodicies of the great theologians, Julian's thought appears most thoroughly grounded in Anselm's satisfaction theory (Baker 17-19).[13] First, satisfaction theory is only realizable through the interaction of consoling a God with the redeemable soul. As Russell notes, "The essence of the argument is that God's fairness and rectitude restore to harmony a human nature that we had distorted by original sin," and that "salvation is no longer an abstract cosmic transaction between God and the Devil, but a free act involving real human beings" (*Lucifer* 170). According to Anselm, Christ's Passion is a sacrifice offered to God by the God/Man, a sacrifice "freely willed" by Christ. God in his mercy chooses to save us. Anselm also moves predestination and God's foreknowledge outside the debate by asserting that God's knowledge transcends causality and time, an effect Julian achieves by focusing on the anagogic reading of the fall. Like Julian, Anselm also grants the Devil, as a consequence of the fall, "limited powers to tempt and punish humanity," but no actual rights over us. The careful reader of Anselm has no choice but to conclude that "in the scenario of satisfaction theory Lucifer has little role" (Russell, *Lucifer* 170-171). The most one should expect of Julian's theodicy, then, are images of the frustrated and impotent devil of the fifth revelation, the pitiful and pitiable object of "scorne and game and ernest" (13.349) [sport and scorn and seriousness (202)]. While it is certainly true that Lucifer works mostly on the margins of Julian's showings, one also cannot deny that her portrait of Lucifer is expanded in the long text, that his image is concretized, and that he becomes more immediate and threatening. Focusing upon the parables of the lord and servant, Jesus as mother, and Julian's version of the fall in which the devil plays no role, theologically grounded studies of Julian's thought do not account adequately for what Julian offers her audience in the sixteenth revelation: the story of her temptation, in which a potent, threatening devil takes center stage, a Lucifer more reminiscent of that described by Gregory the Great, who sees the world as a "battleground in which we, as soldiers of Christ, stand continually in the front lines" (Russell, *Lucifer* 100).

Julian's life marks the end of England's spiritual insularity.[14] Beginning in her final years "several works by and about Continental women visionaries like Bridget of Sweden, Catherine of Siena, and Mechtild of Hackeborn began to arrive in England," even as "the writings of male mystics such as Suso and Ruusbroec" were appearing for the first time in vernacular adaptations (Watson 653). It therefore seems not unreasonable to examine *vitae* from continental spirituality in which the devil plays a central role. Particularly interesting parallels to Julian's experience can be found in the *vita* of Christina of Stommeln, a Rhenish Beguine from the second half of the thirteen century, the only contemporary nun's life included in the *Prosalegendar*, a collection of hagiography used for refectorial readings in Ötenbach or Töß,[15] and the *vita* of Ita von Hohenfels, whose role as the convent's patroness-savior and exemplar of productive suffering dominates the first part of the Ötenbach *Schwesternbuch*.[16] I shall also draw upon Suso's *Exemplar* and *Little Book of Divine Wisdom* for material on suffering and spiritual progress. My goal in all of this is simply to give Julian's devil his due.

II. The Enemy Within

In order to grasp the significance of Julian's encounter with the fiend, it is necessary to understand the peril with which each journey undertaken by a practitioner of affective spirituality to "stand alone before God" was fraught. Enclosure offered only limited protection. Suso's description of the three circles of spiritual protection, the cell, the monastery, and the world in which the cell brings reasonable security, whereas the world turns the soul into an "animal in the wilds . . . surrounded by hunting dogs" (*The Exemplar* 137), remains comforting only as long as one forgets that the hunting dogs could come from within. Nor was each vision, no matter how nurturing, an occasion for unambiguous harmony of the soul within the Divine. Each encounter, each "shewyng" could just as easily become an occasion for self-deception, temptation, or terror, and therefore had to be carefully analyzed. Christina of Stommeln's mentor Petrus de Dacia, citing Augustine's Genesis-commentary, reminds her that rapture could have a purely physical cause, as in the case of the insane or a cause removed from the body, or a spiritual cause, either characterized by the work of the devil who takes the soul into his possession with the aim of spreading false prophecy or by the hand of God, who moves lips to speak of higher mysteries.[17] Gregory the Great, too, admits a multiplicity of causes for spiritual visions: "They are generated either by a full stomach or by an empty one, or by illusions, or by our thoughts combined with revelations" and warns that they are often "diabolical illusions."[18] He urges caution and suspicion: "Seeing, then, that dreams may arise from such a variety of causes, one ought to be very reluctant to put one's faith in them, since it is hard to tell from what source they come" (262). Even true revelation is no sure safeguard against the devil's designs, because Lucifer "is clever enough to foretell many things that are true in order finally to capture the soul by but one falsehood" (262).[19]

Julian is fully aware of the spiritual dangers of what she has experienced. She provides her readers with a tripartite interpretive framework, namely, "oure feyth is contraryed in dyverse maner by oure owne blyndnesse and oure gostely enemys within and withoute" (71.654) ["our faith is opposed in various ways by our own blindness and our spiritual enemies, internal and external" (318)].[20] Indeed, Lucifer's assault on her soul is informed by all three elements. Her showing follows a fall into darkness which corresponds to "oure owne blyndnesse":

> And sodeynly all my body was fulfyllyd with sycknes lyke as it was before, and I was as baryn and as drye as I had nevyr had comfort but lytylle, and as a wrech mornyd hevyly for feelyng of my bodely paynes, and for fautyng of comforte gostly and bodely . . . . A, loo how wrechyd I was! (66.632, 634)

> [and suddenly all my body was filled with sickness as it was before, and I was as barren and dry as if the consolation which I had received before were trifling, and, as the wretched creature that I am, I mourned grievously for the bodily pains which I felt, and for lack of spiritual and bodily consolation. . . . See how wretched I was. (310, 311)]

When the devil appears to Julian, the impression of this "gostely enemy withoute" is immediate and threatening. After the devil vanishes,

Julian's first response is to analyze what has befallen her. Thinking of others, she works to eliminate the possibility of a physical cause for her dream, focusing upon the "greete heet" and "foul stynch," and whether there was during the night "a bodely fyer that shuld a burne vs all to deth" (67.637) ["actual fire, which would have burned us all to death" (312)]. When her companions confirm that there was no fire, indeed, that they smelled and felt nothing, she is actually relieved--"I seyde: Blessyd be god!" The heat and stench allow her to dismiss the possibility of divine intervention, hence the relief embodied in the words, "it was the fende that was come only to tempte me" (637-8)]. This relief is meant to console the reader with the message "Thou shalt nott be ovyrcom" (68.646) ["You will not be overcome" (315)], through the healing power of revelation; comfort is to be found in what the Lord has just shown her as well as in, she is careful to say "the feyth of holy church" (70.650). Almost immediately she is "brought to grete reste and peas" ["brought to great rest and peace"].

This process of fear, uncertainty, exegesis, and deliverance transcends anachronistic categories of fantasy and reality. As Michael Camille reminds us, "Evil was not an idea to medieval people. It was real and had bodies. These bodies were devils" (63). Furthermore, "for every medieval Christian, possession by demons was a common experience, a means of accounting for a host of physical and psychological afflictions through an external agency of evil" (123). One should also keep in mind that, for Julian, the Devil and suffering are real but evil is not. Julian's readers certainly would have taken her report--that the devil "helde me in the throte, and woulde a stoppyd my breth and kylde me" (67.636)-- at face value, as "reality" in the modern sense, but they also would have sought parallels for diabolical strangulation among medieval traditions surrounding Lucifer. One explanation is found in the story of the hypocritical monk of Ton Galathon, which Gregory recounts in his fourth dialogue. This monk enjoys a false reputation for sanctity based on his ability to fast for long periods. Yet the entire time he was secretly stealing food. As his death is imminent, his brothers gather around to hear inspiring words; the situation parallels Julian's. Instead the monk must make a terrifying confession. "I have been handed over to the dragon to be devoured. His tail is now coiled around my feet and knees and, with his head to my mouth, he is stealing the breath of life from me" (247). The point is not that Julian's readers would consider the possibility of her hypocrisy, but rather that they would reflect upon the power of the devil to "steal the breath of life," associating this with a situation in which the soul is in real danger, thereby making Julian's exemplary victory all the more significant. Given Julian's self-proclaimed status as one of the elect, and given that she is battling the devil's attempt at final possession of her soul, her audience would also have immediately associated her terrifying tale with similar tales of possession and exorcism from a variety of sources. Breathing was, from the earliest Christian times, along with prayer, laying on of hands, or the sign of the cross, one of the tried and true methods of exorcism (Camille 123). In this sense, the stopping of breath is an attempt to stop, at its source, one of the weapons of God against demons.[21]

Let us now turn our attention from strangulation to stench. Julian's images of light and darkness and of the Lord's sweet fragrance and the devil's stench may be considered commonplaces in hagiographic accounts. Indeed, their conventionality serves to authenticate for the reader the degree of peril that Julian had to face. But what of the "enemy within"? Although Julian does not confide in her audience, the iconography of the devil and diabolical lore provide some grounds for speculation concerning the precise nature of her temptation. The source is another "near-death" experience, the soldier of Rome's vision of hell, which Gregory relates to his discipulus Peter at the conclusion to his fourth dialogue. This soldier is struck ill by the plague, dies briefly, and then returns to life. He tells of a "river whose dark waters were covered by a mist of vapors that gave off an unbearable stench." The bridge over this river to a land of green meadows and beautiful flowers is a final test of sin and sainthood. Sinners slip off of the bridge and are dragged by demons into the muck. The soldier tells of seeing a certain Stephen, a high-ranking church official, caught in a tug of war between a group of white-robed men trying to pull him up and a group of demons pulling him down. Gregory reveals to Peter that this same Stephen was similarly caught in life between his "lustful tendencies" and "love for almsdeeds."

Gregory's exegesis is as one would expect. He tells, for example, that "the just were seen passing over a bridge to a beautiful meadow, because the road that leads to eternal life is narrow," and that "the soldier saw a river of polluted water because the noisome stream of carnal vices continues daily to flow on toward the abyss" (242). More pertinent to the exegesis of Julian's stench, however, is Gregory's direct association of the "mist and stench from the river" with those who are "stained by sins of the flesh through the pleasures of thought" (242-3). Gregory continues, "It is, therefore, no more than right that an evil-smelling vapor would surround them hereafter since sensual thoughts delighted them in this life," citing Job's words, "May worms be his sweetness" (243). He also notes that "delights of the flesh darken the mind they infect, making any clear vision of the true light impossible" (243). Finally, Gregory confirms that "sins of the flesh are punished with foul odors," reminding Peter of the story of Sodom from the book of Genesis (243). If one proceeds from this association and also considers that Julian's devil appears as a "yonge man . . . longe and wonder leen," whose visage is marred by "foule blacke spottes" and "here was rede as rust," it is entirely possible that Julian's readers might have associated the darkness and stench she describes with "thoughts of the delights of the flesh." According to this reading, Julian's fall into blindness is the supremely painful sin of turning away from God, her outer enemy is Lucifer, and her inner enemy is the deadly sin of lust.

III. Suffering and the Devil

In Julian's universe, "nothyn is done by happe ne by aventure, but alle by the for(eseing) wysdom of god" (11.336-37) ["nothing is done by chance, but all by God's prescient wisdom" (137)], sin has no real substance, and suffering is its only outward manifestation: "I saw nott synne, for I beleue it had no maner of substance . . , ne it myght not be knowen but by the payne that is caused therof" (27.406) ["But I did not see sin, so I believe that it has no kind of substance . . , nor can it be recognized except by the pain caused by it" (225)]. Such suffering is necessary, Julian argues, "for it nedyth vs to falle, and it nedyth vs to see it; for yf we felle nott, we shulde nott knowe how febyll and how wrechyd we be of oure selfe, nor also we shulde not so fulsomly know þe mervelous loue of oure maker" (61.603) ["for we need to fall, and we need to see it; for if we did not fall, we should not know how feeble and how wretched we are in ourselves, nor, too, should we know so completely the wonderful love of our creator" (300)]. The limits of human wretchedness are determined by Julian's image of the divided soul.

We haue in vs oure lorde Jhesu Cryst vp resyn, and we haue in vs
the wrechydnesse and the myschef of Adams fallyng. . . . And by
Adams fallyng we be so broken in oure felyng on dyverse manner
by synne and by sondry paynes, in which we be made derke and
so blynde that vnnethys we can take any comforte. (52.546-7)

[We have in us our risen Lord Jesus Christ, and we have in us the
wretchedness and the harm of Adam's falling. . . . And we are so
afflicted in our feelings by Adam's falling in various ways, by sin
and by different pains, and in this we are made dark and so blind
that we can scarcely accept any comfort. (279)]

Consolation rests on the prospect of redemption through the tripartite
scheme of spiritual development. "By contryscion we be made clene, by
compassion we be made redy, and by tru longyng to god we be made
wurthy. Theyse be thre menys, as I vnderstode, wher by that alle soules
com to hevyn, that is to sey that haue ben synners in erth and shalle be
savyd" (39.451-2) ["By contrition we are made clean, by compassion we
are made ready, and by true longing for God we are made worthy.
These are three means, as I understand, through which all souls come to
heaven, those, that is to say, who have been sinners on earth and will be
saved" (245)]. Suffering caused by sin is essential to the soul's progress,
"for it purgyth and makyth vs to know oure selfe and aske mercy"
(27.406-7) ["for it purges and makes us know ourselves and ask for
mercy" (225)]. Progress is also assured by the essential role of penance, as
enumerated in the paradigm of "falling, keeping, and raising"
exemplified by David, Paul, Mary Magdalene, and John of Beverly
(Baker 73). Each soul, then, has the obligation to assume the role of its
own wrathful judge.

Julian is not Job. In her theodicy, suffering brings self-knowledge.
It should not surprise us that she understands her moments of weariness
and temptation more as a gift from God than a test of faith. Indeed,
Julian's showings and Lucifer both come in response to her fervent desire
for the divine gift of illness. Here she aspires to a form of universal
suffering much more common to the spiritual journeys of continental
spirituals when she asks "to haue all maner of paynes, bodily and
ghostly, that [she] should haue if [she] should haue died, all the dredys
and temptations of fiendes, and all maner of other paynes, saue the out

passing of the sowle" (2.287) ["to have every kind of pain, bodily and spiritual, which I should have if I had died, every fear and temptation from devils, and every other kind of pain except the departure of the spirit" (178)].²² Elsbeth Stagel's experience in the first stage of the spiritual journey she undertakes under the guidance of Henry Suso provides one context in which to understand Julian's desire for "bodily paynes."²³ As Elsbeth embarks on the *via purgativa*, she misunderstands the lessons of the Desert Fathers and begins to "subjugate herself and to torture herself with hair shirts, ropes and terrible bonds, with pointed iron nails and many other things" (Tobin 139).²⁴ Suso forbids this drastic reenactment of Christ's sufferings, advising Stagel to "choose only a part of all this that you can successfully accomplish, given your frail constitution, so that wickedness might die in you but that you might live a long time" (Tobin 139-140).²⁵ When Stagel challenges this judgment, God inflicts Stagel with illness, which the Suso immediately identifies as her ultimate trial. In Stagel's case, illness provides a form of suffering acceptable to the *cura monialium* and an exemplary warning to extreme practitioners of self-mortification such as Elsbeth von Oye. For Julian, illness provides insight into the proper path her desires should take. As a consequence of her gift of nearly fatal illness, she asks no longer for a "bodily sight ne no maner schewing of god," but prays only for "compassion as me thought that a kynd sowle might haue with our lord Jesu" (3.292-3) ["any bodily vision or any kind of revelation from God, but the compassion which I though a loving soul could have for our Lord Jesus" (181)] as the primary mode of suffering, so that she may receive God's grace. Julian's moderation of desire from a bodily sight to mere compassion is meant to exemplify for her readers both the essential function of suffering in the soul's progress and the essential requirement of confining self-imposed suffering within reasonable limits. Stagel undergoes a similar transformation of desire, but under Suso's tutelage. Julian reaches this insight on her own.

A helpful context for understanding the fiend's place in Julian's theodicy of consolation may be found in the spiritual journeys of Christina von Stommeln and Ita von Hohenfels.²⁶ Like Julian and Elsbeth von Oye, Christina is chosen by God. When she is twelve, Christ speaks to her in a vision: "Just as my mother Maria was given the gift of becoming your mother in eternal wisdom, so you have been chosen to be my bride. But first you must endure much suffering in my name."27 This is significant, because it indicates that all suffering that follows is part of God's plan, with the devil as his instrument. Lucifer torments her from the time she is fifteen until she is transported into heaven at age forty-five. He appears to her in the body of Saint Bartholomew and tries to persuade her that suicide is the only form of true martyrdom. She is subsequently assailed at mass by doubt and despair whenever she sees the priest elevate the host. Finally, the devil falls back upon dietary threats, secretly introducing into her food and drink worms which are meant to allow him entry into her body and possession of her. When God displays his favor by inscribing three crosses into her living flesh, the Devil responds with his own inscriptions. This battle for the body pits divine inscription against diabolical mutilation. A series of abductions follows, in which demons torment Christina in ways reminiscent of Christ's passion and she saves the souls of seven murdering robbers. The Devil himself reappears to provide her final ordeal. He takes a sharp knife and, in the delicate words of the biographer, guts her as one would a fish that one wished to broil over a fire. She must then endure bleeding for six months, stanching her wounds with linen cloths, until Christ himself appears and takes her away to heaven.

Of particular interest here is the Dominican ideal of spiritual martyrdom, as set forth in the prologue to the *Prosalegendar,* in which Christina's *vita* is the only contemporary account.28 This martyrdom is achieved through an ethos of suffering which, in and of itself, makes possible the soul's progress.29 The nuns are remanded to "flee all dear friends, to love suffering inflicted by the devil, to despise all worldly goods, to seek out discomfort, to desire disgrace, to break one's will in all things, [and] to suffer without complaint. This will make you a companion of the high martyrs."30 In his dialogical "Little Book of Divine Wisdom," Suso elevates suffering, whether of diabolical or of divine origin, to the chief means of spiritual progress. Eternal Wisdom confides to the soul that suffering even elevates men above the angels because it brings a dimension of experience that angels have never seen (Tobin 246-50). In reading of suffering and the joy accompanying the awful deaths of martyrs such as Christina, nuns should be inspired to become martyrs in their daily lives. For these nuns suffering is life, consolation is deferred until death, and the ultimate agent of suffering is the devil. In such a culture, one actually desires the attentions of the devil as an ultimate test of suffering's ability to shield the soul until death. For the readers of the *Prosalegendar*, as for Julian, sin and suffering are part of God's plan and function because of the fall as the means to eternal life. Unlike Julian, Christina's chronicler would have asserted that suffering is sufficient in and of itself.

Christina's main source of suffering is external and diabolical. Christina's ultimate test comes when the devil sends a band of demons to her cell, who bind her with a chain of fire and transport her three hundred miles into a dark wood inhabited by seven murdering thieves. There the demons nail Christina to a tree and taunt her about the absence of her bridegroom and protector. When the murderers come to witness the spectacle, they are so formidable that they frighten away the demons. They are, of course, no match for Christina. Moved by the power of her presence, they fall to their knees and confess their crimes, which comprise a catalogue of mortal sins. At her behest they turn themselves in to the authorities and are impaled to death. Angels then convey her back to her cell, whereupon the demons make one final attempt. Once again they abduct Christina, bring her to the site of execution, remove the stakes from the murderers' corpses and drive the stakes through her body. When she endures this awful fate successfully, angels appear to rescue her. The reader then learns that through Christina's intercession the murderers have won a spot in purgatory and the hope of salvation. She is permitted to imitate Christ in the sacrifice of her body and in the salvation of lost souls.

These not unconventional motifs reveal some interesting features of the diabology as presented in the *Prosalegendar*. First, whereas Julian depicts the devil as God's adversary and the battle between good and evil in almost Manichean terms of light and darkness, Christina's devil acts explicitly as God's instrument through which she earns salvation for herself and purgatory for others whom one might consider irrevocably lost. The Devil's evil is good, one might argue, just as suffering is joy, and death is life. Second, at work is a kind of *quid pro quo* spirituality. Christ chooses Christina. She is assured of salvation, but she must be prepared to endure thirty years of agony. Just as Julian is chosen to be a seer, Christina is a sufferer. Personal salvation is assured by the ability to effect the salvation of others, not by any sort of explicitly internal development, as is described in the *vitae* of Henry Suso and Elsbeth Stagel (Tinsley 126-9). Third, Christina's suffering is depicted in terms of what one might call reverse incarnation. The Devil begins by tempting her intellectually, through false advice and disputation, then tries to take possession of her body by means of diabolical worms, before settling finally upon disfigurement, that is, ripping chunks of flesh from her body, thereby defiling the wholeness that defined sanctity for the Christian Middle Ages. The highest form of suffering is external, mutilation imposed by the Devil and his minions, the lowest form is spiritual. This reverses the conventional hierarchy of transcendental suffering espoused by Suso, in which the purgative power of self-mortification represents only the initial stage of development, which culminates in a community of universal sufferers who have distanced themselves from the corporeal. In Julian, the reassuring vision of the impotent devil precedes her potentially deadly encounter with the lean young man, as if to remind the reader of the fiend's omnipresence.

True to Suso's dismissal of intention and source, God--through his willing agent, the devil-- imposes suffering upon Ita of Hohenfels not as retribution for sins, nor as a means of self-knowledge, but simply as a condition for worldly existence. Following Ita's conversion and entry into the convent of Ötenbach, two faces appear to her during mass.[31] God tells her that one of the faces is that of Lucifer and warns her that her trials are about to begin. "With that she fell into the challenge of doubt so profound that she thought no one could ever withstand it as long as he lived, unless he were in a state of grace like that of Adam when he was created. And the entire time it was as if hell itself stood open to her and that she was so created that she would have to enter it, and that her chair was placed next to that of Lucifer."[32] In this phase of doubt, Ita, in essence, becomes a demon. For five years she must endure Lucifer's companionship, only finding momentary relief through revelation. Julian, too, falls into blindness and alienation --"hevynes and werynes of my life and irkenes of my selfe" (15.354), but her rise and triumph are assured by the primacy of sin and the certainty of forgiveness.

Ita must also endure despair brought about by the devil's attempts to weaken her resolve with the arguments of the dualists.

> You claim that God is good, but He is not. For He is evil and everything that is evil came from him, for He knew quite well when He created the angel (Lucifer) that he would become the

evil fiend. And He knew of Eve and Adam and that all human beings would stray from his just teaching.33

Only after she is shown a vision of Christ's passion and recognizes Christ's consolation, does Ita regain her equilibrium. Whereas Julian learns in her revelation to scorn the devil's malice, Ita experiences such preeminence and levity only through a life of trial. The Devil inflicts years of suffering upon her, appearing in the guise of a wolf and eating his way through her body. But the chronicler writes that this happens so often that the Devil's power wanes. At the end he is reduced to stealing her clothing and possessions and hiding them. He has, in a sense become the object of "scorne and game and ernest."

IV. Death and Deliverance

The proximity of death is for Julian the beginning of spiritual life; the fear of "domys day" brings the revelations that promise eternal bliss. Near-death also forms the foundation of her *auctoritas* (Watson, 652). Her subsequent desire for "paynes, bodily and ghostly, that I schould haue if I schould haue died" is particularly worthy of note when viewed in the context of Gregory the Great's fourth dialogue, in which similar "near-death" experiences are recounted and analyzed as evidence for the relationship between soul and body. Gregory relates an entire series of such occurrences, which are occasions for revelations, especially concerning impending death or the fate of one's soul.34 He reminds us: "It often happens that the saints of heaven appear to the just at the hour of death in order to reassure them. And, with the vision of the heavenly company before their minds, they die without experiencing any fear or agony." In the case of prophecy, he states: "frequently, knowledge of the future is given to the dying by revelation." He tells of Gerontius, a monk of his own monastery, to whom men in shining white robes appear during a severe illness and reveal to him which monks will die and when. In the following account, a young man appears to a monk Mellitus and gives him a letter, which he commands him to read. Therein he finds his own name and the names of all of his brothers who had been baptized on the same day he had, all of whom then die. The news is not always bad, of course. Other souls "at the time of death have a foretaste of the mysteries of heaven, not through dreams, but in a state of full awareness" (204). The example Gregory cites is of the servant boy of an attorney, Valerian by name, who appears to die of the plague, only to reawaken and report that he had visited heaven. The proof of his journey is his suddenly acquired ability to converse with all foreigners in their native tongue.

For Ita of Hohenfels, in contrast, death actually transcends the devil as an ultimate test of suffering (Lewis, *Sister Books* 166-170). God gives her a most awful, long, and lingering death. She feels constantly as if "in her sleep fifty arrows were being shot into her body."[35] Only through the reassurance of angels can she endure it. Some time after her death it is revealed to another nun that there were two reasons for this final agony.

> One was that God wished to take all of her pain from her while she was still on this earth. The other reason that her death was so bitter was that God wished to grant by means of her ordeal the possibility to other souls that she could lead them, too, into the kingdom of heaven and that they would keep her company.[36]

Ita's death becomes thereby the occasion for granting others eternal life. Death is an anticlimax for Christina because she has been permitted in life to emulate Christ. Her crucifixion at the hands of the demons allows the murderers to enjoy the fate of Christ's good thief. Christ himself rips her from the devil's clutches and brings her to her eternal reward.

While Julian would have agreed that the earth is a vale of tears--"The swylge of the body betokenyth grette wretchydnesse of oure dedely flessch" (64. 623) ["The pit which was the body signifies the great wretchedness of our mortal flesh" (306)]--and that suffering is necessary in life--"It is fulle blesfulle man to be taken fro payne more than payne to be taken fro man; for if payne be taken from vs, it may come agayne" (64.624) ["It is most blessed for man to be taken from pain, more than for pain to be taken from man; for if pain be taken from us, it may return" (307)]--she differs significantly from the two views expressed above in three key aspects of her presentation of suffering, sin, death and the devil's place therein. First, in the thirteenth revelation she is careful to differentiate between suffering and sin and to make sin, not suffering, the primary determinate of good and evil:

For if it were leyde before vs, alle the payne þat is in hell and in purgatory and in erth, deed and other, than synne we shulde rather chese alle that payne than synne. For syn is so vyle and so mekylle for to hate that it may be lyconnyd to no payne whych payne is not synne. And to me was shewed none harder helle than synne, for a kynd soule hatyth no payne but synne; for alle is good but syn, and nought is yvell but synne. (40.458)

[For if it were laid in front of us, all the pain there is in hell and in purgatory and on earth, death and all the rest, we should choose all that pain rather than sin. For sin is so vile and so much to be hated that it can be compared with no pain which is not itself sin. And no more cruel hell than sin was revealed to me, for a loving soul hates no pain but sin; for everything is good except sin, and nothing is evil except sin. (247)]

For Ita and Christina, suffering is a means of transcendence. For Julian, suffering is the inevitable result of sin. It is to be endured but not to be glorified. Second, the greatest suffering one can endure in this life is to be shown, that is, to experience through God's intervention, the pain of Christ's passion: "with alle the paynes that evyr were or evyr shalle be, I vnderstode the passion of Criste for the most payn and ovyr passyng" (27.406) ["with all the pains that ever were or ever will be, I understood Christ's Passion for the greatest and surpassing pain" (225)]. This devalues both the self-imposed suffering glorified in Ita and Christina--"Synne is the sharpest scorge þat ony chosyn soule may be smyttyn with" (39.449) ["Sin is the sharpest scourge with which any chosen soul can be struck" (244)]--and even any suffering the devil may inflict--"And to me was shewed none harder helle than synne" (40.458) ["And no more cruel hell than sin was revealed to me" (247)]. Third, Julian offers the certainty of divine consolation. Although the servant is bound to fall (and to suffer), the consolation of God the Lord and Christ the Mother is immediate, accessible in the world, and ultimately decisive against any fiendish intervention.

Julian's experience of Christ's passion, which she calls the ultimate suffering, is immediately followed by her sharing of divine joy. Her experience of evil is tempered by the reassuring phrase, "Here with is the feende ovyr come" (13.346) first in the world --

And thus he occupyed me alle that nyght and on þe morow tylle it was about pryme day, and anon they were alle goone and passyd, and there lefte nothyng but stynke; and that lastyd styll a whyle. And I scornede hym, and thus was I delyured of hym by þe vertu of Crystes passion. (170.651)

[And so he occupied me all that night and into the morning, until it was a little after sunrise, and then all at once they had gone and disappeared, leaving nothing but their stench, and that persisted for a little while. And I despised him, and so I was delivered from him by the strength of Christ's Passion. (316)]

--and, ultimately as well: "I saw he schalle be scornyde at domys day generally of all that schal be savyd, to whos saluacion he hath had grett envye. For then he shall see that all the woo and tribulacion that he hath done them shalle be turned in to encrese of ther joy without ende" (13.350) ["I saw that on Judgment Day he will be generally scorned by all who will be saved, of whose salvation he has had great envy. For then he will see that all the woe and tribulation which he has caused them will be changed into the increase of their eternal joy" (202)]. Christina, too, is assured of consolation, but knows only that it will come after suffering and death. Ita experiences only the fleeting consolation of divine presence and no assurance whatsoever of ultimate salvation.

Julian attributes the success of her fight against the devil to her ability to stay free of sin. The devil's second assault is more serious. The stench of his presence assails her, fueled, if one gives credence to Gregory's exegesis, by thoughts of lust. She also hears voices which she cannot understand, but they seem to her "as they scornyd byddyng of bedys which are seyde boystosly with moch faylyng" (69.648) ["as if they were mocking the recitation of prayers which are said imperfectly" (Colledge and Walsh 648. n. 8)], thereby invalidating one of the sinner's strongest weapons against possession. Julian is able to resist Lucifer by focusing on the cross, engaging her tongue in the "spech of Christes passion," and trusting in God. The first method harks back to the image of the shining cross in the midst of demon-infested darkness which accompanied her illness. God's consolation prompts her to consider becoming a vessel of consolation herself. Ultimately, though, Julian refs her audience back to the strategy of "scorne" she had analyzed in the fifth revelation. "And I scornede hym, and thus was I delyured of hym by þe vertu of Crystes passion" (70.651) ["And I despised him, and so I was delivered from him by the strength of Christ's Passion" (316)].

Let us take a moment to consider the efforts of other triumphant soldiers of Christ. The example of Benedict, as told by Gregory, has the devil appear "in the form of a little blackbird, which began to flutter in front of his face" (59-60). He drives it away with the sign of the cross, but then he is immediately seized "with an unusually violent temptation," in which his lust-filled thoughts recall the image of a woman. Benedict is about to succumb when he throws himself into the sharp thorns and stinging nettles: "There he rolled and tossed until his whole body was in pain and covered with blood." This act of self-mortification "served to drain the poison of temptation from his body. Before long, the pain that was burning his whole body had put out the fires of evil in his heart. It was by exchanging these two fires that he gained the victory over sin" (60). Free from these temptations, Benedict joins the elect, in that he is qualified to instruct others in the practice of virtue. His example explains Julian's inclusion of her own temptation: she seeks authority not only through revelation but also through exemplary virtue. If one has not conquered Lucifer, how may one instruct others, especially when failing to sin is the basis for the soul's progress?

In contemplating the link between suffering and temptation, Julian's audience would have drawn on an astounding diversity of sources. Benedict's disguised devil evokes images of the trickster common to medieval lore, rather than that of the long, lustful youth of Julian's showing. In both cases the devil awakens thoughts that may lead to sin. For Benedict, self-imposed suffering serves as a "backfire" to the fire of evil. "So complete was his triumph that from then on . . . he never experienced another temptation of this kind" (60). This represents a single and final victory for Benedict. Julian can make no such claim. According to her theodicy, the sinner may always fall back into alienation and sorrow. She does so herself on two occasions (66.632; 74.672-3). For Christina of Stommeln, suffering actually displaces temptation. At the behest of her bridegroom she must display the stoic endurance of the martyrs. Impaling at the hands of demons makes the ultimate *imitatio Christi* possible. Her vision of purgatory allows her to reassure other sinners by authenticating the murderers' redemption. In the most extreme example, Ita of Hohenfels is denied the reassurance of deliverance. She must endure alienation from God and from her own soul; as a demon she is permitted a vision of hell. She does not dismember her body to resist the devil, rather the devil rips chunks from her flesh as part of her "trial" sent by God. Her life consists of suffering, reflecting the ideals espoused by Suso and developed from the ethos of the desert fathers. Her awful, lingering death is a final form of martyrdom, in which she is allowed to suffer more in order to free the souls of others.

Julian's pain, bodily and ghostly, must have been as keenly felt as that of Ita or Christina. After all, even though she describes it as "lytylle," it does cause her to leave "for þe tyme the comfort of alle this blessyd shewyng of oure lorde god" (67.634) ["to abandon so imprudently the strength of all this blessed revelation from our Lord God" (311)] and sets the stage for the fiend. Yet, unlike Elsbeth von Oye, Ita, or Christina, her suffering, for all of its intensity, remains vicarious. Bynum draws this distinction most clearly: "Women's efforts to imitate this Christ involved *becoming* the crucified, not just patterning themselves after or expanding their compassion toward, but *fusing* with the body on the cross" (131). Pain comes to Julian indirectly, at the vision of God's dismemberment. She herself is not dismembered. Christ's blood washes away her sins. She does not have to bleed as He did. In the tradition of Bernard and Bonaventure, she meditates on the passion, she does not relive it.

At the conclusion to the sixteenth revelation, Julian offers some final reflections on her battle with the devil. Consistent with her theodicy, Julian defines suffering as the outward sign of privation, using her own exemplary fall: "For it is þe most payne þat the soule may haue, to turne fro god ony tyme by synne" (76.685) ["For the greatest pain that the soul can have is at any time to turn from God through sin" (328)]. She warns her readers of the dangers of contrition, the most infernal instrument of all. The fiend works with human folly to engender a state of "false drede of oure wrechydnesse, for payne that he thretyth vs by. . . . For it is his menyng to make vs so hevy and so sory in this þat we schuld lett outt of mynde þe blessydfull beholdyng of oure evyrlastyng frende" (76.688) ["false suggestions of fear about our wretchedness because of the pain which he threatens us with. For it is his purpose to make us so depressed and so sad in this matter that we should forget the blessed contemplation of our everlasting friend" (329)]. Having said this, Julian has nothing but words of consolation for the elect. Lucifer may well win victories, but he is no match for charity and meekness (77.689-90). The potent Lucifer of the sixteenth showing who plagues Julian with the smoke and stench of lust reverts to the impotent, miserable, envious devil of the fifth showing who truly deserves her sobriquet of scorn.

It should not be said that the flight to God has no unpleasant consequences, given the state of the world--"This place is pryson, this lyfe is pennannce" (77.693)--and Adam's claim on behalf of the soul. As Julian reminds us, "we be synners and do many evylles that we ouȝte to leue, and leue many good dedys vndone that we ouȝte to do, wherfore we deserve payne, blame and wrath" (46.492-3) ["we are sinners and commit many evil deeds which we ought to forsake, and leave many good deeds undone which we ought to do, so that we deserve pain, blame and wrath" (259)]. Indeed, her words might well have been taken from the *Schwesternbüchern*. Julian's God may not know Augustinian wrath, as Baker asserts, but she depicts a stern and just God who punishes errant souls (77.691). Even Jesus as Mother does not lack Mosaic tendencies: "And when it is wexid of more age, she sufferyth it that it be chastised in brekyng downe of vicis, to make the chylde receyve vertues and grace" (60.599) ["And when it is even older, she allows it to be chastised to destroy its faults, so as to make the child receive virtues and grace" (299)]. Just as Christ teaches Christina, Julian, too, learns that the elect must suffer gladly (77.691-2), for suffering is the price of divine insight: "For this lytylle payne that we suffer heer we shalle haue an hygh endlesse knowyng in god, whych we myght nevyr haue without that. And the harder oure paynes haue ben with hym in hys crosse, the more shalle our worschyppe be with hym in his kyngdom" (21.381) ["for this little pain which we suffer here we shall have an exalted and eternal knowledge in God which we could never have without it. And the harder our pains have been with him on his cross, the greater will our glory be with him in his kingdom" (215)].

V. The Avatar of Evil

In the fifth revelation Julian is granted insight into the nature of evil. The key to Julian's diabology is the image of the impotent, suffering devil. Words of triumph inaugurate her message "Here with is the feende ovyr come" (13.346). Unlike Christina and Ita, she must face only a tiny portion of the devil's arsenal. Although Julian stresses that Lucifer has the same malice as he had before the Incarnation (201), and that his efforts are unceasing, the devil is robbed of potency. Shame and sorrow are his lot. This sorrow does not end even when the devil is successful, for as Julian notes, "he hath as mech sorow when god gevyth hym leue to werke as when he workyth nott" (13.347) ["And he has as much sorrow when God permits him to work as when he is not working" (201)]. For this reason, Julian bids us to imitate God in our response to Lucifer. "Also I saw oure lorde scornyng hys mays and nowghtyng hys vnmyght, and he wille that we do so" (13.348) ["Also I saw our Lord scorn his malice and despise him as nothing, and he wants us to do so" (201)]. God's scorn evokes Julian's joy at the devil's defeat. Her fall into sadness comes not from anxiety regarding the devil or remorse at human frailty, but is a gesture of compassion with Christ:

> And after this I felle in to a sadnes, and sayde; I see thre thynges, game, scorne, and ernest. I see game, that the feend is ovyrcome, and I se scorne, that god scorneth hym, and he shalle be scornyd, and I se ernest, þat he is overcome by the blessydfulle passion and deth of oure lorde Jhesu Crist, that was done in fulle grette ernest and with sad traveyle. (349-50)

> [And after this I became serious again, and said: I see three things: sport and scorn and seriousness. I see sport, that the devil is overcome; and I see scorn, that God scorns him and he will be scorned; and I see seriousness, that he is overcome by the blessed Passion and death of our lord Jesus Christ, which was accomplished in great earnest and with heavy labour. (202)]

Like Julian, Ita of Hohenfels is granted a vision of the devil and his minions. She is transported to a beautiful meadow where she is shown the essence of good and evil, the essential differences between the religious and the secular life, and the distinction between venial and cardinal sins. Finally, she is granted a brief and terrifying vision of the devil's disciples, described "as numerous as flies."[37] She then is allowed to become the vessel of God's wisdom for just a moment before returning from her enraptured state. Julian and Ita also both report revelations surrounding the flowing and healing blood of Christ. Whereas Julian sees its redeeming qualities descending "downe in to helle" to "brak her bondes," working on earth "redy to wash all creatures of synne," and also ascending "vp into hevyn in the blessed body of our lorde Jesu Crist, and ther is in hym, bledying, preyeng for vs to the father" (12.344) ["It descended into hell and broke its bonds . . . overflows all the earth, and it is ready to wash from their sins all creatures who are, have been and will be of good will . . . ascend[ing] into heaven in the blessed body of our Lord Jesus Christ, and it is flowing there in him, praying to the Father for us" (200)]--Ita's vision stresses the bond that Christ's flowing blood creates among saints, martyrs, and the divine:

> And after this she was enraptured in her prayer and saw how the blood and flesh of Jesus Christ is made one with the saints and with the souls such that God's blood and his flesh illuminate through each individual soul with wondrous decoration and their holy lives, just as it was on earth with the martyrs or with special purity or with the virtue that they practiced with extraordinary wonders had shone with wondrous light and illuminated the blood and body of our Lord and how great and joyous the union was. And she saw how the body and blood of Christ fell into the souls and how the souls then fell into his flesh and blood just as if they were one.[38]

For Julian, the healing power of Christ's blood compensates for the terror of his passion. For Ita, Christ's blood signifies an eternal spiritual connection between the Godhead and the individual soul, in which the individual's bloody suffering may reach that of the divine.

Most striking is the effect that these visions of evil have on each visionary. Julian's vision of "game, scorne and ernest" brings consolation which arises in certainty of the fiend's impotence and in the experience of "mervelous melody in endelesse loue." Julian is then permitted to see "thre degrees of blysse that ylke saule schalle hafe in hevene" (14.352) ["three degrees of bliss that every soul will have in heaven" (203)] followed by a "souerayne gastelye lykynge," accompanied by "euerlastande suerness, myghtlye festnyd withou3t any paynefulle drede

. . . so goostly that I was in peese" (15.354) ["supreme spiritual delight, (an) everlasting surety, powerfully secured without any painful fear . . . so spiritual that I was wholly at peace" (204)]. This consolation is only temporary. Then Julian reports being "turned and left to my selfe in hevynes and werynes of my life and irkenes of my selfe" (15.354) ["then I was changed, and abandoned to myself, oppressed and weary of my life and ruing myself" (204)]. This cycle of joy and sorrow is "nedefulle," Julian explains, "For it is goddes wylle that we holde vs in comfort with alle oure myght; for blysse is lastyng withou3t ende, and payne is passyng, and shall be brought to nowght" (15.356) ["For it is God's will that we do all in our power to preserve our consolation, for bliss lasts forevermore, and pain is passing, and will be reduced to nothing" (205)]. Julian wishes here to reassure her readers that, even for the elect, bliss becomes eternal only after death and entry into the kingdom. The sinner on earth, even one assured of salvation, remains in the temporal pit bound to the pendulum of Paul's rapture and Peter's despair. Julian finds consolation in the promise of salvation and in visions of beatitude. Ita's *vita* offers an entirely different message. When her vision ends, her soul is reunited with her body. This results in such shock and disgust on the part of her soul that she falls deathly ill for months. The message is plain and much less reassuring. Unlike for members of the elect like Julian and Christina, the human condition for Ita is characterized by an enduring state of alienation between soul and body. Each vision has its price. No bliss is possible without despair. As long as the spirit is still bound to the world, even divine consolation may be the occasion for suffering. Ita's consolation lies in martyrdom.

All three exemplars' spiritual progress finds expression in the visions that God grants them of eternal life. [39] Just as Julian's awful showing of Christ's pain is relieved by the sense of God's joy at humankind's salvation, her vision of the fiend's impotence is reinforced by a showing of "our lorde god as a lorde in his owne howse" (14.351), where she is permitted to experience "thre degrees of blysse that ech soule shalle haue in hevyn" (14.352). When Julian asks for a vision of hell and purgatory in order that she "myght haue seen for lernyng in alle thyng that longyth to my feyth, wher by I my3t lyue the more to goddes wurschyppe and to my profy3te" (33.427) ["to have seen for instruction in everything which belongs to my faith, whereby I could live more to God's glory and to my profit" (234)], God refuses her. Ita von Hohenfels is forced to sit at the fiend's feet and look directly into hell. Her life of suffering presages hell and her lingering death prepares the eternal way for others. The martyr Christina of Stommeln occupies the middle of this pantheon. Her ability to follow the progress in purgatory of her seven contrite murderers both authenticates her sainthood and reassures those in the audience who have fallen into deadly sin.

In the context of pan-European affective spirituality, the mystical journeys of Julian of Norwich and Elsbeth of Oye have more in common than one might have guessed. Although their theodicies remain diametrically opposed, both pray to a God who requires that suffering be endured with the "mekenes of a synnfulle soule." Because Julian enjoys the confidence and the consolation of the elect, she can endure the suffering borne of her sin and the penance imposed by God. The transitoriness of her suffering is assured. Eternal bliss is certain. Elsbeth's compensation rests alone in God's assurance that her awful suffering brings Him immediate joy. When she asks for her eternal reward, she is told to suffer further so that God may rejoice. For Julian, the devil's greatest threat lies in his ability to engender contrition, so that the blinded soul focuses on its sinfulness and falls away from the promise of salvation. For Elsbeth, whose existence is marked by suffering when she wears her cross of nails and intolerable guilt whenever she lays it aside, resisting the devil means enduring despair. What links these two worlds, one ruled by a benevolent lord and caring mother, the other by an insatiable and oblivious suitor, is the indispensability of the Adversary.

NOTES

1. For useful introductions and extensive bibliographies, see Richard Kieckhefer, "Major Currents in Late Medieval Devotion," *Christian Spirituality. High Middle Ages and Reformation*, ed. Jill Raitt (New York: Crossroad, 1988) 75-108; Caroline Walker Bynum, "Religious Women in the Later Middle Ages," *Fragmentation and Redemption* (New York: Zone, 1991) 121-139; and Alois M. Haas, "Schools of Late Medieval Mysticism" in Jill Raitt, ed., *Christian Spirituality*, Vol. 2 (New York: Crossroad, 1988) 140-175. See also Elizabeth Petroff's introduction to *Medieval Women's Visionary Literature* (Oxford: Oxford UP, 1986); Peter Dronke, *Women Writers of the Middle Ages* (Cambridge: Cambridge UP, 1984); and Peter Dinzelbacher, *Mittelalterliche Frauenmystik* (Paderborn: Schöningh, 1993).

2. Kieckhefer's categories (76), which I use here, become problematical when one considers that most practitioners of affective spirituality on the continent were immersed in forms of devotional piety.

3. The English Channel has remained a seemingly impenetrable bulwark between the conservatism that characterizes English spiritual writing and the radicalism of the continent. Nicholas Watson, "The Composition of Julian of Norwich's *Revelation of Love* ," *Speculum* 68 (1993) 637-683, provides a bibliography on continental and English spirituality as well as a thoughtful discussion of cross-fertilization. See also Denise Despres, "Ecstatic Reading and Missionary Mysticism," in *Prophets Abroad. The Reception of Continental Holy Women in Late-Medieval England*, ed. Rosalynn Voaden (Cambridge: Brewer, 1996) 141-160, on the reception of Catherine of Siena in England. Eamon Duffy, *The Stripping of the Altars* (New Haven and London: Yale UP, 1992) 68-77, and Gail Gibson, *The Theater of Devotion* (Chicago: U of Chicago P, 1989) 19-46, describe the social and historical background that could give rise to a brilliant thinker like Julian.

4. Ritamary Bradley and Valerie Lagorio, *The 14th-Century English Mystics. A Comprehensive Annotated Bibliography* (New York: Garland, 1981), is a reliable source for literature before 1980. See Denise Baker, *Julian of Norwich's Showings : From Vision to Book* (Princeton, N.J.: Princeton UP, 1994) 3; and Watson, "Composition" 642-657, for recent primary and secondary sources on Julian. My article, "The Spirituality of Suffering in the Revelations of Elsbeth von Oye," *Mystics Quarterly* 21 (1995): 121-147, is the only extensive treatment of Elsbeth in English. SeeWolfram Schneider-Lastin, "Das Handexemplar einer mittelalterlichen Autorin," *Editio* 8, (1994): 53. On the transmission of her revelations, see Peter Ochsenbein's two articles, "Die Offenbarungen Elsbeths von Oye als Dokument leidensfixierter Mystik," in *Abendländische Mystik im Mittelalter. Symposium Kloster Engelberg,* ed. Kurt Ruh (Stuttgart: Metzler, 1986) 423-442; and "Leidensmystik in Dominikanischen Frauenklöstern des 14. Jahrhunderts am Beispiel der Elsbeth von Oye," *Religiöse Frauenbewegung und mystische Frömmigkeit im Mittelalter,* ed. Peter Dinzelbacher and Dieter Bauer (Köln: Böhlau, 1988) 353-372 for a catalogue of her motifs. See also Hans Neumann, "Elsbeth von Oye," in *Die deutsche Literatur des Mittelalters. Verfasserlexikon,* Vol. 2 (Berlin: De Gruyter, 1980) 511-514. See Gertrud Jaron Lewis, *Bibliographie zur deutschen Frauenmystik des Mittelalters* (Berlin: Schmidt, 1994), for a comprehensive bibliography of the women mystics of Teutonia.

5. In this essay the terms "Lucifer," "the fiend," and "the devil" are used interchangeably, in the sense understood by both Julian and the Dominican nuns of the fourteenth century, that the agent of evil could have many avatars. Jeffrey Burton Russell's two volumes, *The Devil: Perceptions of Evil from Antiquity*

to *Primitive Christianity* (Ithaca: Cornell UP, 1977); and *Lucifer: the Devil in the Middle Ages* (Ithaca: Cornell UP, 1984), are a useful introduction to the history of evil. See also Gustav Roskoff, *Geschichte des Teufels* (Leipzig: Brockhaus, 1869); and Elaine Pagels, *The Origin of Satan* (New York: Random, 1995).

6. "Swaz ich geliten han von dem kruze, daz ich uzzerlich truog, alz an dizem buochlin geschribin ist, daz dunkit mich ein kleinis liden wider dem wezzin kruze, daz ich in mir trage." All references to the writings of Elsbeth von Oye are taken from a transcription of the Zurich manuscript by Wolfram Schneider-Lastin of the University of Basel, who is preparing the critical edition. I am indebted to Dr. Schneider-Lastin for making the transcription available as well as copies of his articles on the progress of the edition. I also thank the Zentralbibliothek Zurich for providing the microfilm copy of the Zurich manuscript.

7. "In alzo toedmiger angst unt sterbender not strebit min herze gar emziclich tag unt nacht."

8. "Unt ist mir denne, recht alz ime glichin ogenblich mich der vigint bisizzin welle unt mir ellu minu gelit zerzerrin welle, unt diz ist ein alz unsaglich pin, daz ich ez nit zi wortin kan bringen" (135.14-137.2).

9. Edmund Colledge and James Walsh, *A Book of Showings to the Anchoress Julian of Norwich* (Toronto: Pontifical Institute of Mediaeval Studies, 1978), cite scriptural precedents for all of Julian's motifs (168-74). In their view, "she is merely echoing Paul and John in their cosmic visions of the struggle between death and life, light and darkness, good and evil" (172).

10. Brad Peters' predominantly descriptive portraits of Julian's devil, "Julian of Norwich and Her Conceptual Development of Evil," *Mystics Quarterly* 17 (1991): 181-188; and "The Reality of Evil with the Mystic Vision of Julian of Norwich," *Mystics Quarterly* 13 (1987): 195-202, offer no solution to the conundrum of the sixteenth revelation, either in the context of Julian's theodicy or the larger context of English spirituality. See also Frances Beer, *Women and Mystical Experience in the Middle Ages* (Woodbridge, Suffolk: Boydell, 1992) 143-151.

11. Russell, *Lucifer* 66-76, provides a rich catalogue of motifs drawn from folklore.

12. Russell emphasizes in particular the *vita Martini* of Sulpicius Severus (154).

13. If we accept the interpretation that "Julian's anxiety about sin impelled her revision of the showings as her solution to the problem of evil became clear to her over nearly a quarter-century of contemplation" (Baker 64), we look to the Long Text for Julian's ultimate vision of the devil's place in the soul's progress. My

discussion in this section attempts to synthesize Baker's arguments, which I find plausible, with several of Russell's insights. See also the sources discussed by Baker in Footnote 9 of her Introduction.

14. Watson argues for the possibility that Julian composed her Short Text in the 1380's, with work on the Long Text continuing as late as 1413. Baker holds to the conventional dating of Colledge and Walsh, who posit a completion date of the 1370's for the short text and the mid-1390's for the long text.

15. For a comprehensive listing of sources and spiritual motifs surrounding the life of Christina von Stommeln, see Anna Martin, "Christina von Stommeln," *Mediävistik* 4 (1991): 179-263, which devotes three sections to the devil. Unfortunately, Christine Ruhrberg's monograph, *Der literarische Körper der Heiligen. Leben und Viten der Christina von Stommeln (1242-1312)* (Tübingen: Francke, 1995), could not be consulted in time for this article. I chose the *Prosalegendar* as my principal source because of its close connection to the same fourteenth-century Dominican cloister culture that produced the revelations of Elsbeth von Oye and the Sister Books.

16. Gertrude Jaron Lewis, *By Women. For Women. About Women. The Sister-Books of Fourteenth Century Germany* (Toronto: Pontifical Institute of Mediaeval Studies, 1996) 125-127, reports that the devil is "not given the great importance found in contemporary legends," nor does he appear "as the lascivious seducer," his usual role in the *Vitas Patrum*. Thanks to her inclusion of the texts of eight of the Schwesternbücher on microfiche, readers can now see for themselves. For further discussion of Ita's *vita*, see Tinsley, "Elsbeth von Oye" 132-3, and Otto Langer, *Mystische Erfahrung und spirituelle Theologie: zu Meister Eckharts Auseinandersetzung mit der Frauenfrömmigkeit seiner Zeit* (Munich: Artemis, 1987).

17. Martin, "Christina" 217-18.

18. Gregory the Great, *Dialogues*, Trans. Odo John Zimmerman. Vol. 39 (New York: Fathers of the Church, 1959) 261.

19. Compare Watson, "Composition" 647, on the veracity of visions.

20. Compare this account with that of Brad Peters, "Reality of Evil," who makes several problematical assertions, among them that Julian differentiates between sin and evil (195), and that evil is an entity, namely Satan (197).

21. Hagiography offers several examples of saints using their own breath or wind that they summon from nature to destroy idols, a favorite resting place of demons, as recounted in the legends of St. Martin and St. Felix. See Michael

Camille, *The Gothic Idol. Ideology and Image-making in Medieval Art* (Cambridge: Cambridge UP, 1989) 122.

22. See Frank Tobin, ed., *Henry Suso: The Exemplar with Two Sermons* (New York: Paulist, 1989) 13-51 and 407-9, on Henry Suso's life and works. Alois Haas, "'Trage Leiden geduldiglich.' Die Einstellung der deutschen Mystik zum Leiden," in *Gottleiden-Gottlieben. Zur volkssprachlichen Mystik im Mittelalter* (Frankfurt: Insel, 1989) 127-52; and Gertrude Jaron Lewis, *Sister-Books* 159-161, cite numerous examples of this motif from continental spirituality.

23. See Lewis, *Sister-Books* 177-201, and Ursula Peters, *Religiöse Erfahrung als literarisches Faktum. Zur Vorgeschichte und Genese frauenmystischer Texte des 13. und 14. Jahrhunderts* (Tübingen: Niemeyer, 1988) 101-176, for thorough treatments of the *cura monialium*.

24. "Daz si nah der alten veter strenger wise iren lip oh mit grosser kestgung soelti ueben, und vie an, ir selben ab ze brechene und sich ze pingen mit herinen hemdern und mit seiln und grulichen banden, mit scharpfen isninen nageln und dez gelich vil." *Deutsche Schriften,* ed. Kark Bihlmeyer (Stuttgart: 1907; rpt. Frankfurt: Minerva, 1961) 107. See Williams-Krapp, "'Nucleus totius perfectionis.' Die Altväterspiritualität in der 'vita' Heinrich Seuses," in *FS Walter Haug und Burghart Wachinger*, ed. J. Janota, Vol. 2 (Tübingen: Niemeyer, 1992) 402-421, on the Dominican reception of the Desert Fathers. See also Lewis, *Sister-Books* 254-8, on extreme forms of "discipline."

25. "Du solt usser dem allen dir selb och ein vaht nemen, daz du wol mugest erzuegen mit deinem kranken libe, daz diu untugend in dir sterbe und mit dem libe lang lebest" (Bihlmeyer 107).

26. All references to the *vita* of Ita von Hohenfels are taken from my transcription and translation of the Ötenbach Sister Book. I am indebted to the Nürnberg City Archives for allowing access to the manuscript and providing microfilms. All quotations from the *vita* of Christina von Stommeln are taken from my transcription and translation from the *Prosalegendar*. I am indebted to the Solothurn (Switzerland) city library for allowing me access to the manuscript. Research was funded by a Martin-Nelson grant from the University of Puget Sound.

27. "Als mir min muoter Maria vurshen und geben wart ze eurer mroter in der ewigen wisheit, also bist du geordnet zeeiner gemahlen. Du muost aber als vil umb minen namen liden."

28. See Donald Weinstein and Rudolph Bell, *Saints and Society. The Two Worlds of Western Christendom, 1000-1700* (Chicago: U of Chicago P, 1982), for a

catalogue of martyrs. See also Marianne Wallach-Faller, "Ein mittelhochdeutsches Dominikanerinnen-Legendar des 14. Jahrhunderts als mystagogischer Text?" in *Abendländische Mystik im Mittelalter*, ed. Kurt Ruh (Stuttgart: Metzler, 1986) 388-401, on the *Prosalegendar* .

29. For useful background and bibliographical references, see Jean LeClercq, "The Dominican Crusade," in *The History of Christian Spirituality*, Vol. 2, *The Spirituality of the Middle Ages* (New York: Seabury, 1968) 315-343. See also Ellen Ross, "'She Wept and Cried Right Loud for Sorrow and for Pain.' Suffering, the Spiritual Journey, and Women's Experience in Late Medieval Mysticism," in *Maps of Flesh and Light. The Religious Experience of Medieval Women Mystics*, ed. Ulrike Wiethaus (Syracuse: Syracuse UP, 1993) 45-59.

30. "Lieb frunt flien. vnd leide vijent minnen. al zerganklich hab lassen. vngemach suchen. Versmecht begeren. sinen eigennen willen in allen dingen brechen. Liden ane widersprechen. Dv machent der hohen martrer genos."

31. Russell, *Lucifer* 68, gives more examples of the motif of Lucifer's two faces.

32. "Und mit dem viel si in die anefechtung der verzweifflung als größlichen das si des daucht das niemant möchte behalten werden wie wol er lebte, er were denn in der reinikeit als adam do er geschaffen ward. Und was ir alle zeit wie die helle vor ir offen stünde, und si darein geschaffen were das si darein müste und das ir stul were geseczet zu luciffers stul" (126r).

33. "Du sprichest das got gut sey. Des enist er nit. Wann er ist übel und alles übel ist von im kummen wann er west wol da er den engel geschuff das der ze einen pößen veint solt werden. Und Eva und Adam und alles menschlich geslecht von seinen rat fallen sölt" (127r). Baker sees Julian denying the dualist doctrine, as well (65).

34. Peter Dinzelbacher, *Mittelalterliche Visionsliteratur* (Darmstadt: Wissenschaftliche Buchgesellschaft, 1989), is still the best source on visions in the Middle Ages. See also Lewis, *Sister-Books* 88-111, on visions, and especially Watson, "Composition" 647-653.

35. "Do was ir in dem schlaff wie funffzig pfeil in irn leib geschossen wurdent" (129v).

36. "Eine sach das ir got hie in zeit wolt ab nemen alle ir pein. Das ander dar umb was ir tod als pitten das got ander selen mit ir arbeit bereitten wolt das si mit ir ze himelreich fürent und mit ir geselschafft leistetten" (129v-r).

37. "Als fliegen."

38. "Dar nach ward si aber verzucket in iren gepet und sah wie das plut und fleisch Jhu xri vereinpert ist mit den heiligen und mit den selen also durch ein ieckliche sel gottes plut und sein fleisch leuchtet mit sunderlicher gezierd und ir heilig leben als es auff ertrich was mit der martter oder mit sunderlicher reinikeit oder waz tugent si sünderlichen geuebet hetten die schein auch sünderlich aus und leucht aussers unsers herrn plut und fleisch und was die vereinigung als gros und als wunniklichen. Und sie sah wie das plut und fleisch Jhu xri wiel in die selen und wie die selen wider in sein fleisch und in sein plut wielend recht als es ein ding were" (127r-v).

39. Lewis, *Sister-Books* 171-5, discusses visions of the hereafter.

"In the Lowest Part of Our Need": Julian and Medieval Gynecological Writing

Alexandra Barratt

Medical discourse and the writings of the mystics seem today far removed from each other, indeed even antipathetic. In the Middle Ages, however, the gap was not quite so great, for all forms of knowledge were set within an overarching religious framework. While for some medical writers this might represent little more than a need to pay lip service to a Christian world-view, at the other extreme Hildegard of Bingen the German twelfth-century visionary and prophetess wrote extensively in both mystical and medical genres. This is not necessarily surprising as both discourses were concerned with the human person and his or her physical as well as spiritual aspect, as part of God's creation.

This paper will attempt to read Julian's great mystical text *A Revelation of Love*, which has so much to say about the motherhood of God, in the light of a Middle English gynecological and obstetrical treatise that dates from the early fifteenth century and which Julian might therefore conceivably have read. It will suggest that Julian, already known as an acute observer of her visions which she describes with clinical precision, may have had a rather more "scientific" outlook than has previously been allowed. The medical text, which for convenience we will call *The Knowing of Woman's Kind*, is found in Oxford Bodley MS Douce 37 and four other manuscripts. It was probably translated from the French, possibly in part from the text found in London British Library MS Sloane 3525 ff. 246ᵛ-253.[1] It also contains elements from the Latin text *Cum auctor*, traditionally attributed to the eleventh- or twelfth-century gynecologist Trotula, and from the Latin text of Muscio, who drew on the writings of the Alexandrian Greek physician Soranus.

The Knowing of Woman's Kind begins with an elaborate Prologue that places all that follows within the Christian world view: "Ovre lorde God, whan he had storid þe worlde of all creaturis, he made manne and woman . . . and badde hem wexe and multiply and ordende þat of þem too schulde cume þe thurde . . . so that . . . þe chylde schulde be engendy[r]de" (MS Douce 37, f. 1) ["When our Lord God had furnished the world with all created things, he made man and woman... and commanded them to increase and multiply, and decreed that from the two of them should issue the third . . . so that . . . the child should be engendered"]. But in spite of this opening reference to God as Creator and the presentation of reproduction as divinely ordained, this account of the process by which human beings are generated is purely physical: they result from a reasonable and balanced admixture ("tempure") of the four elements of hot and cold, moist and dry. The text makes no attempt to account for the creation of the soul, and nowhere does it broach the topic of the stage at which the embryo becomes "ensouled." Nonetheless, the whole process is presented as the direct result of God's action.

This emphasis on human activity operating within divine parameters is reinforced when, after its opening account of divine creation, *The Knowing of Woman's Kind* goes on to claim a charitable motive for its composition and translation, presenting itself as written specially for women, for women literate in English to read to the illiterate, so that they need not involve men in the treatment of women's diseases.[2] Any men who may happen to read it are sternly warned not to despise women because of their physical complaints, as "they have no other euelys that nov be alyue than thoo women hade that nov be seyntys in heuyn" ["they that are now living have complaints no different than those women who are now saints in heaven"]. After this determinedly pious opening, however, the text soon becomes strictly practical and, in the Douce version at least, ends (rather than concludes) with a recipe for the expulsion of the "secundine" or afterbirth.

In contrast to this blending of the physical and the spiritual found in *The Knowing of Woman's Kind*, Julian is careful to distinguish the creation of the body, which she describes in traditional Biblical terms, from the creation of the soul. God makes the body out of something material, mud in fact, but he simply creates the soul out of nothing: "whan God shuld make mans body he tooke the slyppe of erth, which is a matter medlid and gaderid of all bodily things, and therof he made mannys bodye; but to the makyng of manys soule he wold take ryte nought, but made it" ["when God was about to make the human body he took mud, which is a form of matter compounded and collected from all physical things, and out of it he created the human body; but for making the human soul he wished to take nothing at all, but [simply] made it"].3 And again in contrast to *The Knowing of Woman's Kind*, Julian's text takes the body and its weaknesses as its starting point: the body of Christ, suffering in his Passion, and the body of the visionary, sick unto death at the age of thirty. But it concludes with an assertion of the love of God as manifested in his creation:

> Thus was I lerid that love was our lords mening . . . ere God made us he lovid us. . . . And in this love he hath don all his werke. . . . In our making we had beginning, but the love wherin he made us was in him from withoute beginning; in which love we have our beginning. (103)

> [In this way I was taught that Our Lord's meaning was love . . . before God made us he loved us. . . . And he has done all his work in this love. . . . We had our beginning in our creation, but the love in which he created us existed in him without any beginning; we have our beginning in this love.]

For Julian it is God's love that is supremely important and towards which her text moves, away from the suffering body, just as the suffering Christ is miraculously transformed at the end of the Eighth Showing.

There is no doubt that one of the most prominent themes in *A Revelation of Love* is that of pain and sickness, both the visionary's own and Christ's. This forms another link with medical discourse, for pain and sickness are the principal reasons for its existence. *The Knowing of Woman's Kind* asserts that such suffering is to be alleviated if at all possible. Like most medieval medical texts, it regards women as inherently more prone to pain and disease than men, for simple physiological reasons: women are cold and wet while men are hot and dry. At the very beginning we are told, "for as moche as whomen ben more febull and colde be nature þan men been and have grete travell in chyldynge, þer fall oftyn to hem mo diuerse sykenes than to men and namly to þe membrys þat ben longyng to gendrynge" (f. 1) ["for in as much as women are weaker and colder by nature than men are and have great labour in childbirth, they often suffer more varied sicknesses than men, in particular with respect to the reproductive organs"]. Specifically, there are three types of "anguysch" that "fallyn to women rathyre then to men" (f. 5ᵛ): the pain of childbirth, the pain of various uterine disorders, and the pain of menstruation and its disturbances. Pain is therefore an inherent part of the female condition which cannot be completely eliminated although it can and should be relieved. For this text never suggests that women must suffer in childbirth as punishment for original sin, though it does assert that the only way to avoid the pain of childbirth completely is to refrain from sexual intercourse: as it says rather cynically, "But sche þat wol haue no travyll in chyldynge, let kepe here fro þe recevynge of sede of man and, oon my parell, sche schall nevyre drede þe travelynge of chylde!" (f. 5ᵛ) ["But any woman who does not wish to have labour in childbirth, let her refrain from receiving man's sperm and I can assure her she need never fear the labour of childbirth!"].

Nonetheless this physical pain is not necessarily bad or meaningless: some has a purpose. Menstruation for instance is painful but necessary to purge the female body of the impurities that accumulate as a result of its digestive system, which is inefficient compared to men's: "The flourys of women ys anguysch þat fallyth to euery woman be nature euery month onys and at a certeyn be þey purgyth at her wyket of a mortall poyson þat arysyth in hem of a corrupte blode" (f. 4r-v) ["menstruation is pain that happens to every woman naturally once a month and at a particular [time] they are purged at the opening of the womb of a deadly poison that arises in them from decaying blood"]. Elsewhere the translator describes menstruation as a purgation, "an esporgymente the whyche ys calde þe flourys, wit-outyn whyche may no chylde be engendryde ne conceyvyde" (f. 2) ["a purgation which is called 'the flowers' without which no child can be engendered or conceived"]. Its function is "to purge and clense þe body of euyll humorys and corrupte" (f. 7ᵛ) ["to purge and cleanse the body of evil and rotton humours"]. Its necessity is stressed further by the text when it asserts that if women between the ages of fifteen and fifty (with certain exceptions) fail to menstruate, they will die. So some sorts of pain are essential to continued life.

If according to this medical model suffering is something that all women, by their very nature, share with the Christ of the mystics, are there any similarities in the ways in which their sufferings manifest themselves? Possibly. In her Second Showing, Julian is awed by the discoloration of Christ's face, which she perceives as like its image in the Vernicle, "often chongyng of color. Of the brownehede and blakehede, reulihede and lenehede of this image, many mervel how it might be" (12) ["often changing color. Of the blackness and brownness, the pathos and the emaciation of this image, many wonder how it could possibly be"]. She decides that just as human beings were originally made in God's image, so the Incarnate Christ strove to make himself as close as possible in appearance to fallen humanity, hence appearing as "the image and likenes of our foule blak dede hame wherein our faire, bryte, blissid lord God is hid" (12) ["the image and likeness of our foul black dead outer casing, in which our lovely, bright, blessed Lord God is hidden"]. In the Eighth Showing she also focuses on the changes of color: "I saw his swete face as it was drye and blodeles with pale deyeng; and sithen more pale, dede, langoring, and then turnid more dede into blew, and sithen then more browne blew" (18) ["I saw his sweet face as if it were dry and bloodless with pallid dying; and then more pallid, deadly, sickening and then it turned more deadly to a leaden color, and then a more brownish livid shade"].

This emphasis on pallor is also found in *The Knowing of Woman's Kind* though in a different context, when it describes, among other "sygnes of þe bledyng of þe marys" ["symptoms of the bleeding of the uterus"], "pale colowre as ledde . . . and dryed, and oþer-while þat blode commyth nowth of þe marys but passyth by othyre weyes fro here. þat bledyng commyth of hard delyuerance of chylde" (f. 33ᵛ) ["a pale color like lead . . . and dehydrated, and sometimes that blood does not come out of the uterus but flows out of her through other routes. That bleeding results from difficult delivery of a child"]. Later, "pale colowre, leen of body" is listed among the "sygnes of þe rynnynge of blode of women owt of mesure" (f. 34) ["symptoms of the excessive flow of women's blood"].

Julian's own attitude to pain and suffering is more complex than that of *The Knowing of Woman's Kind* and is an aspect of her thought that modern readers find particularly hard to understand. *A Revelation* begins with three requests. The second, which like the gynecological text associates suffering with purgation, may seem bizarre if not pathological to modern readers. She tells us how she asked God for "bodily sekenesse in youth": "In this sikenesse I desired to have all manier peynes bodily and ghostly that I should have if I should dye. . . . And this I ment for I would be purged be the mercy of God" (2) ["in this sickness I longed to have all the kinds of physical and spiritual pains that I would have if I were to die. . . . And my intention was that I would be purged by God's mercy"]. Her subsequent mysterious sickness is structurally fundamental to the Showings, and Julian describes its circumstances in great detail: she was thirty and a half years old, she was sick for seven nights and six days in all, received the Last Rites on the fourth night, and on the seventh day became numb from waist down, was thought on the point of death and received the Last Rites (3). But more important, it is within the context of this sickness that she received her revelation, consisting of sixteen showings.

That there is an intrinsic connection between her own suffering and Christ's is suggested in the Eighth Showing, where Julian first describes how Christ's appearance seemed to her "as if he had bene seven nighte dede, deyand, at the poynt of out passing away, sufferand the last peyne" (18) ["as if he had been on the point of death, dying, for seven nights, suffering the final pain"]. She then explains that by this ambiguous expression she meant that Christ looked as if he had been dying for seven nights, the very same period during which she was apparently dying herself.

Her suffering is identified with Christ's in other ways too: "I would that his peynes were my peynes with compassion" (4) ["I wished that his pains were my pains though shared suffering"], she writes. Indeed, her request for sickness is inserted between her wish for a greater awareness or consciousness ("mende") of his Passion and for the "three woundes" of contrition, compassion, and desire. Christ's pain becomes fused with hers in the Eighth Showing during which, delivered from her own suffering, she watches Christ dying on the cross: "The which shewing of Cristes peynys fillid me ful of payne. . . . And in al this tyme of Cristes paynys I felte no payn but for Cristes paynys" (20) ["this revelation of Christ's pains filled me full of pain. . . . And in all this time of Christ's pains I felt no pain except for Christ's pains"]. Indeed, pain becomes a unifying bond between Christ and his mother, his disciples and all of us, both good and evil, for "whan he was in payne, we were in payne. And al cretures that might suffre payne suffrid with him, that is to sey, al cretures that God hathe made to our service" (20) ["when he was in pain, we were in pain. And all created beings that were capable of suffering pain suffered with him, that is to say, all created beings that God has made to serve us"]. But Christ's pain is still unique, "for the peynys of Crists passion passen al peynys" (23) ["for the pains of Christ's passion surpass all pains"], and also extreme, "most peyne and overpassing" ["the greatest and most surpassing pain"]. It is seen as inherently good: "the peynes was a nobele, worshipfull dede don in a tyme be the werkyng of love" ["the pains were a noble, honourable action performed at a [particular] time by the operation of love"].

In Julian's world view, however, human pain, which is ubiquitous and inevitable, can be good, bad or morally neutral. Pain may not be bad in itself, but it is closely connected with sin in many passages. For instance, we are told that "synne is cause of all this peyne" (29), and in Chapter 76 that "it is the most peyne that the soule may have, to turne fro God ony time be synne" (92) ["it is the greatest pain that the soul can suffer, to turn away from God at any time through sin"]. Pain can also be the punishment for sin, and in Chapter 38 Julian describes how God showed her that "ryth as to every synne is answeryng a peyne be trewth, ryth so, for every synne, to the same soule is goven a bliss by love" (39) ["just as by justice there is a pain corresponding to every sin, so for every sin there is given a [particular] joy by love"]. Pain can be a manifestation of sin: in Chapter 27, she says, "In this nakid word 'synne' our lord browte to my mynd generally al that is not good" ["In this bare word 'sin' Our Lord brought to my mind in a general sense all that is not good"], which includes "al the peynys and passions of al his creatures" (29). In Chapter 39, she tells us that God considers sin "as sorow and peyne to his lovers in whome he assigneth no blame for love" (40-41) ["as sorrow and pain for those who love him, to whom he attributes no blame because of love"]. In Chapter 72 she reflects that "it semith to us oftentimes as we wern in peril of deth, in a party of hell, for the sorow and peyne that the synne is to us" (87) ["it often seems to us that we were in danger of death, in a part of hell, because of the sorrow and pain that sin represents to us"].

But not all pain is sin: "synne . . . may be liken to no payne, which peyne is not synne" (42) ["sin . . . cannot be compared to any pain, if that pain is not sin"]. Julian also argues that sin has no substance;

earlier, she has said in Chapter 11 that "synne is no dede" (13) ["sin is not an act"], and that it is known only through pain which, in contrast, does have a real existence: "and thus peyne, it is something, as to my syte, for a tyme, for it purgith" (29) ["and in this way pain is [indeed] something, in my view, for a [limited] time, for it purges"]. Pain has a real existence because it can perform an act--in this case, "purge." This metaphor of suffering as a form of purgation is so familiar from didactic, devotional and mystical texts 4 that we perhaps forget that it is at root a medical metaphor. We have already seen how in *The Knowing of Woman's Kind* the "anguish" of women functions literally as a means for their purgation. In Chapter 2, as we have seen, Julian wants a sickness with "all manier peynes bodily and gostly" because she "wold be purged be the mercy of God" (2). In Chapter 74 she describes how certain forms of fear can be salutary, because they purify as does sickness or pain: "the drede of afray . . . doith good, for it helpith to purge man as doeth bodily sekenes or swich other peyne that is not synne" (89) ["fearful dread . . . is beneficial, for it helps purge a person as does physical sickness or some other such pain which is not sin"]. She is also using familiar medical metaphors when she describes contrition, compassion, and true longing as "medycines" that heal the soul's wounds, or in Chapter 82 describes God as "our medecine" (99). *The Knowing of Woman's Kind*, of course, is much taken up with such remedies: for instance, the translator refers to "my medycyns for delyuerance of chylde," which are largely draughts or potions, and elsewhere writes of "medycynys þat will strayne þe blode withinforth" ["medicines that will purify the blood internally"].

The possible influence on Julian of medical discourse is seen in microcosm in one of the best loved and most admired passages in *A Revelation of Love*. In Chapter 5 she describes how Our Lord "shewed a littil thing, the quantitye of a hesil nutt in the palme of my hand" ["showed a little thing, the size of a hazel nut in the palm of my hand"] and when she asked what it was, was "generally answered thus: 'It is all that is made'" (5). The simile has been much admired for its poetic quality, but it has not perhaps been noted that the hazel nut is a standard measurement of size in medieval medical and other recipes. The *Oxford English Dictionary* quotes it, s.v. "hazel nut," as a measure of size from an early fifteenth-century version of Mandeville's *Travels*, "Dyamaundes . . . of þe mykilnes of hesill nuttes" ["diamonds . . . of the size of hazel nuts"]. The *Middle English Dictionary* also quotes from Mandeville, "þer ben summe . . . als grete as and hasell note" ["there are some . . . as large as an hazel nut"], and from a cookery book, "put in the peletes like an hassille nott" ["put in the small pieces like a hazel nut"]. *The Knowing of Woman's Kind* itself uses it as a measure in a medicine for childbirth: "Tak of myrre þe quantite of j hasull not and ȝyf here to drynk in wynne and with-owtyn fayl sche shall be delyuerd a-noon" (f. 13ᵛ) ["Take a [piece of] myrrh the size of one hazel nut and give it to her in wine to drink and infallibly she shall give birth immediately"]. An awareness that the hazel nut simile is not taken from the natural world of wood and forest so much as from women's everyday domestic life is another surprising, yet telling, example of the way in which Julian constantly rewards us if we try to read her in her own cultural context rather than ours.

A quite different, but no less striking, affinity between *A Revelation of Love* and *The Knowing of Woman's Kind*, is a shared model of the process of generation. A great deal of Julian's longer, revised text is devoted to her attempts to elucidate her profoundly radical view of the Trinity; indeed the scribe of the Sloane Manuscript emphasizes this vital aspect when in his explicit he describes the book as "the revelation of love of the blissid Trinite" (102). One of her earlier references to a Trinitarian model comes just after the Fourteenth Showing when Julian describes how the persons of the Trinity are reflected in the "properties" (faculties) of the human soul: "Treuth seith God, and wisedam beholdyth God, and of these ii comyth the thred: that is an holy mervelous delyte in God, which is love. Wher treuth and wisdam is verily, there is love verily comond of hem bothyn, and al of God makyng" (47) ["truth contemplates God and wisdom beholds God and from these two comes the third: a holy, miraculous delight in God, which is love. Where truth and wisdom are truly present, there is love truly coming from them both, and all is of God's doing"]. The phrasing here is astonishingly reminiscent of the medical treatise's description of the generation of the human child: "Ovre lorde god . . . made manne and woman . . . and ordende þat of þem ij schulde cume þe thurde . . . so þat [be] þe tempure of hote and colde, moyste and dry, þe Chylde schulde be engendryde" (47) ["our Lord God . . . created man and woman . . . and decreed that from the two of them should come the third . . . so that by the admixture of hot and cold, damp and dry, the child should be engendered"]. And of course Julian later goes on radically to remodel the Trinity itself on the basis of Father-and-Mother, rather than Father-and-Son.

As countless readers have observed, Julian has much to say on the topic of God as Mother. Much, too, has been written on her theology of the Motherhood of God. But perhaps not enough attention has been paid to Julian's concept of motherhood itself, and the way in which this must have been a product of her own time, for all her originality. Unfortunately *The Knowing of Woman's Kind* does not have as much to say on motherhood itself as one would hope or expect. To summarise its account, the seed comes from the male, who is hot and dry, and is received by the woman, who is cold and moist; between them the child is engendered. The matrice or womb "ys ordende to receyve and holde þe sede of man and þe chylde to conceyue, forme and norsche vnto conuenabyll tyme of hys byrth" (f. 3) ["is designed to receive and contain man's sperm and conceive, form and feed the child until the appropriate time for its birth"]. Some women are more likely to conceive than others; no special treatment is necessary during pregnancy but over-exertion should be avoided from the seventh month. Birth may require some assistance from the midwife; after birth the mother should nurse her own child but wet-nurses may also be employed. The child should be weaned at the age of one or two years. That is just about all that the text has to say on the subject; the treatise pays more attention to uterine and menstrual problems than to normal birth and maternity, which one could perhaps regard as evidence that normal conception, pregnancy, and birth had not been comprehensively medicalized in the Middle Ages.

In considering medieval ideas on motherhood, it is useful to distinguish motherhood as a socially-constructed and learned role from motherhood as a biological fact. Julian uses both concepts; *The Knowing of Woman's Kind* naturally concentrates on the latter, but it does have something to say about the former. When Julian uses the traditional metaphor of the Church as mother and declares, "now I yelde me to my moder holy church as a simple child owyth" (49) ["now I submit myself to my mother Holy Church as a simple child should"], it is the social aspect of motherhood as representing authority and discipline, rather than the biological, nurturing, aspect that she stresses. This implied assumption that mothers wield authority and are defied at the child's own risk, is just as much a social construct as the opposite idea that mothers are by nature merciful and nurturing. Julian appeals to the latter when in her first reference to the motherhood of God in Chapter 48 she says that "mercy is a pitifull propirte which longyth to the moderid [of God] in tendyr love . . . mercy werkyth: kepyng, suffring, quecknyng and helyng, and al is of tendernes of love" (51) ["mercy is a compassionate attribute which pertains to the motherhood in tender love . . . mercy acts: caring, enduring, giving life and healing, and this is all from the tenderness of love"].

But when Julian describes the Blessed Virgin as "our moder in whome we are all beclosid and of hir borne in Christe" ["our mother in whom we are all enclosed and born from her in Christ"], and Christ as "our very moder in whom we be endlesly borne and never shall come out of him" (69) ["our true mother in whom we are endlessly being born and shall never emerge from him"], she is of course thinking of motherhood as a biological event. Julian also uses metaphors of biological motherhood when she describes how Christ takes on human form in order to be our Mother:

he toke the ground of his werke full low and ful myldely in the maydens womb . . . in this low place he raysid him and dyte him ful redy in our pore flesh, himselfe to don the service and the office of moderhede . . . he susteynith us within himselfe in love, and traveled into the full tyme that he wold suffre the sharpist throwes and the grevousest peynes. . . . And whan he had don, and so born us to bliss, yet myte not al this makyn aseth. (73)

[he laid the foundations of his work very humbly and gently in the virgin's womb . . . in this humble place he established himself and dressed himself very readily in our wretched flesh, so that he himself might perform the duties and function of motherhood . . . he bears us up within himself in love, and was in labour until the moment of time when he would undergo the most acute labour pangs and the most severe pains. . . . And when he had finished, and in this way birthed us to glory, still this was not enough.]

Christ is literally born as the biological son of Mary so that metaphorically he can be our true mother, carrying us within himself, going through labour, giving birth and surpassing human mothers in feeding us. For the "moder may geven hir child soken her mylke, but our pretious moder Iesus, he may fedyn us with himselfe" (73) ["mother is able to give the child her milk to suck, but our precious mother Jesus is able to feed us with himself"].

It is easy for us to comprehend these particular images of biological motherhood because we know, as did our medieval ancestors, that the mother carries her unborn child within her, gives birth to it and nourishes it. But we may miss the force of other metaphors because our understanding of gestation and childbirth is not precisely that of the Middle Ages. For instance, the passage from Chapter 48 quoted in the previous paragraph introduces the idea of "quickening," that is, giving life and movement to the embryo. This is a specifically medieval (or at least pre-modern) biological concept, which Julian uses again in Chapter 63 when she writes of Christ that "in the takyng of our kinde he quicknid us, in his blissid deying upon the cross he bare us to endless life" (77) ["in the adoption of our nature he quickened us, in his blessed dying on the cross he birthed us to eternal life"].5 And elsewhere as we have already seen she writes that Christ our mother reforms, restores, and unites us to his substance: "in our moder of mercy we have our reformyng and restoryng, in whom our partes are onyd and all made perfitt man" (71) ["we have our re-formation and restoration in our mother of mercy, in whom our component parts are united and all made a complete human being"]. We may read this as an ethical or moral metaphor but for Julian to re-form, restore, and unify the parts of the body into a viable whole could have been an entirely literal account of what was thought to go on in the mother's womb. *The Knowing of Woman's Kind* stresses the mother's part in "forming" the child: as we have already seen, the translator writes of one of the functions of the uterus being to "form" the child, while he also advises the pregnant woman: "in þe vij monyth let kepe here esyly for þan ys þe Chylde formyde" (f.10) ["in the seventh month let her look after herself for [by] then the child is formed"].

But someone other than the birth mother can carry out the social as distinct from biological roles of motherhood. This is the kind of motherhood Julian has in mind when she writes, "The moders service is nerest, redyest and sekirest" (73) ["the mother's service is most intimate, most prompt and most reliable"], or

To the properte of moderhede longyth kynde love, wysdam and knowing, and it is good; for thow it be so that our bodily forthbrynging be but litil, low and semple in regard of our gostly forthbringing, yet it is he that doth it in the creatures be whom that it is done. The kynde, loveand moder that wote and knowith the nede of hir child, she kepith it ful tenderly as the kind and condition of moderhede will. And as it wexith in age she chongith hir werking but not hir love. (74)

[To the nature of motherhood appertain natural love, wisdom and knowledge, which is good; for though it is true that our physical birth is merely insignificant, humble, and simple in comparison to our spiritual birth, nonetheless it is he who performs it in the [human] creatures through whom it is performed. The natural loving mother who knows and understands her child's needs cares for it very tenderly as the nature and the state of motherhood require. And as it grows older she changes her actions but not her love.]

"Keeping" could be translated as "caring" and Julian uses the term frequently elsewhere: for instance, in Chapter 49 God's goodness "kepith us whan we synne that we perish not" and "we have our kepyng in the endles myte of God" (52) ["we have our caring in God's eternal power"]. *The Knowing of Woman's Kind* gives recommendations for the care or "keeping" of the young child with a whole section entitled, "How ye schall kepe þe chylde þe fyrst yere" (f. 18v). This covers how often the child should be washed (quite frequently!), when it should be fed, and when and how it should be weaned. The section on weaning is a good example of the kind of change Julian might have in mind that is dependent on the child's age and development: "when he ys of age j yere or ij, so þat he have tethe þat he may ete dyuerse metys, than vse hym fro þe bryst" (f. 19) ["when he is one or two years old, as long as he has teeth so that he can eat various foods, then wean him from the breast"].

But these duties would not necessarily be performed by the biological mother in the Middle Ages and *The Knowing of Woman's*

Kind refers from time to time to a "norse." Julian too makes use of the metaphor of the wet- or dry-nurse once or twice. In Chapter 61 she describes how Christ is always ready to welcome us: "the swete gracious hands of our moder be redy and diligently aboute us: for he in al this werkyng usith the office of a kinde nurse and hath not all to don but to entendyn abouten the salvation of hir child" (76) ["the sweet gracious hands of our mother are promply and conscientiously at our service; for in all these actions he performs the duties of a kindly nurse and has nothing to do other than pay attention to the salvation or well-being of her child"]. I have commented elsewhere on Julian's perceptiveness here:[6] usually caregivers have many other duties to perform and it can be a real luxury to be entirely free to look after a single child's well-being and nothing else.

But for a more specifically medieval reading of this passage we could compare it with what *The Knowing of Woman's Kind* has to say about the choice of a nurse and how she should conduct herself: "Tak a norse for hym to kepe þe Chylde þat be yong and in good stat . . . and þat sche lovyth þe Chylde with all here hert . . . but euer let here ete welle and lette here sume tyme travayle þat sche fall not costyff" (f. 17ᵛ) ["Employ a nurse for the child to look after it who is young and in good health ... and let her love the child with all her heart . . . but let her always eat well and let her take exercise from time to time so that she does not become constipated"]. Both texts stress that the nurse must love the child or be "kind," and imply that all details of her life must be focused on the well-being of her charge. The medical text develops this idea more fully: she should eat well and take physical exercise, to stay in good health for the child's sake. For her physical condition--for instance, whether she is constipated or not--can directly impinge on the child's. For the same reason she should be sexually inactive, "for of þat my3ght fall here purgacyon and tak a-way here mylk and mak hym dry" (f. 18) ["because she might menstruate as a result and lose her milk and dehydrate him" (the baby)], and the text goes on to specify the quality of her milk and how it should be tested.

There are no descriptions of childbirth itself in Julian's text. Paradoxically, she plays down physical birth or "our bodily forthbrynging," describing it as "litil, low and semple." Nonetheless it is part of the divine operation or "working": it may be humble, "yet it is he [Christ] that doth it in the creatures be whom that it is done." But her Fifteenth Showing, a vision of the rebirth of the soul in death and its escape from pain, clearly takes its origin from a natural if idealized birth; it is introduced in the Paris Manuscript by the words "all his [God's] blessyd chyldren whych be come out of hym by kynde shulde be brougt agayne in to hym by grace" ["all his blessed children that have emerged from him in the course of nature should be re-integrated into him through the operation of grace"]. Julian describes her vision as follows:

> I saw a body lyand on the erthe, which body shewid hevy and ogyley, withoute shappe and forme. . . . And sodenly out of this body sprang a ful fair creature, a little childe full shapen and formid. . . . And the bolnehede of the body betokenith gret wretchidnes of our dedly flesh, and the littlehede of the child betokenith the clenes of purity in the soule. (79)

> [I saw a body lying on the earth; this body appeared heavy and ugly, without shape and form. . . . And suddenly there leapt out of this body a very beautiful creature, a small child fully shaped and formed. . . . And the swollenness of the body symbolizes the vast misery of our mortal flesh, and the smallness of the child symbolizes the cleanliness of purity in the soul.]

"Hevy" is often used to mean "pregnant" in Middle English, and "bolnehede" suggested an advanced stage of pregnancy. The dead body, then, is like that of a pregnant woman's.

In spite of her reticence about the process of childbirth Julian shows none of the contempt for or disgust with the human body which is usually associated with the Middle Ages. While many ecclesiastical writers urged their readers to see the body as nothing more than a sack of excrement and food for worms, Julian admires its construction and design and is particularly struck by the arrangements made for elimination of digested food. In Chapter 6, where she is reflecting on how the goodness of God "comith downe to the lowest party of our nede" ["condescends to the humble aspects of our need"], the Paris MS alone includes an interesting passage, perhaps omitted by the Sloane MS because its thought is so surprising and unusual:

A man goyth vppe ryght and the soule of his body is sparyde as a purse fulle feyer. And whan it is tyme of his nescessery it is openyde and sparyde ayen fulle honestly. And that it is he that doyth this is schewed ther wher he seyth he comyth downe to vs to the lowest parte of oure nede. For he hath no dispite of that he made, ne he hath no disdeyne to serue vs at the sympylest office that to oure body longyth in kynde, for loue of the soule that he made to his awne lycknesse.

[A man walks erect and the digested food in his body is closed up like a very splendid purse. And when it is time for the call of nature it opens and is closed again in a very seemly fashion. And the fact that it is he [God] who does this is demonstrated where it says that he condescends to us in the humblest aspect of our necessity. For he does not despise what he has made, and he does not disdain to serve us in the simplest function that appertains to our body in nature, for love of the soul that he created in his own image.]7

Julian emphasizes that elimination is done "fulle honestly," that is, honorably or decently, even though it is "low" or "simple"--adjectives as we have already seen that she applies to childbirth in Chapter 61.

The Knowing of Woman's Kind offers a more scientific account of medieval theories of digestion and elimination: "There ys a bouell with-in þe body of manne and woman þat ys clepid 'longaon' by þe wyche þe gret vryne passyth" ["There is a bowel inside the human body which is called 'longaon' through which the solid waste passes"]. He goes on to explain that "alle þe mete þat we receyue goyth in-to þe stomak and þer hit ys sodune and defyede and all þat ys gret and not profitabull to man passyth dovne be þe bouellys þat ys clepit 'longaon' and þer passyth hit a-vay" (f. 7) ["all the food that we absorb goes into the stomach and there it is decocted and digested and all that is gross and not useful for human beings passes down by the bowel that is called 'longaon' and there it is excreted"]. Clearly, Julian did not possess such detailed knowledge of human physiology and anatomy; but her detached and even admiring interest in the workings of the body suggests she might have been the kind of intelligent and informed laywoman for whom *The Knowing of Woman's Kind* was translated.

We have long been aware of the need to historicize texts, that is, read them with reference to their historical and ideological context. But the scientific and medical context of medieval texts is often neglected: such texts enshrine beliefs that we today find bizarre, embarrassing or even ludicrous and which we suspect--and rather hope!--were not widely disseminated or believed even in the Middle Ages. But if we do continue to ignore them, we run the risk of inadvertently falling into the error of essentialism. If on the contrary we confront these ideas and read Julian beside or even against such texts, she will continue to surprise and enlighten us.

NOTES

1 On the distant Greek and Latin sources of this text and the immediate French source, see A. Ellis Hanson and Monica H. Green, "Soranus of Ephesus:I" in *Aufsteig und Niedergang der Römischen Welt: Rise and Decline of the Roman World,* ed. W. Haase and H. Temporini (Berlin and New York: Walter de Gruyter, 1994): 1059. On the text itself, see Monica Green, "Obstetrical and Gynecological Texts in Middle English," *Studies in the Age of Chaucer* 14 (1992): 64-68.

2. This motif is present even in the Latin text of Trotula, *De Passionibus Mulierum*; see *The Diseases of Women by Trotula of Salerno: A Translation of Passionibus Mulierum Curandorum* by Elizabeth Mason-Hohl (New York: Ritchie, 1940): "women on account of modesty . . . dare not reveal the difficulties of their sicknesses to a male doctor. Wherefore I, pitying their misfortunes and at the instigation of a certain matron, began to study carefully the sicknesses which most frequently trouble the female sex" (2).

3. *Julian of Norwich: A Revelation of Love,* ed. Marion Glasscoe (Exeter: University of Exeter P, 1976; rev. 1986) 64. All further references are to this edition unless otherwise stated. Translations are my own. For the reasons for preferring this edition of the Sloane Manuscript to Colledge and Walsh's edition based primarily on the Paris Manuscript, see Marion Glasscoe, "Visions and Revisions: A Further Look at the Manuscripts of Julian of Norwich," *Studies in Bibliography* 42 (1989): 103-20, and Alexandra Barratt, "How Many Children Had Julian of Norwich? Editions, Translation and Versions of Her Revelations" in Anne Clark Bartlett, ed, *Vox Mystica: Essays on Medieval Mysticism* (Cambridge: Brewer, 1995) 27-39.

4. Compare the imagery of various types of purification through suffering that is found in *The Book of Tribulation,* ed. Alexandra Barratt, MET 15 (Heidelberg: Carl Winter, 1984) especially 54: "The thrid seruice of tribulacion, it is that thai seruen þe to purge þe. . . . ther ben fyue maner of purgacions that by reson and by holy writ ben remeued to the seruice of tribulacion." The first of these five types is strictly medical: "by medicyn, outher by bledynge. Bledynge, I say, either by veyne or by garsyng." These three medical forms of purgation are then expounded at length on 53-63.

5. See M. Anthony Hewson, *Giles of Rome and the Medieval Theory of Conception* (London, 1975) and J. Needham, *A History of Embryology* (Cambridge: Cambridge UP, 2nd. ed., 1958) for further details on medieval ideas about quickening.

6. See Alexandra Barratt, *Womens' Writing in Middle English* (London and New York: Longman, 1992) 131.

7. *A Book of Showings to the Anchoress Julian of Norwich,* ed. E. Colledge and J. Walsh (Toronto: Pontifical Institute of Mediaeval Studies, 1978), 2 vols, II: 306/35-307/41.

A Question of Audience: The Westminster Text and Fifteenth-Century Reception of Julian of Norwich

Hugh Kempster

The principal concern of this essay is neither the late-medieval anchoress Julian of Norwich nor the Middle English text she produced, *A Revelation of Love*.[1] Rather, my focus is the early reception of Julian's work and especially the feasibility of identifying one possible fifteenth-century audience. Pivotal to the research has been a largely neglected manuscript, known as the Westminster Text (W), which is the earliest extant witness to the Longer Version (LV) of *A Revelation of Love*. The text is a heavily edited, partial copy of the LV, and as such has been judged to have little to contribute towards Julian studies. In the light of a contemporary shift in methodological focus, from author or text to reader, W takes on a much greater significance.

The only extended commentary on W published to date is found in the introduction to James Walsh and Eric (Edmund) Colledge, *Of the Knowledge of Ourselves and of God*, a modernization of the whole Westminster florilegium. Judged by its hand to have been copied around 1500, the manuscript consists of a series of extracts; two from commentaries on the psalms--*Qui Habitat* and *Bonum Est*--one from Walter Hilton's *Scale of Perfection*, and finally the abridgement of *A Revelation of Love*. Walsh and Colledge make an important differentiation between the scribe who, they argue, mechanically copied the whole manuscript and an earlier editor who undertook the task of piecing together the various extracts. Commenting on the dialectal differences one might expect in the four extracts, Walsh and Colledge conclude:

Such differences, however, have almost entirely disappeared in the Florilegium, which seems to have been copied from another manuscript which had been very carefully translated into the English spoken in the South-Eastern regions of the country, adjacent to London, in the mid-fifteenth century. Neither the extracts from *The Scale* nor those from Julian's *Revelations* show any notable dialectal difference from *Qui Habitat* or *Bonum Est*: and this strongly suggests that the editor was also responsible for this process of translation.[2]

It is the work of this fifteenth-century editor, the first recorded reader and critic of Julian's LV, and particularly what can be inferred of his audience, that will be the focus of this essay.[3]

A parallel reading of the Middle English text of W alongside the two evidential full copies of the LV (London, British Library, Sloane MS 2499 [S1] and Paris, Bibliotheque Nationale, Fonds Anglais 40 [P])[4] uncovers numerous editorial decisions and prompts the question: Why were these changes made? Walsh and Colledge comment only briefly on this aspect of the history of the manuscript: "A reviewer might describe the Florilegium as 'very useful for the *ex professo* contemplative, definitely not for the beginner.'" They add, "the fact that [the editor] does not cite the Latin of the Psalms in the two commentaries (as the other manuscripts invariably do) may support the conjecture that the reader for whom it was intended knew no Latin. One might also argue that this reader must also have been an *ex professo* contemplative" (xv, xvi).

It will be shown in this essay that the Walsh and Colledge supposition that the early reader of W was an "*ex professo* contemplative," which they do not undertake to justify, cannot be sustained. A study of fifteenth-century lay piety points to a potential audience of lay people seeking to pursue what Walter Hilton earlier termed the "mixed life." Read in this context, the editorial construction of W from Julian's full LV affirms the possibility of such an intended audience.

I. A Potential Audience

An important preliminary to the presentation of internal evidence from W concerning its audience is to survey the growth of lay participation in what might be termed the "mixed life" between the late-fourteenth and mid-fifteenth century. Certain writings of the fourteenth-century English mystics suggest that as the century was drawing to a close, debate was taking place over a new form of lay piety. Probably written in the 1380s and addressed to an individual acquaintance or spiritual directee, Hilton's epistle *Mixed Life* marks the beginnings of what was to become a radical redefining of the boundaries of the contemplative life in late-medieval England. The original recipient of the letter seems to have been undergoing a crisis of conscience; on the one hand he felt a strong call to the contemplative life, and yet on the other he was not free to pursue this in the established ways, owing to his secular responsibilities. Hilton's innovative pastoral advice points the wealthy and influential layman beyond the traditional dichotomy of the active and contemplative lives:

þou schalt not vttirli folwen þi desire for to leuen occupacioun and bisynesse of þe world, whiche aren nedefull to vsen in rulynge of þi silf and of alle oþere þat aren vndir þi kepynge, and ȝeue þee hooli to goostli occupaciouns of praiers and meditaciouns, as it were a frere or a monk or an oþir man þat were not bounden to þe world bi children and seruauntes as þou art. . . . þou schalt meedele þe werkes of actif liyf wiþ goostli werkes of lif contemplatif, and þanne doost þou weel.5

[You shall not utterly follow your desire to leave the occupation and busyness of the world, which are necessary in the disciplining of yourself and of all others that are in your keeping, and give yourself wholly to the spiritual occupations of prayers and meditations, like a friar or a monk or another man who is not bound to the world by children and servants as you are. . . . You shall mix the works of an active life with the spiritual works of a contemplative life, and then you will do well.]

In a summary Hilton spells out very clearly what he is advocating: "þou schalt vndirstonde þat þeer is þree maner of lyuynge. Oon is actif. Anoþer is contemplatiyf. þe þredde is maad of boþe, and þat is medeled" (11) ["You shall understand that there are three ways of life. One is active, another is contemplative, the third is made of both, that is, mixed"].

This concept of the "mixed life" was in one sense nothing new; the writings of Augustine and Pope Gregory I had established it as the highest attainable form of Christian living.[6] Where Hilton's work was unique, even radical, was in its deliberate application of traditional teaching on the "mixed life" to a secular, active layperson. Addressing an individual pastoral need, Hilton may have been initially unaware of the potential significance of his teaching. By the mid-fifteenth century, however, the *Mixed Life* had become widely read, providing an important mandate for the democratization of ecclesiastical authority in the areas of contemplative living and access to mystical texts.

It is a matter for debate whether Augustine and Gregory saw the contemplative life as open to all by way of the "mixed life"; certainly by the late-fourteenth century opinion was divided on the matter. The *Cloud of Unknowing* shows an unfavorable attitude towards any idea of mixing the two lives. In an allegorical exegesis of Luke 10:38-42, found in Chapter 21, the *Cloud* author writes:

> Bot whiche ben þees þre good þinges, of þe whiche Marye chees þe best þre lyues ben þey not, for Holi Chirche makiþ no mynde bot of two--actyue liif and contemplatyue liif; þe whiche two lyues ben priuely vnderstonden in þe story of þis Gospel by þees two sisters, Martha and Mary.[7]

> [But what are these three good things, of which Mary chose the best? They are not three lives, for Holy Church recognizes only two--the active life and the contemplative life; these two lives are figuratively understood, in the story of this Gospel, by these two sisters--Martha and Mary].

Seemingly in response to an external debate, or at least offering an alternative to the position taken by Hilton in his *Mixed Life*, the *Cloud* author emphatically denies the existence of a third way of life. His stance assumes ecclesiastical backing, and is thrust home with the symbolism of Scripture; after all there were only two sisters in the story, not three!

The argument does not rest there, however, the *Cloud* author goes on to repeat a section of teaching from Chapter 8 in order to push home the point (29-30, see also 17-18). What the *Cloud* author sees as a misinterpretation, perhaps even a heterodox exegesis of Scripture, has to be further explained in terms of the established orthodox framework. Mary did not choose one of three lives, the *Cloud* author asserts, rather she chose from three "partyes" [parts] or elements within the two established ways of living. Of these parts the lowest is the purely active life and the highest the purely contemplative. In the middle exists a part of the contemplative or active life, not a separate life as such. This part represents either the highest state an active person may aspire to, or the lowest possible state for a contemplative. The awkward complexity and defensiveness of this repeated argument makes most sense if it is seen as an apology. While not specifically mentioning Hilton's work, the passage could be read as a counter argument to the third way of Christian living posited in the contemporaneous *Mixed Life*.

The *Cloud* author's conservative stance suggests that this form of lay piety was in its early stages as the fourteenth century drew to a close. In his translation of the *Meditationes Vitae Christi*, written principally for the laity, Nicholas Love makes specific mention of the "mixed life" alongside the more established lay office of recluse. Towards the end of Chapter 3, Love cuts short the *Meditationes'* discussion on the active and contemplative lives and instead suggests any contemplative readers should look to Hilton's work for further instruction:

> Whereof and oþer vertuese exercise þat longeþ to contemplatif lyuyng, and specialy to a recluse, and also of medelet life, þat is to sey sumtyme actife and sumtyme contemplatif, as it longeþ to diuerse persones þat in worldly astate hauen grace of gostly loue who so wole more pleynly b[e] enfourmed and tauht in english tonge; lete hym loke þe tretees þatþ þe worþ clerk andholi lyuere Maister Walter Hilton þe Chanon of Thurgarton wrote in english by grete grace and hye discrecion.[8]

> [Concerning these and other virtuous exercises that belong to contemplative living, and especially for a recluse, and also someone of the mixed life (that is to say sometimes active and sometimes contemplative, as belongs to various persons who in worldly estate have the grace of spiritual love) who would be more fully informed and taught in the English tongue, let them look at the treatise that the worthy cleric and holy liver, Walter

Hilton the canon of Thurgarton, wrote in English by great grace and high discretion.].

It is not specified which text a recluse or someone of a "mixed life" should read, but the implications are clear: pious lay readers would do well to seek further instruction from contemplative writing such as Hilton's. Unlike the *Cloud*, Love's widely read text (officially sanctioned in 1410 by Archbishop Arundel) openly acknowledges the "mixed life" as a viable option for lay people interested in contemplation.

Although Love earlier suggests that the would-be contemplative "shal be betturtauht by experience, þen by writyng or teching of man" (124) ["shall be better taught by experience, than by the writing or teaching of people"] there is a specific connection made between the "mixed life" and the reading of contemplative treatises--in particular Hilton's work. It would push the point too far to equate lay ownership of, or interest in, a mystical text with pursuit of the "mixed life," but a degree of correlation cannot be denied. While the growth of the "mixed life" as a fifteenth-century lay movement is difficult to systematically trace, ownership of vernacular mystical texts is an observable phenomenon, and arguably a manifestation of such a movement.

A study of wills shows a small but steady increase in lay ownership of mystical texts over the fifteenth century. This coincides with an increased interest in the "mixed life" and certainly indicates a growing potential audience for contemplative works, such as the Westminster florilegium, among the fifteenth-century laity. Norman Tanner's study, *The Church in Medieval Norwich 1370-1532*, provides a useful breakdown of books bequeathed in Norwich. 9 While Norwich is outside the geographical area of interest for the production and early use of W, Tanner's study provides accessible insight into orders of magnitude and trends in what was probably England's second city at that time. The conclusions drawn from this geographically specific study will be compared with other more general studies of book ownership in late-medieval England, particularly that of Margaret Deanesly. A brief excursus concerning Margery Kempe will also be presented to emphasize the wider picture beyond extant records of textual ownership.

Tanner tabulates 167 wills from the laity and 96 clerical bequests between the years 1370 and 1439 (193-197). Of this sample 5.3% of lay people bequeathed books, as contrasted with over a third of all clerics. Of the 16 books left by lay people in this period, 13 were of a liturgical nature, two were legal works and one was scriptural. This suggests that in early fifteenth-century Norwich very few, if any, lay people owned contemplative texts.

Considering this absence of any record of lay-owned mystical literature, one might conclude that the "mixed life" was a rarity or even non-existent in the Norwich area. This could have been a reasonable assumption had not record been found of a resident of neighboring Bishop's Lynn who is portrayed as living what might well be described as a "mixed life." In *The Book of Margery Kempe*, Margery (the narrator and implied author) bears witness to some of the obstacles that might have faced someone seeking to follow this new form of lay piety.[10] Chapter by chapter Margery struggles to forge a new way, to integrate the contemplative and active lives, often at considerable personal cost.

The centrality of *lectio*, or reading, in the traditional monastic approach to contemplation was probably a barrier for many lay people in this period, particularly women and those of the lower and middle classes.[11] Margery is portrayed as the daughter of a wealthy merchant and leading burgess of Lynn, John Brunham, who served as mayor five times and also sat in parliament on several occasions. Despite her father's wealth and social standing Margery claims she was not able to read or write in English, let alone Latin. Whether or not this holds for Kempe (the actual author) we cannot say for sure, but certainly Margery's declared level of literacy was characteristic of many of her contempories.[12]

In Chapter 58 of the *Book*, Margery writes of the deep spiritual hunger she experienced in her contemplation after the loss of a spiritual director. She pleads in prayer: "Alas, Lord, as many clerkys as þu hast in þis world, þat þu ne woldyst sendyn me on of hem þat myth fulfillyn my sowle wyth þi word and wyth redyng of Holy Scriptur" (142) ["Alas, Lord, as many clerics as you have in this world, and you will not send me one of them who might fill my soul with your word and with reading of Holy Scripture"]. God then answers Margery and sends her a new spiritual director: "He red to hir many a good boke of hy contemplacyon and oþer bokys, as þe Bybyl wyth doctowrys þer-up-on, Seynt Brydys boke, Hyltons boke, Bone-ventur, Stimulus Amoris, Incendium Amoris, and swech oþer. . . . þe forseyd preste red hir bokys þe most part of vij ʒer er viij ʒer." (143) ["He read to her many a good book of high contemplation, and other books, such as the Bible with doctors' commentaries on it, St Bride's book, Hilton's book, Bonaventura's *Stimulus Amoris, Incendium Amoris*, and others similar. . . . The said priest read books to her for the most part of seven or eight years"]. Earlier, in Chapter 17, Margery makes passing reference to the same four mystical works, which were probably Bridgit of Sweden's *Revelations*, Hilton's *Scale of Perfection*, James of Milan's *Stimulus Amoris*, and Richard Rolle's *Incendium Amoris*. This clear familiarity with, and use of, at least four key contemplative texts presents Margery (whether an historical figure, or fictional archetype) as a pioneering representative of this new "mixed life" tradition.

Neither Tanner's evidence of wills nor Kempe's *Book* present the "mixed life" as a popular movement in early-fifteenth century Norfolk. Between 1440 and 1489 Tanner records a single, but very significant, contemplative book owner in Norwich, Margaret Purdans (112). A bourgeois widow who made her will in 1481, Margaret bequeathed three mystical texts. The Franciscan nuns at Bruisyard in Suffolk were to receive "Le Doctrine of the Herte," probably a translation of *De Doctrina Cordis* usually ascribed to Bishop Grosseteste (c. 1168-1253) of Lincoln. Another religious community, the Benedictine nuns at Thetford, were left an "English book of Saint Bridget," and one Alice Barly was bequeathed "a book called Hylton." It is of interest to note that two of the three books coincide with Margery's list. Although a solitary figure among the 525 testators from this period, Purdans may well have been another representative of the new class of devout, literate laypeople seeking to pursue the "mixed life."

Looking at patterns throughout England as a whole, Margaret Deanesly's observations are comparable to those made by Tanner.[13] In comparison with the years 1400 to 1525, she describes the period prior to 1400 as almost "bookless," by comparison with the years 1400 to 1525, identifying only two clear-cut cases of lay ownership of contemplative texts in the whole country. The earliest example was a member of the London gentry, Sir William Thorp, who bequeathed a "book composed by Richard the hermit" in 1391. In 1399 a copy of the *Prick of Conscience*, attributed around this time to Rolle, is mentioned in the will of Sir Thomas Roos of Igmanthorpe.

Examples of lay book ownership across fifteenth-century England are more numerous and start earlier than do the Norwich records. In 1401 Isabella, daughter of Baron Henry Percy, left a book which, although not strictly contemplative, suggests an interest in the "mixed life": *Liber Gallicus de Duc Lancastrie*. The text was written in 1354 by another Henry, the first Duke of Lancaster, whose interest in the contemplative life is also evidenced by his founding of a reclusarium.[14] Around this time Joan Game wrote her name in a copy of the *Gracia Dei*, a compilation consisting of extracts from such contemplative works as the *Ancrene Wisse* and *The Abbey of the Holy Ghost*, an English translation of the French *Sainte Abbaye* (Carey 375). It is not until a decade or two after Archbishop Arundel's licensing of Love's *Myrrour*, however, that the trickle of lay owners of mystical texts starts to grow into a small but steady stream. In 1422 Lady Peryne Clanvowe bequeathed a copy of the *Pore Caitiff*, another compilation of texts that included Rolle's writings and the *Ancrene Wisse*. Then in 1432 Robert Helperby is recorded as leaving an English translation of Suso's *Horologium Divinae Sapientiae*. Two years later a burgess of Yarmouth left the *Prick of Conscience* to Agnes Paston, and in 1438 Lady Eleanor Roos bequeathed to her nephew "an English book called the first book of master Walter" in turn given to her by the rector of Kirk Deighton, Yorkshire (Deanesly 355).[15] Lady Eleanor also owned *On the Passion* by Rolle, and the *Revelations of St Maud* that was given to a Joan Courtenay (Hughes 292).

1448 saw Agnes Stapleton bequeath an English text, the *Chastising of God's Children*, that was probably a Carthusian reworking of what Ruysbroeck himself had translated from Latin.[16] Agnes, the widow of Sir Brian Stapleton, also left *The Prick of Conscience, Vices and Virtues*, and a book called *Bonaventura* that was probably Love's *Myrrour*. (Carey 377). Between 1450 and 1451 Deanesly identifies no less than five lay owners of mystical texts, one of whom, Mercy Ormsby, may have shared an interest in the "mixed life" with her husband. The Lincolnshire lawyer Arthur Ormsby died several years after his wife leaving a bequest of "my boke called bonaventure de Christi" to the Archbishop of York (Hughes 107, 297). From the mid-fifteenth century the incidence of lay ownership of mystical texts increased significantly, as did the size of some of the libraries of their owners. Sir Thomas Cumberworth of Somerby owned, among other books, Rolle's Psalter, Hilton's *Mixed Life*, *Gracia Dei*, Love's *Myrrour* and a variety of prayers and meditations. In a will dated 1458, Sir Thomas Chaworth bequeathed an equally large library of mystical and other religious texts, including a service book which he notes "I always have by my side when riding" (Hughes 294). Another owner of a sizeable collection of mystical texts was Elizabeth Sewerby, an East Riding widow and daughter of Sir Henry Vavasour, whose will from 1468 provides some illuminating valuations of her books. The text of Bridget's *Revelations* was estimated at 66s 8d, an expensive aid to devotion when compared to the copy of Rolle's *Meditations on the Passion* which seems to have been an early version of the "paperback edition" at only 4d (Hughes 93).

Although not mentioned by Deanesly, Robert Thornton is considered in some more recent studies to be an exemplar of the new class of devout literate laypeople.[17] The word bibliophile might equally be used to describe Thornton, but it is hard to imagine him not finding some degree of identification with the temporal lord of Hilton's *Mixed Life*, which he transcribed. Starting around 1420 this member of the northern gentry was responsible for copying 65 texts, a considerable portion of which were contemplative, over a period of some thirty years.

The textual achievements of another possible proponent of the "mixed life," Dame Eleanor Hull, are perhaps even more noteworthy than Thornton's and yet have gone largely unnoticed until recently.[18] Demonstrating a knowledge of both French and Latin, Eleanor is twice identified by Richard Fox as the translator of works contained in a Middle English devotional text he was copying. Widowed at an early age from John Hull, a retainer of John of Gaunt, Eleanor developed close ties with the Benedictine Abbey of St. Albans while continuing her courtly connections. It would seem that the aristocratic widow decided to integrate her contemplative calling with an active life rather than join a religious order. Alexandra Barratt points to Eleanor's comparative anonymity alongside the likes of Margery Kempe and Julian of Norwich, a surprising fact when the volume of extant documentary evidence concerning her is considered. For example, Barratt writes, Eleanor is "the only 'Middle English mystic' for whom we possess a tax return" ("Dame Eleanor," 88, note 2).

Although the more wealthy gentry and aristocracy tend to dominate the evidence of wills, there are indications that by the mid-fifteenth century an interest in mystical writing, and thus possibly the "mixed life," had become an equally significant feature of bourgeois piety.

Margery Kempe's *Book* and a handful of vernacular manuscript bequests from the middle classes have already been referred to above. Another indicator of the widespread appeal of contemplative texts is found in a type of manuscript known as the "common-profit" book. Wendy Scase records an inscription from one such book informing the reader how this compilation of contemplative and other writings was to be used:

> This booke was made of þe goodis of John Collop for a comyn profite, that þat persoone þat hath þis booke committid to him off þe persoone þat haþ power to committe it haue þe vse þerof þe teerme of his lijf prayng for þe soule of þe seid John. And þat he þat haþ þe forseid vse of commyssioun, whanne he occupieth it not leene it for a tyme to sum oþer persoone. Also þat persoone to whom it was committid for þe teerme of lijf vnder þe forseid condiciouns delyuere it to anoþer persoone þe teerme of his lijf, and so be it delyuered and committed fro persoone to persoone man or womman as longe as þe booke endureth. (261)

> [This book was commissioned from the goods of John Colop for common profit, so that the person who has this book committed to them (by the person who has power to commit it) has its use for life, praying for the soul of the said John. And that the person who has the aforesaid use of commission, when not using it, may lend it for a time to another person. Also that person to whom it was committed for life, under the aforesaid conditions, may deliver it to another person for life, and so it is delivered and committed from person to person, man or woman, as long as the book endures.][19]

The circulation of John Colop's book was of "comyn profite" to the souls of both the donor, who was guaranteed prayers so long as the book lasted, and the reader who otherwise might not have had access to such literature. Of the many texts that could have been chosen, the preponderance of mystical writings is a significant indicator of interest among the middle and even lower classes.

Little is known of John Colop, although there is evidence that suggests he was the uncle of a London stationer, Richard Colop, whose name appears in another "common-profit" book. The penultimate flyleaf of Lambeth Palace 472 records instructions "þat þis boke be deliuered to Richard Colop Parchemanere of Londoun after my discesse" (Ogilvie-Thomson xiii) ["that this book be delivered to Richard Colop, stationer of London, after my death"]. The original owner of the book, John Killum, was a London grocer who died in 1416, and his text is a compilation of works attributed to Walter Hilton. The manuscript opens with the *Scale* and then preserves a version of the *Mixed Life*. After a translation attributed to Hilton, *The Eight Chapters on Perfection*, there then follow two commentaries on the psalms *Qui Habitat* and *Bonum Est*, and a stylistically similar commentary on the *Benedictus*. There are obvious parallels with the Westminster florilegium in the choice of material. Such "common-profit" manuscripts demonstrate a sophisticated taste in contemplative literature among a small group of London merchants early in the fifteenth century.

Even more remarkable than these, admittedly few, manuscripts is evidence of a "common-profit" library. Scase notes that following the death in 1423 of London's famous mayor, Richard Whittington, a lawyer by the name of John Carpenter was commissioned to found a library at Guildhall (268-70). The library was innovative on two counts: it was the first to extend the "common-profit" concept to an entire collection, and equally significantly it was under civic rather than ecclesiastical authority. Quite who among the lower classes had access to the library is not known, although Scase suggests the poorer secular clergy as most likely to benefit from the theological works (268). Given the growing lay audience, however, and their interest in even specialist contemplative literature, one could speculate on a much wider patronage. Whoever the audience, the mere existence of a civic library symbolizes the fifteenth-century secularization and democratization of what had for centuries been a principally monastic or at least professional ecclesiastical domain.

In summary then, one thing may be stated with some certainty: when considering the audience of a fifteenth-century contemplative Middle English text it cannot be automatically assumed that the audience was "*ex professo* contemplative." An increasing number of laity, from a wide section of society, had an active interest in contemplative literature. The editor of W would have had a substantial potential audience amongst the laity, for whom he may well have been working. In order to explore Julian's early reception further we must now turn to the text of W itself, and from internal data test the hypothesis that the intended audience of W included, or indeed was aimed at, laity pursuing the "mixed life."

II. An Intended Audience

In opening this section of the essay it is worth noting that the word "reuelacion," so central to Julian's full text, is not found once in W.[20] Similarly the word "vision," used seven times in S1, is not found in the chosen vocabulary of the W editor. The word "shewyng" does occur five times in W, but considering the 92 appearances in S1 even this suggests an editorial policy. The contents of the full LV, as outlined in the opening chapter of both P and S1, make very clear the framework around which the original work was constructed: "This is a reuelacion of loue that Jhesu Christ . . . made in xvi shewynges"(1.281.2-3).[21] From the fourth chapter this revelation is systematically narrated and then analyzed in a pedagogical manner. No trace of this bi-polar structure is found in W. The editor has carefully removed all mystical narrative, leaving only Julian's contemplative teaching.

The dialogue between the narrative and the didactic in Julian's full version of *A Revelation of Love* is almost without parallel amongst vernacular mystical texts available to the lay populace of late-medieval England.[22] Margery Kempe's *Book* provides a useful starting place to test this claim to the originality of Julian's structural style. As mentioned earlier, the repetition of four key contemplative texts in Chapters 17 and 58 suggests a basic canon as far as one lay woman was concerned. Of the four there is only one text by a woman, Bridgit of Sweden's *Revelations*; this shares the narrative visionary nature of the LV but, unlike Julian's text, does not go on to reflect theologically on the experience.[23] Walter Hilton's *Scale of Perfection* and James of Milan's *Stimulus Amoris* are principally didactic in the way they approach contemplative prayer.[24] Kempe's *Book* itself fits neatly into the visionary narrative genre, but as with Bridgit's text she does not develop the narrative theologically in the way Julian does.

The only text that comes anywhere near to Julian's style is Richard Rolle's *Incendium Amoris*. Although originally written in Latin the text was translated into Middle English by Richard Misyn in 1435 and does make occasional didactic use of personal mystical narrative. Rolle's prologue, for example, sets the theme for the whole treatise: "Mor haue

I meruayled þen I schewe, fforsothe, when I felt fyrst my hert wax warme, and treuly, not ymagynyngly, bot als it wer with sensibyll fyer, byrned" (2) ["I cannot tell you how surprised I was the first time I felt my heart begin to warm. It was real warmth too, not imaginary, and it felt as if it were actually on fire"].[25] Rolle's use of mystical narrative is sporadic, however, and beside Julian's tight structure of sixteen showings with interspersed theological commentary, the *Incendium* reads as a fairly conservative didactic work with some personal illustrations.

A similar dichotomy between the narrative and didactic emerges from a study of Robert Thornton's canon of devotional writings as found in the Lincoln Cathedral manuscript. The principal contemplative texts in this collection are of a purely didactic nature, such as *The Mirror of St Edmund*, Hilton's *Mixed Life*, and the *Abbey of the Holy Ghost*.[26] Various psalms, prayers and poems punctuate these, and there is one text of the narrative visionary genre: *A Revelation Showed to a Holy Woman*. There are, however, no individual texts which mix the didactic and the visionary.

Turning to one other group of vernacular contemplative texts available to the fifteenth-century laity, "common-profit" books, the same pattern is affirmed. Hilton's works are frequently found in these manuscripts, as are devotional compilations such as *The Pore Caitiff*, but there is no sign of a text seeking to integrate narrative visionary experience with teaching on mystical theology in the way that Julian's LV does.[27] It would seem that a lay person interested in mystical literature could expect a contemplative text to fit into one of two genres. The work would either give an edifying narrative account of a visionary experience (usually that of a woman) or it would be more strictly didactic (with a male author).

Contrary to the established genres of late-medieval contemplative literature, and in particular the gender roles of such writing, Julian presents her readers with an intricate mix of visionary narrative and mystical theology. It is significant that neither of the two earliest extant copies of her work reproduce this unusual integration of mystical prose genres. The Amherst manuscript (mid-fifteenth century) preserves a copy of Julian's Shorter Version of *A Revelation of Love*, which sits fairly comfortably in the visionary narrative genre. The editor of W goes to considerable length to construct a purely didactic text which nestles unobtrusively at the end of a collection of texts usually ascribed to

Hilton. It is not until some two hundred years after Julian's death that copies of the full LV emerge, preserving both the narrative and the didactic material.

Building on the literary sociology of Eric Auerbach, Hans Robert Jauss suggests that "there are works that at the moment of their appearance are not yet directed at any specific audience, but that break through the familiar horizon of literary expectations so completely that an audience can only gradually develop for them."[28] If the number and nature of early copies is anything to go by, it would seem that Julian's LV was one such text. That is not to suggest that the LV was a personal diary or spiritual journal written with no reader in mind. Rather it would seem that once the LV was out of Julian's hands and in those of later scribes and editors, the forces of conservatism and orthodoxy were too great for the highly original text to remain intact for a fifteenth-century active lay audience.[29]

As we have seen, Hilton's writings feature prominently in many of the florilegia and individual texts available to the laity. Texts that were originally written for recluses and other professional contemplatives were rapidly gaining an active lay audience. Michael Sargent notes:

> Within perhaps two decades of their author's death . . . Walter Hilton's *Scale of Perfection* and *Of Mixed Life* were being copied for, and presumably read by, devout, prosperous London businessmen--and one suspects that it was specifically the addition of the *Mixed Life* that facilitated the appropriation of the *Scale* to its new audience. (lxii)

The contents of the Westminster manuscript as a whole fit well into this literary horizon. Folios 1^r to 25^r and 25^r to 35^v are compiled from the two commentaries on the Psalms, *Qui Habitat* and *Bonum Est*, written in a style similar to Hilton's. Then follows an extract from the *Scale of Perfection* (folios 35^v to 72^r), after which W draws the 112 folio manuscript to a close. Within this context, any retention of the original structure of the LV would have stood out markedly from the style of the other texts. In carefully unpicking Julian's weave of the narrative and didactic, the W editor creates a text that fits neatly into the established genres of the time. Put another way, the W editor seems to purposefully

"Hiltonize" Julian's work--perhaps for an intended audience of active lay people.

Symbolic of this Hiltonization of Julian's text is an editorial amendment found near the opening of W, which reads: "For truely our louer desyrith þat þe soule *clyme* to hym, with all the mygthes, and þat we be euyr *clymyng* to his goodnes" (f. 79ʳ) ["For truly our lover desires that the soul climb to him, with all its strength, and that we are always climbing to his goodness"].[30] P records a significantly different reading: "For truly oure lovyr desyereth that the soule *cleue* to hym with all the myghtes, and that we be ever more *cleuyng* to hys goodnes" (6.307-8).[31] S1 too disagrees with the W editor's version, paralleling P: "for treuly our lover desireth that our soule *cleve* to hym with all the might and that we be evermore *clevand* to his godenes" (6.7).[32] The agreement of both P and S1 against W make it most likely that Julian's holograph read "cleue" and not "clyme." There are essentially two possible explanations for the variant. Firstly, if the editor's (or conceivably a copyist's) archetype used the spelling "clyue" rather than "cleue," there may have been a simple misreading of "m" for "u." Alternatively the W editor may have purposefully inserted the word "clyme" in order to evoke images previously encountered in the *Scale* extracts.[33] Either way the variant, whether conscious or not, demonstrates in a small way the pervasive influence of Hilton's language and metaphor on the extract from Julian's text.

In order to examine further this claim of editorial intention I will now turn from a generalized argument to specifics. The opening section, or prologue, of W is highly edited and one of the best examples of the editor as "author." Although by necessity somewhat heavy going, the next part of this essay will examine in some detail the process by which the narrative components of Julian's LV have been removed. Editorial patterns established in the prologue hold almost invariably throughout the remainder of W and consolidate the case for an intended audience of those pursuing the "mixed life."

When compared with the opening chapters of the full LV the prologue of W is almost unrecognizable as Julian's work. It represses the Christocentric visionary narrative, and in its place presents the soul of Saint Mary as a model of contemplation for the reader. Although constructed almost word for word from the LV, the patchwork of W's prologue is in effect a creation of the editor. Turning first to the opening sentence of W:

> Oure gracious and goode Lorde God shewed me in party þe wisdom and þe trewthe of þe soule of oure blessed Lady, Saynt Mary; wherein I vnderstood þe reuerent beholdynge þat she behelde her God þat is her maker, maruelynge with grete reuerence þat he wolde be borne of her þat was a simple creature of his makyng. (f.72ᵛ)

> [Our gracious and good Lord God showed me, in part, the wisdom and the truth of the soul of our blessed Lady, Saint Mary. In this I understood the reverent contemplation with which she beheld her God, who is her maker, marveling with great reverence that he would be born of her, a simple creature made by him].

Julian's entire introduction, with its narrative background and Christocentric focus, has been omitted by the W editor. There is no mention of the sixteen showings, no dating, no claim to be "vnlettyrde" (2.285); in fact the editor has included very little at all that would point the uninformed reader in Julian's direction. Even with the LV at hand, the reader has to turn to the end of the fourth chapter in order to locate the source of the material. Nestled within a brief passage referring to Mary are found the words: "Also god shewed me in part the wisdom and the truth of her sowle . . . a symple creature of his makyng" (4.297).

Describing the inaugural showing, Chapter 4 is very significant in the structure of the LV, but its reference to Mary is little more than an aside. The chapter opens with a vivid image of the suffering Christ: "And in this sodenly I saw the reed bloud rynnyng downe from vnder the garlande, hote and fryshley, plentuously and liuely, right as it was in the tyme that the garland of thornes was pressed on his blessed head"(4.294) ["And at this, suddenly I saw the red blood running down from under the crown, hot and flowing freely and copiously, a living stream, just as it was at the time when the crown of thorns was pressed on his blessed head" (181)]. The reader is told that this showing evoked in Julian an understanding of the Trinity: "for wher Jhesu appireth the blessed trinitie is vnderstand, as to my sight"(4.295-6) ["for where Jesus appears the blessed Trinity is understood, as I see it" (181)]. Only after further reflection on her reaction to this does the anchoress make mention of Mary as she draws the chapter to a close.

The opening paragraph of W is uplifted directly from this section of the LV (4.297). Then, after copying Julian's recollection of Luke 1:38: "Loo me here, gods handmayden" ["Behold me here, God's handmaiden"] the editor of W emerges again from behind the scenes, cutting and pasting a sizeable section from Chapter 7 of the LV. To the reader unfamiliar with Julian's full text a break is hard to detect, but the shift in theological emphasis as a result of the insertion is significant. Opening with the doublet "wysdom and truth" (7.310) the editor neatly links the additional material with the former appearance of the same doublet in the first sentence of W. God's greatness and nobility are then stressed, and contrasted with Mary's littleness and poverty. The W editor copies from Chapter 7 as far as the reference to Mary's meekness as reason for her grace and virtue, and the observation that she "passyth alle creatours" (7.311) [surpasses all creatures], before returning to the original excerpt from Chapter 4 (4.297): "In this syght I vndyrstod sothly þat she is more þan all þat God made beneth her in worthynes and in fulhed; for aboue her þer is nothyng þat is made, but þe blessed manhed of Criste, as to my syght" (f.73ᵛ) ["In this sight I understood truly that she is more than all that God made beneath her in worthiness and fullness; for above her there is nothing that is made, except the blessed humanity of Christ, as I see it"]. When looking for what is referred to by "this syght," the reader of W naturally tends to turn to what immediately precedes. It is the characteristics of Mary's soul, her simplicity, meekness and reverent fear, that justify exaltation above all else but the humanity of Christ. This reiterates what Julian herself adds in Chapter 7 but appears to be a deliberate theological reworking of Julian's original meaning in Chapter 4.

For readers of the full LV, the object of "this syght" is quite different. The W editor's focus on the soul of Mary is seen to be a careful construction. Omitted in W, the opening LV reference to Mary begins with a semi-corporeal vision of the Annunciation: "I saw her ghostly in bodily lykenes, a simple mayden and a meeke, yong of age, a little waxen aboue a chylde, in the stature as she was when she conceivede" (4.297) ["I saw her spiritually in her bodily likeness, a simple, humble maiden, young in years, grown a little taller than a child, of the stature which she had when she conceived" (182)]. Only secondarily is the "wisdom and the truth of her sowle" shown to Julian, and "in part" at that (4.297). Reaching a climax with the familiar scriptural recollection of Mary's words to Gabriel, Julian then concludes with her praise of the mother of Christ: "In this syght I did vnderstand verily that she is more then all that God made"(4.297-8). Mention is made of the "greatnes of her maker and the littlehead of her selfe" (4.297) but without the additional excursus from Chapter 7 this emphasis is secondary to the central theme of the Incarnation. It would seem that in this particular passage Julian is primarily drawing attention to Mary's conception of the Christ child, not her "smallness" and "reverent dread," as the reason for her exalted place in creation. If this is the case, why did the editor of W choose to make such a significant theological alteration? Why focus on the soul of Mary, rather than the Annunciation? And what might this tell us of the editor's intended audience?

In the search for answers I will focus on the W editor's policy of simplifying Julian's complex theological themes and then examine an interesting link between W (and the LV) and the Lay Folk's Prayer Book. In order to address the first issue we need to look at the wider picture of Julian's Marian theology, as found in the LV. At the end of Chapter 25 Julian presents a synopsis of the preceding three showings of Mary found in Chapters 4 (and 7), 18 and 25: "The furst was as she conceyvyd, the secunde as she was in her sorowes vnder the crosse, and the thurde was as she is now in lykynge, worschyppe and joy" (25.401) ["The first was as she conceived, the second was as she had been under the Cross, and the third was as she is now, in delight, honor and joy" (223)]. Most of what precedes this statement concerns Jesus' question to the anchoress, "Willt thou see her?" (25.398). In the mirth and joy of this eleventh revelation Jesus' question is playful, almost a tease for Julian who struggles to resolve the conflict of conscience it evokes: "But here of am I nott lernyd to long to see her bodely presens whyle I am here, but the vertuse of her blyssydfulle soule, her truth, her wysdom, her cheryte, wher by I am leern to know my self, and reuerently drede my god" (25.399) ["But in this matter I was not taught to long to see her bodily presence whilst I am here, but the virtues of her blessed soul, her truth, her wisdom, her love, through which I am taught to know myself and reverently to fear my God" (222)]. In the LV Julian skillfully plays with the tension evoked by this dialectic. Orthodoxy teaches her to focus on Mary's soul, but in this part of the revelation Jesus himself seems to tempt her away from what she has been taught. Such speculation could easily be misinterpreted by a lay audience untrained in theological debate, but for Julian it is one of the tools of the trade.

Throughout her writing Julian displays a technical understanding of what Nicholas Watson terms the "Augustinian hermeneutic," that is, a means of interpreting and classifying visionary experience derived from Augustine's three categories of "corporeal," "spiritual" and "intellectual" vision.[34] Differentiating between the corresponding showings of "bodily sight," "gostly sight," "eye of my vnderstanding," and a variety of shades in between, Julian makes use of this hermeneutic to articulate the complexities of her experience.[35] Jesus' question seems to give Julian (and perhaps the reader) permission to admit to an unorthodox longing to see a vision of the bodily presence of Mary. In characteristic accordance with the Church's teachings, however, Julian finally resolves the tension by recalling that she was given only a "gostly shewyng" in her visions of Mary (25.401). The somatic vision, or "bodily sight," appears to be reserved for showings of Jesus alone.

The hermeneutical intricacies of Julian's mystical theology are carefully removed by the editor of W. Choosing to include only the first of the three Marian visions, the editor cuts and pastes the relevant passages in such a way as to exclude the key technical term "ghostly in bodily lykenes" (4.297). In place of a showing of the young Virgin as she was "when she conceivede," with all its subtle somatic ambiguities, the W editor opens with a safe portrayal of the characteristics of her soul. Superseded by the spiritual concerns of the insert from Chapter 7, the somatic impact of Mary's words "Lo me here, God's handmaiden" is lost. By removing all hints of a bodily vision of Mary, the editor of W creates a simplified vision of Mary's soul quite alien to Julian's carefully constructed semi-corporeal showing.

This careful and no doubt painstaking simplification of Julian's work must have been undertaken for a reason. If the text was being prepared for a purely contemplative reader, such as a recluse, the detailed editing would not have been necessary; any theological difficulties that arose could easily have been ironed out by that person's spiritual director. Enclosed within the strictly controlled environment of an anchorhold, the church authorities generally felt safe about these lay theologians.[36]

An active lay audience, however, would have been quite a different matter.

Julian herself displays a keen awareness of the bounds of orthodoxy. Colledge and Walsh's commentary on Julian's struggle with the desire to see a somatic vision of Mary reads: "*But here of am I nott lernyd to long to see her bodely presens*: this is a plain warning against aspiring to 'bodily sights'"(25.399 and note). They go on to quote from an English translation of Ruysbroek's *Spiritual Espousals* where the author warns against certain "enthusiasts" who "desiren of god sum special ӡifte aboue other, eiþer of worchynge myraclis, or visions, eiþer reuelacions or sum oþer specialte; wherfor ofte tymes þei bien disceyued of þe deuel" ["desire of God some special gift above others, either of working miracles, or receiving visions or revelations, or some other speciality; for which reason they are often deceived by the Devil"]. This would indeed appear to have been an orthodox position. Walter Hilton, for example, in Chapter 10 of the first book of his *Scale* is less condemning but clearly judges such piety as inferior:

> By this that I have said mayst thou somewhat understand that visions or revelations of any manner spirit, in bodily appearing or in imagining, sleeping or waking, or else any other feeling in bodily wits made as it were ghostly . . . are not very contemplation; nor they are but simple and secondary though they be good, in regard of ghostly virtues, nor of this ghostly knowing and loving of God. (Underhill 19)

These comments derive from a traditional understanding of the Augustinian hermeneutic explored earlier, particularly the clause that points to the existence of "a hierarchy in these visions, one being superior to another. For spiritual vision is more excellent than corporeal, and intellectual vision more excellent than spiritual" (Taylor 12.24.213). But is Julian really offering a "plain warning" against the heterodoxy of "bodily sights," or is her theology more subtle than this?

In Chapter 2 Julian clearly states "I desyred a bodely sight" and the resultant opening vision of Christ's bleeding head is classified as a "bodely syght" (2.286 and 7.311). As discussed earlier, Chapter 25 records Julian's confession of a similar longing for a bodily sight of Mary, despite being taught to the contrary. Julian embraces the tension between mystical experience and traditional orthodoxy, and a deeper theological understanding is born as a result. Far from presenting a "plain warning," Julian appears to be demonstrating the dynamic questioning and probing of a skilled theologian.

Whether she read any of the writings of Thomas Aquinas is a matter open to debate, but it is worth comparing Julian's excursus with a similar passage in the *Summa Theologica*:

> *Objection I.* It seems that the angel of the Annunciation should not have appeared to the Virgin in a bodily vision. For *intellectual vision is more excellent than bodily vision*, as Augustine says . . ..
> *Reply Obj. I.* Intellectual vision excels merely imaginary and merely bodily vision. But Augustine himself says (*ibid.*) that prophecy is more excellent if accompanied by intellectual and imaginary vision, than if accompanied by only one of them. Now the Blessed Virgin perceived not only the bodily vision, but also the intellectual illumination. Wherefore this was a more excellent vision.[37]

Aquinas is faced with a dilemma: traditional Augustinian orthodoxy holds that the highest form of vision is intellectual, yet the most Christologically significant biblical vision, the Annunciation, is profoundly corporeal. He resolves the tension by affirming the scriptural observation that "The angel of the Annunciation appeared in a bodily vision to the Blessed Virgin" but backs this up with a broader reading of Augustine's theology--Mary also received an intellectual vision, and even Augustine agrees that two visions are better than one!

In these instances both Aquinas and Julian move beyond a simplistic understanding of Augustinian mystical theology in order to reconcile their fresh insight with traditional orthodoxy. Alongside the traditional hermeneutical model, both theologians construct an original and lively re-interpretation. An unavoidable difference, however, is that one theologian is a man writing in Latin, the other a woman writing in the vernacular. The Marian theology of the LV appears no less orthodox than Aquinas', but then Julian's thought was not protected linguistically from misinterpretation by those unversed in theology.

The editor of W works hard to minimize misunderstanding, displaying a keen awareness of the potential dangers of Julian's text for his audience. A scribal warning that draws the last chapter of S1 to a close shows similar concern:

> I pray almyty God that this booke com not but to the hands of them that will be his faithful lovers, and to those that will submitt them to the feith of holy church . . . for this revelation is hey divinitye and hey wisdam, wherefore it may not dwelle with him that is thrall to synne and to the devill. And beware thou take not on thing after thy affection and liking and leve another, for that is the condition of an heretique. (86.103)

> [I pray to almighty God that this book may not come into the hands of any but those who will be his faithful lovers, and those who will submit themselves to the faith of Holy Church . . . for this revelation is high theology and high wisdom; for which reason it should not reside with a person who is a slave to sin and to the Devil. And beware that you do not take on board one thing that appeals to you and leave another, for such is the disposition of a heretic.]

Although the editor of W may not have seen this particular addition to the text, the principle of approaching mystical texts with care would have been familiar to any expert in the area. The prologue of the *Cloud* makes the same point at some length, noting: "For, parauenture, þer is som mater þerin, in þe beginnyng or in þe middel, þe whiche is hanging and not fully declared þer it stondeþ . . . ȝif a man saw o mater and not anoþer, parauenture he miȝt liȝtly be led into errour" (Hodgson 1) ["For, perhaps, there is some discussion here, in the beginning or in the middle, which is left hanging and not fully expounded where it stands . . . if a person saw one part of the discussion and not another, perhaps that person might easily be led into error"]. Julian's LV is the work of a skilled mystical theologian, what is more a female theologian, and as such it would have required careful editing before it could be used by a fifteenth-century active lay audience. Given the consistent and careful policy of simplification established in the prologue, and followed almost invariably throughout the text, it seems highly likely that the W editor's intended audience was the active laity, or one such person, rather than a professional recluse or religious.

In addition to his policy of simplification, the W editor's choice of a Marian motif in place of Julian's Christological focus invites further examination. Although the horizon of literature available to the fifteenth-century laity was increasing, certain works were far more widespread than others. One such text was the primer, or lay folks' prayer book. In considering the W editor's focus on Mary, it is of interest to note that the principal offices in the primer are the Hours of the Blessed Virgin.[38] Wills across the social classes attest to the widespread use of the primer amongst laity, as does the travel journal of a late fifteenth-century Italian visitor: "any who can read tak[es] the Office of our Lady with them, and with some companion recit[es] it in the church verse by verse in a low voice after the manner of the religious."[39] It was probably this office, amongst others, that Margery Kempe found so hard to keep up with when working on her book:

Whan þis booke was first in wrytyng, þe sayd creatur was mor at hom in hir chambre wyth hir writer and seyd fewer bedys for sped of wrytyng þan sche had donȝerys be-forn. and, whan sche cam to chirche and xulde heryn Messe, purposyng to seyn hir Mateyns and swech oþer deuocyons as sche had vsyd a-for-tyme, hir hert was drawyn a-wey fro þe seying and set mech on meditacyon. (216)

[When this book was first being written the said creature was more at home in her chamber with the man doing the writing, and said fewer beads than she had done for years before, in order to speed the writing. And when she came to church to hear mass, intending to say her matins and such other devotions as she had performed before, her heart was drawn away from recitation and much set upon meditation.]

The primer grew out of Latin monastic offices, but by the late-fourteenth and early-fifteenth century there were English versions and a growing lay audience. Fears over the threat of Lollardy meant that from the mid-fifteenth century vernacular primers became a rarity, but surprisingly the popularity of the Latin primer continued to grow amongst the laity.[40]

In a study of the influence of the primer on English Passion lyrics, Barratt concludes: "It is most likely that the prymer, rather than any other source, acted as a convenient quarry for the lyrics' authors. Furthermore, this suggests that other mediæval lyrics on subjects other than the Passion--and those devoted to the Blessed Virgin in particular-- were also indebted to the prymer to an appreciable extent."⁴¹ If this was so for authors of lyrics, it is highly likely that someone such as the W editor, catering for the contemplative interests of the laity, was also influenced by the primer.

In focusing on Mary's meekness, W's prologue does seem to echo the theme of the opening sentence of the *Sancta maria, piarum* from the office of matins: "Seynt marie, mekest of alle meke wymmen! preie for us" (vol.1, 5) ["Saint Mary, meekest of all meek women! Pray for us"]. Even more striking is the repeated responsory that follows:

> [R] Blessid art þou, maide marie, þat bar oure lord! *þou broʒtest forþ þe makere of þe world þat made þee*, þou bileuest maide wiþ-outen ende.
> [V] Hail, marie, ful of grace! þe lord is wiþ þee.
> [Repeet] *þþou broʒtest forþ þe makere of þe world þat made þee*, and þou bileueuest maide wiþ-outen ende. (Littlehales 6)

> [[R] Blessed are you, maid May who bore our Lord! You brought forth the maker of the world who made you. You remain a virgin without end.
> [V] Hail May, full of grace! The Lord is with you.
> [Repeat] You brought forth the maker of the world who make you, and you remain a virgin without end.]

Julian's words, carefully chosen by the W editor for his prologue, bear a distinct resemblance:

> I vnderstood þe reuerent beholdynge þat she behelde her God þat is her maker, maruelynge with grete reuerence *þat he wolde be borne of her þat was a simple creature of his makyng.* For this was her meruelyng, *þat he þat was her maker wolde be borne of her þat is made.* (f.72v)

[I understood the reverent contemplation with which she beheld her God who is her maker, marvelling with great reverence that he would be born of her who was a simple creature of his making. For this was her marvelling, that he who was her maker would be born of her who is made] (emphasis added).

Colledge and Walsh suggest that this repetition, found also in P, is "plain case of dittography" (4.297 and note). Given the fact that S1 is the only text which omits the repeated phrase (A, W, and P all agree), it seems more likely to be a case of haplography on the part of the S1 scribe. The hint of a parallel between Julian's writing and the primer affirms this explanation.

The presence of this wording in the LV could well be due to the fact that Julian herself used the Hours of the Blessed Virgin, and thus made use of its language where appropriate.[42] This characteristic of Julian's work is then chosen and foregrounded by the W editor for his audience. It is of interest to note that this liturgical influence in W is more characteristic of late fourteenth-century piety than fifteenth, with the move to a Latin primer and perhaps reflects a grassroots response to the removal of the English primer from circulation among lay people. If the intended audience of W were laity with an interest in contemplative literature, it could be assumed that many of them made use of the primer. It is also of interest to note that the W editor includes an extract from Hilton's teaching on contemplative liturgy in his florilegium:

The prayer most fitted to the special needs of every soul . . . is the "Our Father," together with the psalms and hymns and the rest of the liturgy of Holy Church. The soul does not then pray as it used to do . . . the soul is in the spiritual presence of God; and therefore every word and every syllable of its prayer is made with savour and sweetness and delight, and with a perfect harmony between heart and lips. For then the soul is turned into a fire of love.[43]

Although this does not conclusively identify the intended audience of W, it further affirms the likelihood of an active lay audience with an interest in contemplative literature.

This study of the prologue demonstrates editorial policy by which excerpts from Julian's LV were carefully selected and woven together to create W. A detailed study of the remainder of W is beyond the limits of this current essay, but it may suffice to say that the same policy holds throughout. Julian's Christocentric visionary narrative is systematically removed, leaving only selected didactic material and the occasional philosophical showing such as "god in a poynte" (11.336). The W editor consistently simplifies Julian's technical mystical language, as if for a lay audience, and removes all traces of the anchoress' speculative theology. The resultant text fits well into a florilegium dominated by extracts from Hilton's teaching--with one exception.

Some ten folios into W, one sentence seems to decimate all editorial policy so carefully established up to that point: "Also in the nyneth shewyng our Lord God seyd to her thus: 'Art þou well payed þat I sufferd for thee?'" (f.83ᵛ) ["Also in the ninth showing our Lord God said to her: 'Are you well pleased that I suffered for you?'"]. The LV reads significantly differently: "Then seide oure goode lorde askyng: Arte thou well apayd that I sufferyd for thee?"(22.382). Even in the prologue the raw material of the LV is the editor's sole source. Occasional link words are introduced, but only for the purpose of a smooth transition from one passage to another. Here, however, the W editor appears to construct half a sentence. The narrative is changed from the first to the third person, and perhaps most peculiar is the addition of the words "nyneth shewyng." In one sentence the editor seems to reveal all that he has previously repressed so rigorously. The reader is suddenly aware that the original author was a woman, and that she is writing about a series of showings of which we have just reached the ninth.

Considering the careful attention to detail and consistent editorial policy established in the prologue and followed throughout the rest of W, it is most likely that the irregularity is not due to editorial choice but rather an error of some sort. Such a scenario requires a brief, and clearly speculative, exploration of the process of production. The W editor was evidently well acquainted with the full LV and no doubt wrote notes to himself (or another scribe or copyist) as he shuffled, marked and collated the carefully chosen extracts. One such note in an early draft at this point could have read: "Also in the nyneth shewyng our Lord God seyd to her." It is conceivable that the intention was for the final manuscript to read "Also our Lord God seyd," but that this was not picked up by the editor's scribe or secretary. If this was the case, the editorial gloss may have mistakenly slipped through the final proof reading and so been reproduced in the Westminster florilegium several decades later. This sentence aside, the remainder of the extracts from Julian's LV accord remarkably consistently with editorial policy established in the prologue of W.

In conclusion, then, this consideration of the question of audience affirms the possibility of an active lay audience for W. The word "possibility" is carefully chosen, as there are clearly difficulties in making confident assertions concerning authorial or editorial intention. What is clear, however, is that the early audience for *A Revelation of Love* can no longer be assumed to consist entirely of professed contemplatives. To the contrary, there are many indications, both internal and external to the text, that W may have been produced specifically for a lay audience of those seeking the "mixed life." In W we are given a unique glimpse of what an early critic of Julian's considered to be both useable and unusable. It opens up a window into fifteenth-century lay piety, and provides an important early step in tracing the long process of reception of Julian's LV of *A Revelation of Love*.

NOTES

This essay is based on my Master of Theology thesis, "Julian of Norwich: The Westminster Text of *A Revelation of Love* Examined in the Light of its Intended Audience," Melbourne College of Divinity, 1996. Thanks are due to St John's Theological College, Auckland, for funding the research and to Dr Michael J. Wright of Auckland University for supervising the project. An edition of the text of W is currently being prepared for publication in *Mystics Quarterly*.

1. Printed editions and translations of Julian's work come under a variety of titles, from Serenus Cressy's seventeenth-century *XVI Revelations of Divine Love*, to Edmund Colledge and James Walsh, eds., *A Book of Showings to the Anchoress Julian of Norwich* (Toronto: Pontifical Institute of Mediaeval Studies, 1978). I find Marion Glasscoe's well-reasoned choice of title most convincing; see Marion Glasscoe, ed., *Julian of Norwich: A Revelation of Love* (Exeter: U of Exeter P, 1976) xi.

2. James Walsh and Edmund Colledge, trans., *Of the Knowledge of Ourselves and of God: A Fifteenth-Century Florilegium* (London: Mowbray, 1961) vii.

3. Given the style of W it is probable, as Walsh and Colledge assume, that the editor was a man. Note, however, the concluding comments in Alexandra Barratt, "Dame Eleanor Hull: A Fifteenth-Century Translator," in *The Medieval Translator: The Theory and Practice of Translation in the Middle Ages*, ed. Roger Ellis (Cambridge: Brewer, 1989): "if so unlikely a text turns out to have been the work of a woman, we should be wary of automatically excluding the possibility of a woman's authoring of *any* medieval text on *a priori* grounds" (101).

4. Glasscoe, *A Revelation*, uses S1 as her copy text; Colledge and Walsh, *A Book*, base their edition on P; the edition of W is my own.

5. S. J. Ogilvie-Thomson, *Walter Hilton's Mixed Life: Edited from Lambeth Palace MS 472*, Elizabethan and Renaissance Studies 92/15 (Salzburg: Universität Salzburg, 1986) 9-10. Translations are my own.

6. A history of the idea of the "mixed life" is beyond the scope of this essay. For an introductory analysis see Cuthbert Butler, *Western Mysticism: The Teaching of SS. Augustine, Gregory and Bernard on Contemplation and the Contemplative Life* (London: Arrow, 1960) 217-220, 227-238, 242-43. See also Jonathan Hughes, *Pastors and Visionaries: Religion and Secular Life in Late Medieval Yorkshire* (Woodbridge: Boydell, 1988) 251-253; Walter H. Beale, "Walter Hilton and the Concept of 'Medled Lyf,'" *American Benedictine Review* 26 (1975): 381-394; and Hilary M. Carey, "Devout Literate Lay People and the Pursuit of the Mixed Life in Later Medieval England," *The Journal of Religious History* 14 (1986-7): 361-381.

7. Phyllis Hodgson, ed., *The Cloud of Unknowing and Related Treatises on Contemplative Prayer* (Exeter: Catholic Records Press, 1982) 29. My translation.

8. Michael G. Sargent, ed., *Nicholas Love's Mirror of the Blessed Life of Jesus Christ* (New York: Garland, 1992) 124. My translation.

9. Norman P. Tanner, *The Church in Late Medieval Norwich 1370-1532* (Toronto: Pontifical Institute of Mediaeval Studies, 1984).

10. Sanford Brown Meech and Hope Emily Allen, eds., *The Book of Margery Kempe*, EETS, os 212 (London: Oxford UP, 1961). My translations are based on B.A. Windeatt, trans., *The Book of Margey Kempe* (London: Penguin, 1985). It has long been assumed that *The Book* is unmediated autobiography. Lynn Staley's significant study, *Margery Kempe's Dissenting Fictions* (Pennsylvania: Pennsylvania State UP, 1994), questions this and draws a distinction between

Margery, the subject, and Kempe, her author. See also David Lawton's comments on Kempe's literacy and even Latinity, "Voice, Authority, and Blasphemy in *The Book of Margery Kempe*," in *Margery Kempe: a Book of Essays*, ed. Sandra J. McEntire (New York: Garland, 1992) 93-115.

11. On the traditional monastic triad of *lectio, meditatio* and *oratio,* see Vincent Gillespie, "*Lukynge in haly bukes: Lectio* in some Late Medieval Spiritual Miscellanies," *Spätmittelalterliche Geistliche Literatur in der Nationalsprache,* Analecta Cartusiana 106/2 (1984): 2-3.

12. There is evidence, for example, in Lollard communities of only 3ff of women being able to read, even with their emphasis on the written word. Shannon McSheffrey, "Literacy and the Gender Gap in the Late Middle Ages: Women and Reading in Lollard Communities," in *Women, the Book and the Godly*, eds. Lesley Smith and Jane H. M. Taylor (Cambridge: Brewer, 1995) 162.

13. Margaret Deanesly, "Vernacular Books in England in the Fourteenth and Fifteenth Centuries," *The Modern Language Review* 15 (1920): 349-358. What follows is based on a chronological overview of the key data from Deanesly's "Vernacular Books" 352-58, with additional references.

14. E. J. Arnould, ed., *Le Livre de Seyntz Medicines: The Unpublished Devotional Treatise of Henry of Lancaster* (Oxford: Blackwell, 1940). For further comment see Hughes, *Pastors and Visionaries* 66-67.

15. See also Hughes 102. Deanesly records the name as "Ross" which is presumably a spelling variant.

16. On the circulation of Ruysbroek's writings in late medieval England, see Edmund Colledge, "*The Treatise of Perfection of the Sons of God*: a fifteenth-century English Ruysbroek translation," *English Studies* 33 (1952): 49-66.

17. See for example George R. Keiser, "'To Knawe God Almyghtyn': Robert Thornton's Devotional Book," *Spätmittelalterliche Geistliche Literatur in der Nationalsprache,* Analectica Carthusiana, 106/2 (Salzburg: Universität Salzburg, 1984): 103, 122. Hughes 295.

18. Barratt, "Dame Eleanor" 87, notes only three other published references at that time. For an edition of Dame Eleanor's work, see Barratt, ed., *The Seven Psalms: A Commentary on the Penitential Psalms translated from French into English by Dame Eleanor Hull*, EETS 307 (Oxford: Oxford UP, 1995).

19. Wendy Scase, "Reginald Pecock, John Carpenter and John Colop's 'Common-Profit' Books: Aspects of Book Ownership and Circulation in Fifteenth-Century London," *Medium Ævum* 61 (1992): 261. My translation. The text includes several Lollard treatises as well as the more conservative mystical excerpts.

20. The word "revelation" occurs 17 times in S1 for example. My thanks to Dr. Michael Wright for making his computer edition of S1 available.

21. All general references to the LV are taken from Edmund Colledge and James Walsh, *A Book of Revelations*, the numbers in parentheses referring to chapter and page. Translations, when necessary, are from Colledge and Walsh, trans., *Julian of Norwich, Showings* (New York: Paulist, 1978) and are cited by page.

22. For an overview of all extant mystical MSS, see Valerie M. Lagorio and Michael G. Sargent, "English Mystical Writings," in *A Manual of the Writings in Middle English 1050-1500*, vol. 9, gen. ed. Albert E. Hartung (New Haven: Connecticut Academy of Arts and Sciences, 1993) 3049-3137.

23. William Patterson Cumming, ed., *The Revelations of Saint Birgitta*, EETS os 178 (London: Oxford UP, 1929).

24. Evelyn Underhill, trans., *The Scale of Perfection by Walter Hilton* (London: Watkins, 1923); H. Kane, ed., *The Prickynge of Love*, 2 vols, Salzburg Studies in English Literature: Elizabethan and Renaissance Studies 92/10 (1983).

25. Margaret Deanesly, ed., *The Incendium Amoris of Richard Rolle of Hampole* (Manchester: Manchester UP, 1915) 2. Ralph Harvey, ed., *The Fire of Love*, EETS os 106 (London: Kegan Paul, 1896). Translation is from Clifton Wolters, trans., *The Fire of Love* (Harmondsworth: Penguin, 1972).

26. For the devotional contents of the Thornton MS, Lincoln Cathedral Library A.1.17, see C. Horstman, ed., *Yorkshire Writers: Richard Rolle of Hampole, an English Father of the Church, and His Followers*, vol. 1 (London: Swan Sonnenschein, 1895) 184-85.

27. For a list of "common-profit" manuscripts and their contents see, Scase, "'Common-Profit' Books" 261.

28. Hans Robert Jauss, *Toward an Aesthetic of Reception*, trans. Timothy Bahti (Brighton: Harvester, 1982) 26.

29. On the relationship between author and scribe, see Chapter One of Lynn Staley's, *Dissenting Fictions*. On the "Conservatism of English Spirituality," see Nicholas Watson, "The Composition of Julian of Norwich's *Revelation of Love*," *Speculum* 68 (1993): 642-657.

30. References to W are from my own edition, at present being prepared for publication in *Mystics Quarterly*, and are located by folio number.

31. Colledge and Walsh, *A Book*, is the source of extracts from P.

32. References to S1 are from Glasscoe, *A Revelation*, located by chapter and page.

33. For an example of Hilton's ascent/descent imagery, see Walsh and Colledge, *Knowledge* 35.

34. See this volume 59-88. See also John Hammond Taylor, trans., *St. Augustine: The Literal Meaning of Genesis*, vol. 2 (New York: Newman, 1982) book 12, 185ff.

35. See for example Colledge and Walsh, *A Book* 293, 299, 300, 323, 514.

36. Note, however, the exception of the anchoress Matilda of Leicester who was imprisoned on suspicion of heresy. Anne K. Warren, *Anchorites and their Patrons in Medieval England* (Berkeley: U of California P, 1985) 80.

37. Fathers of the English Dominican Province, trans, *The "Summa Theologica" of St. Thomas Aquinas*, part 3, no. 2 (London: Washbourne, 1914) Q.30, article 3, 46-47.

38. Henry Littlehales, ed., *The Prymer or Lay Folk's Prayer Book*, EETS os 105, vol. 1 (London: 1895) 1-36.

39. A. Trevisano, ed., *A Relation, or Rather, a True Account of the Island of England about the year 1500*, Camden Soc. XXXVII (1847) 23, cited in Eamon Duffy, *The Stripping of the Altars: Traditional Religion in England 1400-1580* (New Haven: Yale UP, 1992) 212; Duffy also surveys the evidence of wills.

40. See Duffy, *The Stripping of the Altars* 209-265, 213.

41. Alexandra Barratt, "The Prymer and Its Influence on Fifteenth-Century English Passion Lyrics," *Medium Ævum* 44 (1975): 278.

42. For an outline of "The Anchoresses' Horarium," see Robert W. Ackerman and Roger Dahood, eds., *Ancrene Riwle: Introduction and Part I* (New York: Medieval and Renaissance Texts and Studies, 1984) 37.

43. Walsh and Colledge, *Knowledge* 34.

Leaving the Womb of Christ: Love, Doomsday, and Space/Time in Julian of Norwich and Eastern Orthodox Mysticism

Brant Pelphrey

In her *Revelations of Divine Love* Julian of Norwich explores several themes which are especially interesting to Eastern Orthodox readers. Among these are the ontological character of divine Love as the mutual indwelling of the Persons of the Trinity; Doomsday (the judgement) as a positive step in the process of salvation; and the notion that Christ is "pregnant" with the saints and the saints with Christ. In this context Julian develops a view of the divine relationship to space/time which is reminiscent of Orthodox mysticism and also opens the door to a unique dialogue with contemporary physics.

Although she was an English mystic, Julian of Norwich holds a special place of interest for Eastern Orthodox readers. With simplicity and depth, she explores the mystery of divine love in ways reminiscent of Sts. Symeon the New Theologian and Maximus the Confessor. Orthodox theologians have noted that her theology is neither scholastic on the one hand, nor emotional on the other--two problems which, from an Orthodox perspective, tend to mar the spiritual writings of the Christian West.[1] Points of theological correspondence between Julian and Eastern Christian mystics seem especially felicitous because Julian is best known for her feminine theology, in which she does not hesitate to refer to God as "Mother" and in which she does not see any wrath in God--concepts which, at first blush, might not seem at home with the Byzantines. But in fact she echoes themes which are present both in Orthodox spiritual writings and also in the Orthodox liturgy itself.

The Revelations of Divine Love also provides an opportunity for dialogue between Christianity and other world religions and ideologies, and even contemporary physics. Julian is not fuzzily inclusive or "New

Age," as is sometimes alleged; but her observations about human nature, the problems of suffering and death, love and the Being of God seem to transcend ordinary theologies to reach out to other religions, while remaining distinctly Christian. This, too, can be said to have an Orthodox character, since Orthodoxy historically has approached the mystery of salvation and the Church in cosmic terms.

Of particular interest is Julian's view of how God relates to space/time and her understanding of the Last Things, or "Doomsday," in light of it. Today popular Christianity tends to portray the eschaton almost exclusively in terms of God's judgment of sinners, resulting in their eternal punishment at the end of time. Julian, however, understands the judgment as God's final act of love towards all creation. Doomsday is part of the cosmic mystery of salvation, as important for the world as Christ's crucifixion and resurrection or indeed as creation itself. Its meaning is related to the mystery of the incarnation, in which the creator of the universe was contained in the womb of Mary. The miracle of Mary's womb, finally, is recapitulated in every faithful soul. To understand how, and to explore Julian's theological "physics" which is implied, it is necessary to begin with her deep analysis of divine love.

I. Love as Being

Underpinning all Julian's theology is her understanding of love. Julian's most important realization through her revelations is that love is an ontological reality, not merely a psychological one. Divine love is identical with divine being. More specifically, love is Being-in-communion, the mode of being of the Trinity. This way of existing, in which the divine Persons exist in and through one another, ultimately transcends human understanding. Nevertheless, it is possible for human beings to experience in a small way the communion of the Trinity in the sharing which is called "love" and which was made visible in Jesus Christ.

Early in her experience of the revelations Julian realizes that although she is seeing the face of Christ, she should understand the Trinity:

The trinitie is our maker, the trinitie is our keper, the trinitie is our everlasting louer, the trinitie is our endlesse ioy and our bleisse, by our lord Jesu Christ, and in our lord Jesu Christ. And this was shewed in the first syght and in all, for wher Jhesu appireth the blessed trinitie is vnderstand, as to my sight. (4.295)

[The Trinity is our maker, the Trinity is our protector, the Trinity is our everlasting lover, the Trinity is our endless joy and our bliss, by our Lord Jesus Christ. And this was revealed in the first vision and in them all, for where Jesus appears the blessed Trinity is understood, as I see it. (181)][2]

Julian's point is not that the face of Jesus symbolizes the Trinity in her visions but rather that the whole of the Trinity is present to her whenever Jesus is present. Christ reveals the Father: "For the furst hevyn, Crist shewyd me his father, in no bodely lycknesse but in his property and in hys wurkyng. That is to sey, I saw in Crist that the father is" (22.383) ["For the first heaven, Christ showed me his father, not in any bodily likeness but in his attributes and in his operations. That is to say, I saw in Christ that the Father is" (216)]. However, only the divine Son of God became incarnate and suffered on the cross, and only the divine Son is visible: "Alle the trinyte wrought in the passion of Crist, mynystryn habonndance of vertuse and plente of grace to vs by hym, but only the maydyns sonne sufferyd, werof all the blessed trynyte enjoyeth" (23.391-92) ["All the Trinity worked in Christ's Passion, administering abundant virtues and plentiful grace to us by him; but only the virgin's Son suffered, in which all the blessed Trinity rejoice" (219)].

Here Julian's theology recapitulates a Byzantine concept known as *perichoresis* (περιχώρησις), literally, "running around." Eastern theologians coined this unusual term to mean that the Father dwells "in" the Son, the Son "in" the Father, the Spirit "in" the Son, the Son "in" the Spirit, and so on. The relationship of divine indwelling is not simply the overlapping of some divine qualities, but is a mystery in which the whole of each Person actively lives in the whole of each Other.[3]

While the *perichoresis* of the Trinity defies ordinary logic, it is revealed in the incarnation. In the incarnational perichoresis, the eternal Logos is located "in" humanity and human nature is now located permanently "in" God.[4] Thus Julian first realizes that in her visions she should understand the mystery of the Trinity where Jesus appears; but later she realizes that similarly, the Son of God has chosen to dwell permanently in human nature:

> Owre good lorde shewde hym to his creature in dyverse manner both in hevyn and in erth; but I saw hym take no place but in mannes soule. He shewde hym in erth in the swete incarnacion and hys blessyd passion. . . . He shewde hym dyuerse tymes reignyng, as it is a fore sayde, but pryncypally in mannes soule; he hath take there his restyng place and his wurschypfulle cytte. Oute of whych wurschypfully see he shalle nevyr ryse ne remeve withoute ende. (81.713-4)

> [Our good Lord revealed himself to his creature in various ways, both in heaven and on earth; but I saw him take no place except in man's soul. He revealed himself on earth in the sweet Incarnation and his blessed Passion. . . . He revealed himself several times reigning, as is said before, but principally in man's soul; he has taken there his resting place and his honourable city. Out of this honourable throne he will never rise or depart without end. (336-37)]

Greek theology refers to the mystery of shared existence in God as *koinonia* (κοινωνία), communion: many becoming one. Julian refers to it as "onyng," in which the Persons of the Trinity are seen to be One, and also the lover of God becomes one with God. It is also "charite," divine love which is the nature of God's being and which is actively shared in and with humanity:

> I had iij manner of vnderstondynges in this lyght of (c)ha(r)ite. The furst is charite vnmade, the seconnde is charyte made, the thyrde is charyte gevyn. Charyte vnmade is god, charyte made is oure soule in god, charyte gevyn is vertu, and þat is a gracious gyfte of wurkyng, in whyc we loue god for hym selfe, and oure selfe in god, and alle þat god lovyth for god. (84.727)

> [I had three kinds of understanding in this light of charity. The first is uncreated charity, the second is created charity, the third is given charity. Uncreated charity is God, created charity is our

soul in God, given charity is virtue, and that is a gift of grace in deeds, in which we love God for himself, and ourselves in God, and all that God loves for God. (341)]

Like the Eastern Fathers, Julian does not attempt to analyze the mystery of Trinitarian love too carefully because it is ultimately beyond comprehension. It takes us beyond thought, like a Buddhist koan.[5] Nevertheless, the Christian assertion is that God has entered into absolute communion with humanity, and for this reason the mystery of communion within God can be known.

In both Julian and Orthodox mysticism, the dynamic indwelling and relationship of the Persons of the Trinity is what constitutes personhood in God. In other words, God is "personal" precisely because of the way the Persons of the Trinity relate and act, and personhood is neither static nor merely a psychological reality. Father, Son and Spirit are so-called because the Son relates to the Father in terms of Sonship, the Spirit relates to the Father in terms of spiritual procession, and so on. Human personhood, similarly, derives from the mystery of coinherence in God.[6] Julian builds the concept throughout the *Revelations* in different ways, showing the link between human nature--to which she refers as "kynd"-- and the indwelling of the Second Person in human nature, and the indwelling of the Persons of the Trinity in one another. An example is the following, in which she refers to the special work of the Son as "mercy" and the special work of the Holy Spirit as "grace":

> I had in perty touchyng, and it is growndyd in kynd, þat is to say: oure reson is groundyd in god, whych is substanncyally kyndnesse. Of this substancyall kyndnesse mercy and grace spryngyth and spredyth in to vs, werkyng all thynges in fulfyllyng of oure joy. Theyse be oure groundys, in whych we haue oure beyng, oure encrese and oure fulfyllyng. For in kynde we haue oure lyfe and oure beyng, and in mercy and grace we haue oure encres and oure fulfyllyng. (56.573-4)

> [I had partial touching, and it is founded in nature, that is to say: Our reason is founded in God, who is nature's substance. From this substantial nature spring mercy and grace, and penetrate us, accomplishing everything for the fulfillment of our joy. These

are our foundations, in which we have our being, our increase and our fulfillment. For in nature we have our life and our being, and in mercy and grace we have our increase and our fulfillment. 289-90)]

Because Julian sees divine love ontologically in terms of coinherence or the relationship of the divine Persons, she avoids a tendency in western theology after Augustine to psychologize divine love or to view love as only one of the divine attributes. It is, rather, the very being of God. She also avoids the tendency to view divine love as the peculiar operation of the Holy Spirit, another tendency in the West with Augustinian roots. Eastern theology never depicts the Holy Spirit as merely a "love-bond" between the Father and the Son, nor love as the special role of the Spirit only.

By establishing divine Being/Love as the interaction of the Persons of the Trinity, and therefore of the Trinity with humanity, Julian lays a groundwork for the other important themes in Christian doctrine. Creation, evil, sin, salvation, faith, judgment, and so on are all approached in ontological terms--as modes of dynamic being--rather than psychologically as matters of the will or perception or affection. This general approach allows Julian to view human love itself in terms of participation in God rather than as mere emotion or attachment to persons or things.

Julian's trinitarian theology also presents a model which is familiar to modern atomic physics. If contemporary physicists were theologians, they might say with Julian that the Trinity is an absolute interpenetration or reciprocity of Persons. Scientists speak of matter as composed of interacting sub-particles which swarm like bees, more like concentrations of energy than substantial objects. These sub-particles are so dynamic that in a sense they cannot be said to "be" anywhere, unless they are viewed as everywhere-at-once in their spheres of possibility. Similarly, Julian sees the Persons of the Trinity as continually in and with one another, not identical but never separated.

II. Being and Energy

Julian understands Love in terms of divine Being, but divine Being is also divine energy. Divine Love generates existence outside of itself:

God creates everything that exists; God loves it, and God sustains it constantly (Ch. 5). These are dynamic terms, not static. Unlike many medievals, Julian speaks of God in terms of what God does and how God relates to creation, rather than in terms of divine essence or divine properties. Therefore Julian frequently refers to God as "Maker, Lover, Keeper," referring both to God's being but also to God's deeds.

As her theology unfolds through the *Revelations*, Julian draws a distinction--unusual in the West--between the essence of God, which cannot be understood, and God's deeds or "workings" which are shared with creation. Julian becomes aware that there are two aspects of her showings, two dimensions of theology, one of which is open and evident in Christ and the other which is never revealed:

> He gaue vnderstondyng of ij partyes. That one party is oure saviour and oure saluacyon. Thys blessyd parte is opyn, clere, feyer and lyght and plentuouse, for alle mankynde that is of good wylle and that shalle be is comprehendyd in this part. . . . And thus may we see and enjoye oure parte is oure lorde.
>
> That other is hyd and sparryd fro vs, that is to sey alle that is besyde oure saluacion; for that is oure lordes prevy conncelle, and it longyth to the ryalle lordschyppe of god to haue hys pryvy connceles in pees, and it longyth to his saruanntes for obedyence and reverence nott wylle to know hys connceyles. (29.414-5)

> [He gave understanding of two portions. One portion is our saviour and our salvation. This blessed portion is open, clear, fair and bright and plentiful, for all men who are of good will are comprehended in this portion. . . . And so we may see and rejoice that our portion is our Lord.
>
> The other portion is hidden from us and closed, that is to say all which is additional to our salvation; for this is our Lord's privy counsel in peace, and it is fitting to his servants out of obedience and respect not to wish to know his counsel. (228)]

The "pryvy connceles" are not merely things which God does and which human beings do not understand, but pertain also to the Being of God which is beyond comprehension. Thus the Father cannot be seen except through the incarnate Son: "But man is blyndyd in this life, and therefore we may nott se oure fader god as he is. And what tyme that he of hys goodnesse wylle shew hym to man, he shewyth hym homely as man. . . ." (51.525) ["But man is blinded in this life, and therefore we cannot see our Father, God, as he is. And when he of his goodness wishes to show himself to man, he shows himself familiar, like a man . . . ." (272)].

The self-revealing of God in Christ is God's "workings" or activity towards humanity. Julian identifies the "workings" as certain teachings which the lover of God receives in prayer--what she elsewhere identifies as the gracious work of the Holy Spirit (Ch. 80). Here she seems to refer to her own revelations. But more fundamental are the ways in which God interacts with the world in creation, incarnation, salvation and judgment. As seen above, Julian understands the Incarnation as the center of the divine works: ". . .Crist shewyd me his father, in no bodely lycknesse but in his property and in hys wurkyng" (22.383) ["Christ showed me his Father, not in any bodily likeness but in his attributes and in his operations" (216)].

The Church and sacraments are also the works of God. All these do not merely teach about God but actually draw the saints into the Being of God, which is uncreated love or charity. Again, "Charyte vnmade is god, charyte made is oure soule in god, charyte gevyn is vertu, and þat is a gracious gyfte of wurkyng" (84.727) ["Uncreated charity is God, created charity is our sould in God, given charity is virtue, and that is a gift of grace in deeds" (341)].

The "workings" are seen continually in creation, but they intensify in mystical prayer, that is, for the soul who seeks and waits for God. This is the special role of the Holy Spirit: ". . .for it is his wille þat we know that he shall aper sodenly and blyssydefully to all his lovers. For his workyng is prevy, and he wille be perceyved, and his aperyng shalle be swet(h)e sodeyn" (10.335) ["it is his will that we know that he will appear, suddenly and blessedly, to all his lovers. For he works in secret, and he will be perceived, and his appearing will be very sudden" (196)].

Julian uses the term "workings," literally equivalent to the Greek *energeia* (ἐνέργεια), "energies." In Eastern Christian theology the distinction between the essence of God and the divine (uncreated) energies of God is viewed as crucial for understanding the nature of the Trinity and the divine relationship to humanity. In this view the essence of God cannot be known by created beings; however, the divine nature is indeed accessible to human beings because God enters into relationship with creation exactly through the divine energies.

Julian surely did not know it, but the essence/energies distinction was articulated in Orthodoxy during her own lifetime. In the fourteenth century a controversy arose between St. Gregory Palamas, representing the monastic traditions of Mount Athos, and a Calabrian named Barlaam, an Orthodox whose schooling had been in the West. Certain monks of Mt. Athos were said to have seen divine light, recalling Jesus' transfiguration, during their experience of prayer. Barlaam assumed that such experiences were phantasms or visions of created light, since God cannot be seen; but the essence of God should be sought through reason. For Gregory, on the other hand, the essence of God cannot be known through human reason, but the light seen by the so-called hesychastic monks (practitioners of a type of silent prayer linked to the breath) was said to be uncreated, a transfiguring "energy" emanating from God.[7]

In Palamite theology, as for Julian, God is understood as a paradox of essential stillness (without-change) and essential dynamism, an *ekstasis* in which God encounters humanity. The paradox explains how God is both inaccessible and accessible at once. The essence/energy distinction also has other implications for understanding the Christian life. For example, if the divine relationship to the cosmos is understood in dynamic terms as divine energies or "workings," then salvation is a dynamic process, not a state of being.

A static concept of God and salvation would imply that individual persons are either "saved" or "unsaved," members of one category or another. This is precisely the view articulated in various doctrines of predestination in the Middle Ages and in what came to be known to Calvinists in the Protestant Reformation as "positional atonement." By contrast, for Julian as for the Byzantines, salvation is not a state of either/or, saved or unsaved but a process of growth. It is the transformation or completion of humanity into the image of the divine Son. For Julian the process is like the formation of an infant in the womb; in eastern theology it is more often described as transfiguration or deification, but it is also seen as a process of maturation into the likeness of God in Christ.[8]

Another implication of dynamic theology is the way in which the mystery of the Incarnation is explained. Christians believe that the eternal Son of God was born as man; therefore Christ is both divine and human. In a static model, Christ appears to be an artificial fusion of two static and opposite natures, divinity and humanity. This model tends to see humanity as distant from God and even "against" God's nature. A dynamic approach, on the other hand, is to see a never-ending reciprocity between complementary natures. In the latter view humanity is seen positively, as created in the divine image for the purpose of the incarnation--which is to say, in order that humanity might become one with God:

> God the blyssydfull trynyte, whych is evyr lastyng beyng, ryght as he is endlesse fro without begynnyng, ryghte so it was in his purpose endlesse to make mankynde, whych feyer kynd furst was dyght to his owne son, the second person; and when he woulde, by full accorde of alle the trynyte he made vs alle at onys. And in oure makyng he knytt vs and onyd vs to hym selfe, by which oonyng we be kept as clene and as noble as we were made. (58.582)

> [God the blessed Trinity, who is everlasting being, just as he is eternal from without beginning, just so was it in his eternal purpose to create human nature, which fair nature was first prepared for his own Son, the second person; and when he wished, by full agreement of the whole Trinity he created us all once. And in our creating he joined and united us to himself, and through this union we are kept as pure and as noble as we were created. (293)]

III. The Problems of Sin and Blame

An important implication of Julian's ontological approach to divine love is her ontological approach to the nature of sin and evil. Wondering why God has allowed sin to exist and observing that God does everything, Julian wonders whether God can be said to be the cause of sin (Ch. 11). Naturally, it seems impossible for God to sin or to create evil. She concludes, therefore, that evil is not something which God does; it has no positive existence in itself. Evil is the absence of good, just as sickness is the absence of health. It is non-being, whatever is not-God. Likewise, Julian reports that she could not see sin itself. She concludes that this is because it does not have positive existence: "But I saw nott synne, for I beleue it had no maner of substannce, ne no part of beyng, ne it myght not be knowen but by the payne that is caused thereof" (27.406) ["But I did not see sin, for I believe that is has no kind of substance, no share in being, nor can it be recognized except by the pain caused by it" (225)].

Julian's characterization of evil in terms of non-being is ancient. Echoing a tradition presaged in ancient Greek philosophy, the first Christian theologians characterized evil as *ouk on* (οὐκ ὄν), non-being or a malevolent chaos. Sin is falling away from being itself, a participation in non-being. Following this tradition St. Athanasius writes simply, "...it is God alone Who exists, evil is non-being, the negation and antithesis of good"; Maximus the Confessor argues that evil is non-being, "the privation of being--but not of being properly so called, for it has no contrary--but of true being by participation." The Eastern concept of evil as privation of being was developed at some length by the mysterious sixth-century Syrian writer known as Dionysius the Areopagite, at least some of whose works were known in the West in translation, both in Latin and in English, by Julian's time.9

Then what is sin? On the simplest level Julian suggests that one should not characterize "sins" as deeds or thoughts. Sin gives rise to these things, but it is really a condition of helplessness which has left all humanity broken and incomplete. Julian's concrete vision of the Fall is of Adam, God's "seruannt," falling into a ditch of his own making from which he cannot rise and from which he can no longer even see the face of God (Ch. 51). The vision is not merely of Adam himself but of all humanity:

The lorde that satt solemply in rest and in peas, I vnderstonde that he is god. The seruannt that stode before hym, I vnderstode that he was shewed for Adam, that is to se oone man was shewed that tyme and his fallyng to make there by to be vnderstonde how god beholdyth alle manne and his fallyng. For in the syghte of god alle man is oone man, and oone man is alle man. (51.521-2)

[I understood that the lord who sat in state in rest and peace is God. I understood that the servant who stood before him was shown for Adam, that is to say, one man was shown at that time and his fall, so as to make it understood how God regards all men and their falling. For in the sight of God all men are one man, and one man is all men. (270]

Through the revelations Julian comes to a new appreciation of the true nature of sin as a cosmic injury of devastating consequence. Nevertheless, God shows Julian that she should not despair about sin because "alle shalle be wele, and alle shalle be wele, and alle maner of thynge shalle be wele" (28.405). This prompts Julian to ask how all things can be well in the face of the great injury which creation has suffered due to sin (Ch. 28-29). Julian is aware that sin has affected all creation because of the special role humanity has as caretaker of the Earth. But if sin is a cosmic fall, then salvation also has a cosmic dimension. Salvation in Christ means that the sin of Adam is healed in mankind; therefore, everything "that is less" shall also be made well in salvation (Ch. 29).

Like the Byzantine theologians, Julian is careful to point out that ultimately it is impossible for created beings to understand the character of evil or why it exists, any more than it is possible to understand the essence of God. Nor should we try. To attempt to look too deeply into the problem is itself dangerous. However, it is possible to see that if the divine nature is love, then love does not change in the face of evil. Instead, evil becomes the opportunity for love to prove itself. Therefore, ". . .I saw an hygh mervelous prevyte hyd in god, whych pryuyte he shalle opynly make and shalle be knowen to vs in hevyn. In whych knowyng we shalle verely se the cause why he sufferde synne to come, in whych syght we shalle endlessly haue joye" (27.407) ["I saw hidden in God an exalted and wonderful mystery, which he will make plain and we shall know in heaven. In this knowledge we shall truly see the cause why he allowed sin to come, and in this sight we shall rejoice forever" (226)].

Julian's theology here moves away from Augustinian thought regarding the nature of sin. Augustine recognized that sin must lack positive being because God cannot be said to have created it. However, his primary question was a psychological one: with St. Paul he wondered, "Why do I do what I do not want to do?" (Romans 7:15). Ultimately Augustine answered this question in psychological and legal terms: in the fallen state there is concupiscence or lust for the things of the world, a bent in the will which is inevitably contrary; it is disobedience.[10]

St. Paul argues that the "wages of sin is death" (Romans 6:23). Following Augustine, western theology tends to see in Paul's statement a psychological response on God's part to the offense of sin: death is God's punishment for disobedience. Julian views sin and judgment differently, and her perspective is easily understood in terms of Byzantine theology.

In Julian's view, death and hell represent ultimate despair in the face of divine love. Hell is a malapropriation of the graces of God on the part of human beings who choose fear, wrath, and contrariness in life rather than faith, kindness, and divine love. Punishment is not God's will for any human being; indeed there is no wrath in God. God's desire, in the face of the tragedy of sin, is not to punish sinners but to heal the pain of sin. This is accomplished as God draws near to the sinner, and indeed there is no place where one will not ultimately encounter the presence of God (Ch. 10).

For those who love God, the divine presence chastises and cleanses one from sin. For those who are wrathful, the presence of God (in whom there is no wrath at all) is experienced as caustic, engendering despair (Ch. 17). It is hell. Byzantine theology, similarly, understands the caustic fires of hell to be the malapropriation of divine love, the "fire" of the presence of the Holy Spirit which cannot be tolerated by sinners, and in which sin is not tolerated by God.[11]

Julian's theology also recapitulates the Byzantine concept that if sin is not merely psychological, neither can sin be remedied by blame, punishment, or any merely psychological repair. St. Athanasius argues that salvation requires the remaking of humanity and conquering of death and for this reason could not have been achieved even by human repentance. The reason is not the greatness of the "crime" of sin against God (as, for example, in Anselm's theology) but that the real enemy is death and non-being:

> Had it been a case of a trespass only, and not of a subsequent corruption, repentance would have been well enough; but when once transgression had begun men came under the power of corruption proper to their nature and were bereft of the grace which belonged to them as creatures in the image of God.[12]

IV. God, Space and Time

A scribe made the annotation to the *Revelations* that it is impossible to understand Julian's theology unless all of it is taken togther. This is especially true with regard to her view of divine Judgment. It is necessary to evaluate her account of Doomsday in light of her treatment of the divine relationship to space and time. The key is found in Julian's allegorical vision of a "seruannt" or gardener, noted above, who ran to do the will of his master, fell into a ditch and was mortally wounded (Ch. 51). After considerable reflection Julian realizes that the vision of the gardener comprehends both Adam and Christ and also all humanity:

> In the servant is / comprehendyd the seconde person of þe trynyte, and in the seruannt is comprehendyd Adam, that is to sey, all men. And therefore whan I sey the sonne, it menyth the godhed whych is evyn with the fader, and whan I sey the servannt, it menyth Crystes manhode whych is ryghtfull Adam. (51.532-3)

> [In the servant is comprehended the second person of the Trinity, and in the servant is comprehended Adam, that is to say all men. And therefore when I say "the Son", that means the divinity which is equal to the Father, and when I say "the servant", that means Christ's humanity, which is the true Adam. (274)]

The human nature of the Son of God comprehends all humanity because all humanity is comprehended in Adam, and also because the incarnation weds the divine nature to all human nature. Because of this mystical unity, Julian observes, there is also an overlapping of time and events: "When Adam felle [into the chasm of sin], godes sonne fell. . . . Goddys son fell with Adam in to the slade of the meydens wombe, whych was the feyerest doughter of Adam, and that for to excuse Adam from blame in hevyn and in erth" (51.533-4) ["When Adam fell, God's son fell. . . . God's son fell with Adam, into the valley of the womb of the maiden who was the fairest daughter of Adam, and that was to excuse Adam from blame in heaven and on earth" (274-75)].

Julian's main theological point is that in the incarnation human nature has been permanently joined to the divine nature in a way which cannot be broken apart even by sin. More subtly, she is also arguing that from the divine perspective the incarnation is simultaneous with the fall of humanity into sin. Even the creation of every human being may be said to be simultaneous with the creation of Adam, which in turn was for the sake of the (future) incarnation itself: ". . .it was in [God's] purpose endlesse to make mankynde, whych feyer kynd furst was dyght to his owne son, the second person; and when he woulde, by full accorde of alle the trynyte he made vs alle at onys" (58.582) ["just so was it in his eternal purpose to create human nature, which fair nature was first prepared for his own Son, the second person; and when he wished by full agreement of the whole Trinity, he created us all once" (293)].

This rather startling concept has great implications for Christian faith and life. Questions which occupied medieval theologians as well as many Christians today suddenly become irrelevant: for example, whether God knew in advance that Adam would sin, or why God waited so long after the fall of Adam to send his Son to save the world. Julian concludes that from the divine perspective there is only the one time, a single event of creation/fall/redemption/eschaton, in which God "made us all at once" and in which mystical union with God occurred simultaneously.

Julian realizes that because God sees time as all-at-once, those who draw near to God will also experience space/time differently. Her visions reaffirm the teaching of St. Paul that the faithful participate mystically in the fall of Adam as well as in the resurrection of Christ, in this life (cf. Romans 6:2-4, Colossians 2:12). Lovers of God begin to share in the future of the cosmos, anticipating the joy and perfection which still are to come. Therefore for them the eschaton becomes a current event, not merely something in the future. Those who love God lead a mixed life, in which they participate in the pain of sin and contrition, but also in the bliss which is to come:

> For þe tyme of this lyfe we haue in vs a mervelous medelur both of wele and of woo. We haue in vs oure lorde Jhesu Cryst vp resyn, and we haue in vs the wrechydnesse and the myschef of Adams fallyng. Dyeng by Cryst we be lastynly kept, and by hys gracyous touchyng we be reysed in to the very trust of saluacyon. (52.546)

[During our lifetime here we have in us a marvellous mixture of both well-being and woe. We have in us our risen Lord Jesus Christ, and we have in us the wretchedness and harm of Adam's falling. Dying, we are constantly protected by Christ, and by the touching of his grace we are raised to true trust in salvation. (279)]

Similar observations are made by Julian with regard to space. In her vision of a little ball like a hazelnut in her hand (Ch. 5), Julian realizes that she is seeing all that exists. Nevertheless, it is presented as the way the cosmos might appear to God: small and frail. She immediately wonders why it does not disappear altogether. The frailty of the little ball of light indicates the invasion of evil into the realm of created being. If left to itself the created cosmos would disappear quickly into nothingness. Julian learns in this vision that the cosmos continues to exist only because the God who made it also loves it continually and thereby keeps it from falling into nothing.

The next lesson is that God is at the heart of all that exists. Julian says, "And after this I saw god in a pynte, that is to say in my vnderstanding, by which syght I saw that he is in althyng. I beheld with avysement, seeyng and / knowyng in that syght that he doeth alle that is done" (11.336) ["And after this I saw God in a (point), that is to say in my understanding, by which vision I saw that he is present in all things. I contemplated it carefully, seeing and recognizing through it that he does everything which is done" (197)].[13] The meaning of this vision is that she cannot go anywhere, even to the bottom of the sea, without encountering God's presence. Therefore the "point" is both dimensionless and also pan-dimensional: it is every point of space, encompassing all points of three-dimensional space equally.

As will be evident below, Byzantine theologians treat space/time in a similar way, especially in the divine liturgy and the icons of the Church. In eastern theology time is transcended by the fact of the incarnation of the Son of God. The present moment exists only in light of the future time in which Christ will come again. In the meantime the believing soul exists in a new aeon, the "new Age." Therefore the present is informed by the future, and in the liturgies of the Church the faithful are already participating in the future. Space, too, is transformed so that in the iconography of the Church the dimensions of this world no longer apply.[14]

V. The Mystery of the Eucharist

Eternal life begins in the present, and participation in eternal life in this life is a process of formation. For Julian, as for Orthodoxy, the means by which lovers of God are transformed, transcending space/time and sharing in the Age which is to come, is the practice of prayer and sharing in the sacramental life of the Church. Prayer joins us to God: "Prayer onyth the soule to god, for though the soule be evyr lyke to god in kynde and in substance restoryd by grace, it is ofte vnlike in condescion by synne of mannes perty" (43.475) ["Prayer unites the soul to God, for though the soul may be always like God in nature and in substance restored by grace, it is often unlike him in condition, through sin on man's part" (253)]. And the sacraments actually are the presence of God in Christ:

> Wherfore hym behovyth to fynde vs to nourish us, for the deerworthy loue of moderhed hath made hym dettour to vs. The moder may geue her chylde sucke hyr mylke, but oure precyous moder Jhesu, he may fede vs wyth hym selfe, and doeth full curtesly and full tendyrly with the blessyd sacrament . . . and so ment he in theyse blessyd wordys, where he seyde: . . . All the helth and the lyfe of sacramentys, alle þe vertu and þe grace of my worde, alle the goodnesse that is ordeynyd in holy chyrch to the, I it am. (60.596-7)

> [Therefore he must needs nourish us, for the precious love of motherhood has made him our debtor. The mother can give her child to suck of her milk, but our precious Mother Jesus can feed us with himself, and does, most courteously and most tenderly, with the blessed sacrament . . . and so meant in these blessed words, where he said: . . . All the health and the life of the sacraments, all the power and grace of my word, all the goodness which is ordained in Holy Church for you, I am he. (298)]

It is interesting that Julian's language regarding Christ as mother, feeding us with himself in the Sacrament, is anticipated as early as the second century. St. Irenaeus of Lyon writes:

> He could have come to us in his indescribable glory; we, however, could not have borne the greatness of his glory. For this reason, the one who was the perfect bread of the Father offered himself to us as milk for children: he came in human form. His purpose was to feed us at the breast of his flesh, but nursing us to make us accustomed to eat and drink the Word of God, so that we would be able to hold in ourselves the one who is the bread of immortality, the Spirit of the Father.[15]

Orthodox theologians instinctively relate theological themes to the Divine Liturgy because it is here that Christian faith and prayer are most clearly articulated. Julian, who as an anchoress observed the Mass daily from her cell, also seems to have written with the liturgy in mind.

At every celebration of the Eucharist the ancient Christian liturgies express a puzzling concept of space and time in which all of time seems to be collapsed into one time, and all space into one space. This new space/time is not the timeless "now" of Zen Buddhism, in which there is no past and no future but only the Now; nor the spaceless "no-thing" in which there is no dimension but only Emptiness or Horizon (*sunyata*).[16] Rather, it is a "pregnant" space/time in which all the past and all the future are here-at-once, and in which the whole universe is collapsed into a single point.

In the western Mass this "point" is of course understood to be the Host, and in the Orthodox East, the bread and wine comingled in the chalice and presented as the Body and Blood of Christ.[17] Here Christ, who is seated at the right hand of the Father beyond all space-time, is said to make himself present to the faithful within space and time, at a particular place and time, in the bread and in the wine.

A medieval question was how to understand the divine presence at the Eucharist. If bread still appears to be bread, and wine still appears to be wine, in what sense did they become the Body and Blood of Christ? How is Christ present "in" them? Western scholastics attempted to answer these questions in terms of Aristotelean physics: the "accidents" of bread and wine remain unchanged, the "substance" is transmuted. In the

Christian East, however, the question of how the bread and wine might be or contain Christ was not analyzed but accepted as mystery.

The heart of the Orthodox liturgy is the affirmation that Christ is mystically present, that is, one cannot say how. There is no adequate physics in which to conceptualize it. Moreover, Christ is understood to be present at every place and time, yet his presence is unique at the Eucharist. In the Orthodox liturgy the priest, turning to the deacon, says, "Christ is in our midst." The greeting is echoed by the parishoners, who say, "He is and always shall be." Moreover the divine presence is said to intensify through the liturgy. At the Great Entrance the choir sings of the entrance of Christ "mystically upborne" and escorted by the Seraphim and Cherubim.

One of the most dramatic expressions of the divine relationship to space/time in the Orthodox liturgy occurs in the prayers quietly said by the priest in preparation for the Eucharist. In the prayers before the prothesis the priest acknowledges the central mystery of divine presence: that Christ, unbound by space and time as we know them, was simultaneously everywhere,

> in the tomb bodily,
> but in hell with the spirit as God,
> and in paradise with the thief,
> you were, O Christ, filling all places at once;
> for you cannot be circumscribed.[18]

In Orthodox liturgical physics, the exact location of Christ's body is beyond definition. It is both visible and invisible at once. It is visible in the people themselves, who are the assembled Church, the Body of Christ. It is visible, too, as the tangible elements of bread and wine. On the other hand, it is invisible as the mystical Presence which we cannot see but which is acknowledged by faith; and Christ is present in bread and wine, but also filling all places, and at the right hand of the Father.

Because the Son of God is the Creator of All and is at the center of all that exists, his presence brings with it the presence of all that is contained by God. Thus the eucharist mystically represents--or may be said to "contain"--every point of space in the universe, of which Christ is the center. When bread (*prosphora*) is prepared for Orthodox consecration it is marked in such a way as to represent Christ in the center, surrounded by the Mother of God, the saints, martyrs, bishops, and all the Church, including those who have died. In this sense all the world is located there and is prayed for before the mystery of the Eucharist can begin.

In the same way, in eucharistic space/time all time is present at once. Thus the liturgical prayers acknowledge that the moment of Eucharist "contains" the moment of creation, and the moment of our salvation, and also the moment of our death and of our judgment. Every Sunday is the day of Resurrection; every Feast of the Nativity is the night in which the Virgin gives birth to the One who created the heavens; every Holy Thursday Vespers becomes, by anticipation, the day on which the Creator of all space and time is himself subjected to death and the cessation of time. And worshippers are present every Sunday when the women come, bearing spices, to the tomb.

Evidence of the collapse of space/time still exists in the western eucharistic rites. In the "Mystery of Faith," recited by the faithful just before the consecration, past, present and future are deliberately represented at once: "Christ has died, Christ is risen, Christ will come again." But the mystery of collapsed time is most movingly expressed at the Paschal Vigil on Easter Eve. Here, as if moving backwards through time, worshippers pass through their own exorcism and baptism once again. They are present at the crucifixion and at the resurrection itself. Worshippers hear that this is the night in which heaven and earth are joined. The Sarum liturgy, probably that which Julian heard from her cell, includes the following for the Paschal Vigil:

Hec sunt enim festa paschalia in quibus uerus ille agnus occiditur eiusque sanguine postes consecrantur . . .Hec nox est in qua destructis uinculis mortis christus ab inferis uictor ascendit. Nichil enim nobis nasci profuit nisi redimi profuisset. O mira circa nos tue pietatis dignacio. O inestimabilis dilectio caritatis ut seruuum redimeres filium tradidisti. O certe necessarium ade peccatum et nostrum quod christi morte deletum est. O felix culpa que talem ac tantum meruit habere redemptorem. O certe beata nox que sola meruit scire tempus et horam in qua christus ab inferis resurrexit.[19]

Although not an exact rendering, this English version reflects how tenses shift back and forth or are ambiguous:[20]

> For this is the Paschal feast, in which that true Lamb is slain, and the door-posts are consecrated by his blood. . . .
> This is the night in which Christ burst the bonds of death, and rose a conqueror from the grave.
> For it had advantaged us nothing to be born except we had the advantage of redemption.
> O marvellous condescension of thy loving-kindness concerning us!
> O inestimable tenderness of love! Thou gavest up thy Son to redeem thy servant.
> O truly necessary sin of Adam and of ourselves, which was blotted out by the death of Christ!
> O happy guilt, the desert of which was to gain such and so great a Redeemer!
> O truly blessed night, to the desert of which alone was granted to know the time and the hour in which Christ rose from the grave!

It is perhaps from the Easter Vigil that Julian obtains her famous phrase, "sin is behovabil," i.e. somehow necessary or beneficial (Ch. 27). In the Paschal Vigil the sin of Adam is seen to be both, because it gives rise to the opportunity for so great a salvation.

While the Paschal mystery is certainly the center of the liturgical life of the Church, the Feast of the Nativity also gives evidence of the collapse of space/time in eucharistic thought. In the Sarum liturgy the offices for Christmas Eve treat the Nativity as a present event: "To-day ye shall know that the Lord will come and save you,/ and in the morning, then ye shall see his glory." And again: "Tomorrow the iniquity of the earth shall be blotted out,/ and the Savior of the world shall reign over us." And again: ". . .Who was before all time/ Is born of purest Maid;/ Glory to God in heights sublime,/ Peace comes the world to aid" (93-4; 99).

In Orthodoxy there is a similar awareness that because the Son of God comprehends all space/time, the mystery of the incarnation in Mary's womb also comprehends all space/time. Orthodox hymns for Christmas-Lent (the seven weeks of fasting before Christmas) locate the drama of Bethlehem in the present, as the faithful move towards the stable which will become the Throne of the Son of God. In the Orthros prayers and hymns in weeks preceding Nativity, hearers are reminded that Mary's womb was "stretched" to contain the heavens. The theme is echoed in liturgical hymns sung the weeks before Pascha (Easter).

In the East the holy icons, finally, are said to be non-spacial depictions of the reality of Christ and the saints. The icons do not depict depth or ordinary perspective but seem to reverse the rules of realistic drawing and painting to follow the rules of "heavenly space." Objects and saints are shown larger or smaller depending upon their role or importance, not upon distance; all things are equally distant; the saints are never inside any enclosure; light comes from "inside" the icon itself. And the icons draw the viewer into the reality of the event or saint depicted, actually in some sense making the view present to them and vice-versa. The mystery of the incarnation is depicted in the icon above the altar, called Platytera, in which the Theotokos (Mother of God) appears with the words, "greater than the heavens," indicating the presence of Christ who contains all space, within her womb.[21]

VI. The Womb of Mary and of Christ

In one of her more unusual feminine images, Julian describes the mystical sharing in divine space/time by the faithful in terms of pregnancy. The Virgin's pregnancy with Christ also comprehends the faithful, because Christ comprehends humanity. But Christ himself is the true divine Mother who is "pregnant" with humanity. This present life is our formation in the divine womb:

> Thus oure lady is oure moder, in whome we be all beclosyd and of hyr borne in Crist, for she that is moder of oure savyoure is mother of all þat ben savyd in our sauyour; and oure savyoure is oure very moder, in whome we be endlesly borne and nevyr shall come out of hym.
> . . .We be all in hym beclosyd, and he is beclosyd in vs. (57.580-581)

> [So our Lady is our mother, in whom we are all enclosed and born of her in Christ, for she who is mother of our saviour is

mother of all who are saved in our saviour; and our saviour is our true Mother, in whom we are endlessly born and out of whom we shall never come.

. . . We are all enclosed in him, and he is enclosed in us. (292)]

However, while earthly mothers deliver their children into a world which ends in death, Jesus the true Mother delivers the saints into a world which does not end: "We wytt that alle oure moders bere vs to payne and to dyeng. A, what is that? But oure very moder Jhesu, he alone beryth vs to joye and to endlesse levyng. . . . Thus he susteyneth vs with in hym in loue and traveyle, in to the full tyme pat he wolde suffer. . . ." (60.595-6) ["We know that all our mothers bear us for pain and for death. O, what is that? But our true Mother Jesus, he alone bears us for joy and for endless life. . . . So he carries us within him in love and travail, until the time when he wanted to suffer. . . ." (297-98)].

Thus the "point" at which all the divine acts of salvation come together is the point of the incarnation, the entry of the divine Son into the womb of Mary. In a sense this is salvation, because it is the ontological union of humanity with the divine nature. This is God's corrective to the tragedy of sin, a "knitting together" of humanity with divinity. As noted above, Julian boldly argues that human nature was created for the Son of God and not first of all for ourselves (6.58). Human beings share in Christ's humanity, not vice-versa. Thus the entry of the Son of God into humanity is the real source of salvation.

Julian speaks of the natural human state as "kind," making a pun on the medieval word. The natural or "kind" way of life is loving or "kind," reflecting the nature of God, for our true nature or Kind is established ontologically in Christ. In this life humanity, including human emotions and perceptions, is changeable; but the inevitable instability of this life due to sin will eventually be overcome. Thus salvation--in the working of grace--is the process of growing in the womb of Christ, into the fulness of humanity, which through the incarnation is actually located in God: "Here may we see that we be all bounde to god for kynd, and we be bounde to god for grace. Her may we see that vs nedyth nott gretly to seke ferre out to know sondry kyndys, but to holy church into oure moders brest, that is to sey in to oure owne soule, wher oure lord dwellyth" (62.612) ["Here we can see that we are all bound to God by nature, and we are bound to God by grace. Here we can see that we do not need to seek far afield so as to know various natures, but to go to Holy Church, into our Mother's breast, that is to say into our own soul, where our Lord dwells" (303)]. Paradoxically, every believer is also "pregnant" with Christ in this life: "Plentuously, fully and swetely was this shewde; and it is spoken of in the furst, wher it seyde we be all in hym beclosyd, and he is beclosyd in vs" (57.580) ["Plenteously, fully and sweetly was this shown; and it is spoken of in the first revelation, where it says that we are all enclosed in him, and he is enclosed in us" (292)].

Orthodox mysticism too asserts that every soul which is being saved is a bearer of Christ. In Christ the "space" of creation, incarnation, resurrection, and judgment is collapsed to a single point, which point is both Mary's womb and the soul of the lover of God. St. Gregory of Nyssa comments,

> What happened in the stainless Mary when the fulness of the Godhead which was in Christ shone out through her, that happens in every soul that leads by rule the virgin life. No longer indeed does the Master come with bodily presence . . . but, spiritually, He dwells in us and brings His Father with Him, as the Gospel somewhere tells.[22]

And in his Commentary on the Our Father, St. Maximus the Confessor presages Julian exactly:

> By this power [of humility and dispassion], Christ is always born mysteriously and willingly, becoming incarnate through those who are saved. He causes the soul which begets him to be a virgin-mother who, to speak briefly, does not bear the marks of nature subject to corruption. (109)

By nurturing Christ within, the faithful soul "expands" to fill the universe as Christ fills it. Such lovers of God join the saints in worship "at all times and in all places" praising God. Finally, as has been seen, the collapse of space/time in the Liturgy presages the Second Coming or

Judgment at the end of time. The faithful already participate in the end of time, even though it is not-yet.

VII. The Omega Point

At least one contemporary physicist has proposed a concept which is strangely reminiscent of Julian's Doomsday theology. Called the Quantum Omega Point Theory, the concept proposes a future convergence of space/time which is the beginning, but also the "end" of space/time. Theoretically, Omega Point would be a vantage point from which a conscious being would simultaneously apprehend all space/time at once. At this vantage point, conscious being would therefore be absolute, but it would not interact with space/time in terms of cause/effect. The Omega Point would suggest that a general resurrection from the dead is not only possible but necessary in terms of physics.[23]

The question of cause/effect is important theologically. An important question for the scholastics, raised in the Augustinian controversy with Pelagius, was whether God merely knows in advance all that is going to happen, or actually causes all that happens. In Julian's theology, however, the question itself already betrays misunderstanding.

As Julian saw it in her revelations, divine Love cannot be characterized in causal terms. Love creates love in others, and love even condemns sin--by the fact that it is love. Love, however, cannot be coerced and love is not coercive or wrathful. In this light, to think of God in terms of causality misses the point. At the same time, the nature of God is to relate constantly to all that is created. Therefore, while God is intimately related to everything and "does all things" (in Julian's terminology), God does not "cause" in any impersonal sense. Rather, God--who is almighty and Creator of all--relates to the cosmos in absolute humility:

> Thus it faryth by oure lord Jhesu and by vs, for verely it is the most joy that may be, as to my syght, that he that is hyghest and myghtyest, noblyest and wurthyest, is lowest and mekest, hamlyest and curtysest. . . . For þe most fulhede of joy that we shalle haue, as to my syght, ys thys marvelous curtesy and

homelynesse of oure fader, that is oure maker, in oure lorde Jhesu Crist, that is oure broder and oure sauior. (7.314-5)
[So it is with our Lord Jesus and us, for truly it is the greatest possible joy, as I see it, that he who is highest and mightiest, noblest and most honourable, is lowest and humblest, most familiar and courteous. . . . For the greatest abundance of joy which we shall have, as I see it, is this wonderful courtesy and familiarity of our Father, who is our Creator, in our Lord Jesus Christ, who is our brother and our saviour. (188-89)]

Similarly, when the soul which loves God participates in the divine nature, causality disappears: there is no wrath, no judgment, no coercion, but only a dynamic sharing of "kindness" and sensitivity. Thus the lover of God becomes open to all people in all places and times, by participating in God. St. Maximus sees divine humility as the mark of bearing Christ:

If the indestructible might of the unfading kingdom is given to the humble and the meek, who would at this point be so deprived of love and desire for the divine gifts as not to tend as much as posssible toward humility and meekness to become, to the extent that this is possible for man, the image of God's kingdom by bearing in himself by grace the exact configuration in the Spirit of Christ, who is truly by nature and essence the great King? (Berthold 108)

Eventually all human beings will experience the divine presence and meekness, though some unpleasantly owing to their pride and, to use Julian's word, the "contrariness" of sin.

It will be interesting to see whether in future years physics will provide a mathematical model for Julian's ontological mysticism. In any case it seems apparent that Julian's theological approach merits further study, not merely in the context of medieval mysticism and not merely as a guide for personal piety or daily prayer. For the present, it is perhaps enough to explore the Day of Doom in a new way: not as the beginning of everlasting torture, but the fulfilment of our ontological participation in the cosmic event of salvation and Love.

It is fitting to end with a word of peace from Pseudo-Macarius and from Julian. Preaching perhaps in the 380's, Macarius says:

When God wishes, he becomes fire, burning up every coarse passion that has taken root in the soul. "For our God is a consuming fire". . . . When he wishes, he becomes an inexpressible and mysterious rest so that the soul may find rest in God's rest. When he wishes, he becomes joy and peace, cherishing and protecting the soul.[24]

And Julian:

I haue menyng of th(re) manner of cherys of oure lorde. The furst is chere of passion, as he shewde whyle he was with vs in this lyfe dyeng; and though this beholyng be mornyng and swemfulle, yet it is glad and mery, for he is god. The seconde manner of chere, it is pitte and ruth and compassion, and this shdwyth he to all his louers withsekernesse of kepyng that hath nede to his mercy. The thyrde is þe blessydfulle/ chere as it shalle be with outyn ende, and this was oftenest shewyd and longeste contynuyd. (71.656-7)

[I recollect three kinds of demeanour in our Lord. The first is that of his Passion, as he revealed when he was with us in this life, dying; and although to contemplate this be sorrowful and grievous, still it is glad and joyful, because he is God. The second is pity and ruth and compassion, and this he reveals to all his lovers, with the certainty of protection which necessarily belongs to his mercy. The third is that blessed demeanour as it will be without end, and this was most often revealed, and continued the longest time. (319)]

NOTES

1. Julian has been cited in recent years by Orthodox authors to explain eastern concepts. See for example Bishop Kallistos Ware, *The Orthodox Way,* St. Vladimir's Seminary Press, Crestwood, 1995) 47, 83. I have treated various of these themes elsewhere: cf. *Julian of Norwich: Christ Our Mother* (Wilmington. DE:

Glazier, 1989; and *Love Was His Meaning: The Theology and Mysticism of Julian of Norwich,* (Salzburg: Universität Salzburg, 1982).

2. All citations from the text of the Revelations in this essay are taken from the critical edition by Edmund Colledge and James Walsh, *A Book of Showings to the Anchoress Julian of Norwich* (Toronto: Pontifical Institute of Mediaeval Studies, 1978). Translations are from *Julian of Norwich: Showings,* trans. and eds. Edmund Colledge and James Walsh. Classics of Western Spirituality. (New York: Paulist, 1978). Subsequent citations will be provided parenthetically within the text.

3. St. Athanasius uses this terminology in *Ad Serapionem* 1:16. See *Athanasiana,* ed. George Dragas (London: Archdiocese of Thyratira, 1980) 69.

4. The Greek verb perichoreo (περιχωρέω) and its attendent noun, perichoresis (περιχώρησις), were used first (e.g. by St. Gregory the Theologian) with reference to Christology, meaning "to interpenetrate" in the sense that the human and divine natures of Christ are located in one another. They were later applied by the Church fathers (e.g. John of Damascus, Maximus the Confessor, Cyril of Alexandria) to the Persons of the Trinity relating to one another.

5. Both the Christian Trinity and Buddhist enlightenment are traditionally understood to be beyond thought. Buddhist "emptiness" (*sunyata*) and the Trinity have been compared, though not with reference to Julian of Norwich, by Roger Corless and Paul Knitter in *Buddhist Emptiness and Christian Trinity* (New York: Paulist, 1990). See also William Johnston, "All and Nothing: St. John of the Cross and Buddhist-Christian Dialogue," *Areopagus* 2.2 (Easter, 1989) 18 and 24; and note 16, below.

6. A contemporary Orthodox exploration of communion as ontological reality, constituting both being and personhood, is developed by (Metropolitan) John Zizioulas, *Being as Communion* (New York: St. Vladimir's Seminary Press, 1985).

7. The history and theological issues involved are presented in John Meyendorff, *St. Gregory Palamas and Orthodox Spirituality* (St. Vladimir's Seminary Press, 1974) esp. 86 ff.

8. Orthodoxy understands redemption in terms of theosis, deification, which is also depicted as the process of transfiguration into the divine image, and a growth into mature humanity (following Irenaeus of Lyons, d. 200). These dogmas in turn relate to the understanding of human person in relation to divine Person as pure communion. See for example Vladimir Lossky, *In the Image and Likeness of God* (London: Mowbrays, 1967), 97 ff.

9. Athanasius, *On the Incarnation,* (Crestwood, NY: St. Vladimir's Orthodox Theological Seminary, Crestwood, NY, 1944 [repr.1982]) 30. Maximus, "Four

Centuries on Love," *Maximus Confessor: Selected Writings,* trans. George Berthold, (New York: Paulist, 1985) 65.

The Dionysian treatment of evil may be seen in *Dionysius the Areopagite: The Divine Names and The Mystical Theology,* trans. C. E. Rolt (London: SPCK, 1940; repr. 1977) 111 ff. Dionysius raises the question of why evil exists and answers that "Evil cometh not of the Good; and if it cometh therefrom it is not evil." Julian may have been familiar with Dionysius' Mystical Theology, available in England as the *Hid Diuinity.*

10. Cf. Augustine's treatment of evil, sin and original sin in Faith, Hope, and Charity, also known as the Enchiridion. In the Augustinian view humans commit sin because of ignorance and weakness of will (Ch. 22), which are both understood psychologically. Louis Arand, *St. Augustine: Faith, Hope and Charity,* Ancient Christian Writers (New York: Newman, n.d. [1947?]) 81 ff.

11. For an extended discussion of the Orthodox view of hell and punishment, see Hierotheos, Metropolitan of Nafpatkos, *Life After Death,* trans. Esther Williams, Birth of the Theotokos Monastery (Levadia, Greece, 1996), esp. 249 ff.

12. Athanasius 33.

13. Colledge and Walsh suggest in footnotes (226 and 336) that the phrase "in a poynt" does not here refer to the center of the universe, but to "an instant of time." While either interpretation seems possible and both point to Julian's concept of the collapse of space/time in her visions and in the divine perspective, she seems here to be making the point that God is at the heart of all that occurs in the universe, i.e at the mid-point of everything and also of each point of space/time.

14. The Orthodox view of space/time as it appears in the liturgy and the iconography of the Church is discussed by Constantine Kalokyris, *The Essence of Orthodox Iconography,* Holy Cross School of Theology, 1971. See also Paul Evdokimov, *The Art of the Icon: A Theology of Beauty,* trans. Fr. Steven Bigham (Redondo Beach, CA: Oakwood Publications, 1993) 127-42.

15. *Against Heresies,* Book IV, cited in J. Patout Burns, S.J., *Theological Anthropology* (Philadelphia: Fortress, 1981) 23.

16. For a clear discussion of dimensionlessness and nothingness as understood in Zen, see T. P. Kasulis, *Zen Action Zen Person* (Honolulu: U of Hawaii P, 1981). The idea of dimensionless "space" has been discussed in the context of Buddhist-Christian dialogue by the contemporary Japanese Buddhist philosopher Maseo Abe, following the philosopher Nishitani.

17. In the Eastern churches the bread or Host (called the Lamb) is placed in the chalice which already contains wine and warm water, and the faithful are communed with a spoon.

18. This translation is taken from the *Service Book of the Holy Eastern Orthodox Catholic and Apostolic Church*, Antiochian Orthodox Christian Archdiocese of North America, 6th ed., 1980.

19. J. Wickham Legg, ed., *The Sarum Missal Edited from Three Early Manuscripts* (Oxford: Oxford UP, 1916) 118.

20. Vernon Staley ed., *The Sarum Missal in English, Parts I and II* (London: Moring, 1911) 271-272.

21. See Kalokyris 85 ff..

22. *Gregory of Nyssa,* trans. Phillip Schaff and Henry Wace, Nicene and Post-Nicene Fathers of the Christian Church, Second Series, Vol. V (Grand Rapids: Eerdmans, 1976) 344.

23. The theory is proposed at some length by Frank J. Tipler, *The Physics of Immortality* (New York: Doubleday,1994).

24. George Maloney, ed., *Pseudo-Macarius: The Fifty Spiritual Homilies and the Great Letter* (New York: Paulist, 1992) 55.

Works Cited

Primary Sources

Anchoritic Spirituality. Ancrene Wisse and Associated Works. Trans. Anne Savage and Nicholas Watson. New York: Paulist, 1991.

Ancrene Riwle: Introduction and Part I. Ed. Robert W. Ackerman and Roger Dahood. New York: Medieval and Renaissance Texts and Studies, 1984.

Aquinas, Thomas. *The "Summa Theologica" of St. Thomas Aquinas.* Part 3, no. 2. Trans. Fathers of the English Dominican Province. London: Washbourne, 1914.

Arnould, E.J., ed. *Le Livre de Seyntz Medicines: The Unpublished Devotional Treatise of Henry of Lancaster.* Oxford: Blackwell, 1940.

Athanasius. *Athanasiana.* Ed. George Dragas. London: Archdiocese of Thyratira, 1980.

---. *On the Incarnation.* New York: St. Vladimir's Seminary P, 1944. Repr. 1982.

Augustine. *The City of God.* Trans. M. Dods with G. Wilson and J. J. Smith. *Basic Writings of Saint Augustine.* Vol. 2. Ed. Whitney J. Oates. New York: Random, 1948.

---. *Confessions.* Trans. Vermon J. Bourke. Washington, DC: Catholic U of America P, 1953.

---. *On Christian Doctrine.* Trans. D. W. Robertson. Indianapolis: Bobbs-Merrill, 1958.

---. *On Genesis.* Trans. Roland Teske. Washington, DC: Catholic U of America P, 1901.

---. *St. Augustine: The Literal Meaning of Genesis*. Trans. John Hammond Taylor. Vol. 2. New York: Newman, 1982.

---. *The Trinity*. Trans. Stephen McKenna. The Fathers of the Church 45. Washington, DC: Catholic U of America P, 1963.

Barratt, Alexandra, ed. *The Book of Tribulation*. MET 15. Heidelberg: Winter, 1984.

---, ed. *The Seven Psalms: A Commentary on the Penitential Psalms Translated from French into English by Dame Eleanor Hull*. EETS 307. Oxford: Oxford UP, 1995.

---. ed. *Women's Writing in Middle English*. London and New York: Longman, 1992.

Bazire, Joyce, and Eric Colledge, eds. *The Chastizing of God's Children*. Oxford: Blackwell, 1957.

The Booke of Gostlye Grace of Mechtild of Hackeborn. Ed. Theresa A. Halligan. Toronto: Pontifical Institute of Mediaeval Studies, 1979.

Bridget of Sweden. *The Liber Celestis of St. Bridget of Sweden*. Ed. Roger Ellis. EETS os 291. Oxford: Oxford UP, 1988.

---. *The Revelations of Saint Birgitta*. Ed. William Patterson Cumming. EETS os 178. London: Oxford UP, 1929.

Chaucer, Geoffrey. *The Riverside Chaucer*. 3rd ed. Ed. Larry D. Benson, et al. Boston: Houghton, 1987.

---. *A Variorum Edition of the Works of Geoffrey Chaucer, Volume II: The Canterbury Tales, Part Twenty: The Prioress's Tale*. Ed. Beverly Boyd. Norman, OK: U of Oklahoma P, 1987.

The Cloud of Unknowing and Other Works. Trans. Clifton Wolters. London: Penguin, 1961. Rpr. 1978.

Davies, R. T., ed. *Medieval English Lyrics: A Critical Anthology*. Evanston, IL: Northwestern UP, 1964

Dinzelbacher, Peter, ed. *Mittelalterliche Visionsliteratur. Eine Anthologie*. Darmstadt: Wissenschaftliche Buchgesellschaft, 1989.

Dionysius. *Dionysius the Areopagite: The Divine Names and the Mystical Theology*. Trans. C. E. Rolt. London: SPCK, 1940.

The Diseases of Women by Trotula of Salerno: A Translation of Passionibus Mulierum Curandorum. Trans. Elizabeth Mason-Hohl. New York: Ritchie, 1940

Geoffrey of Vinsauf. *Poetria Nova of Geoffrey of Vinsauf.* Trans. Margaret F. Nims. Toronto: Pontifical Institute of Mediaeval Studies, 1967.

Gregory I. *Dialogues*. Translated by Odo John Zimmerman. Vol. 39. New York: Fathers of the Church, 1959.

Gregory of Nyssa. *Gregory of Nyssa*. Ed. Phillip Schaff and Henry Wace. Nicene and Post-Nicene Fathers, Vol. V. Grand Rapids, MI: Eerdmans, 1976.

Hilton, Walter. *The Prickynge of Love*. Ed. Harold Kane. 2 vols. Salzburg Studies in English Literature: Elizabethan and Renaissance Studies 92/10. Salzburg: U Salzburg, 1983.

---. *The Scale of Perfection*. Trans. Evelyn Underhill. London: Watkins, 1923

---. *Walter Hilton: The Scale of Perfection*. Trans. John P. H. Clark and Rosemary Dorward. Classics of Western Spirituality. New York: Paulist, 1991.

---. *Walter Hilton's Mixed Life: Edited from Lambeth Palace MS 472*. Ed. S. J. Ogilvie-Thomson. Elizabethan and Renaissance Studies 92/15. Salzburg: U Salzburg, 1986.

Hodgson, Phyllis, ed. *The Cloud of Unknowing and The Book of Privy Counselling*. EETS 218. London: Oxford UP, 1944.

---, ed. *The Cloud of Unknowing and Related Treatises on Contemplative Prayer*. Exeter: Catholic Records P, 1982.

Horstman, C., ed. *Yorkshire Writers: Richard Rolle of Hampole, an English Father of the Church, and His Followers*. Vol. 1. London: Swan Sonnenschein, 1895.

Julian of Norwich, *A Book of Showings to the Anchoress Julian of Norwich*. 2 vols. Eds. Edmund Colledge and James Walsh. Toronto: Pontifical Institute of Mediaeval Studies, 1978.

---. *Julian of Norwich: A Revelation of Love*. Ed Marion Glasscoe. Exeter: U of Exeter, 1976; rev. 1986.

---. *Julian of Norwich: Showings*. Trans. and eds. Edmund Colledge and James Walsh. Classics of Western Spirituality. New York: Paulist, 1978.

---. *Julian of Norwich's Revelations of Divine Love: The Shorter Version*. Ed. Frances Beer. Heidelberg: Winter, 1978.

---. *Revelations of Divine Love*. Trans. Clifton Wolters. London: Penguin, 1966.

---. *The Revelations of Divine Love of Julian of Norwich*. Trans. James Walsh. Wheathampstead: Clarke Books, 1973.

---. *The Shewings of Julian of Norwich.* Ed. Georgia Ronan Crampton. TEAMS Middle English Texts Series. Kalamazoo, Michigan: Medieval Institute, 1994.

Kempe, Margery. *The Book of Margery Kempe.* Ed. Sanford Brown Meech and Hope Emily Allen. EETS os 212. London: Oxford UP, 1940. Rpt. 1961.

---. *The Book of Margery Kempe.* Trans. B. A. Windeatt. Harmondsworth, England: Penguin, 1985.

Littlehales, Henry, ed. *The Prymer or Lay Folk's Prayer Book.* 2 vols. EETS os 105. London, 1895.

Lombard, Peter. *Sententiae. Patrologiae Latinae.* Vol. 192. Ed. J. P Migne. Turnholt: Brepols, 1844-1864.

Love, Nicholas. *Nicholas Love's Mirror of the Blessed Life of Jesus Christ.* Ed. Michael G. Sargent. New York: Garland, 1992.

Maximus the Confessor. *Maximus Confessor: Selected Writings.* Trans. George Berthold. New York: Paulist, 1985.

Mechtild of Hackeborn. *The Booke of Gostlye Grace of Mechtild of Hackeborn.* Ed. Theresa A. Halligan. Toronto: Pontifical Institute of Mediaeval Studies, 1979.

Meister Eckhart. *Meister Eckhart: Teacher and Preacher.* Ed. Bernard McGinn with Frank Tobin and Elvira Borgstadt. Classics of Western Spirituality. New York: Paulist, 1986.

Of the Knowledge of Ourselves and of God: A Fifteenth-Century Florilegium. Trans. James Walsh and Edmund Colledge. London: Mowbray, 1961.

Piers Plowman. Ed. A. V. C. Schmidt. London: Everyman, 1978.

Pseudo-Macarius. *Pseudo-Macarius: The Fifty Spiritual Homilies and the Great Letter.* Trans. George Al Maloney. New York: Paulist, 1992.

Rolle, Richard. *The Fire of Love.* Trans. Ralph Harvey. EETS os 106. London: Kegan, 1896.

---. *The Incendium Amoris of Richard Rolle of Hampole.* Ed. Margaret Deanesly. Manchester: Manchester UP, 1915.

The Sarum Missal Edited from Three Early Manuscripts. Ed. J. Wickham Legg. Oxford: Oxford UP, 1916.

The Sarum Missal in English, Parts I and II. Ed. Vernon Staley. London: Moring, 1911.

Service Book of the Holy Eastern Orthodox Catholic and Apostolic Church.
Antiochian Orthodox Christian Archdiocese of North America. 6th.
ed., 1980.

Silverstein, Theodore, ed. *English Lyrics before 1500.* York Medieval
Texts. Evanston: Northwestern UP, 1971.

Suso, Henry. *Deutsche Schriften.* Ed. Karl Bihlmeyer. Stuttgart: 1907.
Rpt.: Frankfurt: Minerva, 1961.

---. *The Exemplar with Two Sermons.* Ed. Frank Tobin. Classics of
Western Spirituality. New York: Paulist, 1989.

The Women Troubadours. Ed. Meg Bogin. New York and London:
Paddington, 1976.

Secondary Sources

Aers, David. *Community, Gender, and Individual Identity: English
Writing 1360-1430.* London: Routledge, 1988.

Aers, David, and Lynn Staley. *The Powers of the Holy: Religion, Politics,
and Gender in Late Medieval English Culture.* University Park, PA:
The Pennsylvania State UP, 1996.

Alford, John A. *A Companion to Piers Plowman.* Berkeley: U of
California P, 1988.

Anderson, J. F. *St. Augustine and Being: A Metaphysical Essay.* The
Hague: Martinus Nijhoff, 1965.

Arand, Louis. *St. Augustine: Faith, Hope and Charity.* Ancient
Christian Writers. New York: Newman, n.d.

Baker, Denise Nowakowski. *Julian of Norwich's Showings: From Vision
to Book.* Princeton: Princeton UP, 1994.

Bakhtin, M. M. *The Dialogic Imagination.* Austin, TX: U of Texas P,
1981.

---. *Rabelais and His World.* Bloomington, IN: Indiana UP, 1984.

---. *Speech Genres and Other Late Essays.* Trans. Vern McGee. Austin:
U of Texas P, 1986.

Barratt, Alexandra. "Dame Eleanor Hull: A Fifteenth-Century
Translator." *The Medieval Translator: The Theory and Practice of
Translation in the Middle Ages.* Ed. Roger Ellis. Cambridge:
Brewer, 1989. 87-101

---. "How Many Children Had Julian of Norwich? Editions,
Translation and Versions of Her Revelations." *Vox Mystica: Essays*

on *Medieval Mysticism*. Ed. Anne Clark Bartlett. Cambridge: Brewer, 1995. 27-39.

---. "The Prymer and Its Influence on Fifteenth-Century English Passion Lyrics." *Medium Ævum* 44 (1975): 264-279.

Beale, Walter H. "Walter Hilton and the Concept of 'Medled Lyf.'" *American Benedictine Review* 26 (1975): 381-394.

Beer, Frances. *Women and Mystical Experience in the Middle Ages.* Woodbridge: Boydell, 1992.

Bell, David N. *The Image and Likeness: The Augustinian Spirituality of William of St Thierry.* Kalamazoo, MI: Cistercian, 1984.

Blamires, Alcuin, ed. *Woman Defamed and Woman Defended.* Oxford: Clarendon, 1992.

Bloch, Howard. *Medieval Misogyny and the Invention of Western Romantic Love.* Chicago: U of Chicago P, 1991.

Bolton, Brenda. "Mulieres Sanctae." *Women in Medieval Society.* Ed. Brenda Bolton, et al. Philadelphia, U of Pennsylvania P, 1976. 141-158.

Bond, H. Lawrence. "Nicholas of Cusa and the Reconstruction of Theology: The Centrality of Christology in the Coincidence of Opposites." *Contemporary Reflections on the Medieval Christian Tradition.* Ed. George H. Shriver. Durham, N.C: Duke UP, 1974. 81-94.

Børresen, Kari. *Subordination and Equivalence. The Nature and Role of Women in Augustine and Thomas Aquinas.* Washington, D.C: University P of America, 1981.

Bradley, Ritamary. "Christ, the Teacher, in Julian's Showings: The Biblical and Patristic Traditions." *The Medieval Mystical Tradition in England.* Exeter: U of Exeter P, 1982. 127-42.

--- and Valerie Lagorio. *The 14th-Century English Mystics. A Comprehensive Annotated Bibliography.* New York: Garland, 1981.

Brewer, D. S. "Courtesy and the *Gawain* Poet." *Patterns of Love and Courtesy.* Ed. John Lawlor. Evanston, IL: Northwestern UP, 1966. 54-85.

Budick, Sanford. "Chiasmus and the Making of Literary Tradition: The Case of Wordsworth and 'The Days of Dryden and Pope'." *English Literary History* 60 (1993): 961-987.

Bullough, Vern L. "On Being a Male in the Middle Ages." *Medieval Masculinities: Regarding Men in the Middle Ages.* Ed. Clare A.

Lees, et al. Medieval Cultures, vol. 7. Minneapolis: U of Minnesota P, 1994. 31-46.

Burns, Patout. *Theological Anthropology*. Philadelphia: Fortress, 1981.

Butler, Cuthbert. *Western Mysticism: The Teaching of SS. Augustine, Gregory and Bernard on Contemplation and the Contemplative Life.* London: Arrow, 1960.

Bynum, Carolyn Walker. "Religious Women in the Later Middle Ages." *Fragmentation and Redemption. Essays on Gender and the Human Body in Medieval Religion.* New York: Zone, 1991. 121-39.

Cadden, Joan. *Meanings of Sex Difference in the Middle Ages: Medicine, Science, and Culture.* Cambridge: Cambridge UP, 1993.

Camille, Michael. "Fallen Angels: Demonic Images." *The Gothic Idol. Ideology and Image-making in Medieval Art.* Cambridge: Cambridge UP, 1989. 57-73.

Carey, Hillary M. "Devout Literate Lay People and the Pursuit of the Mixed Life in Later Medieval England," *The Journal of Religious History* 14 (1986-7): 361-381.

Carruthers, Mary J. *The Book of Memory: A Study of Memory in Medieval Culture.* Cambridge: Cambridge UP, 1990.

---. *The Search for St. Truth: A Study of Meaning in Piers Plowman.* Evanston, IL: Northwestern UP, 1973.

Cixious, Hélène and Catherine Clément. *The Newly Born Woman.* Trans. Betsy Wing. Minneapolis: U of Minnesota P, 1986.

Clark, Elizabeth A. *Women in the Early Church.* Message of the Fathers of the Church. Vol 13. Wilmington, DE: Glazier, 1983; rpt. 1987.

Clark, John P.H. "Fiducia in Julian of Norwich, II." *Downside Review*, 95 (1979). 214-29.

---. Introduction. *Walter Hilton: The Scale of Perfection.* Trans. John P. H. Clark and Rosemary Dorward. Classics of Western Spirituality. New York: Paulist, 1991. 13-68.

Clark, Gregory. *Dialogue, Dialectic, and Conversation: A Social Perspective on the Function of Writing.* Carbondale: Southern Illinois UP, 1990.

Colledge, Edmund. "*The Treatise of Perfection of the Sons of God*: A Fifteenth-Century English Ruysbroek Translation." *English Studies* 33 (1952): 49-66.

Collins, Marie. "Feminine Response to Masculine Attractiveness in Middle English Literature." *Essays and Studies* 38 (1985): 12-28.

Corless, Roger. "Comparing Cataphatic Mystics: Julian of Norwich and T'an-Luan." *Mystics Quarterly* 21 (1995): 18-27.

--- and Paul Knitter, eds. *Buddhist Emptiness and Christian Trinity: Essays and Exploration.* NY: Paulist, 1990.

Cousins, Ewert H. "Bonaventure, The Coincidence of Opposites and Nicholas of Cusa." *Studies Honoring Ignatius Charles Brady.* Ed. Romano Stephen Almagno and Conrad L. Harkins. St. Bonaventure, NY: Franciscan Institute, 1976. 177-197.

Crane, Susan. *Gender and Romance in Chaucer's Canterbury Tales.* Princeton: Princeton UP, 1994.

Cranny-Francis, Anne. "Gender and Genre: Feminist Subversion of Genre Fiction and its Implications for Critical Literacy." *The Powers of Literacy: A Genre Approach to Teaching Writing.* Ed. Bill Cope and Mary Kalantzis. Pittsburgh: U of Pittsburgh P, 1993. 90-115.

Davies, Oliver. *God Within: The Mystical Tradition of Northern Europe.* New York: Paulist, 1988.

---. "Transformational Process in the Work of Julian of Norwich and Mechthild of Magdeburg." *The Medieval Mystical Tradition in England.* Ed. Marion Glasscoe. Cambridge: Brewer, 1992. 39-52.

Dean, Ruth J. "Manuscripts of St. Elizabeth of Schonau in England." *Modern Language Review* 32 (1937). 62-71

Deanesly, Margaret. "Vernacular Books in England in the Fourteenth and Fifteenth Centuries." *Modern Language Review* 15 (1920): 349-358.

Despres, Denise. "Ecstatic Reading and Missionary Mysticism: *The Orchern of Syon.*" *Prophets Abroad. The Reception of Continental Holy Women in Late-Medieval England.* Ed. Rosalynn Voaden. Cambridge: Brewer, 1996. 141-160

---. *Ghostly Sights: Visual Meditation in Late-Medieval Literature.* Norman, OK: Pilgrim, 1989.

Dictionary of Saints. Donald Attwater. Middlesex: Penguin, 1965.

Dinshaw, Carolyn. *Chaucer's Sexual Poetics.* Madison: U of Wisconsin P, 1989.

Dinzelbacher, Peter. *Mittelalterliche Frauenmystik.* Paderborn: Schöningh, 1993.

Dronke, Peter. *Women Writers of the Middle Ages.* Cambridge: Cambridge UP, 1984.

Duffy, Eamon. *The Stripping of the Altars: Traditional Religion in England 1400-1580.* New Haven: Yale UP, 1992.

Eco, Umberto. *Semiotics and the Philosophy of Language.* Bloomington, IN: U of Indiana P, 1984.

Ellis, Roger. "'Flores ad Fabricandum . . . Coronam': An Investigation into the Uses of the Revelations of St. Bridget of Sweden in Fifteenth-Century England." *Medium Aevum,* 51 (1982). 163-86.

---. "Revelation and the Life of Faith: The Vision of Julian of Norwich." *Christian,* 6 (1980). 61-71.

Emerson, Caryl, and Michael Holquist. Introduction. *Speech Genres and Other Late Essays.* Ed. Caryl Emerson and Michael Holquist. Austin, TX: U of Texas P, 1986. ix-xxiii.

Encyclopaedia Judaica. 13 vols. Jerusalem: Keter, 1972.

Evdokimov, Paul. *The Art of the Icon: A Theology of Beauty.* Trans. Fr. Steven Bigham. Redondo Beach, CA: Oakwood, 1993.

Finke, Laurie A. *Feminist Theory, Women's Writing.* Ithaca: Cornell UP, 1992.

---. "Knowledge as Bait: Feminism, Voice, and the Pedagogical Unconscious." *College English* 55 (January 1993): 7-27.

---. "Mystical Bodies and the Dialogics of Vision." *Maps of Flesh and Light: The Religious Experience of Medieval Women Mystics.* Ed. Ulrike Wiethaus. Syracuse, NY: Syracuse University Press, 1993. 28-44

Gasché, Rodolphe. "Introduction." *Readings in Interpretation: Hölderlin, Hegel, Heidegger.* Ed. Andrzej Warminski. Minneapolis: U of Minnesota P, 1987. ix-xxvi.

Gibson, Gail McM. *The Theater of Devotion. East Anglian Drama and Society in the Late Middle Ages.* Chicago: U of Chicago P, 1989.

Gillespie, Vincent. "Idols and Images: Pastoral Adaptations of *The Scale of Perfection.*" *Langland, the Mystics and the Medieval English Religious Tradition: Essays in Honour of S. S. Hussey.* Ed. Helen Phillips. Cambridge: Brewer, 1990. 97-123.

---. "'Lukynge in haly bukes': Lectio in some Late Medieval Spiritual Miscellanies." *Spätmittelalterliche geistliche Literatur in der Nationalsprache.* Analecta Cartusiana 106/2 (1984): 1-27.

---. "Postcards from the Edge: Interpreting the Ineffable in the Middle English Mystics." *Interpretation: Medieval and Modern.* Ed. Piero Boitani and Anna Torti. Cambridge: Brewer, 1993. 137-165.

---. "Vernacular Books of Religion." *Book Production and Publishing in Britain, 1375-1475*. Ed. Jeremy Griffiths and Derek Pearsall. Cambridge Studies in Publishing and Printing History. Cambridge: Cambridge UP, 1989. 317-44.

--- and Maggie Ross. "The Apophatic Image: The Poetics of Effacement in Julian of Norwich." *The Medieval Mystical Tradition in England*. Ed. Marion Glasscoe. Cambridge: Brewer, 1992. 53-77.

Glasscoe, Marion. "Means of Showing: An Approach to Reading Julian of Norwich." *Analecta Cartusiana* 106 (1983). 155-77.

---. "Visions and Revisions: A Further Look at the Manuscripts of Julian of Norwich." *Studies in Bibliography* 42 (1989): 103-19.

Gray, Douglas. *Themes and Images in Medieval English Religious Lyric*. London: Routledge, 1972.

Green, Monica. "Obstetrical and Gynecological Texts in Middle English." *Studies in the Age of Chaucer* 14 (1992): 53-88

Grundmann, Herbert. *Religiöse Bewegungen im Mittelalter*. Hildesheim: Olms, 1961.

Haas, Alois M. "Schools of Late Medieval Mysticism."*Christian Spirituality*. Vol. II. *High Middle Ages and Reformation*. Ed. Jill Raitt, et al. New York: Crossroad, 1988. 140-75.

---. "'Trage Leiden geduldiglich.' Die Einstellung der deutschen Mystik zum Leiden." *Gottleiden-Gottlieben. Zur volkssprachlichen Mystik im Mittelalter*. Frankfurt: Insel, 1989. 127-52

Hagen, Susan K. *Allegorical Remembrance: A Study of The Pilgrimage of the Life of Man as a Medieval Treatise on Seeing and Remembering*. Athens: U of Georgia P, 1990.

---. "Feminist Theology and 'The Second Nun's Tale': or St. Cecilia Laughs at the Judge." *Medieval Perspectives* 4-5 (1989-90): 42-52.

Hamburger, Jeffrey M. "The Visual and the Visionary: The Image in Late Medieval Monastic Devotions." *Viator* 20 (1989): 161-82.

Hanson, A. Ellis, and Monica H. Green, "Soranus of Ephesus: Methodicorum princeps." *Aufsteig und Niedergang der Römischen Welt: Rise and Decline of the Roman World*. Ed. W. Haase and H. Temporini. Berlin and New York: de Gruyter, 1994.

Hearn, Michael. *Medieval Thought: The Western Intellectual Tradition from Antiquity to the Thirteenth Century*. New York: St. Martin's, 1985.

Heimsoeth, Heinz. *The Six Great Themes of Western Metaphysics and the End of the Middle Ages.* Trans. Ramon J. Betanzos. Detroit: Wayne State University Press, 1994.

Hewson, M. Antony. *Giles of Rome and the Medieval Theory of Conception.* London: Athlone, 1975.

Hierotheos, Metropolitan of Nafpatkos. *Life After Death.* Trans. Esther Williams. Levadia, Greece: Birth of the Theotokos Monastery, 1995.

Hughes, Jonathan. *Pastors and Visionaries: Religion and Secular Life in Late Medieval Yorkshire.* Woodbridge: Boydell, 1988.

Jantzen, Grace. *Julian of Norwich.* London: SPCK, 1987.

---. *Julian of Norwich: Mystic and Theologian.* New York: Paulist, 1988.

---. *Power, Gender, and Christian Mysticism.* Cambridge Studies in Ideology and Religion 8. Cambridge: Cambridge UP, 1995.

Jauss, Hans Robert. *Question and Answer: Forms of Dialogic Understanding.* Trans. Michael Hays. Minneapolis: U of Minnesota P, 1989.

---. *Toward an Aesthetic of Reception.* Trans. Timothy Bahti. Brighton: Harvester, 1982.

Johnston, William. "All and Nothing: St. John of the Cross and Buddhist-Christian Dialogue." *Areopagus* 2.2 (Easter, 1989): 18 and 24.

Jones, Catherine. "The English Mystic Julian of Norwich." *Medieval Women Writers.* Ed. Katharina M. Wilson. Athens: U of Georgia P, 1984. 269-277.

Kalokyris, Constantine D. *The Essence of Orthodox Iconography.* Trans. Peter A. Chamberas. Brookline, MA: Holy Cross School of Theology, 1971.

Kasulis, Thomas P. *Zen Action-Zen Person.* Honolulu: U of Hawaii P, 1981.

Keiser, George R. "'To Knawe God Almyghtyn': Robert Thornton's Devotional Book." *Spätmittelalterliche geistliche Literatur in der Nationalsprache.* Analectica Carthusiana 106/2 (1984): 103-129.

Kieckhefer, Richard. "Major Currents in Late Medieval Devotion." *Christian Spirituality.* Vol. II. *High Middle Ages and Reformation.* Ed. Jill Raitt, et al. New York: Crossroad, 1988. 75-108.

Knight, Stephen. *Geoffrey Chaucer.* Oxford: Blackwell, 1986.

Laato, Antti. "The Composition of Isaiah 40-55." *Journal of Biblical Literature* 109 (1990): 207-228.

Lagorio, Valerie M. and Michael G. Sargent. "English Mystical Writings." In *A Manual of the Writings in Middle English 1050-1500*. Vol. 9. Gen. ed. Albert E. Hartung. New Haven: Connecticut Academy of Arts and Sciences, 1993. 3049-3137.

Langer, Otto. *Mystische Erfahrung und spirituelle Theologie: zu Meister Eckharts Auseinandersetzung mit der Frauenfrommigkeit seiner Zeit*. Munich: Artemis, 1987.

Lanham, Richard A. *A Handlist of Rhetorical Terms*. Berkeley: U of California P, 1968.

Laskaya, Anne. *Chaucer's Approach to Gender in the Canterbury Tales*. Cambridge: Brewer, 1995.

Lawton, David. "Voice, Authority, and Blasphemy in *The Book of Margery Kempe*." *Margery Kempe: A Book of Essays*. Ed. Sandra J. McEntire. New York: Garland, 1992. 93-116.

Leclercq, Jean. *The Love of Learning and the Desire for God: A Study of Monastic Culture*. Trans. Catharine Misrahi. New York: Fordham University Press, 1982.

---. Preface. *Julian of Norwich. Showings.* Trans. Edmund Colledge and James Walsh. NY: Paulist, 1978. 1-14.

---, Francois Vandenbroucke, and Louis Bouyer. "The Dominican Crusade." *The History of Christian Spirituality*. Vol. 2. *The Spirituality of the Middle Ages*. Trans. Benedictines of Holme Eden Abbey (Editiones Montaigne: 1961). New York: Seabury, 1968. 315-43.

Lermack, Annette. *Visual Sources in the Visions of Julian of Norwich*. MA Thesis: Northern Illinois University, 1993.

Lerner, Gerda. *The Creation of Feminist Consciousness: From the Middle Ages to Eighteen-seventy*. Oxford: Oxford UP, 1993.

Lewis, Gertrud Jaron. *Bibliographie zur deutschen Frauenmystik des Mittelalters*. Bibliographien zur deutschen Literatur des Mittelalters, 10. Berlin: Schmidt, 1994.

---. *By Women. For Women. About Women. The Sister-Books of Fourteenth Century Germany*. Toronto: Pontifical Institute of Mediaeval Studies, 1996.

Lichtmann, Maria R. "'I Desyrede a Bodylye Syght': Julian of Norwich and the Body." *Mystics Quarterly* 17 (1991): 12-19.

Lochrie, Karma. *Margery Kempe and Translations of the Flesh.* Philadelphia: U of Pennsylvania P, 1991.

Lossly, Vladimir. *In the Image and Likeness of God.* London: Mowbrays, 1967.

Louth, Andrew. *The Origins of the Christian Mystical Tradition.* Oxford: Clarendon, 1981.

Lunsford, Andrea. "On Reclaiming Rhetorica." *Reclaiming Rhetorica: Women in the Rhetorical Tradition.* Ed. Andrea Lunsford. Pittsburgh: U of Pittsburgh P, 1995. 3-8.

Martin, Anna J. "Christina von Stommeln." *Mediävistik* 4 (1991): 179-263.

Masson, Cynthea. "Crossing the Chasm: The Rhetoric of the Ineffable in Margery Kempe and Julian of Norwich." Diss. McMaster U, 1995.

McAlpine, Monica E. *The Genre of Troilus and Criseyde.* Ithaca and London: Cornell UP, 1978.

McFague, Sallie. *Models of God. Theology for an Ecological, Nuclear Age.* Philadelphia: Fortress, 1987.

McGinn, Bernard. "The Changing Shape of Late Medieval Mysticism." *Church History* 65 (1996): 197-219.

---. "The Human Person as Image of God II: Western Christianity." *Christian Spirituality: Origins to the Twelfth Century. World Spirituality: An Encyclopedic History of the Religious Quest.* Vol 16. Ed. Bernard McGinn and John Meyendorff. New York: Crossroad, 1985: 312-30.

---. "Love, Knowledge, and Unio Mystica in the Western Christian Tradition." *Mystical Union and Monotheistic Faith: An Ecumenical Dialogue.* Ed. Moshe Idel and Bernard McGinn. New York: Macmillan, 1989. 59-86.

---. *The Presence of God: A History of Western Christian Mysticism.* Vol. 1. *The Foundations of Mysticism.* New York: Crossroads, 1992.

McNamara, Jo Ann. "The *Herrenfrage*: The Restructuring of the Gender System, 1050-1150." *Medieval Masculinities: Regarding Men in the Middle Ages.* Ed. Clare A. Lees, et al. Medieval Cultures, Vol. 7. Minneapolis: U of Minnesota P, 1994. 3-30.

---. "The Rhetoric of Orthodoxy." *Maps of Flesh and Light.* Ed. Ulrike Wiethaus. Syracuse: Syracuse UP, 1993. 9-27.

McSheffrey, Shannon. "Literacy and the Gender Gap in the Late Middle Ages: Women and Reading in Lollard Communities." *Women, the Book and the Godly.* Ed. Lesley Smith and Jane H.M. Taylor. Cambridge: Brewer, 1995. 157-170.

Mermall, Thomas. "The Chiasmus: Unamuno's Master Trope." *PMLA* 105 (1990): 245-255.

Meyendorff, John. *St. Gregory Palamas and Orthodox Spirituality.* New York: St. Vladimir's Seminary P, 1974.

Minnis, A.J. *Medieval Theory of Authorship.* London: Scolar, 1984.

Mirrer, Louise. "Representing 'Other' Men: Muslims, Jews, and Masculine Ideals in Medieval Castilian Epic and Ballad." *Medieval Masculinities: Regarding Men in the Middle Ages.* Ed. Clare A. Lees, et al. Medieval Cultures, vol. 7. Minneapolis: U of Minnesota P, 1994. 169-186.

Molinari, Paul. *Julian of Norwich.* London: Longman, 1958.

Murphy, James. *Rhetoric in the Middle Ages: A History of Rhetorical Theory from Saint Augustine to the Renaissance.* Berkeley and Los Angeles: U of California P, 1974.

Nänny, Max. "Chiasmus in Literature: Ornament or Function?" *Word and Image: A Journal of Verbal Visual Enquiry* 4.1 (1988): 51-59.

Needham, J. *A History of Embryology.* Cambridge: Cambridge UP, 2nd. ed., 1958

Neumann, Hans. "Elsbeth von Oye." *Die deutsche Literatur des Mittelalters. Verfasserlexikon.* Vol. 2. Berlin: De Gruyter, 1980. 511-514.

Newman, Barbara. *From Virile Woman to WomanChrist.* Philadelphia: U of Pennsylvania P, 1995.

Norrman, Ralf. *Samuel Butler and the Meaning of Chiasmus.* London: Macmillan, 1986.

Nuth, Joan M. *Wisdom's Daughter: The Theology of Julian of Norwich.* New York: Crossroad, 1991.

Ochsenbein, Peter. "Leidensmystik in Dominikanischen Frauenklöstern des 14. Jahrhunderts am Beispiel der Elsbeth von Oye." *Religiöse Frauenbewegung und mystische Frömmigkeit im Mittelalter.* Ed. Peter Dinzelbacher and Dieter Bauer. Cologne: Böhlau, 1988. 353-372.

---. "Die Offenbarungen Elsbeths von Oye als Dokument leidensfixierter Mystik." *Abendländische Mystik im Mittelalter.*

Symposium Kloster Engelberg. Ed. Kurt Ruh. Stuttgart: Metzler, 1986. 423-442.

Oxford Latin Dictionary. Ed. P. G. W. Glare. Oxford: Clarendon, 1982.

O'Faolain, Julia and Lauro Martines, eds. *Not in God's Image.* NY: Harper, 1973.

Pagels, Elaine. *Adam, Eve, and the Serpent.* NY: Random, 1988.

---. *The Origin of Satan.* New York : Random, 1995.

Panichelli, Debra Scott. "Finding God in the Memory: Julian and the Loss of the Visions." *Downside Review* 104 (1986): 299-317.

Park, Trajei. "Reflecting Christ: The Role of Flesh in Walter Hilton and Julian of Norwich." *The Medieval Mystical Tradition in England: Exeter Symposium V.* Ed. Marion Glasscoe. Cambridge: Brewer, 1992. 17-37.

Pegis, Anton Charles. *St. Thomas and the Problem of the Soul in the Thirteenth Century.* 1934. Repr. Toronto: Pontifical Institute of Mediaeval Studies, 1976.

Pelphrey, Brant. *Julian of Norwich: Christ our Mother.* Collegeville, MN: Liturgical, 1989.

---. *Love Was His Meaning: The Theology and Mysticism of Julian of Norwich.* Salzburg Studies of English Literature. Salzburg: University of Salzburg, 1982.

Peters, Brad. "Julian of Norwich and Her Conceptual Development of Evil." *Mystics Quarterly* 17 (1991): 181-188.

---. "The Reality of Evil with the Mystic Vision of Julian of Norwich." *Mystics Quarterly* 13 (1987): 195-202.

Peters, Ursula. *Religiöse Erfahrung als literarisches Faktum. Zur Vorgeschichte und Genese frauenmystischer Texte des 13. und 14. Jahrhunderts.* Tübingen: Niemeyer, 1988.

Petroff, Elizabeth Alvilda. *Body and Soul: Essays on Medieval Women and Mysticism.* Oxford: Oxford UP, 1994.

---. *Medieval Women's Visionary Literature.* Oxford: Oxford UP, 1986.

Poliakov, Léon. *The History of Anti-Semitism.* Trans. Richard Howard. New York: Vanguard, 1965.

Radday, Yehuda T. "Chiasmus in Hebrew Biblical Narrative." *Chiasmus in Antiquity: Structures, Analyses, Exegesis.* Ed. John W. Welch. Hildesheim: Gerstenberg, 1981. 50-117.

Ragland-Sullivan, Ellie. *Jacques Lacan and the Philosophy of Psychoanalysis*. Chicago: U of Illinois P, 1986.

---. "The Sexual Masquerade: A Lacanian Theory of Sexual Difference." *Lacan and the Subject of Language*. Ed. Ellie Ragland-Sullivan and Mark Bracher. New York: Routledge, 1991. 49-80.

Riehle, Wolfgang. *The Middle English Mystics*. Trans. Bernard Standring. London: Routledge, 1981.

Robertson, Elizabeth. "Medieval Medical Views of Women and Female Spirituality in the *Ancrene Wisse* and Julian of Norwich's *Showings*." *Feminist Approaches to the Body in Medieval Literature*. Ed. Linda Lomperis and Sarah Stanbury. Philadelphia: U of Pennsylvania P, 1993. 142-67.

Robertson, D. W., Jr. *A Preface to Chaucer: Studies in Medieval Perspectives*. Princeton: Princeton UP, 1962.

Rorem, Paul. *Pseudo-Dionysius: A Commentary on the Texts and an Introduction to Their Influence*. Oxford: Oxford UP, 1993.

Roskoff, Gustav. *Geschichte des Teufels*. Leipzig: Brockhaus, 1869.

Ross, Ellen. "'She Wept and Cried Right Loud for Sorrow and for Pain.' Suffering, the Spiritual Journey, and Women's Experience in Late Medieval Mysticism." *Maps of Flesh and Light. The Religious Experience of Medieval Women Mystics*. Ed. Ulrike Wiethaus. Syracuse: Syracuse UP, 1993. 45-59.

Ruhrberg, Christine. *Der literarische Körper der Heiligen. Leben und Viten der Christina von Stommeln (1242-1312)*. Tübingen: Francke, 1995. Bibliotheca Germanica 35.

Russell, Jeffrey Burton. *The Devil : Perceptions of Evil from Antiquity to Primitive Christianity*. Ithaca: Cornell UP, 1977.

---. *Lucifer: The Devil in the Middle Ages*. Ithaca: Cornell UP, 1984.

---. "Mystical Bodies and the Dialogics of Vision." *Maps of Flesh and Light. The Religious Experience of Medieval Women Mystics*. Ed. Ulrike Wiethaus. Syracuse: Syracuse UP, 1993. 28-44.

Ryder, Andrew. "A Note of Julian's Vision." *Downside Review* 96 (1978). 299-304.

Scase, Wendy. "Reginald Pecock, John Carpenter and John Colop's 'Common-Profit' Books: Aspects of Book Ownership and Circulation in Fifteenth-Century London." *Medium Ævum* 61 (1992): 261-274.

Schneider-Lastin, Wolfram. "Das Handexemplar einer mittelalterlichen Autorin. Zur Edition der Offenbarungen Elsbeths von Oye." *Editio* 8 (1994). 53-100.

Scholem, Gershom. *On the Kabbalah and Its Symbolism.* Jerusalem, 1941; repr. New York: Schocken, 1961.

Sells, Michael A. *Mystical Languages of Unsaying.* Chicago: U of Chicago P, 1994.

Shook, Laurence K. Foreword. Trans. Margaret F. Nims. *Poetria Nova of Geoffrey of Vinsauf.* Toronto: Pontifical Institute of Mediaeval Studies, 1967. 7-8.

Sonnino, Lee A. *A Handbook to Sixteenth-Century Rhetoric.* London: Routledge, 1968.

Staley, Lynn. *Margery Kempe's Dissenting Fictions.* Pennsylvania: Pennsylvania State UP, 1994.

Tanner, Norman P. *The Church in Late Medieval Norwich 1370-1532.* Toronto: Pontifical Institute of Mediaeval Studies, 1984.

Thomson, David. "Deconstruction and Meaning in Medieval Mysticism." *Christianity and Literature* 40.2 (1991): 102-121.

Tinsley, David F. "The Spirituality of Suffering in the Revelations of Elsbeth von Oye." *Mystics Quarterly* 21 (1995): 121-147.

Tipler, Frank J. *The Physics of Immortality: Modern Cosmology, God, and the Resurrection of the Dead.* NY: Doubleday, 1994.

Torrell, J.-P. *Theorie de la prophetie et philosophie de la conaissance aux environs 1230: La Contribution d'Hughes de Saint-Cher.* Spicilegium Sacrum Lovaniense, Etudes et documents, 40. Louvain, 1977.

Trachtenberg, Joshua. *The Devil and the Jews: The Medieval Conception of the Jew and Its Relation to Modern Antisemitism.* New Haven: Yale UP, 1943.

Tuve, Rosemund. *Allegorical Imagery: Some Medieval Books and Their Posterity.* Princeton: Princeton UP, 1966.

Wallach-Faller, Marianne. "Ein mittelhochdeutsches Dominikan-erinnen-Legendar des 14. Jahrhunderts als mystagogischer Text?" *Abendländische Mystik im Mittelalter. Symposium Kloster Engelberg.* Ed. Kurt Ruh. Stuttgart: Metzler, 1986. 388-401.

Ware, Kallistos. *The Orthodox Way.* Crestwood, NY: St. Vladimir's Seminary P, 1979; repr. 1995.

Warren, Anne K. *Anchorites and Their Patrons in Medieval England.* Berkeley: U of California P, 1985.

Watson, Nicholas. "Censorship and Cultural Change in Late Medieval England: Vernacular Theology, the Oxford Translation Debate and Arundel's Constitutions." *Speculum* 70 (1995): 822-64.

---. "The Composition of Julian of Norwich's *Revelation of Love*." *Speculum* 68 (1993): 637-683.

---. *Richard Rolle and the Invention of Authority*. New York: Cambridge UP, 1991.

---. "The Trinitarian Hermeneutic in Julian of Norwich's *Revelation of Love*." *The Medieval Mystical Tradition in England: Exeter Symposium V*. Ed. Marion Glasscoe. Cambridge: Brewer, 1992. 79-100.

---. "'Yf wommen be double naturelly'": Remaking 'Woman' in Julian of Norwich's Revelation of Love." *Exemplaria* 8 (1996): 1-34.

Watson, Wilfred G. E. "Further Examples of Semantic-Sonant Chiasmus." *Catholic Biblical Quarterly* 46 (1984): 31-33.

Weinstein, Donald, and Rudolph Bell. *Saints and Society. The Two Worlds of Western Christendom, 1000-1700*. Chicago: U of Chicago P, 1982.

Welch, John W., ed. *Chiasmus in Antiquity: Structures, Analyses, Exegesis*. Hildesheim: Gerstenberg, 1981.

Williams-Krapp, Werner. "'Nucleus totius perfectionis.' Die Altväterspiritualität in der 'vita' Heinrich Seuses." *FS Walter Haug und Burghart Wachinger*. Ed. J. Janota. Vol. 2. Tübingen: Niemeyer, 1992. 402-421.

Windeatt, B.A. "Julian of Norwich and Her Audience." *Review of English Studies* 28 (1977): 1-17.

Woolf, Rosemary. *English Religious Lyric in the Middle Ages*. Oxford: Clarendon, 1968.

Wright, Richard E. "The 'Boke Performyd': Affective Technique and Reader Response in the *Showings* of Julian of Norwich." *Christianity and Literature* 36 (1987): 13-32.

Yates, Frances A. *The Art of Memory*. London: Routledge, 1966; Chicago: U of Chicago P, 1968.

Zizioulas, John D. *Being as Communion: Studies in Personhood and the Church*. Crestwood, NY: St. Vladimir's Seminary P, 1985.

Index

2003.02.12   80.00 (18.98)